T0385574

Islamic Law in
Contemporary Indonesia

Ideas and Institutions

Harvard Series in Islamic Law

Islamic Law in Contemporary Indonesia

Ideas and Institutions

Edited by

R. Michael Feener
Mark E. Cammack

Published by the
Islamic Legal Studies Program, Harvard Law School
Distributed by Harvard University Press
Cambridge, Massachusetts
2007

Library of Congress Control Number: 2007936108

ISBN 978-0-674-02508-0

For Dan Lev —

In recognition of his role in generating these discussions, as well as his generous criticisms along the way

CONTENTS

viii CONTENTS

Part III. APPENDIX

ACKNOWLEDGEMENTS

It has become cliché to remark on the fact that Indonesia is home to the world's largest Muslim population while lamenting the relative dearth of serious academic studies of Islam in that country in prefaces to work on this subject. In fact, however, over the past decade there has been a remarkable rise in the amount of such work produced in the fields of history and anthropology, Islamic and legal studies. The perception of its neglect may in some ways be understood as reflecting the dramatically interdisciplinary nature of such work, as most scholars who publish in specialist Indonesian studies journals such as *Bijdragen tot de Taal-, Land- en Volkenkunde* do not regularly read *Islamic Law and Society*, and vice versa.

This volume contains a selection of papers based upon presentations prepared for the first international conference to focus specifically on Islamic law in modern Indonesia, hosted and generously supported by the Islamic Legal Studies Program at Harvard Law School on April 17 and 18, 2004. That meeting was organized in order to bring together in one place diverse perspectives on Islamic law in Indonesia, including academics from a broad range of disciplinary backgrounds, as well as practicing jurists and Muslim activists of various ideological orientations. This ambitious and successful attempt at generating new conversations on the subject would not have been possible without the help of many generous colleagues, for whose contributions, advice and assistance we are very grateful. This extends not only to those who produced papers for publication in this work, but also to other participants whose input contributed to the direction and development of our discussions, including Clark Lombardi, Engseng Ho, Mitsuo Nakamura, Hisako Nakamura, Mastuhu, Mun'im Sirry, Ibrahim Assegaf, Yudian Wahyudi, Dadi Darmadi, Robert Hefner, Ismail Yusanto, Ulil Abshar Abdalla, and Dan Lev. In particular we would like to thank Peri Bearman and Frank Vogel for the great amount of time, effort, and resources that they devoted to making this conference possible. Through the generous efforts of all of these colleagues, we have been able to assemble a volume that we hope will serve to both disseminate information about—and stimulate further interest in—the legal, intellectual, social, and political dimensions of Islamic law in modern Indonesia.

R. Michael Feener
Mark E. Cammack

Introduction

ISLAMIC LAW IN INDONESIA: FORMATIONS OF A MODERN TRADITION?

R. Michael Feener and Mark E. Cammack

For over seven centuries, Muslim communities in the Indonesian Archipelago have creatively engaged with a complex and changing array of ideas and institutions in developing their own distinctive understandings of Islamic law. The pace of religious, cultural, and legal change accelerated considerably in the early twentieth century, however, as technological advances and institutional innovations facilitated the rapid modernization of local educational and political structures.[1] This in turn fostered the development of new contexts within which to conceptualize and apply law in modern Indonesian society. This volume presents a series of overviews of some of the major developments of various facets of Islamic law in modern Indonesia—legal thought, fatwas, legal education, and the formal judiciary—as well as a number of more detailed case studies of particular ideas and institutions involved with Muslim understandings and practices of religious law in the country.

The essays published in this collection are based upon papers presented at a 2004 conference held by the Islamic Legal Studies Program at Harvard Law School. This meeting was the largest international conference on Islamic law in Indonesia to date, and in planning it a deliberate decision was made to include discussions of a broad range of phenomena from legal theory to formal systems of implementation.

"Islamic law" or a Muslim legal tradition?

The past two decades have witnessed remarkable developments in the study of Islamic law and society. Nevertheless one continues to find ongoing tensions between those who adopt "essentialist" views of Islamic law and those whose analyses proceed from what might be characterized as a "disintegrative" perspective. Each tries to grapple with the fact that different regions have developed very different institutions to address questions of Islamic

law. Significantly different versions of Islamic law co-exist in different parts
of the world and, indeed, within particular regions. Essentialist views identify one particular manifestation of Islamic law as "authentic" (usually an
iteration of some "classical tradition" as practiced in particular parts of the
Middle East) and view everything else as a corrupted form of the original.
The disintegrative approach challenges essentialist views by first pointing
out that it is arbitrary to favor one interpretation of Islamic law over others. It is then argued that because there is no basis for preferring one form
of Islamic law over any other, all interpretations are equally valid, with
the result that the concept of "Islamic law" itself becomes largely meaningless, since there are no criteria for deciding which interpretations qualify for that label.

The studies presented in this volume illustrate the shortcomings of both
essentialist and disintegrative approaches to Islamic law for understanding
developments in the Indonesian setting. Southeast Asia generally, and
Indonesia in particular, provides us with the paradigmatic example of a
region that has embraced a range of interpretations of Islamic law that are
extraordinarily different from those that dominated the Middle East in the
classical period. Indonesian Muslims have developed a number of distinctive Islamic institutions, interpretive theories, and political theories. Since
Indonesia is by far the most populous, and arguably one of the most diverse
Muslim countries in the world, it would seem to provide the greatest ammu-
nition for those who would argue against essentialist paradigms of Islamic
legal studies, preferring that we instead talk about "Muslim legal systems."
That said, as the various contributions to this volume also make clear,
Indonesian Muslims themselves do not feel disassociated from the Islamic
tradition or from classical Middle Eastern approaches to Islamic legal reasoning and adjudication. They consider themselves to be part of a global
community that embraces the same foundational texts and that is engaged
in a common struggle to develop methods of interpreting these texts in
ways that make sense in the world at large as well as in the context of
particular cultural realities.

The problem of determining which (if any) version of "Islamic law" is
most authentic can be largely avoided if one examines efforts to develop
approaches to law based on Islam within the framework of "traditions."
In elaborating the notion of tradition as a means of conceptualizing developments of Islamic law in modern Indonesia it may be useful to start by
considering the ideas of Alasdair MacIntyre. Addressing the concept in the
context of Aristotelian, Augustinian, Scottish, and liberal traditions, MacIntyre
defines a "tradition" as

an argument extended through time in which certain fundamental agreements are defined and redefined in terms of two kinds of conflict: those with critics and enemies external to the tradition who reject all or at least key parts of those fundamental agreements, and those internal, interpretive debates through which the meaning and rationale of the fundamental agreements come to be expressed and by whose progress a tradition is constituted. (MacIntyre 1988, 12)

By viewing the Islamic tradition through this lens, one can avoid essentialist and disintegrative approaches to Islamic law and can recognize why Indonesians believe that their interpretation of Islam is part of a larger religious phenomenon that manifests significant aspects of both coherence and diversity. The definition's emphasis on the existence of a set of fundamental agreements or shared understandings as the focal point of a tradition explains its coherence and continuity. Conversely, the ongoing debate over the meaning of those understandings is the source of the tradition's diversity and vitality.

Talal Asad's work adds to MacIntyre's approach and brings the discussion of "tradition" to bear on the study of Islam. Pursuing MacIntyre's insight that a religious tradition can be seen as an "argument," he has suggested an approach to the study of Islam that recognizes it as a discursive tradition. "Although Islamic traditions are not homogeneous, they aspire to coherence, in the way that all discursive traditions do." (Asad 1986, 17–18) In his more recent work, Asad reminds us that when approaching diverse conceptions from a comparative perspective, "the important thing is not origins— but the forms of life that articulate them." (Asad 2003, 17) The history of "Islamic law" must thus be examined contextually within complex constellations of factors involved in debates over the form and content of law in modern Muslim societies. In Indonesia, the predominant mode of "Islamizing" society often involves the integration of contemporary indigenous and "Western" secular elements and structures of thought. Aspects of these dynamics are even evident within attempts at the imposition of various essentialized visions of "Islam" upon local praxis. It is in this sense, perhaps, that one might speak of the modern formation of a distinctively Indonesian "tradition" of Islamic law emerging in the modern period.

Re-evaluating the concept of tradition from the perspective of comparative law, H. Patrick Glenn (2000) stresses the diversity, complexity, and dynamism of the world's major legal traditions in arguing for what he calls "sustainable diversity in law." The essence of tradition, according to Glenn, consists in "the extension of the past into the present." (Glenn 2000, 11) Glenn observes that the mechanism by which the past is "captured" and made accessible to the present must be a process of human communication. He rejects the view of tradition as consisting of "an indefinite series of repetitions of an action," arguing that identification of tradition with actions or process confuses the result or expression of the tradition with the tradition itself. A tradition manifests itself in a series of actions, but the tradition that produces that result is best thought of in terms of the instructions, knowledge or know how, that guides those actions. "That which is brought from the past to the present," according to Glenn, "is information." (Glenn 2000, 12)

Glenn's focus on the cognitive content of traditions is helpful in understanding the dynamics of change and interaction within and among traditions. But his choice of the term "information" to describe the content of legal traditions is potentially misleading insofar as it could be taken to suggest that legal traditions are comprised of a defined body of doctrine or a set of explicit rules. Although Glenn does not elaborate on the specific kind of information that comprises a tradition, his broader discussion does dispel any suggestion that he intends the term to be understood in that narrow sense. The pool of information that makes up a legal tradition invariably includes legal rules, but the information that defines and characterizes a particular tradition is of a distinctly different order. As John Henry Merryman, another comparative lawyer, has written, the essence of a legal tradition is "a set of deeply rooted, historically conditioned attitudes about the nature of law, about the role of law in society and the polity, about the proper organization and operation of a legal system, and about the way law is or should be made, applied, studied, perfected, and taught." (Merryman 1985, 25)

It is adherence to a common approach to such foundational issues that defines a particular legal tradition and distinguishes one tradition from another. But as Glenn has also pointed out, traditions cannot effectively control the capture of new information, and old and complex traditions can incorporate a diverse range of interpretations of the tradition's core themes. "Different levels of understanding, different means of interpretation of existing sources, different opinions, will all contribute to a variety of statements of current elements of the tradition." (Glenn 2000, 14) The world's major legal traditions, according to Glenn, are successful precisely because of their ability to accommodate diversity and contradiction. Once it is recognized that traditions are made up of information and that they lack the means to enforce complete uniformity in the information that enters the tradition, the conventional association of tradition with a static social order and resistance to change is no longer tenable. "Tradition becomes rather a resource from which reasons for change may be derived, a legitimating agency for ideas which, by themselves, would have no social resonance." (Glenn 2000, 22) This process of reform, renewal or reinterpretation of existing sources together with the acquisition of new information can even give rise to wholly new traditions.

The concept of tradition as it is elaborated by the thinkers above is useful for understanding Islamic law in Indonesia. "Islamic law," thus understood, is not a fixed body of rules or set of doctrines, but rather a discursive practice that occurs around a set of fundamental agreements or shared understandings and addresses itself to a particular arena of social life. By using this paradigm, we can better understand and contextualize the distinctive constellations of ideas and institutions that are discussed in this book. As these chapters make clear, Islamic law in general and Indonesian Islamic law in particular is a site of conflict and exchange with other traditions addressing themselves to the same problems but based on a discourse with different core assumptions. Indeed, given the diverse sources informing legal practice among Muslims in Indonesia, some of the most articulate voices elaborating visions of Islamic law there are not those of authorities who restrict themselves exclusively to any one particular tradition—be it "Islamic," "indigenous," or "imported" from the modern West. Rather, some of the most important contributions to contemporary developments are being advanced by those Indonesians who undertake the even more demanding work of building upon strong foundations within one particular tradition in order, as MacIntyre himself has expressed it, "to become involved in the conversation between traditions, learning to use the idiom of each in order to describe and evaluate the other or others." (MacIntyre 1988, 398) In his recent work John Bowen (2003) has demonstrated the extent to which this kind of dynamic movement across discourses of public reasoning has been characteristic of modern Indonesia, while highlighting also the development of each of the traditions involved over time.

Summary of contents

The essays published here address a range of issues that we have grouped into two broad categories dealing with intellectual and institutional elements of Islamic law in modern Indonesia. At various points, some of them evoke and provide data that will be of considerable interest to students of comparative Islam. However, rather than making comparison the primary lens through which to view the developments discussed here—an approach that might unintentionally reinforce the essentialist critique of Indonesian Islam as "marginal"—these studies closely examine the internal dynamics of Indonesian Islamic legal thought and institutions. Taken together, they provide a series of substantive introductions to important developments in both the theory and practice of law in the world's most populous Muslim society.

The first chapters focus on developments in the area of Islamic legal theory, both in terms of its historical development in the modern period and focused examinations of the work of specific groups of scholars and jurists. Michael Feener's essay provides a general overview of Indonesian Islamic thought on law and society over the past century, tracing developments from early calls for a reformist agenda of *ijtihād* through mid-century attempts at forging a distinctly "Indonesian *madhhab*" and subsequent trends in Islamism, neo-modernism, and critical re-engagement with aspects of traditional *uṣūl al-fiqh* methodology. The chapter that follows by Nelly van Doorn-Harder looks at specific developments in modern Indonesian Muslim legal thought with a particular focus on the discussions of women's issues among liberal sectors of the mass Islamic organization Nahdlatul Ulama (NU)—discussions that often include members of NGOs as well as scholars, or *'ulamā'*. Her contribution analyzes some innovative ways in which aspects of the diverse heritage of Islamic legal thought are being re-evaluated and deployed by contemporary Indonesian Muslim men and women interested in issues of "gender justice."

The next two chapters of this group are comprised of studies of fatwas and fatwa-issuing bodies. As recent scholarship has demonstrated, fatwas can and have played a vital role in the interaction between theoretical discourses of jurist-scholars and the practical implementation of Islamic law in various Muslim societies.[2] Kees van Dijk's chapter examines the complex relationships between religious and political authority through an overview of the history of various fatwa institutions in Indonesia. He focuses particularly on the Majelis Ulama Indonesia (MUI) and its fatwas on a selection of highly-publicized issues ranging from the definition of "religion" (as opposed to "belief," *kepercayaan*), to the permissibility of family planning and the permissibility of a national sports lottery. In this chapter, Van Dijk contextualizes these opinions in relation to broader patterns of fatwa-requesting (*iftā'*) and its relation to the authority of the state in other Muslim countries of the region in a way that highlights the complexities and ambiguities of the Indonesian case. The considerable diversity of modern Indonesian fatwa institutions is highlighted in Michael Laffan's chapter, which examines a collection of fatwas produced by a Sufi organization, the Jam'iyah Ahlith Thoriqoh al-Mu'tabaroh (JATM). Through a discussion of the form and content of a number of specific fatwas, Laffan opens up a window into the social history of the organization, particularly in its attempts to legitimate certain forms of Sufi practice in terms of established models and rules from traditional Muslim jurisprudence. At the same time, however, the fatwas discussed there shed light on important aspects of the relationships between Islamic legal opinions and political developments of Nahdlatul Ulama (NU) during the "New Order" regime of President Suharto, who ruled the country from the mid-1960s until he was forced to resign in 1998.

The second half of this volume looks at concrete manifestations of Islamic law in modern Indonesia, including court systems, positive law, the drafting of new "Islamic" legislation, and contemporary debates over the implementation of the Shari'a. Rifyal Ka'bah's chapter begins this section with a survey of the principal institutional forms of Islamic law in contemporary Indonesia together with the sources and modes of reasoning on which those institutions rely. The first half of the chapter deals with decisions of the Islamic courts, examining the mix of classical and contemporary authorities on which courts base their decisions. The focus then shifts from court decisions to fatwas, contrasting the sources and styles of reasoning reflected in the work of the fatwa-issuing bodies of Indonesia's two largest mass Muslim organizations—the NU and Muhammadiyah.

That study is followed by two chapters on substantive law. The chapter by Mark Cammack, Helen Donovan, and Tim Heaton addresses divorce—a subject that makes up the overwhelming bulk of the work of Indonesia's Islamic courts. In the first part of the chapter the authors trace a decades-long process of judicial and administrative reinterpretation of the divorce provisions of the 1974 Marriage Act whereby Muslim divorces have quietly and gradually been brought more closely under state control. In the second part of the chapter the focus shifts from the law of divorce to divorce practice. Comparing divorce statistics from the courts with survey data on the number of self-reported divorces, the authors show that many Indonesian Muslims are bypassing the courts and "divorcing" through means regarded as religiously valid but not recognized by the state. In her contribution, Musdah Mulia discusses a highly controversial proposal to reform the law of marriage for Indonesian Muslims. Referred to as the Counter Legal Draft (CLD), the proposal was prepared as an alternative to the Compilation of Islamic Law, a code of marriage, inheritance, and charitable endowment rules drafted by the Department of Religion and the Supreme Court in the 1980s and promulgated in 1991 for use by the Islamic courts. Adopting a contextual approach to the interpretation of the primary sources on Islamic marriage, the CLD proposes a fundamental reconceptualization

of marriage in which the rights and obligations of men and women are
fully equal. After discussing the jurisprudential approach and substantive
content of the CLD, the chapter concludes with an account of the passionate reactions evoked by the draft upon its release in late 2004.

   The next two chapters in this section offer different perspectives on
Indonesia's nation-wide system of Islamic courts. Mark Cammack first provides a broad overview of the origins, organization, powers, and operation
of the Islamic judiciary. After sketching the early history of the courts, the
chapter examines fundamental changes made to the organization, staffing,
and administrative supervision of the Islamic judiciary in response to an
expansion of the courts' functions and caseloads following enactment of a
national marriage law. The chapter then presents a broadly drawn profile
of the current composition, caseload, and functioning of the courts. This
broad-brush description of the Islamic judiciary is followed in the next
chapter by a close look at the operation of one particular court. John
Bowen draws on more than a quarter-century of ethnographic study of
Islam in the Gayo region of northern Sumatra to paint a fine-grained por-
trait of the Islamic court in the highland town of Takèngën. Focusing on
land disputes, Bowen shows how Islamic judges on the Takèngën court
invoke multiple normative resources in attempting to construct locally res-
onant renderings of Islamic inheritance law.

   Other developments in Aceh are the subject of the last two chapters of
this book. Aceh merits such extensive consideration in this volume because
of the special powers over Islamic law that have recently been granted to
the Acehnese provincial government. While the jurisdiction of Indonesia's
national system of Islamic courts extends only to marriage law, inheritance,
and the charitable trust (*waqf*), legislation enacted in 1999 and 2001 grants
special autonomy status to Aceh and gives the regional government expan-
sive authority to implement Islamic Shari'a. The special treatment afforded
Aceh was part of the Indonesian government's efforts begun in the immediate post-Suharto period to settle Acehnese demands for independence
from Indonesia. At the time the contributors to this volume met in Cambridge
in April of 2004 fighting between the separatist Free Aceh Movement, or
GAM (Gerakan Aceh Merdeka), and the Indonesian military was ongoing
and, at that time, prospects for settlement of the conflict seemed slight.
However, the situation in Aceh changed drastically as a result of the deadly
tsunami that struck the region in December of 2004, and against all expectations a peace agreement between GAM and the Indonesian government
was concluded in July of 2005. In the months since the peace agreement
was signed events have moved quickly in Aceh, and chapters on Aceh

included here reflect the situation as it existed in early 2006, and thus can serve to inform an understanding of the recent background of subsequent developments.

The two studies on the implementation of Islamic law in Aceh illustrate in different ways the complex political dynamics of the "Shariʿatization" process, and show how the politics of the process give meaning to recent legal developments. M. Nur Ichwan focuses primarily on the dynamic between Aceh and Jakarta. Based on an examination of the process leading to the special autonomy designation, he concludes that the impetus for granting Shariʿa to Aceh as the answer to the region's separatist demands originated with the Indonesian government in Jakarta, rather than from demands by the Acehnese. Lindsey and Hooker also consider aspects of the Aceh-Jakarta dynamic, but their main focus is on processes occurring within Aceh. Tracing the links between modern institutional structures for implementation of the Shariʿa and historic cleavages between established social groupings of local elites, they examine the effects of the Shariʿatization program on contemporary power relations within Aceh. The authors of both chapters see the Shariʿa program in Aceh as serving primarily symbolic ends, with considerable uncertainty remaining as to any future emergence of a system of coercive enforcement of religious obligations.

Finally, Azyumardi Azra's contribution discusses changes in Muslim higher education as one of the principal institutional bases for the development of Islamic legal thought in modern Indonesia. This appendix traces the history of the emergence of new institutions of Islamic legal education in the Archipelago over the course of the twentieth century, with a particular emphasis on the development of the State Islamic Education Institutes (IAINs) as the nation's premier centers of Muslim higher education and their role in the development of what has been described by various parties as a distinctively Indonesian approach to Islamic law.

The Harvard Islamic Legal Studies Program conference at which these papers were originally presented brought together leading scholars from around the world to focus specifically on Islamic law in modern Indonesia. It is our hope that the publication of this volume will both provide a foundation for understanding the material and, more importantly, stimulate further interest in pursuing future studies of the subject in which conversations can be developed between specialists concerned with Indonesian law and society and those interested in modern developments of Islamic law more generally.

Note on transcription

In attempting to produce a volume for both Indonesia specialists and scholars of Islamic studies more broadly, the issue of transliteration needs to be
addressed. The technical language of Islam draws heavily from Arabic. At
the same time, when used in scholarly treatments of modern religious discourses in the Indonesian language—or other Muslim vernaculars for that
matter—hyper-Arabization of technical terminologies can be considerably
misleading and obscure important aspects of specific local usages. When
dealing with the uses of these terms in their Indonesian context, then, one
is forced to decide whether to present them in a format recognized in
English-language scholarship for the transliteration of the Arabic terms from
which they are ultimately derived, or to simply render them in their contemporary Indonesian form. Those who adopt the first approach may not
only over-technicalize their presentations, but also risk conveying the impression that the terms they are using imply all the same fields of meaning in
Indonesian as they do in the original Arabic. Those who opt for the second method, on the other hand, are in danger of making their work appear,
cosmetically at least, less acceptable to other scholars who work on various aspects of Muslim societies outside of Southeast Asia and, more con-
sequentially, to miss opportunities to connect local discussions of particular
issues to broader discourses elsewhere in the Mulsim world. The editors of
this volume have opted for something of a middle course in which, when
dealing with the contents of specific Indonesian texts in which Indonesianized
Arabic terms are being used in distinctive ways, they are reproduced in
the form in which they were presented in the text immediately under discussion. In more general discussions, however, as well as in dealing with
Indonesian-language examples in which certain Islamic technical terms are
being used in direct dialogue with Arabic sources and debates carried out
in that language, they will be given full diacritics following the Arabic
transliteration system used by the Middle East Studies Association (MESA).

Part One

ISLAMIC LEGAL THOUGHT, EDUCATION, AND THE
PRODUCTION OF FATWAS

One

MUSLIM LEGAL THOUGHT IN MODERN INDONESIA: INTRODUCTION AND OVERVIEW

R. Michael Feener

Introduction

In recent years various aspects of Islam in Indonesia have received increased attention in both popular media and international scholarship. Scholars working in fields such as anthropology and political science—disciplines which have been dominant in North American-based Indonesian area studies for over half a century—are now being joined by colleagues trained in Islamic studies at established institutes in Europe, Australia, and Indonesia, where in recent years a considerable number of theses, dissertations, and other works have focused on particular figures or organizations important to the intellectual, cultural, and political history of Islam in Indonesia.[1]

Such studies have in many cases contributed significant new and detailed information to the expanding corpus of knowledge on Indonesian Islam. However, there is still a lack of more comprehensive works that could serve to construct a broader framework for integrated discussions of modern Indonesian Muslim intellectual history. This chapter will sketch a provisional outline of some of the major developments of modern Indonesian Muslim legal thought in an attempt to provide narrative contextualization for the more detailed discussions in the chapters that follow.[2]

The world of Muslim Southeast Asia was undergoing tremendous social, economic, cultural, and intellectual changes at the turn of the twentieth century. It was a time when a number of external influences, although long in evidence both from the West and various areas of the wider Muslim world, were becoming increasingly pronounced as they interacted with a complex array of local institutions to produce new expressions of Islam in the region. While the resulting changes were many, some general pattern of their effects can be seen in the appearance of three new, or newly reformulated, institutions in Muslim Southeast Asia: the school, the voluntary association, and the print media. The interactions of these new institutions came to radically alter not only the physical and economic landscape of the region, but its intellectual and cultural vistas as well.

In recent years a number of scholars have remarked upon changes in the patterns of religious and cultural discourse in a number of Muslim societies in terms of the emergence of a class of "new Muslim intellectuals" who have come to challenge the position of the established scholars (*'ulamā'*) as authoritative interpreters of Islamic tradition.[3] This breaking of the monopoly on religious discourse previously maintained by the *'ulamā'* made room for a new type of Muslim scholar to enter into debates on Islamic law. In Indonesia as well, a number of new figures emerged in the early decades of the twentieth century contributing alternative voices to public discussions of religious and social issues, thus creating a new style of intellectual leadership for the community. The implications of such developments have had epistemological as well as socio-political implications that pose interpretive challenges both to Islamicists and to scholars of other fields dealing with the intellectual and cultural history of modern Muslim societies. Within the Muslim community itself, it has also created situations in which new influences from outside the traditional curriculum of Muslim scholarship in the region enter into the developing debates and discussions of *fiqh* and other areas.

Calls to *ijtihād*

During the twentieth century a new, more broad-based interest in the study of legal theory and methodology (*uṣūl al-fiqh*) and the pursuit of *ijtihād* (independent jurisprudential reasoning) emerged in Indonesia within contexts of rapid modernization.[4] Working in the milieu of newly reformed institutions of education, especially those sponsored by various new voluntary associations, new Muslim intellectuals explored significantly different orientations to and new formats for their popular published work, thereby establishing a new paradigm of authority in Indonesian Islam.[5] These developments had a pronounced impact upon the study of law and jurisprudence over the course of the twentieth century.

The radical changes in the form of Islamic legal debates have resulted not only in an exponential expansion of the number of participants in the discourse, but also the inclusion of a much more broadly pluralistic body of contributors. The pros and cons of this development may be debated, but advocates of neither side can afford to dismiss the social reality of this situation. The inclusion of an increasingly greater number of non-*'ulamā'* into public debates over the interpretation of Islamic law and the development of Islamic legal theory has substantially altered both the tone and content of this discourse.

These developments in some ways started from a radical call for vigorous *ijtihād* by authors associated with reformist organizations such as the scripturalist-reformist Muslim voluntary association known as PERSIS, whose major public intellectuals were A. Hassan and Moenawar Chalil.[6] Hassan was born at Singapore in 1887 where his father was a journalist, writer, and publisher of Tamil books and newspapers. Moving to Surabaya in 1921, Hassan pursued a series of odd jobs until eventually becoming associated with PERSIS and other reform-minded activists in Java. He quickly established himself in these circles, and within a few years became the most prolific author and ideological spokesman for PERSIS, using his writing skills and experience in publishing to greatly expand the influence of this organization. Hassan's call for a radical *ijtihād*, which ideally reaches back directly into the Qur'an and Sunna, demanded a reinvigorated study of these primary sources. Toward this end Hassan composed his own Qur'anic commentary (*tafsīr*) in the form of an Indonesian translation of the Qur'an, as well as an annotated Indonesian translation of Ibn Ḥajar al-'Asqalānī's (d. 1449) work on prophetic Tradition (*ḥadīth*), *Bulūgh al-Marām*.[7] In addition to these works, Hassan also produced a treatise expounding his scripturalist legal theory entitled *al-Boerhan*, which became the first popular monograph on Islamic legal theory written in modern, Roman-script Indonesian (Hassan 1928). Hassan dedicated his attention to *uṣūl al-fiqh* because he believed that by undertaking a critical study of the sources of law and the methods used to apply them, Muslims could free themselves from the shackles of "blind *taqlīd*" (adherence to established rulings), and purify their religion from unnecessary and even dangerous human innovations (*bidʿa*).

Another leading reformist of Hassan's generation was Moenawar Chalil. Chalil was born into a prominent family of traders and religious scholars at Kendal, Central Java in 1908.[8] Like Hassan, Chalil began his religious education under his father; however, he then continued on through a thorough course of studies in the formal Islamic religious sciences under other prominent local religious teachers (J. *kyai*). Unlike Hassan, however, Chalil never combined this "traditional" style of Javanese Muslim religious education with studies in a "modern" style school.

In his own writings Chalil devoted considerable energy to producing works of *tafsīr* and *ḥadīth* study to serve as a foundation for his larger project of legal reform, which he outlined and presented thematically in his signature work, *Kembali kepada Al Qur'an dan As-Sunna* ("Return to the Qur'an and the Sunna"), first published in 1956.[9] Despite the title of this work, Chalil's approach to Islamic law went beyond simple scripturalism. In fact, the second section of this book features chapters devoted to establishing the relationship between rulings based directly on the Qur'an and Sunna and those arrived at through such extra-scriptural legal sources as consensus (*ijmā'*) and analogy (*qiyās*) as well as the debates on *ijtihād*, *taqlīd*, *ittibā'* (informed acceptance of a jurist's decision), adherence to one of the four orthodox schools of law, and the consideration of public interest (*istiṣlāḥ*) as a source of law.[10]

Chalil undertook a critical evaluation and re-envisioning of previous work in the scholarly traditions of Muslim jurisprudence while maintaining a qualified respect for the authority of established interpretations of the *'ulamā'*. Thus, for all his radical rhetoric of returning directly to the scriptural sources of the tradition, Chalil remained convinced that the task of legislating in accordance with the Qur'an and Sunna is best left to those with specialized training in the religious sciences. Such a model of authority is one in which Chalil, with his background in the tradition of Javanese Muslim scholarship that entitled him to use the title of *kyai*, would comfortably fit.[11] It is a model of authority that would not appear to be as accommodating to Chalil's contemporary, Hassan, with his limited formal education and checkered career as a printer, petty trader, and tire vulcanizer.

In Chalil we can see something of a moderation of the more radical reformism of Hassan, and this qualified scripturalism seems to have left a much more enduring, broad-based impression upon subsequent developments in movements for the reform of Indonesian Islam. From the writings of Hassan to those of Chalil one can notice a shift in orientation which came to have significant consequences for debates in the area of *fiqh* and *uṣūl al-fiqh*. For Chalil's understanding of *ijtihād* did not necessarily mean a blanket rejection of the tradition of Muslim legal scholarship. Rather, he suggested that such legacies could be constructively used in the formation of a new legal theory and a revitalization of *fiqh* that would be responsive to the changing needs of the times (Chalil 1955).

Local custom in a "national" madhhab

Times were changing rapidly during the lives of Hassan and Chalil, and the leading Muslim authors of the generation that followed them found themselves living and working in a dramatically different setting. Over the first few decades following independence in 1945, a new struggle faced the fledgling nation of Indonesia: a struggle no longer for sovereignty in the face of colonial control, but rather an internal struggle to define the new nation for itself. In this arena, conflicts among the three most powerful groups of Nationalists, Socialists, and "Islamists" were often most pronounced in debates over the constitutional basis for the state and the model of law promulgated by it.

Some of the principal debates over the role of Islam in the Indonesian state were expressed in the disputes over the "Jakarta Charter" (*Piagam Jakarta*). This early preamble to the 1945 constitution included the controversial pronouncement that the Republic was to be founded on a set of principles, the first of which was: "The belief in God, with the obligations for adherents of Islam to practice Islamic law."[12] The second clause in this phrase, referring to the Shari'a, was later struck from the preamble as part of a series of political compromises amongst various segments of the Indonesian independence movement. This move was viewed by some Indonesians as a testament to the triumph of nationalist over communitarian religious ideas, consistent with the non-sectarian political ideology of President Soekarno, known as *Pancasila*. Others in the Muslim community, however, viewed the decision to delete the reference to the Shari'a as a compromise of their aspirations for an autonomous Muslim-majority nation and even as a betrayal of their own participation and sacrifice in the struggles that led to achieving independence.

Without a constitutional statement legitimizing the formal establishment of Islamic law in the administration of the young republic, Indonesia's legal system came to be established primarily according to the legal ideologies and institutions of the Dutch colonial system that preceded it. However, this did not end Muslim endeavors directed toward expanding the sphere of influence for Islam upon various aspects of life in modern Indonesia. Some took to armed struggle for the formal establishment of an "Islamic state" in the various Darul Islam movements across the archipelago, some turned to party politics, while others attempted to further the Islamization of Indonesian society through the work of Muslim social welfare and educational organizations. Over the middle decades of the twentieth century, various groups of this kind attracted the energy of many young and committed Muslims, including one who was to become a major national figure through his prolific production of textbooks and other popular writings on Islam: Hasbi Ash Shiddieqy.

Hasbi was active in a number of capacities within the Indonesian system of State Islamic Colleges (IAIN) following his appointment as a lecturer at Yogyakarta in 1951. In addition to his teaching and administrative work at the IAIN, Hasbi also worked more than any other single Indonesian author of his day toward the production of materials to be used in the curriculum of these institutions. Many of his writings have been reprinted multiple times since his death in 1975.[13] In these works, Hasbi drew on a wide variety of medieval and modern authorities in a conscious attempt to expand the corpus of Muslim scholarship studied in Indonesia. Some of the most prominent influences visible in Hasbi's works are the medieval Maghrebi Maliki jurist al-Shāṭibī, the eighteenth-century *mujtahids* al-Ṣanʿānī, al-Shawkānī, and Shāh Walī Allāh, as well as the twentieth-century Egyptian reformists Muḥammad Muṣṭafā al-Marāghī, ʿAbd al-Wahhāb al-Khallāf, and Maḥmūd Shaltūt.

In the story of Hasbi's life and works we see many parallels between his activities and those of activist autodidacts like A. Hassan a generation earlier. Both shared a similar concern with the problems facing the Indonesian Muslim community of their day, and both strove to improve the situation through calls for a rethinking of religion and of its place in society. For Hassan the solution to the dilemmas facing the Muslim community was to be found in a purified Islam, a religion stripped of all its illogical and scripturally-unfounded accretions. Hasbi, on the other hand, felt that such a minimalist and scripturalist understanding of Islam would be in itself incapable of addressing the problems posed by the complexity of modern life in Indonesia. It was this concern that prompted Hasbi's advocacy of moving beyond simply the "purification" of Islam, seeing that as merely the first step in a more constructive project directed toward the creation of a new system of "Indonesian *fiqh*" (Ind. *fikih Indonesia*).[14]

At about the same time another movement for the establishment of a school of distinctively modern Indonesian Muslim jurisprudence was being elaborated in the form of a proposal for the formation of a new "National School of Law" (*madzhab nasional*) being advanced by Hazairin, a Dutch-trained scholar of customary law (*adat*).[15] Coming to the task of developing a specifically Indonesian *fiqh* through different avenues than Hasbi, Hazairin attempted to work out new models of *fiqh* grounded in the realities of Indonesian cultural contexts through his ethnographic studies of *adat*. Along these lines he advocated the creation of a newly reformulated Muslim jurisprudence, or, more properly, a new national model of Islamic law that would take greater account of the social and historical contexts of Indonesia.

The raw materials for the creation of such a school were to include not only considerations of local geography and culture, but also elements from the other schools, not only that of al-Shāfiʿī which has historically been dominant in the archipelago. In his *Hukum Islam dan Masyarakat*, we see Hazairin's elaboration of a critique on *taqlīd*, which he describes in part as the conflation of adherence to Arabian custom with following Islamic law (Hazairin 1951, 8). Thence he argued that Indonesians needed to be critical of legal formulations that would impose Middle Eastern cultural norms upon Indonesian adherents of Islam. Hazairin's specialized training in *adat* law is clearly reflected in his differentiation between *agama* (religion) and *adat* (custom). However, while he applied aspects of this methodology in his consideration of local custom as a source of law, Hazairin also reacted sharply to the dominant mode of Dutch *adat* law studies, which held that only those Islamic laws that had been fully "received" into local custom could be considered as valid. This left Islamic law with no inherent author-ity of its own, and it was in reaction to this that Hazairin railed against the "reception theory" of Dutch *adat* law as "the theory of the devil" (*teori Iblis*).

One of the defining contributions of Hazairin's work was in the area of inheritance law.[16] Based upon his ethnographically-oriented study of *adat* law, Hazairin determined that a number of the larger ethnic groups of the Indonesian archipelago traditionally distributed estates along the lines of both parents. He then noted the discrepancies between these bilateral sys-tems and the patrilineal model of Arabian society that had been so influential in early formulations of *fiqh*. Hazairin argued that the inclusion of these patrilineal features resulted from historical accidents arising from the place and time in which God's last messenger lived, and thus elements of Arabian customary practice contained within classical Islamic jurisprudence were not part of the revealed Law.

Hazairin maintained that in order for Islamic law to become realized as the actual "living law" of Indonesian society, it would have to be reinter-preted according to Indonesian cultural conditions, and not according to some other foreign and historically distant situation. In short, he proposed the establishment of a new system of inheritance based on an elaboration of the scriptural precepts of the Qur'an and Sunna in terms of a bilateral, rather than a patrilineal, model of kinship.[17] In the formulation of such interpretations, one can perceive something of the orientational shift that has occurred between Hazairin and the other figures discussed previously. Even Hasbi, writing at the same time as Hazairin, tended to discuss such issues primarily in terms of the Islamic reformist rhetoric of *sunna* and *bid'a*. Hazairin, however, reformulated the issue in terms of the modern social science categories of "religion" and "custom."

Islamist ideology in Indonesian legal debates

The complex relationships between Islamic religious and Indonesian cul-tural values were later radically rethought by one of Hazairin's doctoral students, Anwar Harjono.[18] However, Harjono's writings on legal issues differed significantly from those of his teacher, as they dealt not so much with how the law of Islam is to be interpreted and applied, as with the nature of Islamic law itself. Anwar Harjono is today more widely known as an activist than as an Islamic legal theorist. Until his death in 1999, he led the Dewan Dakwah Islamiyah Indonesia (DDII), and before that he was an active member of the Muslim political party Masjumi.

In both of these organizations, he was a close associate of M. Natsir— arguably the most powerful Muslim politician in modern Indonesian history.[19] During a 1957 address to the Constituent Assembly, Natsir had put forward a model of state that he referred to as "Theistic Democracy"—a system in which the sovereignty of the people was to be exercised within certain limits that had been determined by God. The word Natsir used to refer to these limits was ḥudūd, a term which in Islamic legal discourse and Islamist political rhetoric is usually used to refer to canonically-established penalties for certain offenses. Here, however, Natsir spoke of ḥudūd as "universal moral principles" in a manner reminiscent of Western discourses on natural law (Ihza 1995, 143–44).

In the notes accompanying the text of his 1957 Constituent Assembly address, Natsir even pointed out the origins of such an approach to natural law in the work of Thomas Aquinas (d. 1274).[20] Natsir's citation of a medieval Roman Catholic theologian in establishing his own modern Muslim conception of "natural law" raises questions about just what he had in mind when deploying such a reference and, more generally, what he found appealing in certain forms of natural law reasoning. Modern revivals and reinterpretations of natural law theory flourished in the middle decades of the twentieth century, not only in Europe and the United States, but in many parts of the world in an atmosphere marked by the United Nation's Universal Declaration of Human Rights in 1948 and processes of decolonization in many parts of Asia and Africa (Crowe 1977, 251).[21]

During those years religious intellectuals from various confessional backgrounds were engaged in developing modern interpretations of natural law theory. The modern Roman Catholic philosopher Jacques Maritain, for example, put forward a new model which held that the most basic principles of natural law were not known through reason, but "connaturally" or "by inclination" and that these impressionistic bases for understanding natural law are ultimately beyond question (Maritain 2001, 9). Such potentially arbitrary and authoritarian conceptions of natural law appear to have been also at work in subsequent Indonesian Muslim writings produced by Natsir's ersatz successor Anwar Harjono, who built upon Natsir's later

thoughts on natural law recast in terms of "the Way of God" (*Sunnatullah*).[22]
In one of his essays, Harjono builds upon a series of Qur'anic usages of
this term to construct a definition of *Sunnatullah* as: "A law that is not made
by human beings, but influences and in fact serves to order human society, with or without their agreement to it."[23] Harjono argued that God's
law, as made known through the Qur'an and Sunna, must be appealed to
directly and established as a "living law" through the practice of *ijtihād*,
rather than relying on the man-made *fiqh* of the established schools.

Rather than any particular methodology of jurisprudence, then, Harjono
called for a scripturalist project of "capturing the spirit" of the Qur'an and
Sunna in a way that is "impressionistic and always up to date" (Harjono
1968, 101–06). However, the practical possibility of implementing a working system of law with the degree of flexibility implied by this statement
seems at the same time to be undercut by the emphasis he places on the
need for the codification and formal implementation of Islamic law in both
civil and criminal courts. For Harjono maintained that any "law" without
governmental power to enforce it is not really law at all (Harjono 1995,
129, 27–8, 87)—an assertion of a model of Muslim politics that reveals the
lineage connecting the cultural Islamization programs of DDII with their
roots in Masjumi and that party's struggles to formalize a place for Islamic
law in the Indonesian constitution through appeals to the Jakarta Charter.

Under Suharto's New Order, however, direct political action was a non-
option for Muslim organizations as the mandatory affirmation of *Pancasila*
as the sole ideological basis of all political parties forced them to withdraw
from the political arena and to redirect their activities toward the fields of
social welfare and education. These social and cultural activities became
the central pursuits of a number of movements that gained strength toward
the end of the New Order. Many such movements saw themselves as
involved in *daʿwa*, which came to be understood in diverse ways as a means
of furthering the Islamization of the social and cultural spheres of Indonesian
life in the later twentieth century.

Anwar Harjono's thinking on Islamic law and other issues was popu-
larized through the activities of the DDII, which continued to advocate
the formalization of Islamic practices and institutions in Indonesian society through means that avoided direct involvement with party politics.[24]
This agenda was pursued aggressively through various means, including
publishing ventures, preaching activities, and educational programs. However,
the DDII was not the only, nor even the most popular and influential,
Muslim organization engaged in such endeavors, for during the last quarter of the twentieth century, a vibrant Muslim public sphere developed as

a place to give voice to activists and scholars of widely divergent ideological orientations who had studied in various kinds of schools making up the rapidly expanding system of colleges and universities in the country.

Renewal and "reactualization"

The rapid expansion of Islamic higher education in Indonesia during this period resulted in the further exponential growth in the number of potential participants in debates over issues of religion, law, and society. Some of the most influential developments regarding these issues were taking place within the growing system of IAIN campuses throughout the country. Under the administrations of reforming Ministers of Religious Affairs Mukti Ali (1971–1978) and Munawir Sjadzali (1983–1993), facilities at various IAIN branches expanded to include post-graduate studies and other programs to upgrade teaching staff for the religious sciences in an interdisciplinary format. Such programs had a marked effect on the kinds of religious scholars produced in Indonesia during the later twentieth century. In fact, one can see a marked shift in orientation of the institutes from the earliest years when faculty were exchanged with Egypt[25] to the 1970s when IAIN began looking more to the West for training and methodological approaches. This started with the sending of trainees to Canada, Australia, the Netherlands, Germany, and the United States in the 1970s and continued over subsequent decades on a much larger scale and in cooperation with such international partners as the Indonesian-Netherlands Co-operation in Islamic Studies (INIS) and the McGill Indonesia project.

Some of the changes at IAIN during the first decades of the New Order—accompanied as they were by the promotion of developmentalist agendas by the Suharto regime—facilitated the rise to prominence of a new corps of intelligentsia that approached religious questions from a viewpoint radically different from that of their forbears. Many of these new Muslim intellectuals had advanced training in such fields as communications, economics, and the social sciences, and a number of them held advanced degrees in Islamic Studies from universities in Europe, Canada, and the United States. Their influence transformed earlier patterns in Indonesian understandings of Islam by introducing approaches and conceptual categories from the academic study of religion into the mainstream of Indonesian public religious discourse.

One of the most prominent Indonesians with such training was Nurcholish Madjid, who completed his dissertation under Fazlur Rahman at the University of Chicago. He has been characterized by a number of scholars as a "Neo-Modernist" in his attempt to re-evaluate Muslim tradition in a constructive reformulation that drew selectively upon those aspects of the tradition that seemed most beneficial and relevant to the needs of contemporary society.[26] This trend in contemporary Islamic thought is most often referred to within Indonesia as *Pembaharuan* (Renewal), and while Madjid's work is not primarily focused on law or legal theory, the dynamic atmosphere fostered by the *Pembaharuan* movement that he pioneered in contemporary Indonesia has had considerable impact on developments over the past two decades. This has not simply created an Indonesian school of Rahman-style Neo-Modernists, but rather has facilitated the expression of a wide range of other voices articulating divergent views on Islamic law and legal theory.

One of Madjid's major contributions in this was his role in the establishment of the Paramadina foundation which publishes works of progressive Islamic scholarship and hosts seminars and discussions on religious and social issues attended by many of Indonesia's leading public intellectuals. A prominent participant in these discussions at Paramadina during the late 1980s was the Indonesian Minister of Religious Affairs, Munawir Sjadzali (Van Dijk 1991), a career diplomat who held assignments in the Middle East, London, and Washington. Sjadzali pursued graduate work in political science at both Exeter and Georgetown, and later drew on his studies of religion and politics when appointed Minister of Religious Affairs in 1983. He held that office for a decade, during which time he publicly proclaimed his program for the "Reactualization" (Ind. *Reaktualisasi*) of Islam (Sjadzali 1988).

Sjadzali's writing on *Reaktualisasi* elaborated some of the more general aspects of *Pembaharuan* specifically in the sphere of Islamic law.[27] The general progressive tendencies of Indonesian Neo-Modernism were reflected in particular positions put forward by the Minister. In support of his stance on issues such as gender equality in Islamic inheritance law, Sjadzali relied heavily upon a radical reinterpretation of Qur'anic exegetical principles such as abrogation (*naskh*). As a result of the liberties that Sjadzali was perceived to have taken with this sub-discipline of Qur'anic studies and other aspects of Islamic jurisprudence, his program of *Reaktualisasi* attracted considerable criticism from various fronts.

New directions in "traditionalism"

Subsequently, however, a number of more traditionally-trained Indonesian Muslim scholars have come forward with popular publications that present new ideas that are in a number of ways similar to those of *Pembaharuan*, but presented in more established idioms of traditional Muslim learning. These authors come largely from backgrounds of traditional religious education (*pesantren*), a much-disparaged system in the work of the radical reformism of Hassan, but one that found a new level of appreciation among *Pembaharuan* thinkers in their turn toward new readings of "tradition." In their work these young *pesantren* scholars have sought to adapt their extensive knowledge of both scripture and classical Muslim scholarship into ongoing debates in an effort to contexualize relevant material from traditional Muslim learning with the needs of contemporary Indonesian society. One of the most important figures of this type has been Sahal Mahfudh, a classically-trained *kyai* from Central Java associated with the Indonesian "traditionalist" Muslim organization Nahdlatul Ulama (NU), who pioneered movements among traditionalists for more contextualized applications of classical Islamic religious scholarship.[28]

Mahfudh contends that the true integration of *fiqh* into society involves more than simply "bringing things up to date," as if *fiqh* were some concrete corpus that simply needs tinkering with now and then. Rather he argues that *fiqh* should be thought of not as "a second [closed body of] scripture beside the Qur'an" but instead as a dynamic "counter discourse" (Mahfudh 1994). In explaining the contextual relationship of *fiqh* to other aspects of community life, Mahfudh repeatedly reminds his readers that the first two institutions built by the Prophet in Medina were the mosque and the marketplace. According to Mafudh, this shows that Muḥammad was keenly aware of the need to balance the concerns of this world with those of the world to come. Such a balance of emphasis between this world and the next is a cornerstone of Mahfudh's thought, and serves as a framework for his understanding of *fiqh* methodology as a valuable resource for the Muslim community in confronting the challenges of the contemporary world.

The work of NU religious scholars like Sahal Mahfudh has helped to create a new energy in the "traditionalist" *pesantren* milieu. This was accomplished to a considerable extent through fostering the development of "study circles" (Ind. *halqah*) in which younger scholars were introduced to modern "contextualizing" approaches and encouraged to develop new interpretations of Islamic law that could be relevant to the social and economic needs of the community. One major figure in these developments has been Masdar Mas'udi, who has contributed his extensive knowledge of Islamic law and theology in service of a number of programs dedicated to progressive agendas for social justice. His arguments are well grounded in the *pesantren* tradition of Muslim learning while at the same time being elaborated in a way that makes it possible to communicate with and relate to the concerns of Muslims from a variety of different backgrounds. Since the 1980s, Mas'udi has worked to put his innovative readings of the tradition into practice through the programs of the Muslim NGO known as P3M (Perhimpunan Pengembangan Pesantren dan Masyarakat).

Mas'udi's major work, a treatise on the Islamic alms tax *zakāt* entitled *Agama Keadilan* ("The Religion of Justice") is an "entry into a broader discussion of the 'Social Vision of Islam'" (Mas'udi 1991, 6–7). He chooses the subject of *zakāt* because he sees it as addressing some of the most profound injustices resulting from the dramatic changes brought on by rapid economic and social transformations in Indonesian society. Mas'udi addresses these issues through a careful and critical re-reading of traditional Muslim legal scholarship and a radical redeployment of the classifications of specific scriptural texts as either unambiguously binding (*qaṭ'ī*) or open to human interpretation (*ẓannī*). This aspect of Mas'udi's approach has been adopted by a diverse range of Muslim thinkers in contemporary Indonesia. However, his own prominence in progressive conversations on Islamic law has diminished in recent years, especially following the public acrimony that accompanied his contracting of a polygamous marriage in 2000.

Contextual "traditionalist" approaches to social justice issues have been further pursued by other scholars and activists associated with the NU, including Husein Muhammad and the women of the Yayasan Kesejahteraan Fatayat (Women's Welfare Foundation, or YKF). This organization works to culturally contextualize conceptions of gender justice within the world of the *pesantren*, and devotes considerable energies toward the training of cadres of Indonesian Muslim women who are both able to read classical Arabic texts and familiar with the traditional methodologies of Muslim jurisprudence. Armed with this knowledge of Islamic intellectual heritage, these scholars work together on developing critical readings of traditional materials that can help to re-evaluate Islamic legal thought on gender issues as well as broader concerns.[29] The nuanced and in-depth treatments of the technical workings of Islamic jurisprudence pursued by such thinkers provide alternative visions of a just, modern, and Muslim Indonesian society set alongside those of the scripturalists and modernists.

The current situation in Indonesia is one of increasing public engagement on the foundational constitutional and institutional structures of the state. Whatever their ultimate impact on state legal reformulation, the models of Muslim legal thought developed by Indonesian thinkers over the past century comprise a rich and varied heritage upon which future work may be built. Important aspects of the diverse legacy of Muslim legal thought in modern Indonesia that may be relevant here would include: (1) the encouragement of *ijtihād*, (2) the consideration of local conditions in the way that the Shariʿa is interpreted and implemented, (3) a theoretical sophistication directed toward historical and sociologically-informed understandings of the development of law in society, and (4) an appreciation of aspects of traditional jurisprudential methodologies in Islamic scholarship with a creative eye to ways in which those methodologies may serve to inform contemporary debates. Attempts already made in all of these areas may yet come to serve as important building blocks in the construction of a foundation upon which future work toward legal reformulation may be based. Indeed, these issues may become increasingly crucial as Indonesia seeks to chart its course through a period of transition that presents the nation with some of the most critical questions regarding the nature of the state and its law that it has faced since independence.

Two

RECONSIDERING AUTHORITY: INDONESIAN FIQH TEXTS ABOUT WOMEN

Nelly van Doorn-Harder

Introduction: Discourses

Indonesia is the land of *wacana*, or discourse. Animated discussions concerning religious topics ranging from proper ritual worship (*ʿibādāt*) to the lawfulness of erotic dances performed by *dangdut* singers take place in the press, on radio, on TV, and during numerous seminars.[1] In this context, it is not surprising that the reinterpretation of the Qurʾan and the body of jurisprudence (*fiqh*) concerning certain topics is not limited—as is the case in most Islamic countries—to an elite group of male scholars. During the past decade especially, discussions about women have taken center stage in debates on all levels of society. Myriad books on the topic of "women" fill the bookstores and both those who seek women's liberation and those who oppose it pen their thoughts. Since the fall of the Suharto regime, the debates have become even more energized as Islamist voices have been added to the choir of opinions. Those who advocate polygyny and curtailing the rights of women and non-Muslims joined and intensified the debate. This was not an entirely negative development, however, as they also accelerated the activities of Muslims who sought to strengthen women's position within Islamic legal structures, especially those transmitted through the study of *fiqh*.

This chapter will discuss some of the initiatives to reinterpret Muslim jurisprudence and approaches to modern women's issues that have developed within Indonesia's traditionalist circles connected to the Nahdlatul Ulama (NU), an Islamic organization that claims some thirty million followers. This process started during the 1970s and was spearheaded by the visionary ideas of a group of NU leaders, the most prominent of whom was Abdurrahman Wahid (1940–). Wahid's agenda aimed at promoting religious tolerance, human rights, and the democratization of society, which he saw as an antidote against influences of radical Islam that reached Indonesia via aggressive missionary activities (*daʿwa*) often inspired by Saudi

Arabia. In cooperation with a group of eminent NU scholars of Islam (*kyai*) such as Sahal Mahfudh, Wahid initiated the discussion of how traditionalist Muslim teachings could serve as a force of societal change. In this process they did not see the rules of Islamic jurisprudence as immutable due to the fact that they are based on the divine precepts. Rather, they advocated understandings of *fiqh* as dynamic codes that can reflect changing times and conditions.[2]

These NU thinkers were working against the backdrop of several developments that emerged during the 1970s. Traditionalist NU leaders faced the increasing success of reformist approaches that allowed direct interpretation of the Qur'an and independent legal reasoning (*ijtihād*), to bypass the teachings of the established schools (*madhhab*). As this was simpler to learn than the jurisprudence that required decades of study, NU feared a loss of social relevance, especially since reformist energies were often channeled into the creation of educational institutions. For example, under the leadership of the reform-minded Harun Nasution (1919–1998), the State Institute for Higher Islamic Learning (IAIN) in Jakarta modernized its curriculum in order to combine "studies of traditional Islamic sciences with subjects drawn from modern western educational models, such as sociology, anthropology, comparative religion and secular philosophy."[3] The vision underlying this change was to create an "Islamic state of mind" through a modern, rationalized model of education (Hooker 2003, 36–7).

While positioning themselves vis-à-vis the reformist methods and philosophies of learning, NU leaders reconsidered the significance of their own time-consuming models that included the study of medieval Islamic interpretations. However, rather than ignoring the long tradition of scholarship, NU scholars utilized established approaches such as that proposed by the medieval Maliki jurist Abū Isḥāq al-Shāṭibī (d. 1388) to articulate new paradigms that could lead to fundamental reform of their religious interpretations (Riddell 2001, 252).

Another important element of the context for these developments concerned the limitations the Suharto regime (1966–1998) imposed on Muslim-based political activity. During the 1970s an intense discussion raged within traditionalist circles about the separation of Islam and politics in the context of Suharto's interpretation of Indonesia's state ideology of *Pancasila* that advocated the belief in One God for Muslims, Christians, Buddhists, and Hindus. Ultimately Muslim organizations were forced to steer away from politics, shifting their focus to social, charitable, and missionary activities.

Concurrent with these developments was a demand from NU women that the organization reconsider some of its *fiqh* teachings about women. While in public life NU women were gaining inroads in prominent positions as members of parliament and teachers in the State Institutes for Islamic Studies (IAIN), in private their lives were still ruled by traditional teachings based on a limited number of established *fiqh* texts. These texts had considerable influence on the way preachers spoke about women and shaped the self image of Muslim women all over Indonesia. As the maps of reality and religious theory no longer matched, change became unavoidable and a new legal theory about women's role seemed imperative. This was not an easy task. *Fiqh* texts were not to be taken lightly since they contained texts from Qur'an and *ḥadīth* and were considered sacrosanct by some traditionalist Muslims. Transmission of texts over time had bestowed on them an aura of authority, whether this status was deserved or not, and to this day there are some within the Indonesian Muslim community who maintain that the aura of sanctity is inherent to the texts. Hence there was resistance to revising or adapting the legal injunctions, in this case those concerning the role and rights of women according to the Islamic law.

The problem of religious authority: Shaping authorities

Legal systems are inevitably subject to continuous change as they are connected to and reflect developments in the concrete world of human interactions. In spite of this reality, in the minds of many Muslims and non-Muslims, the system of Islamic law seems immutable and unchanging. Recent scholarship on Islamic law has worked against this perception by showing how, through fatwas and other mechanisms, undestandings of the Shari'a as embodied by the teachings of substantive law (*furū' al-fiqh*), legal methodology (*uṣūl al-fiqh*), and jurisprudence have been subject to historical change. This "development of the Shari'a from below" signified a natural process as it took shape in response to needs and requests from specific Muslim communities (Masud, Messick, and Powers 1996, 4).

The process by which Islamic law was accepted by local communities introduced a degree of flexibility to the Islamic law system. Local interpreters rejected certain texts while ascribing authority to others. Studies such as Brannon Wheeler's *Applying the Canon in Islam* (1996) have pointed out that it is not always the text that matters but the authority assigned to it by the transmitters of the religious and legal system. Wheeler, for example, observed how the early interpreters of Islam manipulated the traditional interpretations in order to establish certain forms of authority (Wheeler 1996, 9). As the tradition thus emerging was transmitted through pedagogical means, the canonical authority of certain texts became fixed

(Wheeler 1996, 2, 3). Wheeler's approach is informed by the writings of the historian of religions Jonathan Z. Smith (1978; 1982), who analyzed the divination process of the Ndembu and concluded that canonical authority is not found in a given text. According to Smith, forming a canon is "about establishing and maintaining certain forms of interpretive authority" (Wheeler 1996, 9).

Similar to the impression that Islamic law is immutable, the idea of fixed traditions (those comprising the body of ḥadīth as represented in the Sunna of the Prophet) has settled in the minds of many Muslims and non-Muslims alike. With particular reference to the role of women in Islam, this has led to instances where Muslim scholars have overlooked Qur'anic injunctions that are egalitarian towards men and women. Instead, they gave preference to texts that denigrate the status and morality of women. Khaled Abou El Fadl has written extensively about traditions concerning women that were deemed weak (ḍaʿīf) or based on singular transmissions but gained disproportionate authority among the early Muslims. As a result of this, transmissions about women prostrating before their husband and fulfilling their obligations toward him gained prominence although they were based on weak links of transmitters. One of the many traditions quoted by Abou El Fadl summarizes several of these themes. Its source is Azhar b. Marwān who reported that when Muʿādh returned from Syria he prostrated before the Prophet.

> The Prophet said, "What are you doing Muʿādh?" Muʿādh said, "I was in Shām and I saw that the people prostrated to their priests and clergy and I wished we could do the same for you." The Prophet said, "If I would have ordered anyone to prostrate before anyone but God, I would have ordered a woman to prostrate to her husband. By God, a woman cannot fulfill her obligations to God until she fulfills her obligations to her husband and if he asks for her [i.e. for sex] while she is on a camel's back, she cannot deny him [his pleasure]." (Abou El Fadl 2001, 211)

Abou El Fadl has pointed out that it is curious that this form of gendered reading of ḥadīth gained precedence over the notion of God's supremacy (one should not prostrate before people) while also ignoring the Qur'anic discourse on marriage (Abou El Fadl 2001, 214). Apart from that, Abou El Fadl has drawn attention to the fact that the structure of these traditions was peculiar as the Prophet spontaneously inserted a remark about women in a question asked by men about the actions of other men (Abou El Fadl 2001, 213). Abou El Fadl has also shown that preferring certain traditions over others might have been the result of internal politics within the early Muslim community where Sunnis waged a battle for authority with Shi'ites (Abou El Fadl 2001, 217). And, finally, he is adamant that many of the weak or suspect traditions originated from Abū Hurayra who was a problematic and contested source. However, since the traditions of the Prophet gained authority based on their transmission, believers stopped questioning the credibility of the transmitters (Wheeler 1996, 11). The next rung on the ladder of authority were the individual interpreters who chose those traditions that suited best their arguments, thus producing new forms of *fiqh* teachings.

Reformist and traditionalist interpretations

During the past three decades, an awareness has grown in the Muslim world that a reinterpretation of the Islamic teachings concerning women is called for. The so-called reformist or modernist mode of Islamic inter-pretation developed by Muḥammad 'Abduh (1869–1905) and his succes-sor Rashīd Riḍā (1865–1935) in the Middle East were further advanced in Indonesia through the work of the Muhammadiyah movement. In the West, especially in the United States, books and articles started to appear by the 1980s analyzing the teachings of women in the Qur'an based on reformist modes of interpretation. Representatives of this trend include, for example, Azizah al-Hibri (1982), Asma Barlas (2002), and Ashgar Ali Engineer (1992).[4] Their reinterpretations relied directly on the Qur'an and mostly ignored the body of texts that processed the teachings of Qur'an, *ḥadīth* and *fiqh*. Since Muḥammad 'Abduh introduced this revolutionary approach at the beginning of the twentieth century it has gained wide adherence. Apart from faster tracks of Islamic learning, it opened up new vistas for Muslim women, as they gained increasing access to education and the workforce.

However, by the end of the twentieth century, Muslim Sunni scholars who were seeking to transform Islam into a societal force of justice and democracy came to realize the limitations of the reformist approach that for the most part ignored the tradition of *fiqh* scholarship. They started to point out that in bypassing the body of jurisprudence and using rulings from the four *maddhab*s selectively, the discourse about women remained laudatory, vague, and often apologetic. The positive picture painted by reformist advocates for women such as Azizah al-Hibri glosses over the difficult realities Muslim women face arising from the laws and interpre-tations that govern their daily lives. Selective optimism in the end carries negative religious and social ramifications for women. For example, Kecia

Ali has drawn attention to the fact that with regards to the marriage contract, the reformist interpretations failed to address the Arab mindset that
had shaped this contract in analogy with that concerning the possession of
slaves (see Ali 2003). Since this mindset still influences men's views on the
status of women in many parts of the Muslim world, it continues to govern women's position in marriage. An approach that does more than highlight the egalitarian texts of the Qur'an ignores the reality that many women
suffer injustices based on the original ideas concerning marriage. The program of progressive scholars who simply put a rosy gloss on teachings that
in principle were shaped through the lens of male bias can never truly lib-
erate women.

A greater awareness of the importance of the continuing influence of
fiqh on the position of women in Islam developed during the late 1990s
among U.S. Muslims who call themselves "progressive." As I have indicated earlier, however, this insight is not entirely new; the importance of
fiqh had been recognized earlier by traditionalist Muslims in Indonesia,
especially those connected with the NU, the umbrella organization for
Muslims following the traditionalist methods of interpreting the holy texts
of Islam. Since the 1980s NU scholars have included the classical *fiqh* texts
when reinterpreting Qur'an and *ḥadīth* in order to highlight teachings that
are of an egalitarian and just nature.

*Creating new legal teachings: Re-reading fiqh texts from below and NU's "Fiqh
Sosial"*

Fiqh has traditionally been studied in the NU Islamic boarding schools, the
pesantren, where students (*santri*) could spend up to two decades before
becoming authorities on Islam. The texts of the *pesantren* curriculum are
called *kitab kuning*, "yellow books," a term referring to their age and dura-
bility that evokes the impression of authority. They are composed in Arabic
or Arabic script forms of local languages, the very form of which is seen
to enhance their authority. By the 1970s, *pesantren*, and their *kitab kuning*
were considered out of sync with modern society. In order to prepare a
new cadre of leaders who could negotiate the rapid changes of modern
society and be instrumental in bringing about social change, NU leaders
realized that they had to modernize the traditional network of *pesantren*.[5]
Their challenge was to transform the *pesantren*'s potential of dedicated people who were well-versed in Islamic knowledge into instruments of change
that could propagate Islam as an innovative way of life. The goal was to

teach Islamic ethics and ideologies that could strengthen the Islamic intellectual potential and concurrently shape community frameworks based on Islamic principles and values (Wahid 2001, 202). These ethics and ideologies were applied in society via the teachings of *fiqh*. Hence a new approach toward *fiqh* texts was needed. This led to the development of the so-called *Fiqh Sosial* school.

Over the past three decades, *Fiqh Sosial* has become one of the hallmarks of NU jurisprudential thinking. Sahal Mahfudh, the Chair of the NU Syuriah, the religious board that issues fatwas, became one of the most influential proponents of this school. The editors of one of his books about the topic, *Nuansa Fiqih Sosial*, outline the agenda of this type of legal thinking. According to them, thinking about *fiqh* in NU has shifted from "being a paradigm of 'orthodox truth'" to "a paradigm of 'social relevance'" (Mahfudh 1994, vii). Thus *fiqh* texts, when reinterpreted within the contemporary context, can provide a system of social ethics that uses philosophical methodologies to analyze cultural and social problems. According to the editors, this means that the interpreters do not follow a *madhhab* in its literal teachings, but in its methods. This approach distinguishes between the "roots" or essential (*pokok*) teachings of the *madhhab*'s legal methodology and its "branches" (*furū'*)—its theoretical aspects. In this way, they consider *fiqh* to be a hermeneutic tool that has the potential to manage a plurality of truths (Mahfudh 1994, viii).

Perhimpunan Pemgembangan Pesantren dan Masyarakat (P3M)

In order to teach the *santri* at the NU *pesantren* about these potentials for *fiqh*, progressive NU leaders set up several institutes during the 1980s. One of these institutes was P3M (Perhimpunan Pengembangan Pesantren dan Masyarakat or "Center for the Development of *Pesantren* and Society," 1983) that was created to help configure the *pesantren* curriculum so that students could gain deeper understanding of social-religious issues. This resulted in a steady stream of seminars about topics ranging from human rights and democracy to the reinterpretation of *fiqh*. It was also at P3M where the discussion about *fiqh* teachings concerning women started. During the 1990s, P3M organized workshops for the women in *pesantren*—both leaders and students—to discuss matters concerning women such as reproductive health and rights, the status of women in Islamic jurisprudence, and its reinterpretation. The focus on women and reproductive rights in Islam was unique at the time—the first initiative of its kind in the Muslim world.

The re-reading and reinterpretation of *fiqh* texts dealing with women's issues led to the project that I have chosen to illustrate the various levels on which these re-readings are emerging and what strategies are used to adopt them into the framework of the legal teachings. Several alumni of the P3M workshops decided that in order to change the attitudes of *pesantren* students concerning women, they had to address the texts that were the source of negative opinions. One of these texts was the *Kitāb ʿUqūd al-luj-jayn fī bayān ḥuqūq al-zawjayn* (*Kitāb ʿUqūd*) by Muḥammad Ibn ʿUmar al-Nawawī al-Jawī written around 1874. It was a text that, according to a respected NU *kyai*, Bisri Mustofa, "went to a man's head" (*membuat lelaki besar kepala*) (Forum Kajian Kitab Kuning 2001, x).[6] The rest of this chapter traces the process that resulted in the publication of a revised and annotated *Kitāb ʿUqūd* and the ensuing projects to apply these new findings in interpreting Islamic law on women's issues.

Initiating new readings

The re-reading of the *Kitāb ʿUqūd* text was based on numerous workshops that were initiated first by P3M and followed by other similar projects. In order to legitimize these activities, P3M's director, Masdar Masʿudi, sought the support of respected *kyai* who helped develop a methodological and philosophical framework based on classical Islamic teachings. He relied heavily on the thinking of Abdurrahman Wahid. Inspired by the ideas of the medieval jurist al-Shāṭibī, Wahid saw the key to Islamic reform in protecting the five basic human needs of life (*al-nafs*), religion (*al-dīn*), offspring (*al-nasl*), property (*al-māl*) and intellect (*al-ʿaql*) (see Riddell 2001, 252). Using this paradigm, Masʿudi, among others, developed an Islamic model to protect women's basic reproductive rights. In spite of the fact that these ideas were unconventional in NU circles, Masʿudi gained the approval of those who did not agree with all of his findings by grounding his concepts firmly within the tradition of *fiqh*.

P3M based its teaching on the assumption that Islam is a just religion but that the position of women in Islamic thought has been shaped by ideas from outside Islam—by culture, society, and the interpretations of texts. Furthermore, P3M identified as the main obstacle for women to be considered as fully human the fact that traditional jurisprudence failed to apply the basic rights allowed to them by the Qurʾan. From this basic philosophy, P3M undertook to redefine the role of women and help them to become knowledgeable about their rights.

These ideas, according to P3M, have the potential to do more than empower Muslim women and men; they would also help create a democratic civil society and form the basis for social systems that eventually could replace the hierarchical model conventional to Indonesia. Masdar Mas'udi explained this as follows:

> In the old days changes in society were brought about by way of a top down model. The king issued a decree and all obeyed. Nowadays we try to initiate change by working from the bottom up by teaching students at the *pesantren* new ideas that eventually will change the way society thinks. That is the P3M model.[7]

This model thus aims at directly applying *fiqh* teachings in society and using them as a tool for societal change. Meetings to create this new social model used methods still unconventional for Indonesia at that time, providing solid information, but also using discussion and role play. Participants analyzed the rules of *fiqh* for women by looking at the original Qur'anic texts, the *ḥadīth,* and the different forms of interpretation.

Part of the inspiration for P3M's ideas came from the writings of the Sudanese intellectual Abdullahi A. An-Na'im who has argued that over time the status of women came to be governed by verses from the Qur'an revealed in Medina, rendering the more egalitarian and universal verses from the Mecca period obsolete (An-Na'im 1990). Following this line of thinking, P3M used the five basic human needs formulated by al-Shāṭibī to develop a set of basic human rights. These are the rights to physical well-being and safety, prosperity, offspring, and freedom of thought and religious belief.[8] Over and above these rights, P3M stresses that the Qur'an guarantees women three rights within the marital relationship: the right to be provided with food, with clothing, and with a place to live. By critically re-engaging traditional jurisprudential categories in light of contemporary concerns and language, and by stressing the rights that are written in the Qur'an, P3M aligned these texts with modern teachings about universal human rights. This strategy has given life to a variety of new initiatives to improve the teachings about women, especially within the *pesantren.*

Reconsidering the texts: Kitāb ʿUqūd

The perception of women within the *pesantren* world has long been dominated by textbooks written by men with views on woman's capacity and psychology that cast her mainly in the role of spouse and mother. After scrutinizing the books traditionally used in the *pesantren,* Masdar Mas'udi concluded that their basic teachings hold men as the standard for everything. Differences between men and women are interpreted such that women never reach the male standard. It is as if a woman exists only to serve the man and fulfill his sexual desires. Man's status, both in this world and the next, is above woman's status. It is as if one man equals two women (Van Bruinessen 1995, 172).[9]

Many argue that the essential problem with the texts concerning women is that they not only reduce the status of women, but also give the impression that all that matters are issues such as "menstruation, ritual purity, the veil and inheritance [woman's share being half of that of a man]. The texts ignore important matters such as women's right to work, the social status of widows, and woman's participation in education, and in economical and political life." (Van Bruinessen 1995, 182) Since the 1980s this has given rise to discussions about the influence of the *pesantren* in creating gender-biased discourses. The reality is that most texts were written before the twentieth century and carry cultural baggage that has long been abandoned in other areas of life. Also, the majority of the texts come from the Middle East, reflecting its specific culture. It is clear that a process of reinterpretation of these texts was called for. This was a complicated matter, however, since these texts cannot simply be cast aside and declared unsuitable; as stated above, they are considered sacrosanct by some Muslims and thus great care must be taken in researching and criticizing them.

Although no single fixed model was used in the research and revision of *fiqh* texts, the process followed by the team that reinterpreted the *Kitāb 'Uqūd* can shed some light on an underexamined aspect of Islamic reform in contemporary Indonesia. The process of reinterpretation is an arduous one, consisting of the following steps: (1) identifying the problematic text; (2) discussing its contents (including holding workshops about detailed elements of the texts); (3) researching its truth claims; (4) reinterpreting the text's quotes from the Qur'an and *hadīth*; (5) editing the original text with footnotes that correct faulty information; (6) introducing the critical version into the *pesantren* and familiarizing NU leaders with its contents via discussions and workshops; and (7) using the revised version in sermons and discussing it with women's and men's Qur'an study groups.

The use of workshops as a means to gather, discuss, and publicize information is practiced widely in Indonesia. From their inception at the beginning of the twentieth century, established Muslim organizations such as NU and Muhammadiyah have held national and local congresses in order to include their members in the decision-making processes and to build and expand their organizations. It was at these gatherings where legal advice and decisions of the organizations' fatwa boards were discussed and transmitted to the organization's constituency. This approach led to a democratization of Islamic knowledge, a trend that was furthered by changes in the educational systems (for example, through the Muhammadiyah schools). Leaders of the organizations became "activist-scholars" who situated their teachings and research within the framework of the needs of their organization and society. In short, shaping Islamic knowledge went hand in hand with transmitting it to a wider audience. The process for the revision of the *Kitāb 'Uqūd* derives from this model; from the outset it was the scholars' intention to bring their findings to a wide audience. However, before this step could be taken, it was vital for the project's scholarly merit to have the approval of authoritative scholars of Islam.

The text of *Kitāb 'Uqūd* went through the entire seven-step process mentioned above. A team of twelve men and women calling themselves FK3 (*Forum Kajian Kitab Kuning*, or "Forum for the Research of Yellow Books"), who specialized in the disciplines of *ḥadīth*, *fiqh*, Qur'anic exegesis, Islamic history, and anthropology, took several years to prepare the new critical edition that came out at the end of 2001.[10] Mrs. Nuriyah Abdurrahman Wahid was one of the driving forces behind the project and became its powerful patron during her time as First Lady (1999–2001). After the book appeared she continued to discuss its contents in the national media.

The critical edition was prepared based on the P3M ideologies, following NU principles of research. For example, in order to separate truth from myth, the *ḥadīth* used in the texts and their chains of transmission were carefully scrutinized. Teams of *ḥadīth* specialists found that more than half of the reports quoted in the text were fabricated or weak. Since the *pesantren* audience had no knowledge of this, the authenticity of these prophetic reports had previously been taken for granted. As a result the teachings of these *ḥadīth* were applied to daily life, with detrimental consequences, especially for women (Mas'udi 1997a, 61).

In explaining passages quoted from the Qur'an, the team followed the NU philosophy that distinguishes between texts that apply to the time and place of the Prophet only, and texts that contain universal ethical values. The texts containing fundamental truths (*qaṭʿī*) are those concerned with basic values such as human equality and justice between men and women. The meaning of these texts is clear and unambiguous at any moment of human history. The texts that are contingent upon time and place (*zannī*) are those concerning matters that are of a private, social, cultural, or political character. These are less clear and need to be interpreted with independent jurisprudential reasoning (*ijtihād*) (A.H. Rofiq et al. 1995, 7). An example of the latter is the requirement in the Qur'an of two female witnesses in lieu of one man when contracting business agreements (Q 2:282). According to many NU scholars, two women were necessary at one time because women were not actively involved in business and therefore the observation of a single female witness could be mistaken due to her lack of experience. Today, however, due to the expansion of education for women these conditions have changed.

According to Masdar Mas'udi, the challenge to contemporary interpreters of the texts from Qur'an and *hadīth* is to make sure that texts that arose from a certain context can be brought in alignment with those that hold eternal truths. Texts that cannot pass this test, he agrees, are not suitable for universal use in the twenty-first century. Those engaged in this process of re-evaluation are allowed to exercise judgment (*ijtihād*). However, *ijtihād* has to be practiced within the NU model of interpretation. Originally, this model was based on the close following (*taqlīd*) of the accepted texts and opinions of the scholars of the school of al-Shāfi'ī. In order to adapt to contemporary needs, NU scholars decided that *ijtihād* could be allowed within the framework of the community of NU scholars at large (Mas'udi 1997, 61–3). The new model meant that *ijtihād* and *taqlīd* would be used simultaneously, as the one approach does not exclude the other. The authority of the medieval scholars supports the authority of the contemporary teachings.

Guided by this combination of classical and new principles, the team annotated the original text of *Kitāb 'Uqūd*. The text was broken up into sections in Indonesian translation of the original Arabic. Then follow the results of the team's research with regard to *hadīth* and the medieval *fiqh* texts. The sections end with commentaries by FK3 members who present the opinions of contemporary Indonesian scholars of Islam such as Quraish Shihab and Tolhah Hasan.

The results of this process of critical reinterpretation can be illustrated with a text which, based on certain *hadīth*, teaches that a woman

> should know that she is like a slave marrying her master, or a weak prisoner who is helpless under someone's power. . . . A wife should feel timid (*malu*) toward her husband, she may not contradict him, she must lower her head and her gaze when in front of her husband, she must obey her husband no matter what he asks her to do, apart from what Islam forbids, she must remain silent when her husband talks, stand up at his coming and going (Forum Kajian Kitab Kuning 2001, 61).

Concerning the above quote, the team comments: "The above passage forces us to scrutinize once again what the goal of marriage is. According to [the medieval scholar] al-Ghazālī, the first goal of marriage, when considered from the point of view of the law (*Sharīʿa*) and the general religious teachings, is to perform one's social duty." The team then proceeds to cite the five benefits of marriage identified by al-Ghazālī: "To procreate, to protect religion and limit one's desires (*nafsu*), to develop closeness to women, to have someone who can take care of the household, and to practice the development of good character."

The segment ends with commentaries by FK3 and quotes from contemporary scholars of Islam. Building on the theories on marriage put forth by al-Ghazālī, one of the most respected scholars in the history of Islam, the team comments: "From the aforementioned explanation [it becomes clear] that there is not one word mentioned that places a woman in the position of a slave." Then the team quotes the two respected contemporary Indonesian Muslim leaders, Quraish Shihab and Tolhah Hasan, who discuss the importance of harmony and mutual understanding within marriage (Forum Kajian Kitab Kuning 2001, 61, 62).

Finally, the team adds some insights of its own. At the end of his work, the author of the *Kitāb ʿUqūd* defends the seclusion of women with a *ḥadīth* that states that the Companions of the Prophet covered the window and holes in the wall so that the women could not spy on the men. The team refutes this particular *ḥadīth* since serious flaws have been found in its chain of transmission. It then levels the following criticism:

> Closing up the house turns the woman into a prisoner. This is not human. Moreover, a house without ventilation is not healthy, especially not for children because no fresh air can enter. A woman becomes like a frog under a coconut shell (*katak dalam tempurung*) who is unable to see how wide the world is and how deep the sea (Forum Kajian Kitab Kuning 2001, 158, 159).

The results of this reinterpretation had to be presented with great tact as the team found that over fifty percent of the *ḥadīth* quoted in the *Kitāb ʿUqūd* were weak or false. This meant that for over a century *pesantren* students had memorized flawed teachings which the students passed on in their sermons once they became *kyai*. Naturally, these teachings greatly influenced thinking patterns, especially about the marital relationship. Even today, *kyai* frequently pepper their sermons to married women with quotes from this text. Women are told: "When a woman does not seek her husband's permission for everything she plans to do, all she does will amount to nothing and she will be cursed by God"; "The best spouse is she who always pleases her husband. Whether there is money or not, she will always smile."[11] This leaves most women utterly confused since it imposes requirements that are unrealistic, at times inhuman. As expressed by some younger *kyai*,

This text harms women. The problem is that it is the only text that covers the
fiqh concerning women. Other books for or about women are considered instruc-
tive or advisory only. Very few *kyai* manage to translate what this text teaches into
the contemporary Javanese context. From the gender perspective it is no longer
suitable as educational material in the *pesantren*.[12]

Yet in many instances tradition can appear to overrule common sense.
Through the pedagogy of transmission the text has gained an undue respect
that is hard to cleanse from the minds of the average leaders of Islam.
Until the new edition reaches them, most *kyai* do not have access to or
are not aware of sources that are less biased. The core problem is that,
in accordance with Brannon Wheeler's observations about how texts gain
authority, texts from the body of "yellow books" are still considered sacred.
In the minds of many students and teachers they are superior to new teachings by contemporary Muslim leaders. Another aspect of the problem is
that debates about women's issues draw less interest from influential *kyai*
because these issues do not belong to core religious concerns, such as worship (*ʿibādāt*).[13] *Kyai* Husein Muhammad, one of the leading researchers of
the annotated revision of the *Kitāb ʿUqūd*, explained this as follows:

Compare it to Catholicism: women cannot become priests but nobody protests
against a female president in Ireland. The *kyai* are more interested in the rule that
forbids women leading the ritual prayers when men are present than they are in
questions of limits to women's careers.[14]

The point that *kyai* seldom rely on the *Kitāb ʿUqūd* when dealing with
matters concerning the public position of women is illustrated by the battle of words about the permissibility of a woman president that erupted
when in 1999 Megawati Sukarnoputri emerged as a leading candidate for
the presidency. In spite of an abundance of religious arguments for and
against a woman president, none of the traditionalist scholars ever referred
to sources such as the *Kitāb ʿUqūd*. This demonstrates the lack of opinion
concerning women's issues in contemporary life in traditionalist circles.
Those advocating the revision of the *Kitāb ʿUqūd* used this to their advantage. Although they were interpreting a classical *fiqh* text, their interpretation touched upon so many contemporary issues that the text no longer
belonged to the domain of religious scholars only, facilitating the transmission of their findings to a wider audience.

Legal discourse at the grassroots level

The distribution of the findings of the FK3 research benefited from the NU's well-established organizational structure. Since the 1970s, several groups within NU had quietly begun working to eradicate teachings that harmed women psychologically, mentally, or physically. This process encompassed several NU-connected organizations. It included the Muslimat NU, its branch for married women that was set up in 1946 to cater to the social needs and education for young women and children of pre-*pesantren* age. Although the majority of its members are now middle aged, Muslimat NU is still charged with the formation of the young female NU members who are associated with the Fatayat NU. These young women have often set up their own initiatives as they find the pace of developments concerning women's issues in Muslimat NU to be too slow. Benefiting from the educational reforms of the Suharto regime, they are more highly educated than any generation before them. The NU organizational system made it possible for the new *fiqh* interpretations to be taught simultaneously to several generations of women, some of whom were scholars and leaders of Islam themselves. They take up the tools traditionally used by NU scholars to question and de-mystify the rules formulated by centuries of scholars. Despite such work by the Muslimat NU, however, the younger generation is not impressed and finds that the older NU members do not push hard enough to bring about change in society where gender bias and religious learning are concerned.[15]

While the Muslimat NU operates in what Alberto Melucci calls a "crisis-oriented" mode, meaning that they try to remedy problems within the existing system, the younger generation, according to Melucci's model, represents a "conflict-oriented" movement. By this he refers to groups who do not accept the status quo but aim at fundamental reorganization of societal conditions (Melucci 1996, 22, 23). The NU-related group of YKF (*Yayasan Kesejahteraan Yogyakarta*) that is based in Yogyakarta is an example of such a conflict-oriented group. It was set up in 1991 with the goal to bring about fundamental change in the status and role of Muslim women. During the past decade YKF developed into a platform for women's issues, especially those related to the *pesantren*. Following the philosophical model and pedagogical approaches of P3M, YKF created programs that advocate for women's reproductive rights. In tune with the discourse developing globally about these rights, they broadened the scope of their interest to include issues such as HIV/AIDS, prostitution, domestic violence, divorce, and early child marriage. This focus translated into myriad workshops and publishing activities, including the publication of a journal (*Mitra*), books, and a newsletter that spread YKF ideas to young NU leaders.

Through its workshops and the journal, YKF involves men and women who are teaching in the *pesantren* in the reinterpretation of the teachings of Qur'an, *ḥadīth* and *fiqh* concerning the rights of women. The essential points of these findings are summarized in handy booklets that those leaders can carry with them when giving talks or sermons.[16] This itself is an innovation. However, YKF's vision reaches beyond the specialists in Islam for whom the study of *fiqh* is a natural part of their training. YKF wishes to educate those who put legal teachings into practice without knowledge of the texts—the general public. To create illustrative material for this group, YKF commissioned a novel called *Perempuan Berkalung Sorban* ("Women Wearing the Turban)" that covered topics within woman's *fiqh* (El Khalieqy 2001). The writer, Abidah El Khalieqy, is a *pesantren* graduate, and brought first-hand information to the novel's contents. Apart from the novel, YKF also organized writing contests for high school students, broadcast a radio show in the rural areas surrounding Yogyakarta, and produced a TV show that questions the practice of polygyny.

Conclusion

Re-reading *fiqh* texts concerning women is not simply an intellectual hobby of NU scholars but carries deep religious, social, cultural, and political consequences in contemporary Indonesia. For those involved there are many real, socially-grounded issues at stake. Not only do they aspire to strengthen the role and position of women within Islam, they also are engaged in strengthening Islam against those who wish to reduce it to a narrow selection of misogynist *ḥadīth*. These traditions often favor Middle Eastern culture as it existed during the early centuries of Islam. Some traditions have become tools in the hands of Muslims who try to reduce a complex and sophisticated religious heritage to a mass of Islamist slogans that at times take precedence over the teachings of the Qur'an. Michael Sells has observed that Saudi-Wahhabi manuals written in the form of popular pamphlets utilize this method of discourse to disseminate their specific interpretation of Islam.[17]

The goal of recapturing NU's relevance in Indonesian society has met with great enthusiasm. NU members across the generations have come to realize that this endeavor is not just a theoretical, legal exercise but will also advance the Islamic goal to provide justice for all. The unexpected outcome has been that NU scholars are producing a new traditionalist legal discourse unique in the Muslim world. Generally, most of what is considered to be "progressive" in modern Muslim thought has come from reformist interpreters while "traditionalist" scholars of Islam are seen as backward and incapable of joining religious discussions that suit the demands of the twenty-first century. Such conventional understandings of contemporary Islam are, however, not supported by the Indonesian evidence discussed in this essay.

The result of the work of NU scholars is a development that emerged both from the leading religious elite and from demands at the grassroots level. It will take years before the outcome of all this crystallizes into clear, authoritative teachings. The process reveals that what is at stake is the determination of where the center of religious authority really lies—a powerful question at a time when a more radical Islamic discourse is vying for center stage in Indonesian Islam and politics. Whatever the outcome of this battle, the religious discussions, or *wacana*, will continue and will involve many layers of society. This by itself is an important exercise in developing new legal theories in Islam.

Three

RELIGIOUS AUTHORITY, POLITICS AND FATWAS IN CONTEMPORARY SOUTHEAST ASIA

C. van Dijk

Presenting an overview of issuing fatwas (*iftā'*) in contemporary Indonesia is a highly complex matter. One of the reasons for this is that the *iftā'* process is not formally state controlled, although during the New Order under President Suharto (1966–1998), the hand of the state in the drafting of some fatwas was discernable in a number of cases. The New Order even created its own fatwa-issuing institution, the Indonesian Council of Ulama (Majelis Ulama Indonesia/MUI). However, precisely because the MUI was a New Order creation, its legal authority was considered by some sections of the Muslim community to be somewhat dubious. The MUI also never succeeded in becoming the sole authoritative fatwa institution in the country; it remained one among many organizations performing this function. Furthermore, due to the diversity of religious inclinations represented on the Council, it could occasionally come up with different opinions in response to similar questions.

In neighboring Malaysia the situation seems much simpler, at least on the surface. In the Malaysian states the sultan is the head of religion, as confirmed by the Constitution, and it is the sultan who appoints the mufti and deputy-mufti. Hierarchically speaking this makes the mufti the second most important religious authority in a state. To quote from the Administration of Islamic Law Enactment of 1989 from the State of Selangor (Art. 30), the mufti is "the chief authority in the State of Selangor after his Royal Highness the Sultan" in all matters of Islamic religious law (*hukum syara'*), except when otherwise decreed. In the Federal Territories (Kuala Lumpur and Labuan) as well as in Penang, Malacca, Sarawak, and Sabah, it is the King of the Federation, the Yang di-Pertuan Agong, who acts as the head of Islamic affairs and appoints the mufti.[1]

The rules for the issuing of a fatwa in the Malaysian states are also well defined. In order for the opinion of a mufti to become a fatwa it must be published in the gazette.[2] Once this has taken place the fatwa is binding on all concerned Muslims in the state; and once a fatwa has been thus published only the mufti or his successor can change or annul it. No "counter-fatwas" are allowed. Disregarding this rule or belittling a fatwa is also considered a punishable offence. In Johor, a maximum fine of 500 ringgit or imprisonment not exceeding three months, or both, is laid down for issuing what is defined as a "false fatwa," that is, "any fatwa whether written or oral in respect of the Islamic religion in any manner contrary to the fatwa issued by the Majlis" (Johore Administration of Islamic Law Enactment, 1978, Art. 167). Similar sanctions are meted out for contempt of religious authority, another section of the law that can be brought into use to silence criticism of fatwas (Art. 172). The maximum sentence for contempt, including bringing into contempt a lawfully issued fatwa, is twice as high as that for issuing false fatwas (Art. 173).

In Indonesia there is no single institution that has such a fatwa monopoly. Aside from the MUI, religious organizations also have their fatwa councils and/or religious advisory bodies. This holds for the two largest and generally moderate organizations of the Nahdlatul Ulama, with its Bahtsul Masail al-Diniyah al-Waqi'iyyah, and the Muhammadiyah, with its Majlis Tarjih, but also for the radical, hard-line Islamic organizations. Among the latter is the Defenders of Islam Front (Front Pembela Islam/FPI), whose members claim to be engaged in "commanding the right and forbidding the wrong" in conducting raids on "places of sin" in Jakarta and other Indonesian cities, which they refer to as "anti-sin processions" (*pawai anti maksiat*). The FPI established its own Fatwa Department in May 2001.[3]

The Majelis Ulama Indonesia

The MUI was founded on July 26, 1975. At that time each of the other recognized religions in Indonesia already had a body which could serve as a forum for internal consultation and as an interlocutor between their respective religious communities and the government. The Protestants had the Communion of Churches in Indonesia (Dewan Gereja-gereja Indonesia/DGI—now the Persekutuan Gereja-gereja di Indonesia/PGI); the Roman Catholics the Bishops Conference of Indonesia (Konferensi Waligereja Indonesia/KWI); the Buddhists the Representation of the Indonesian Buddhist Community (Perwakilan Umat Buddha Indonesia/Walubi); and the Hindus the Hindu Council of Religious Affairs (Parisada Hindu Dharma Indonesia/PHDI—originally the Parisada Hindu Dharma Bali).

During the first decade of the New Order the Islamic community lacked any such vehicle for internal consultation that could also serve as a point

of contact with government. Official history has it that the founding of the
MUI was an initiative of Islamic scholars and intellectuals themselves, who
had gathered at a conference in Jakarta for a meeting which afterwards
came to be known as the first National Congress of the MUI. Looking at
the political realities of the period, however, a slightly different picture suggests itself. The 1970s were the years in which the Indonesian government
attempted with varying degrees of success to simplify (and control) the political landscape. With regard to Islam, Suharto and his political advisers
such as Ali Murtopo aimed for a single political party to represent devout
Muslims who could not be persuaded, gently or otherwise, to support the
government party (Golkar), and, when possible, to have other consolidated
organizations stand for interest blocks such as youth, women, workers, etc.
The founding of the MUI fits this political climate perfectly. Given government concerns over the political potential of Islam, it is also doubtful
that the establishment of an (in principle) authoritative institution such as
the MUI would have been possible without government consent and direction. The *Ensiklopedi Islam* (1993, 122), for example, subtly notes that the
MUI was founded upon the issuance of a mandate (*amanat*) from President
Suharto.

Originally set up as a kind of contact organization for the government
representing the whole Islamic community, the Council also served as a
national fatwa institution, with local branches filling analogous roles in the
provinces and at lower administrative levels of regencies (*kabupaten*) and
larger cities (*kotamadya*).[4] The fatwas issued by the central MUI during the
New Order reflected the political purposes for which it was founded. Rarely
were fatwas issued in response to questions submitted by individual Muslims.
An opinion explaining the correct response of an aircraft traveler to expe-
riencing either two Fridays or no Fridays in a single week is one of the
few fatwas issued by the MUI in reply to a question from an individual
Muslim (MUI 1997, 22–3). More often the MUI simply issued a fatwa
without revealing why it was considered necessary or in response to letters
from central government departments. Most such requests came from the
Ministry of Religion, but one fatwa was issued in reply to a request for
clarification of Indonesian understandings of the meanings of such Arabic
Islamic terms as *jama'a, khalīfa,* and *bay'a* sought by the office of the Attorney
General investigating a group called the Jamaah Muslimin Hizbullah (MUI
1997, 83–5). In other instances questions originated from local administrators and were forwarded to the Council by a regional MUI. At times
the MUI also clearly sprang into action in response to "hot issues." One
such case involved an opinion that the teachings of the Malaysian group

known as Darul Arqam were deviant (MUI 1997, 74–7), though in that case the Council seems to have acted somewhat belatedly since four provincial MUIs, all in Sumatra, had preceded it with opinions of their own on the matter.

The fate of being linked from birth to what in Indonesia is often called "practical politics" has put the MUI in a problematical position—torn, at times, between the desires of the government and the convictions of at least part of the Islamic community. The connection between the MUI and the government in itself militated against it gaining a favorable reputation in some religious circles. But even apart from this, the dual demands of not alienating the government and at the same time satisfying the Muslim mainstream was a difficult, if not impossible, mission. This was made even more difficult by ambitious government policies intended to stimulate economic development and national unity, since these goals occasionally came into conflict with convictions held by segments of the country's religious communities—both Muslim and non-Muslim. For this reason the absence of an MUI fatwa on a particular matter may be as significant, or perhaps even more so, than its issuing one.

Nevertheless, politics is not conspicuously in the forefront in MUI decisions. A fatwa of 1976 supports the "simple living" campaign promoted by the Indonesian government at the time, but this is a borderline case. In one of its fatwas the MUI explicitly stressed that it is not a political institution, but the fatwa in which this statement is made is one of the most politically-charged fatwas the MUI ever gave. The fatwa concerned was issued in early 1978 and addressed the question how local MUIs should respond to the upcoming session of the People's Congress (Majelis Permusyawaratan Rakyat/MPR) in which legislators were expected to include the controversial word *kepercayaan* (belief) in two of the Congress's decrees—the Broad Outlines of State Policy (Garis-garis Besar Haluan Negara) and the Guidelines for the Internalization and Implementation of the Pancasila (Pedoman Penghayatan dan Pengamalan Pancasila). The proposed language created a furor in devout Islamic circles, where it was believed that the government's objective in mentioning the word *kepercayaan* in the same breath with the word *agama* (religion) was to elevate the status of Javanese heterodox variants of Islam (usually referred to as *aliran kepercayaan*) to that of a separate and officially recognized "religion."[5] The consequence of official recognition would be that under legislation on religious propaganda and missionary activities, persons who adhered to the heterodox stream would be legally protected against attempts by orthodox Muslims to have them change their religious views. The MUI fatwa, entitled

"Facing the Upcoming 1978 General Session of the People's Congress" (Menghadapi Sidang Umum MPR 1978), was published in response to the commotion. It did not, however, condemn the government in the unequivocal way that some Muslim groups might have wished. It stated that the MUI "only issued religious fatwas and did not meddle in political problems" (MUI 1997, 97). Though pains were taken to remove any doubt that the MUI rejected a separate status for the *aliran kepercayaan*, the fatwa was first and foremost an appeal to maintain domestic quiet. It was not a statement from which the opponents of the disputed clause could draw much moral support. Rather it was a fatwa about not issuing a fatwa. It begins by reciting that the MUI is presenting a fatwa, after which there appears a list of "considerations" (which normally include grounds for the decision that follows), but the concluding section in which an opinion would typically appear is absent. By drafting its fatwa but not actually giving an opinion, the MUI had found a middle course between ignoring Muslim indignation, which because of the intensity of the outrage it could not do, and offending Suharto, which could have had its own consequences.

Another issue in which the MUI was confronted with conflicting demands from the Islamic community and the government was that of lotteries. The MUI initially functioned to justify government policy on lotteries. For a number of years it did so passively by remaining silent on the issue. Although the MUI itself refrained from taking a stand on the matter, in 1986 the chairman of both the MUI and of its Fatwa Committee, Ibrahim Hosen, gave his full support to a national sports lottery, the Porkas Sepakbola, organized by the Ministry of Social Affairs. It was Hosen's opinion that the sports lottery could be distinguished from (forbidden) gambling (*maysir*) and was thus allowed (Hosen 1987). The subtle distinction underlying the opinion rests on the greater likelihood that gambling might incite division and ill-feeling among the participants. While individuals who play the lottery are not together in the same room when the winners are announced, gamblers are together at the same location, and are therefore able to confront one another, which could provoke feelings of hatred and animosity.

Hosen's fatwa could not but occasion debate and opposition in certain Islamic quarters. The issue became even more emotionally charged when it re-emerged in 1991. A fierce row erupted within the Nahdlatul Ulama when it was revealed in late 1991 that the NU central board had endorsed a subsidy request submitted by a foundation for the purpose of making renovations to a dilapidated *pesantren* the foundation owned in Tuban, East Java.[6] The foundation—the Social Prosperity Dedication Fund Foundation (Yayasan Dana Bhakti Kesejahteraan Sosial/YDBKS)—obtained much of its money from managing the Social Charity Donation with Prizes (Sumbangan Dermawan Sosial Berhadiah/SDSB), the lottery that had replaced the Porkas. The situation was complicated by the fact that the SDSB had been founded by President Suharto's daughter, Siti Hardijanti Rukmana (Tutut). This close link with the Suharto family might help explain why all of the sudden the lottery evoked so much opposition in the form of student demonstrations across the country. As matter of fact, the lottery issue led to one of the few instances of massive Muslim public protests during the New Order—the *kepercayaan* dispute was another one—and was of such intensity that it could hardly be ignored by the government and the leaders of the Islamic community. In November the MUI declared itself against the SDSB. In a joint statement with the All-Indonesia League of Muslim Intellectuals (Ikatan Cendekiawan Muslim Indonesia/ICMI) dated November 12, the MUI stressed that "gambling in all its forms is forbidden by religion" (MUI 1997, 163). Then, on November 23, the MUI issued its own fatwa declaring the SDSB forbidden. In doing so it also made a particular point of noting that the Indonesian Islamic Bank (Bank Muamalat Indonesia) had not purchased shares in the SDSB Foundation.

Fear that the domestic situation might spiral out of control appears to have been a prime motivation prompting the MUI to speak out. In its own fatwa the MUI "[c]alled upon society, especially the Islamic community, to remain calm and not be provoked by matters which could have negative consequences" (MUI 1997, 162). In the joint statement with ICMI it was observed that a number of issues were at play at that time which "did not benefit the development of the nation" (MUI 1997, 163). The MUI and ICMI appealed to "all members of society, especially the younger generation, to strengthen feelings of togetherness (*rasa kekeluargaan*) and the spirit of solidarity within the framework of jointly maintaining national union and unity" (MUI 1997, 163). The SDSB was discontinued in November 1993.[7]

In the cases of *kepercayaan* and SDSB the MUI issued fatwas in the wake of social unrest. In other cases, however, it issued them because the government wished it to do so. One such case was the MUI's October 1983 fatwa that endorsed the government's family planning program. This program was one of the cornerstones of New Order development policy, and its success was a source of pride for the Suharto government. In fact, however, the MUI gave its consent to the policy rather late. Both the Nahdlatul Ulama and the Muhammadiyah had already twice spoken out in favor of family planning—NU in 1969 and 1971 and the Muhammadiyah in 1968 and 1981. Discussions on family planning in Muslim circles elicited such

remarkable scenes as one depicted in a photograph appearing in a monograph about the Nahdlatul Ulama, in which members of the NU Bahtsul
Masail dressed in sarongs and sitting barefoot on the floor look on as one
of the group holds up a condom for inspection by the assembled *kyai* (Anam
1985, 30). As in other fatwas in the Islamic world allowing family planning, the point of departure of the MUI fatwa is that family planning
should not be inspired by the intention to avoid bearing children. Rather,
family planning should be solely for the purpose of lengthening the period
between births. It is often argued that the main reason for postponing a
new pregnancy is to protect the health of mother and child, or that a
smaller number of children will enhance the opportunities for education.[8]
The MUI fatwa mirrors this line of reasoning, emphasizing that Islam is
in essence a "religion of development" and that overpopulation results in
social and economic conflict. The opinion defines family planning as "a
means or effort by people to regulate pregnancy in a family, in a way that
is not against religious law, state law, and Pancasila morality," and states
that the use of family planning is allowed by Islam "to guard the health
of mothers and children [and promote] the education of children so that
they become healthy, intelligent, and devout." The government was asked
to forbid vasectomy, tubectomy, and abortion for the Muslim community,
and was entreated to "increase its vigilance against the misuse of contra-
ceptives which could be used for sinful conduct." Among the other deside-
rata of the MUI was that arrangements be made so that somebody with
understanding of Islam be stationed at each family planning clinic (MUI
1997, 136–48).

What is striking about the MUI's "political" fatwas is that they are among
the lengthier and better-reasoned of the Council's opinions. It is also noteworthy that fatwas addressing politically sensitive issues are permeated with
New Order jargon. That is especially the case with the fatwa on family
planning. It appears that the leaders of the MUI believed that these fatwas needed more extensive justifications, either for their fellow Muslim citizens or for the government.

The changing position of the MUI

The relationship between the MUI and the government remained close
throughout the New Order. Its general chairman, K.H. Hasan Basri, cam-
paigned for the government Golkar party in the 1997 general elections
(and had a first-hand experience of Indonesian election violence when the

hotel in which he was staying in Banjarmasin was attacked by a mob). When the Southeast Asian financial crisis reached its peak in Indonesia in the months that followed, the MUI sought to avert a slide into economic and political chaos, though pressure from the government might have played a role here. The Chief of Staff of the Army had called upon religious leaders with their special status in society to help to overcome the economic crisis by providing society with "correct" information. The MUI then declared hoarding, waste, corruption, and currency speculation to be sinful, arguing that Islam did not allow changing the function of currency from a medium of exchange to a commodity with the aim of making a profit, causing others to suffer. In the spirit of the Aku Cinta Rupiah ("I love the Rupiah") campaign initiated by Suharto's daughter Tutut in January 1998, the MUI also urged people who held dollars to exchange them for rupiahs. A second campaign launched by Tutut in the same month, the Gerakan Cinta Indonesia (Love Indonesia Movement), was given similar support. This time the MUI stressed that currency speculation amounted to gambling, and thus was not permitted by Islam. In February, the MUI called for a holy war (*jihād*) against speculators and corruptors.

Speaking out as it did at that particular moment, the MUI—described at the time as a "government backed Islamic group" (*The Indonesian Times*, January 28, 1998)—joined a patriotic drive led by an elite with whom many in the country had lost faith (if they had ever had any) and whose own love for their country was becoming increasingly questioned. This made the MUI even more susceptible to accusations that it was a mere tool of the government (Van Dijk 2001, 97–103). The criticism also made it clear why during the New Order period the MUI had been so sparing in formally speaking out on political issues, since doing otherwise would have brought it right into the heart of the antagonism that existed between the government and certain segments of the Islamic community. The fatwas that might have resulted certainly would not have satisfied Muslims who continued to bear a grudge against New Order Islamic policy, even after relations between the government and the Islamic community as a whole had improved. It might even be argued that the rapprochement that had become visible since the mid-1980s was essentially one of political and religious elites, and that Muslims who were not part of this elite continued to nurture aspirations and religious beliefs that differed from the line set out by the government.

The reputation of the MUI reached a low ebb in the final days of Suharto's rule. But the Council seemed reinvigorated after Suharto resigned, and appears to be faring well in the new political and religious environment of the post-Suharto era. The MUI gained international notoriety in the days just before and after the start of the American-led invasion of Afghanistan in October 2001 for its strong anti-American stance. On September 25 the Council issued an appeal (technically not a fatwa), co-signed by representatives of 46 other Indonesian Islamic organizations, calling for a jihad should the United States invade Afghanistan, a move that attracted considerable attention both in and outside Indonesia.[9]

A fundamental transformation had occurred with the passing of the New Order. Whereas the MUI had previously been identified with the government, after May 1998 it often voiced opposition. It is telling that after the MUI issued its appeal for jihad, the then Minister of Religion, Prof. Dr. Said Agil Husin Al Munawar, expressed regret that the MUI had not consulted his Ministry before making the statement public. He even complained that "as always the MUI wanted to go its own way [and] never consulted with the Ministry of Religion" (Achmad, Hendrowinoto, and Gunarso 2001, 223).

For most of its existence the MUI remained hesitant to make political statements, but that changed following the collapse of the New Order. To use a New Order expression, the MUI entered the field of "practical politics," and became an active player in the political game. In contrast to its prior approach, there were no longer any limits on public religious discussions. In the run-up to the general elections of 1999 the MUI was one of a score of Islamic organizations which, in joint or separate statements, appealed to Muslims not to vote for the PDI-P, the party of Megawati Soekarnoputri, which they tried to stigmatize as anti-religious. The MUI warned against the danger of a reemergence of communism and secularism, and though the PDI-P was not mentioned by name, it was clear that this was the party the MUI had in mind (Van Dijk 2001, 441–3). Nevertheless, the MUI remained silent on one important issue that had been raised to block the possibility of Megawati becoming president. This was the question whether Islam allowed a woman to become head of state, an issue that generated heated debate at the time. The MUI refrained from formulating an opinion on this issue in spite of the fact that Muslims looked to the organization for a ruling.[10] Exploiting a supposed objection to a female president on religious grounds held by many ordinary Muslims in Indonesia, Abdurrahman Wahid blocked Megawati's chances of being elected. The final outcome was that he himself emerged victorious from the presidential election in the People's Congress.

It was during Wahid's short presidency that the dangers of communism again emerged as a specter to haunt certain Muslim quarters. There was strong opposition to Wahid's suggestion in early 2000 that the General Session of the People's Congress scheduled for August of that year revoke the 35-year-old ban on the Indonesian Communist Party (PKI) and the propagation of Marxism. Among those protesting was the MUI, which thereby joined—or attempted to lead—the country's Islamist opposition. The April 2000 issue of the MUI monthly, *Mimbar Ulama*, in which the stance (*pernyataan sikap*) of the MUI was published, was partly devoted to an exposé of the purported "evil deeds" of Indonesian communists. The cover of the issue carried the slogan *Umat Islam tolak Komunisme*, "The Islamic Community Rejects Communism" (Ichwan 2005).

Abdurrahman Wahid's position on this issue contributed to his rapid downfall. Any suggestion of leniency toward former communists touches raw nerves within elements of the Islamic community whose sentiments the MUI was attempting to articulate. Matters were made worse by the fact that the suggestion came from the president of the country, and what is more, a president whose blunt dismissal of anyone who disagreed with him had enraged segments of the Islamic community whose earlier support had made it possible for him to defeat Megawati in the contest for the presidency. Abdurrahman Wahid's erstwhile supporters were especially offended by the way he responded to Muslim protests against the government's lack of resolve to come to the assistance of the Muslim community in the Moluccas and to Muslim appeals to wage a jihad there. A mass demonstration on the issue was held at the National Monument in Jakarta in January 2000. Proudly described by its organizers as a "campaign of a million Muslims" (*aksi sejuta umat*), the rally featured speeches by, among others, Amien Rais and Hamzah Haz. Abdurrahman Wahid belittled this act of protest as insignificant, attended, he averred, by only 20,000 people. And, when Ja'far Umar Thalib visited him in April of that same year to explain his intention to organize a jihad in the Moluccas and to protest the lifting of the ban on the PKI, an angry Abdurrahman Wahid showed him the door within ten minutes. Having alienated his former supporters, Abdurrahman Wahid was forced to step down mid-term during an Extraordinary Session of the People's Congress held in July 2001.

Megawati Soekarnoputri then succeeded to the presidency, but had the misfortune of beginning her term only a few months before September 11, 2001. Fundamental differences over the position of Indonesia in the American war on terrorism laid extra emphasis on the political role of the MUI during her presidency. The jihad statement—again a "position statement" (*pernyataan sikap*) rather than a proper fatwa—was made when the political temperature in Indonesia had risen considerably. It came on top of similar calls and actual preparations to facilitate the registration of jihad fighters. To make matters worse, there was talk at the time of a "sweeping" of Americans and other Westerners (that is, their abduction and subsequent expulsion by radical Islamic groups). Anti-government demonstrations in response to Megawati's support for Bush's war on terrorism seemed to threaten the stability of the country. All this made it appear likely that Indonesia would once again be plunged into chaos, as it had been throughout 1998 when police and demonstrators had been embroiled in fierce battles. Americans feared for their safety. For their part, Indonesian police were reluctant to intervene in the demonstrations fearing that to do so would provoke a backlash and even more turmoil. In Washington, the State Department considered the situation so critical that it authorized the U.S. embassy in Jakarta to evacuate its non-essential staff, and the American ambassador, Robert S. Gelbard, advised Americans living in Indonesia to consider leaving the country. The Jakarta police prepared emergency plans for when matters really spun out of control, including the evacuation of the foreigners living in Jakarta to safe refuges or to the airport.

By issuing this statement the MUI had put the government, and particularly Vice-President Hamzah Haz and the cabinet ministers who represented more radical Islamic political parties, in a difficult position. Their position was further complicated by Ambassador Gelbard's persistent complaints that the Indonesian authorities were failing to protect American citizens and property. Under these circumstances the secretary-general of the MUI, Din Syamsuddin, and its general chairman, K.H. MA Sahal Mahfudh, succeeded in maneuvering President Megawati into expressing understanding for organizations which called for a jihad against the United States and its allies. After a meeting between Megawati and the two MUI officials on October 16, 2001, Din Syamsuddin reported that Megawati could understand the MUI's call for a jihad because she was aware of the wide meaning of jihad and therefore realized that the MUI statement should not simply be equated with a call for physical warfare.[11]

Some of the most influential national Islamic political and religious leaders, however, were of the opinion that prudence was in order, not only to maintain domestic order but also because a rift with the United States might cost Indonesia dearly, especially economically. Among the organizations urging a cautious approach were the Nahdlatul Ulama and the Muhammadiyah, the two most important Islamic organizations, both claiming a membership of tens of millions. The general chairman of the Muhammadiyah, Prof. Dr. Syafii Ma'arif, advised against using the word "jihad," afraid of the emotions and radicalism the term could evoke. His colleague in the Nahdlatul Ulama, K.H. Hasyim Muzadi, reportedly preferred a "diplomatic jihad."[12] Another important Islamic politician, Amien Rais, who had been a leading figure of the *Reformasi* movement and chaired the People's Congress, also urged Muslims to avoid speaking impulsively about a jihad.

The MUI's fierce denunciation of communism and the Council's participation in drafting the jihad statement are among the indications that the MUI, or at least part of its leadership, was repositioning itself as mouthpiece for opinions prevalent in more radical streams of Indonesian Islam, and in doing so they were sometimes ahead of the game. As its jihad statement indicates, the MUI wished to take the lead on such issues. The new role the MUI has carved out for itself found more recent expression in a decision taken at the December 2003 National Working Meeting (Rapat Kerja Nasional) in Jakarta. One of the major decisions produced there was a proclamation that interest on bank loans and other financial transactions is tantamount to usury (*riba*) and thus forbidden by Islamic law.[13] In a statement to journalists after the meeting, the chairman of the fatwa committee, Ma'ruf Amin (a deputy chairman of the Nahdlatul Ulama), declared that the MUI forbade Muslims to engage in interest-based transactions, but that exceptions to the prohibition were to be determined in accordance with the principle of "emergency" (*ḍarūra*). It is permissible, for instance, for Muslims living in areas where an Islamic bank has not yet been established to use conventional banks, and conventional banks may be used for specific financial services not yet provided by local Islamic banks. Elsewhere, and he mentioned Jakarta as an example, where circumstances were such that the ruling on interest was binding (*wājib*), it was to be implemented immediately (*Republika*, December 17, 2003).

The institutional hierarchy

The MUI ban on the use of interest by Muslims was presented as confirmation of a previously unpublicized decision taken in April 2000 by the National Syari'ah Council (Dewan Syari'ah Nasional/DSN). The DSN was a relatively new institution, established by the MUI in 1997 for the specific purpose of dealing with financial matters. The name given to the new body leaves no doubt about the MUI's aspirations for dominance, at least in the field of Islamic banking. The reason for founding the DSN was the growing number of Islamic financial institutions in Indonesia, each with its own Shari'a Board issuing its own rulings. The creation of the DSN was intended to forestall the confusion inherent in this situation (Muladi 2004, 21).

Whatever the significance of the DSN ruling, the decision by the MUI to declare banking interest unlawful was shrouded in confusion. As soon as the decision was announced, the word "fatwa" began appearing in the media, and within days Sahal Mahfudh and Din Syamsuddin were compelled to explain that matters had not yet reached that stage. It was stated that the decision taken at the MUI meeting had yet to be sanctioned by its Executive Committee and was therefore not final.[14] Ma'ruf Amin backed down, belittling the authority of the decision. In a comment made just days after his earlier explanation, he stated that the fatwa was not binding, and that it was left to individual Muslims to decide for themselves whether to use Islamic or conventional banks. He dismissed the ruling as "just a fatwa," and observed that even the Qur'an is not followed by everybody, much less a mere "fatwa" (*Indo Pos*, December 21, 2003). An MUI fatwa in this sense was nothing more than a directive, an understanding of the term closer to traditional conceptions than to working assumptions of some modern fatwa organizations.[15]

One of the reasons for Ma'ruf Amin's backtracking was probably that the Nahdlatul Ulama and Muhammadiyah disagreed with the MUI's decision on bank interest. Both organizations owned banks that charged interest—the Bank Nusumma and the Bank Persyarikatan, respectively (*Jakarta Post*, December 17, 2003). Members of the central boards of the Muhammadiyah and Nahdlatul Ulama had already expressed their disagreement with the statement Ma'ruf Amin announced several weeks earlier that the MUI planned to issue a fatwa declaring interest forbidden at the end of 2003 or in 2004. At that time Din Syamsuddin (also a chairman of the Muhammadiyah), usually a proponent of the new course the MUI had taken, argued that not all Islamic scholars in the MUI could agree with such a fatwa, and that he was against such a position (Suaramerdeka.com, November 10, 2003).[16] The reason he gave for rejecting publication of the fatwa was that the number of Islamic bank branches in the country was still small. Din Syamsuddin also indicated that he could not agree with a fatwa forbidding interest after Ma'ruf Amin had already intimated that the MUI had taken such a decision. In another reaction, the general chairman of the Muhammadiyah, Syafii Ma'arif, pointed out that the subject of interest was still "controversial" among *'ulamā'*. He added that it had to be acknowledged that the MUI often issued fatwas that afterwards proved to be ineffective (*Koran Tempo*, December 18, 2003). Finally, his colleague in the Nahdlatul Ulama, K.H. Hasyim Muzadi, stressed that his organization had not yet taken a decision on the permissibility of interest or made a determination whether the receiving of interest is among those topics whose status as lawful or unlawful remains uncertain (Ind. *syubhat*). Under these circumstances Muslims could decide for themselves which opinion to follow.

Such confusion about a fatwa was not unique. The previous year a far greater—albeit short-lived—commotion had been caused by a Nahdlatul Ulama fatwa about suicide-bombers. The fatwa had been formulated some three months before the Bali bomb explosions during a July 2002 national conference of NU *'ulamā'* by the committee within the legal commission (Bahtsul Masail) assigned to deal with current political problems. It stated that while suicide is a grave sin, carrying out a suicide bombing could be allowed under certain circumstances, and even be considered an act of martyrdom. For this to be the case, three conditions must be present: first, the only intention of the would-be suicide should be to protect or fight for basic legal rights; second, the individual committing the attack should be convinced of the absence of effective alternative measures involving less grave risk; and, thirdly, the targets of the attack should be those individuals who orchestrate and perpetrate tyranny (which, one member of the Dewan Syuriah of the NU, K.H. Abdul Malik Madani, pointed out excluded as targets children and civilians who were shopping). Though the discussion in the committee was much broader—combatting tyranny by committing suicide and whether a hunger strike is permissible—the debate was really about Palestinian suicide-bombers. It may well be that the members of the committee had been carried away by their pro-Palestinian and anti-Israeli sentiments, and that they had failed to fully appreciate the implications of their fatwa in the Indonesian context—not anticipating, for instance, how the fatwa could be interpreted by Muslims and what it meant for Indonesia's image abroad.

The fatwa was, it is fair to say, an explosive decision. The Islamic magazine *Sabili* captured the gist of the matter with a caption printed on the cover of an issue carrying an article about the NU meeting stating *Bom Syahid di tengah NU*, "A Martyr's Bomb in the Midst of NU" (*Sabili*, August 22, 2002). In view of the mass demonstrations after September 11 and the accusations from Singapore, the United States, and Australia that the Indonesian government was not prepared to act against domestic Islamic terrorism, Indonesia needed to project an image as the home of moderate Muslims. The Nahdlatul Ulama has often been held up as a model and standard-bearer for such moderation. The suicide-bomber fatwa detracted from the organization's image as the paradigm of moderation that some NU leaders like to stress.

The ensuing damage control effort sought to foster the impression that the suicide-bomber fatwa represented a minority opinion within the NU.

A number of the organization's leaders, who themselves may also have been worried by the content of the fatwa, tried to play down its importance. It was argued that "the fatwa was a 'low level' religious order" and that "it was not issued by any of the influential Muslim clerics within the organization" (*The Straits Times Interactive*, July 31, 2002). This raises questions about what those who expressed this opinion thought about the organization's other fatwas, and why the specific individuals who drafted the fatwa had been assigned to the committee that issued it. The general chairman of the NU, Hasyim Muzadi, stressed that what had been agreed upon was not yet an NU fatwa; a valid fatwa must be countersigned by the central board (*pengurus besar*), as indeed is required (*Sabili*, August 22, 2002, p. 71). To dampen fears that the fatwa might have domestic implications, Hasyim Muzadi also told *The Straits Times* that the fatwa "did not signify a change in NU's moderate view of Islam," and that militant groups in Aceh and the Moluccas "could not use the fatwa as an endorsement for suicide bombings" because these conflicts were "neither religious nor international wars" (*The Straits Times Interactive*, July 31, 2002). Another NU leader, Masdar Farid Mas'udi, assured *The Straits Times* that the fatwa would "not encourage radicalism" because it had "to be read in context" (ibid.)—all niceties with which radical Muslims would probably not bother.

The NU suicide-bombers fatwa also went too far for a man like Ja'far Umar Thalib, the leader of the Laskar Jihad and a person regarded by many, especially outside of Indonesia, as a prominent voice of Islamic radicalism and extremism. His opinion was that suicide-bombing, strictly speaking, is forbidden by Islam, since the attacker should allow for the possibility to escape death, however small that chance that might be (*Gatra*, August 10, 2002, p. 27). The MUI itself later spoke out against suicide bombing after the Bali explosions of October 2002, at least one of which was probably committed by a suicide-bomber, as was the bomb attack at the JW Marriott Hotel in Jakarta in August 2003 (thejakartapost.com, November 28, 2002). In a formal ruling issued in December 2003 the MUI declared suicide-bombings to be unlawful, wherever they were committed—in war zones or in zones of peace. This decision was taken at the same meeting in which the disputed ruling about interest was formulated.

Religious authority

The discussion about the fatwas on interest and suicide-bombers illustrates the tension that sometimes exists between religious advisors within an Islamic organization on the one hand and the members of its executive board, who must take non-religious considerations into account, on the other. The same tension is also sometimes felt between members of a fatwa committee and Islamic scholars who sit on the religious advisory boards (*dewan syuriah*). Political considerations are sometimes critical to the decision whether a fatwa shall be made public, as illustrated by an incident during Abdurrahman Wahid's presidency. At a time when voices urging him to step down were gaining momentum, an unofficial gathering of NU '*ulamā*' produced a fatwa declaring that persons demanding Abdurrahman Wahid's resignation were guilty of subversion (*bughot*). For "reasons of public order," however, the fatwa was not made public. The '*ulamā*' who had drafted the fatwa feared that the potentially inflammable domestic situation then prevailing, in which supporters of Abdurrahman Wahid were indicating that they might travel to Jakarta to defend his presidency by force, might get out of hand (*Gatra*, August 10, 2002, p. 33). This raises questions about the value of such a fatwa. The answer may be that it can serve both as moral support and as an instrument of sanction in a dispute between senior politicians. In the first function the subversion fatwa may have succeeded; in the second function it failed.

In the case of the suicide-bombers fatwa, it was political considerations which weighed most heavily. Economic arguments predominated in the discussions about the "fatwa" on the permissibility of interest. Din Syamsuddin was concerned that the Islamic banks were not equipped to accommodate the new customers that a ban on interest might bring them (though some Indonesian economic experts doubted that the influx would be particularly great). Others worried about the consequences for the conventional banks, which had suffered gravely during the financial crisis in the late 1990s. Not unexpectedly for an exchange of views that took place in fatwa-issuing circles, the discussion stayed well within the confines of conventional religious debate and did not touch on more fundamental or broader religious questions. It remained far removed from the "re-actualization" debate of the 1980s, initiated by the then Minister of Religious Affairs, H. Munawir Sjadzali. In those years he and a number of other Muslim intellectuals had stressed that changing social circumstances should be taken into consideration and that in certain aspects of life religious law should follow practices that had become generally accepted in Indonesian society. One prominent issue that was debated broadly was inheritance. The view was expressed by some that with respect to inheritance Islamic lawmakers should take into account the belief, reportedly common at that time, that it was unfair that under Islamic law sons inherited twice as much as daughters.

The permissibility of bank interest was another subject where such considerations were discussed. It was argued that in a society where most people perceived no problem in using the services of a conventional bank, interest should not be declared unlawful. However, these discussions were more or less cut short by the MUI. The Council did not respond to Munawir Sjadzali's campaign for the need to adjust Islamic law to the realities of contemporary Indonesian life, but rather took the lead in establishing an Islamic bank in Indonesia—an initiative that enjoyed the warm support of President Suharto (Van Dijk 1991). The new institution, the Bank Muamalat Indonesia, opened its doors in May 1992.

The Nahdlatul Ulama suicide-bomber fatwa and the fatwa of the MUI on interest illustrate the obvious fact that there is a hierarchy of religious authority in Indonesian Islam, and that the matter of authority has consequences for the drafting of a fatwa. Ranking within this hierarchy is generally determined informally, with some 'ulamā' acquiring greater prominence than others. At times it is also formally acknowledged within the structure of organizations. The procedure followed in the Nahdlatul Ulama and MUI resembles decision-making in the Indonesian People's Congress, the MPR. Decisions taken at the committee stage can be shelved before they reach the general session of the People's Congress or they can be rejected outright. This is an integral part of the political process, and the give-and-take involved mitigates the potential effect on the political status of those involved. But how does this process work with religious authority, and how in turn does this relate to conceptions of political authority? In theory religious authority prevails over political authority in many Indonesian Islamic political, religious, and social organizations, but in actual practice it may well be the reverse.

Internal disagreement is a sensitive phenomenon, especially in the MUI, which was envisaged as a national institution bringing together several streams of Islam, each with different religious practices.[17] Nevertheless, there are organizations representing specific segments of the Indonesian Islamic community that are reluctant to delegate the sole authority to issue fatwas to the MUI. For example, commenting upon the MUI fatwa on interest, Din Syamsuddin stressed that the MUI would take into consideration the views of the Nahdlatul Ulama, Muhammadiyah, and other Islamic organizations, and that the ruling by Muhammadiyah's Majlis Tarjih would be the point of departure for the evaluation of the MUI fatwas.

Islamic religious authority also has an international component. In some situations the opinions of Islamic scholars abroad are actively sought. This can be done for a variety of religious and political reasons. An example of this can be seen in the drafting of a fatwa approving family planning by Islamic scholars in the Philippines, who solicited endorsement and comments of the Grand Mufti of Egypt, the Grand Shaykh of the Al-Azhar University, and other religious scholars in Egypt. Publication of the final draft of the fatwa, which was made official in March 2004, was postponed until the comments from Egypt had been incorporated into the text of the decision.

In other instances political motives are also clearly at play as opinions of authoritative foreign religious figures are brought to bear by governments on issues on which they differ fundamentally with domestic Islamic opposition. Such a course of action can both provide a measure of justification for unpopular government programs and work to convince local Muslims still wavering on particular issues. However, the would-be opposition, which is supposed to be impressed by such foreign authority, is usually unmoved. An acknowledgement by the Grand Shaykh of Al-Azhar University, Dr. Muḥammad Sayyid Ṭanṭāwī, of the right of states to ban headscarves in schools certainly pleases the governments of France and Singapore, but it does not necessarily convince those who defy their governments on the matter.[18] When the Grand Shaykh visited Malaysia in July 2003 and called Malaysia a model for other Islamic countries, it pleased the Malaysian government, but it did nothing to convince Malaysia's Islamic opposition, who considered their country to be anything but an Islamic state. Thus, the then president of the popular Islamist Parti Islam seMalaysia (PAS) expressed disdain; Abdul Hadi Awang said he understood precisely why the Grand Shaykh had called Malaysia an Islamic state, as he had been appointed by the Egyptian government and not by the religious scholars and academics of the University.

In present-day Indonesia such foreign authority usually remains in the background. There is, however, at least one blatant exception. That is the Laskar Jihad, an organization created to come to the assistance of Muslims in the Moluccas who were engaged in a gruesome civil war with the local Christian population. The leaders of the Laskar Jihad, or rather those of its mother organization, the Forum Komunikasi Ahlus Sunnah Wal Jamaah (FK-ASWJ), appear to have taken no decision of any importance without first consulting a number of shaykhs in Yemen and Saudi Arabia.[19] Compared to these Middle Eastern scholars, they considered themselves "still laymen" (*masih awam*) (Baker n.d., 24). At times the Laskar Jihad leaders contacted these scholars by telephone or traveled to the Middle East to meet them personally. The founding of the Laskar Jihad on April 6, 2000 was preceded by a fatwa from the Middle Eastern shaykhs assuring Ja'far Umar

Thalib—who was to become the Laskar's commander or *panglima*—and other FK-ASWJ leaders that: "A jihad in the Moluccas was obligatory to defend Muslims from the attacks by Christians" (Baker n.d., 23).[20]

To the surprise of almost everybody, Ja'far announced the disbanding of the Laskar Jihad on October 14, 2002, two days after the Bali blasts. Since its founding Ja'far had stressed defense of the unitary Indonesian state and complained about the failure of Jakarta to appreciate the gravity of the threat to national unity posed by Christian separatists active in the Moluccas.[21] That Jakarta had finally admitted the reality of the danger was presented as the reason for the disbanding. But there was more. Laskar Jihad leaders expressed sincere regret over mistakes and failures made in the past, especially in the Moluccas and in Poso in Sulawesi, where the Laskar Jihad was also active. It is noteworthy that the errors that were admitted had been brought to the attention of the Laskar Jihad by the same Islamic scholars in the Middle East whose opinions had been requested in the past, and it was after consultation with those scholars that the decision was taken to disband. Among the "moral faults" committed by the Laskar Jihad were that some members had become involved in politics, had failed to abide by the ban on the taking of photographs of living creatures, had besmirched the government, and had a penchant for staging demonstrations (Shoelhi 2002a, 4–6).

The same Middle Eastern shaykhs were also consulted when a member of the Laskar Jihad was found guilty of the rape of a 13-year old girl in Ambon in March 2001. Since the man was married, the verdict for his actions was death by stoning (*rajam*). Accordingly, he was buried to the waist and then stoned to death by members of the Laskar Jihad.[22] Before the execution, Laskar Jihad leaders had sought the advice of their spiritual leaders in the Middle East. One point of uncertainty for the Laskar leadership was whether they had the right to carry out justice themselves or were obliged to leave this to the state. It was determined that, in view of his behavior, Abdurrahman Wahid was an apostate (*murtadd*), and thus the Indonesian government was not headed by a devout Muslim who executed his mandate in a just and proper manner (Shoelhi 2002, 74).

Regional comparisons

In Malaysia and Singapore the issuing of a fatwa (*iftā'*) is firmly embedded in public administration. Nevertheless, the right to issue fatwas is exercised with prudence by the government. When their respective institutions are mobilized to support the government on sensitive issues, the religious councils in Malaysia and Singapore often respond with a fatwa. Another option available to the councils is a public statement by the chairmen endorsing the position of the government or condemning what the opposition said or did as a violation of religious rules.

This was the course adopted by the Majlis Ugama Islam Singapura (MUIS) when, in early 2002, inter-religious relations—as well as relations within the Muslim Malay community—came under stress as a result of the government's position on the wearing of headscarves (*tudung*) by schoolgirls. The parents of four six-year-old girls who were starting school at four different primary schools had demanded that their daughters be allowed to wear the headscarves to school.[23] The school principals were adamant in their refusal to permit this, arguing that a headscarf was not part of the Singapore school uniform. Thus, the four girls were not allowed to enter school unless they removed the headscarf. The Singapore government took the same position. In an effort to break the impasse the MUIS stepped in. It did not issue an opinion, but it advised the parents to set aside their religious objections and send their children to school without a headscarf. The MUIS gave this advice on the suggestion of the mufti of Singapore, Syed Isa Semait, who explained that when forced to choose between education for one's children and wearing a headscarf, the preference of Muslims should be for the more important of the two: education. The MUIS couched its pronouncement in terms of *nasihat* (advice) and *pandangan* (opinion); *penjelasan* (explanation) and *pendapat* (opinion) were the terms used by the mufti.

In Malaysia considerations about whether to issue a fatwa came to the fore when Nik Aziz Nik Mat, the spiritual leader of Parti Islam seMalaysia (PAS), stated in a speech in March 2002 that God ws a "gangster" (*Tuhan samseng*), "arrogant" (*sombong*) and "wicked" (*jahat*), and to a greater degree than any human being (Van Dijk 2002). What ensued could have been predicted. However, Nik Aziz refused to retract his words, explaining that it had been his intention to make clear that nobody can act with the toughness of God. On another occasion he explained the use of those particular descriptive words to point out "how supreme and mighty God is compared with human beings . . . He is superior than [sic] all gangsters in this world" and that among "the Kelantan people, the term *samseng* (gangster) instills much fear unlike the words [sic] *berkuasa* (powerful) which has little impact" (*New Straits Times* Online, August 1, 2002). He and his supporters also stated that "arrogant" and *samseng* were proper translations of the Arabic terms *al-Mutakabbir* and *al-Jabbār*, two of the names of God, which were translated in *The Straits Times* as, respectively, "proud," "boastful" or "The

Almighty," and as "cruel," "mighty," "heavy-handed" or "The Revengeful" (*The Straits Times* Interactive, August 30, 2002; August 31, 2002; *Berita Harian* Online, September 24, 2002).[24]

Leaders of the United Malay National Organization (UMNO), the political and religious rival of PAS, made it clear that they wanted to develop new rules to prevent a repeat of this performance. But what was the best way to go about it? The chairman of the National Fatwa Council for Islamic Matters (Majlis Fatwa Kebangsaan bagi Hal Ehwal Agama Islam), Datuk Dr. Ismail Ibrahim, announced that his institution was contemplating issuing a fatwa about likening the attributes of God to the negative qualities of men.[25] The deputy prime minister of Malaysia, Datuk Seri Abdullah Ahmad Badawi, also indicated that the government was studying the possibility of a fatwa. In his opinion, such a step was necessary to clarify the matter for Malaysian Muslims.

The Director of the Institute of Islamic Understanding (Institut Kefahaman Islam Malaysia/IKIM)—a "think tank" created by the Malaysian government in 1993 to promote the understanding and image of Islam—disagreed with this course of action. The issue, Datuk Dr. Abdul Monir Yaacob said, should be solved politically, not by a fatwa.[26] He argued that legal means should be used to tackle cases in which people compared the attributes of God to those of men or committed blasphemy. Such an approach was needed because the matter was not one specifically concerning religion or ordinary *'ulamā'*, but one involving either *'ulamā'* who had specific political interests or politicians engaged in political speech. If a fatwa in answer to calling God a gangster were issued, the result might be the issuance of another fatwa, and countless additional fatwas would become necessary every time "irresponsible politicians" used offensive words or expressions.[27] Such a series of fatwas would only confuse the ordinary believer. Abdul Monir Yaacob's answer was to have the Election Commission (Suruhanjaya Pilihan Raya/SPR) or the Departments of Islam (Jabatan Agama Islam) of the individual states issue a code of ethics.[28] Only in cases where ordinary *'ulamā'* used such words, he said, was a fatwa needed (*Berita Harian* Online, August 27, 2002; *Utusan Malaysia* Online, August 27, 2002).

In the end the National Fatwa Council decided against issuing a fatwa on this case. Instead, it "advised" all parties to respect the law and to stop comparing the attributes of God with those of men, adding that Muslims who did not honor this advice and divided the Islamic community through the spoken and the written word or who damaged the image of Islam should be prosecuted. The chairman of the Council, Ismail Ibrahim, explained that likening the attributes of God or Muḥammad to those of ordinary men clearly constituted a sin. In such an instance a fatwa was superfluous. The statutory law could deal with it. The National Fatwa Council should not issue a fatwa in the case, and certainly not one which had the status of a verdict. Legal action was the preserve of the civil authorities, and in such circumstances the Council could only give advice (*Berita Harian* Online, September 6, 2002).[29]

One specific reason for restraint in issuing a fatwa in Malaysia is that, unlike in Indonesia, fatwas in Malaysia are considered to be legally binding. All Malaysian courts, secular and Islamic, can also turn to the Majlis Agama for advice. To avoid disputes over a binding fatwa, and also to prevent a confrontation over the relation between secular and religious law, the Council generally chooses to issue advice rather than a fatwa proper (Jusoh 1991, 74–5). However, the media use the word fatwa liberally, equating utterances by religious scholars and politicians with a fatwa. Specialists are also sometimes careless. The recent warning by the Malaysian Prime Minister, Datuk Seri Abdullah Badawi, not to issue fatwas of any kind during the general election campaign alluded to this propensity.

In Indonesia a fatwa is at most morally binding. As already stated, the MUI also does not hold a position comparable to that of the religious councils in Malaysia and Singapore. Other fatwa institutions operate alongside it, which means that issuing fatwas sometimes resembles preaching to the converted but at other times is more like competitive politicking. It also means that when the MUI tries to act as a national institution, it can find itself publicly confronted with the fact that there are "rival" fatwa institutions. The Indonesian situation exemplifies the fact that religion is not a science, and that although the methodologies of Islamic jurisprudence can be very detailed, some terms remain to a considerable degree contested.

Four

LIGHTNING, ANGELS AND PRAYERS FOR THE NATION: READING THE FATWAS OF THE JAM'IYAH AHLITH THORIQOH AL-MU'TABAROH

Michael Laffan

It was during a visit to Jakarta in July 2002 that I met the distinctive Habib Luthfi Ali of Pekalongan. We met at the biannual national conference of the Nahdlatul Ulama (NU), the largest mass organization for Indonesian Muslims. Here the prominent descendant of Hadrami emigrants was an active participant in consultative sessions held to determine fatwas for this body, including one draft on suicide bombing. After long conversations on the general history of Sufism in the archipelago, and Islam in general, I came away with the impression that I had met someone very important but was unable to make sense of where he figured in the world of Indonesian Islam.

I later learned that Habib Luthfi is one of the so-called "paranormal" *kiai*s with a voice on the advisory council of NU. He is also the head of an adjunct organization that claims to be the voice of the traditional Sufi orders in Indonesia, the Jam'iyah Ahlith Thoriqoh al-Mu'tabaroh (JATM), and had presided over the organization in 2000 when it issued ten fatwas for the benefit of his fellow citizens. The topics covered in these pronouncements were diverse, including one especially puzzling fatwa—the very first to be listed—on the nature of lightning:

> In an area there is lightning (Ind. *petir* / Jav. *bledek*).
> (a) It strikes trees and the like such that they are mortally damaged.
> (b) The people of this area call this lightning *paju*.
> (c) When it strikes trees and the like they become singed (Jav. *gosong*).
> (d) Lightning enters a house in the form of a snake or human to strike things in the vicinity.
>
> The question is:
> (a) What in fact is lightning?
> (b) Is it true that *kandari* wood has special protective qualities against lightning?

[Signed] Cilacap.

Answer:
(a) According to the statements of the majority of the *'ulamā'*, lightning is [caused by] the movement of angels under instruction from God, which leads to excessive wind pressure (*ekses benturan hawa*) or a fiery burst/electrical current (*kisikan api/arus listrik*) that gives rise to a "voice" (*suara*).
(b) It is entirely possible to take any form (as is stated by Ibn Kathīr), and trees, flowers or leaves may well ward it off (as is stated by Ibn Kathīr).[1]

This fatwa was then followed by three pages of Arabic source quotations, including passages from the exegesis of al-Bayḍawī (fl. ca. 1293), al-Zurqānī's commentary (*sharḥ*) of the *Muwaṭṭa'* of Mālik b. Anas (ca. 711–96), and the parenthetically cited Ibn Kathīr (ca. 1300–73). In its formal aspects, and by reference to classical jurisprudence, this statement on the nature of lightning resembles the fatwas given by many other Muslim organizations in Indonesia, and indeed jurists from across the centuries. Still I wondered if this could be read as legal text (*fiqh*) at all, and how indeed JATM fitted into the spectrum of Islamic activism in often stormy Indonesia. This chapter is a tentative description of the JATM in light of its own declarations and, more especially, its fatwas.

Background

From the 1910s, competition for the mantle of representing Islamic orthodoxy in Indonesia has been played out between a variety of Islamic organizations. At the most general level, these organizations divide on a nominal, and extremely porous, fault line of traditionalism and modernism (Saleh 2001). And although much of the heritage of this categorization is a colonial construct, what forms Islamic traditionalism in Indonesia today is often identifiable with, or connected to, the practices upheld by NU, which recent surveys have suggested may claim an influence over some 42 percent of the population (see Jamhari 2002, 183–89).

Whereas NU was founded in 1926 to uphold the traditional authority of the *'ulamā'*, including those from the Sufi tradition, it has also trod the boards of the political stage. In the early years of the Republic (1949–52) it was affiliated to the largest political body for Muslims, Masyumi (the Consultative Council for Indonesian Muslims).[2] However, due in part to modernist dominance of the organization, NU withdrew from Masyumi in 1952 and ran in the 1955 election as a party in its own right. Neither NU nor Masyumi secured a clear majority, and the combined "Muslim" vote nationally was a disappointing 43 percent, a proportion never since exceeded.[3]

In the aftermath of the coup of 1965, Suharto repressed any explicit role for Islam in party politics, and in 1973 NU was forcibly incorporated into the United Development Party (PPP). Frustrated by such impediments placed before Muslim politics, and a lack of cohesion in the PPP, a group of NU 'ulamā', including Abdurrahman Wahid (aka Gus Dur, b. 1940), called for a return to the "first principles" (khittah) of the movement at the 1984 congress at Situbondo, East Java. This effectively marked the withdrawal of NU from party politics until the fall of Suharto in 1998.[4]

The somewhat surprising ascension of Gus Dur to the Presidency in October 1999 finally (albeit inadvertently) yielded a short-lived golden age for NU; and it was first met by his partisans with unalloyed delight. An almost messianic hope seems to have been placed in him to deliver Indonesia from the host of problems facing the nation beyond the economic crisis of 1998 and the near collapse of central authority. But Gus Dur's presidency (which ended in July 2001) did not ultimately deliver peace and prosperity under the banner of Islam, but was marred instead by corruption scandals and, more darkly, by the escalation of a vicious fratricide in the Moluccas.[5]

Such issues and events are beyond the scope of this paper. Rather I wish to return to the past by way of the pages of a journal produced as one part of the emergent discourse of Islam under Gus Dur. In April 2000, the monthly journal entitled Sufi: Jalan menuju ilahi made its appearance on Java's news stands and propagated the message that mysticism held many answers for the problems of the nation, but only· if it was properly practiced under the guidance of a recognized teacher (murshid). It was in this connection that the JATM was publicly presented afresh as the coordinating national body for true Sufi activity, that is, Sufism as organized by the traditional orders (Ar. ṭuruq, sing. ṭarīqa; Ind. tarekat, sometimes thoriqah or thoriqoh, etc.) rather than the ever-widening array of traditional healers and "mystical" clinics.

Origins of the JATM

The precise date and circumstances surrounding the foundation of the JATM as an organization are difficult to ascertain. In his work on the history and spread of the Naqshbandiyya order in Indonesia, Martin van Bruinessen discusses the special role of the Pesantren Darul Ulum in Rejoso, Jombang, and the role of senior tarekat leaders of the Naqshbandiyya affiliated with NU in the first incarnation of the JATM in 1957.[6] It convened its first conference in October of that year, an event which I would suggest may have been triggered in part by the fact that a consortium of spiritualist groups had established a national association in 1956 to influence the government.[7]

Certainly the JATM saw itself as playing a very politicized role under the apparent protection of NU star and then national Minister for Education, Saifuddin Zuhri. In an address to the congress of the body, held in Jakarta on July 26, 1962, Zuhri spoke of the task of the JATM to develop the spiritual capacity of the Indonesian people.[8] Splicing appeals into his address to contribute to the "multi-complex revolution" to create a just and prosperous community blessed by God with appeals to be active for the liberation of Irian from the Dutch, Zuhri clearly felt at home with the rhetoric of Sukarno's government. Perhaps more meaningfully, however, he also declared more generally in this short address that any nation without the spiritual strength (of Islam) was like a new hospital building—perhaps modern in style and form, but nonetheless a building filled with sick people. The strength that the Sufi orders offered, therefore, was one founded on the true Divine unicity (*tawḥīd*), with such teaching being properly disseminated by those who followed the dictates of the *ʿulamāʾ* of the pious generation (*ʿulamāʾ al-salaf al-ṣāliḥ*), defined as those of "the respectable way" (*thoriqat jang muʿtabarah*).

Although the JATM has always claimed to represent all "respectable" (i.e., *muʿtabara*) orders, and disseminated a list of 44 *ṭarīqa*s that could claim this appellation, at its inception the JATM was locally dominated by members of the very Indonesian Qadiriyya wa Naqshbandiyya order. Even so, its notions of respectability are shared across *ṭarīqa* boundaries, and are in marked distinction to the welter of mystical movements found in Indonesia (and especially Java). Properly speaking, this validation is earned by a documented connection to the Prophet by way of a genealogy of transmission (*silsila*) and a commitment to the defense of orthodoxy embodied by the *Ahl al-Sunna wa l-Jamāʿa* (as defined by NU).[9]

By 1975 the JATM was under the effective control of Kiai Mustaʿin Romly of Rejoso, then the "most charismatic . . . and most ambitious" of the Sufi masters on Java (Van Bruinessen 1992, 171). However, in the lead-up to the 1977 general elections, Romly openly associated himself with the ruling Golkar Party of Suharto, rather than the PPP with which his peers in NU remained associated. This earned Romly the reputation of having betrayed NU and he was accordingly disavowed as head of the JATM. The initiative for this removal of sanction was led by the Pesantren Tebuireng, which has always had a somewhat ambivalent attitude to the teachings of the mystical orders: neither explicitly adopting them nor stopping students from undertaking them privately.[10]

At the 1979 NU congress held in Semarang,[11] a grouping from within the JATM founded the new, more explicitly NU-affiliated organization, the JATM*N* (Jam'iyah Ahlith Thoriqoh al-Mu'tabaroh *an-Nahdliyyah*). Its leaders include the *kiai*s Adlan Ali, Arwani from Kudus, Muslih from Mranggen, and Hafiz of Pesantren Lasem, Rembang. However, the old JATM of Musta'in itself was never formally dissolved and the latter continued to act as its leader until his death in 1984. With the death of his own teacher, Usman bin Ishaq, Hafiz's students went to pledge their allegiance to his deputy (*khalifa*), Sonhaji, in Kebumen. According to Gus Dur, at that time Chairman of NU, he was approached for support as new fractures emerged between NU partisans, once more divided between PPP and Golkar in the lead-up to the elections of 1987. Despite its ambitions to voice the concerns of the mystical orders on Java, if not ultimately throughout Indonesia, the JATM and its effective successor, the JATMN, have largely been paralyzed by internal conflict and subsumed, for all intents and purposes, under the mantle of NU. In the 1990s, the movement came under the guidance of the then head of the Executive Board (Ketua Tanfidziah), Idham Cholid (1921-2000), before passing, in 1998, into the hands of Habib Luthfi, who has established himself as a weighty presence at its fatwa-giving consultations.[12]

The fatwas of JATM as a window into its social history

Even before their official merger in 1979, the activities of the JATM obviously intersected with those of NU. Most of its luminaries, such as Idham Cholid, were drawn from a subset of NU *kiai*s and gurus. Reminders of this fusion may still be found in the bookstands patronized by the NU, which make JATMN publications available, or in NU literature in general. One fatwa released by NU in 1961 makes reference to an earlier decision given at the second conference of the JATM held in November 1959.[13] In this section I will consider two documents relating to the JATM. The first was a revised compilation of early JATM fatwas and the second the results of the Ninth Congress of the JATMN, held in Pekalongan in February 2000.

(i) al-Fuyūdāt al-rabbaniyya

The first volume referred to above that contains JATM fatwas is a cheaply-produced reprint of material dating from 1982. Entitled in Arabic al-Fuyūdāt al-rabbāniyya fī muqarrarāt al-mu'tamarāt li-jam'īyyat ahl al-ṭarīqa al-mu'tabara al-nahḍiyya ("The Divine Streams: Decisions of the Congresses of the JATM") and glossed in Indonesian as Berbagai masalah agama [thariqah dan fiqih] ("Various Questions of Religion [tarīqa and fiqh]"), this slim volume of 127 pages contains 132 official fatwas of the JATM issued between 1957 and (ostensibly) 1973. Of these, the first 74 resulted from four general conferences (Tegalrejo 1957, Pekalongan 1959, Tulung Agung 1963, and Semarang 1968). The remainder came from two meetings of the Great Consultation (Musyawarah Besar) held in Semarang and Malang in 1973, where, it should be noted, the movement was still declared to be an "all-Java" affair rather than the "all-Indonesia" one that NU now is.

According to the principal editor of NU fatwas, Aziz Masyhuri,[14] the various juridical opinions presented in the Fuyūdāt had actually first been compiled many years previously by the late Abdul Jalil Kudus. However, at the time of his death, this work had not been completed, let alone approved. The project was then passed on to Mahfudh Anwar, who gave it its Arabic title, before the collection was examined and corrected by the long-time Director-General (Rois Am) and chair of the NU executive, Bisri Syansuri (d. 1980). Only after this was the text rendered into Arabic.

This long and carefully-considered process must have presented difficulties for its intended audience, and suggestions were apparently made for the Arabic questions and answers to be dropped in favor of their Indonesian variants, which were in any case the original.[15] According to Masyhuri, this proposal was adopted for the second edition as a means of making a general source available to any party interested in knowing more about the goings-on of the mystical orders. Furthermore, he argues, this will clearly answer the ancient charges of Sufism's critics:

> After reading this book people will become aware and recognize that the people of the orders are not ignorant of the Shari'a. [Rather] they are knowledgeable agents of the dictates of religion. Never are they boorish (ceroboh) in making a legal decision on any matter touching upon religion, nor are they bold enough to declare licit something that is clearly illicit. They will always exercise caution with matters

that are detested (*makruh*) or merely dubious (*syubhat*). Indeed, many of them will never deliberately do anything that is *makruh* or *syubhat* in the slightest, immediately repenting or asking God's forgiveness. As regards the actions of the orders, they are rapidly expanding in the community these days, leading those who know little of them to become antipathetic, incredulous, or quite possibly stirred up against them with little provocation to level charges that the orders will only herd the community (*umat*), and especially the Islamic community (*jama'a*), to their decline and division. Some even dare to charge that [they] are polytheists and unbelievers. We take refuge in God from that! On the contrary, it is those who accuse the orders of sowing dissent themselves who would bring the *umat* far from the truth in carrying out the way of Islam (*syari'at Islam*). It would come to the point where the Islamic community would be deceived by their perfidy [whereupon] the Islamic community would ultimately be unable to realize the true meaning (*hakekat*) of life as a servant of God Almighty (Masyhuri n.d., iv–v).

Masyhuri points out that the affairs of this world and the next are inextricably linked by faith (*iman*). He then goes on to argue that only once someone has become involved in the affairs of the orders, rather than being a skeptical critic on the outside, does he or she realize how the activities of the Sufis are rooted in Islam. In this way, they will find that Sufis root their behavior in the very practice of the Prophet and his Companions; and that this practice has been maintained by the "respectable" orders whose *'ulamā'* maintain direct connections with Muḥammad through their genealogies of instruction.

The practices of the Sufis belonging to orders are therefore presented as being in total harmony with the Shari'a, and it is appropriate then that the vast majority of the fatwas presented in the *Fuyūdāt* relate equally to two topics that are seen as implicitly interrelated: *ṭarīqa* (*masalah thoriqoh*, 45 fatwas) and worship (*masalah ibadah*, 44 fatwas). The remainder of the volume is concerned with questions of social relations (*masalah mu'amalah*, 14), marriage (*masalah munakahat*, 5) and "varia" (*masalah warna warni*, 22). All are presented in the *Fuyūdāt* in a simple manner. The question(s) of the person requesting the fatwa (*mustafti*) and an answer from the otherwise anonymous panel or individual mufti representing the JATM are given in roman-script Indonesian. These are followed by Indonesian references to works of Islamic jurisprudence (*fiqh*), and usually by direct quotations in Arabic from those works (which are listed in an appendix), with the occasional endnote for good measure or to add additional explanation to earlier fatwas requiring clarification.

Here is the first fatwa in the volume as an example.

Rules for joining an order

Q: What is the opinion of delegates (*mu'tamirin*) regarding the rules for joining an order and practising it?

A: If joining an order is done in order to study how to cleanse the heart from base qualities, and to embellish those which are praiseworthy, then such [an act] is an individual duty (*farḍ ʿayn*). This case is like the *ḥadīth* of the Prophet, God's peace and blessings be upon him, the meaning of which is: "Seeking knowledge is obligatory for every Muslim man and woman." Meanwhile, if induction in a respectable order is specifically for the practice of *dhikr* and *wirid* (Ar. *wird*), then it is regarded as the Sunna of the Prophet, God's peace and blessings be upon him.[16] It is incumbent (*wājib*) for one to carry out *dhikr* and *wirid* after having made the pact of obedience (Ar. *bayʿa*) [to the spiritual guide] as that is the fulfilment of a promise. In regard to giving instruction in *dhikr* and *wirid* to a student, [this] is deemed to be Sunna. If the genealogy (*sanad*) of the order connects with the Prophet, God's peace and blessings be upon him, then it is sound.[17]

Naturally enough, similar fatwas declaring that practices of respectable orders are sound, and moreover Sunna, as well as those regulating the orders or relating to their respectability take priority in the compilation. Other such regulatory fatwas concern: the possibility of students moving between orders (no. 2); a spiritual guide (*murshid*) preventing a student giving obedience (*bayʿa*) to another teacher (no. 3); women serving as deputies (*khalifa*, no. 7); or the impossibility of following a teacher who does not live according to the regulations of the Shariʿa (no. 10). There are questions that relate to the practice of reading adulatory texts in praise of the great Sufi master ʿAbd al-Qādir al-Jīlānī (nos. 14, 15, 27); unvocalized *dhikr* (no. 20) and other pious or supererogatory ejaculations such as "'Abd al-Qādir is a friend of God," often said in Sufi gatherings after the Islamic confession of faith (*shahāda*) (nos. 57, 124). Fatwas are given on the possibility of pursuing instruction in more than one order (no. 4); on the possibility for more than one *khalīfa* to operate in a single town (no. 58); and on the dangers of taking instruction from anyone who claims to have witnessed, and even merged with, God (no. 12), or who is merely unable to withstand the intense pressures of Divine Attraction (*jadhba*) and is thus *majdhūb* (no. 93).[18]

Importantly, too, the name and number of orders that may claim to perpetuate proper Shariʿa-oriented practice are defined. It appears, however, that the precise number of respectable orders, much like the names of Java's famous nine saints (*wali songo*), is in some state of flux. According to fatwa no. 9, released after the congress of November 1959, only a teacher who could prove a validated link to the Prophet could carry out instruction. Such orders that maintain verifiable links are then merely described as being "like the Naqshbandiyya, the Qādiriyya and the Khālidiyya," with supporting quotes from the Sufi texts *Khazīnat al-asrār*, *Uṣūl al-ṭarīq* and *Tanwīr al-qulub* that spoke vaguely of connection to the way (*ṭarīq*) of the Salaf and the Prophet.

Further clarification may be found in fatwa no. 16, apparently given at the same meeting. Herein the questioner asks whether there can be more than 42 "respectable" orders as had been determined at the very first meeting at Tegalrejo—though apparently no fatwa had been issued in this regard. Accordingly, reference is made to the *Jamiʿ uṣūl al-awliyāʾ* which designates forty-four orders, although the fatwa duly notes that not all are found in Indonesia.[19] Of those that are, only the Naqshbandiyya, Qādiriyya, and Shaṭṭāriyya could be regarded as prospering while the Shādhiliyya, Tijāniyya, and Sammāniyya are found in only a few areas.

Regardless of how many orders were then present (or yet thriving) in Indonesia, the JATM made sure in 1959 to issue a fatwa that rejected the widespread charges that the orders only cause decline in a community.

> *On the erroneous saying (*ocehan*) "The Sufi order leads to decline"*
>
> Q: What is the opinion of delegates (*muʾtamirin*) regarding a person who says to an aspirant member of an order: "Don't join an order, because the orders only cause decline in religion." As a matter of fact, the orders are the learning (*ilmu*) of the Saints. What ruling should be given on such an utterance?
>
> A: Such is forbidden, and such a person is cursed or will not achieve eternal bliss, such a person intends only to reject and combat [Islam].
>
> Information derived from the *Taqrīb al-uṣūl* of Shaykh [Aḥmad bin] Zaynī Daḥlān [d. 1886]:
>
> [Arabic follows:] *Taqrīb al-uṣūl* of Zaynī Daḥlān, p. 81, the text being: Shaykh Abū ʿUthmān, may God be pleased with him above the leaders of guidance, said: "God's curse be on whoever rejects this path (*ṭarīq*). Whoever believed in God and the last day and said so, God's curse be on him." And he said, "Whoever rejects this path will never prosper." (*al-Fuyūdāt*, fatwa no. 13)

It would thus appear that, as far as the learned members of JATM are concerned, God is on the side of the Sufis who claim to maintain the purest understanding of both the esoteric and exoteric aspects of religious practice.

In terms of its declarations on the matters of ritual, there is some crossover evident in the *Fuyūdāt*. There is also a marked tendency over time for the congresses to take up issues of practice and ritual rather than matters

exclusive to the orders. Ten fatwas deal with the ritual or medical handling of the bodies of deceased persons. There are also diverse fatwas on
playing lotto (no. 76), on allowing tourists into the mosque of Demak (no.
78), or, much later, on relations with Christians (no. 122).[20] Then there
are such interrelated matters as the form by which the word of Islam may
be delivered and received, the use of a tape recorder for the Friday ser-
mon (*khuṭba*) (no. 116) delivering a *khuṭba* in the style of a public address
(no. 117), or applauding by clapping (no. 77).

In most cases there is a strong overlap in both the concerns and methodology of the fatwas of JATM with those of NU more generally. The fusion
itself is made explicitly in the final opinions of the volume, wherein definition
is given for the term *muʿtabara* (no. 128), the reason for the addition of the
term al-Nahdliyyah (no. 129), the date of origin of the JATM (no. 130),
its founders (no. 131), and whether or not an order is an element of Sufism
(*taṣawwuf*) (no. 132). More specifically, the reader of opinion no. 129 learns
that the JATM became the JATMN because:

> (a) its followers always work to enact the worship and recollection of Almighty
> God, their Shariʿa is in accordance with the Ahl al-Sunna wa l-Jamaʿa via one of
> the four schools of law (*madhhabs*), their Sufism follows the teachings of the Pious
> Generation, and they participate in development (*pembangunan*).

> [and]

> (b) the term Nahdliyyah allows one to differentiate those who are not Nahdliyyah.
> Hence it is clear that the JATMN is a part of the NU community [Jamʿiyah
> Nahdlatul Ulama]

With the mention of both the concepts of the Ahl al-Sunna and the idea
of development, this particular opinion subtly blends the lexicons of traditional Islam and political life under Suharto's New Order, where (national)
development was the catch-cry of all social activity deemed positive by the
state. Reference to complicated statutes and regulations couched in bureaucratic language seals the implicit bond between religion and state.

Even if such language is far more redolent of NU in the political and
social context of the latter part of the twentieth century than the JATM
of old, one should not say that the outward forms of statist Islam have
overwhelmed the essential claims of the order to authenticity. Fatwa no.
130 makes plain that the association was founded in 1979 (and thus six
years after the last dated fatwas in the compilation), while fatwa no. 131
attributes the founding of the Thoriqoh Muʿtaborah to two distinct entities:

> (a) The founder(s) of the Thoriqoh Muʿtaborah Nahdliyyah, if considered orga-
> nizationally, are the participants of the 26th NU congress in Semarang.

(b) However, if we look at it in terms of the true founder, then the founder of
the aforementioned Thoriqah is the Messenger of God, God's blessing be
upon him. It was he who made a pact of obedience to the Angel Gabriel,
peace be with him, and the Angel Gabriel, peace be with him, who did so
with God Almighty. (*al-Fuyūdāt*, fatwa no. 131)

As I have noted, there is no appreciable differentiation of these last fatwas in the book from those of 1973, although internal evidence clearly
shows them to be post-factum declarations, or at least to have been edited
at a later stage. In such a presentation, the disastrous split of 1977, the
apparent hiatus in fatwa-giving, and the troubles with personalities such as
Musta'in Romly are effaced. Furthermore, the fatwas issued prior to his
ascension to the leadership of the JATM are appropriated as the general
property of NU in its quest to guide its constituents at a national level,
pursuant with both the practice of the Pious Forebears (*al-salaf al-ṣāliḥ*) and
the politics of development.

(ii) *Hasil-Hasil Muktamar IX*

While not technically a collection of fatwas, the second volume, containing those of 2000, is a vastly different publication. Packaged as an overall
report of the Ninth Congress of the JATMN, this much thicker, glossy
book is an explicit statement of a movement that identifies the broader
Indonesian Muslim community as its target. For example, the heads of the
organization write thankfully (if verbosely) of the services of the JATMN
for

the religion (*agama*), people (*bangsa*) and state (*negara*) of the Republic of Indonesia
as well as for developing *ṭarīqa*-feeling (*mengembangkan syiar thoriqoh*) in the Era of
Reform in keeping with the unfolding demands of the times and the current needs
of the community (Muktamar IX JATMN 2000, i–ii).[21]

Equally the editors write in glowing terms of the mass impact of the congress of 2000, which attracted nearly 2000 delegates—all of whom are
named in the appendix:[22]

Praise be to God, the participants who attended sufficiently represented almost [all
the country] from Sabang to Merauke.[23] Whether they were aged *'ulamā'* or young-
sters, all attended the convention full of enthusiasm. Indeed, it is greatly pleasing
to see that whereas the Jam'iyah Ahlith Thoriqoh al-Mu'taborah an-Nahdliyyah
was once little known, or thought by people to be the most narrow-minded (*kolot*)
[element] in the general community, the orders are now truly understood, approved
of, or indeed [seen as] embodying a goal that is striven for in a positive way
(Muktamar IX JATMN 2000, 1–2).

The printed address of the then Minister of Religion, Muhammad Tolchah Hasan, also echoed the aspirations of Zuhri four decades previously, and dwelt at length on the contribution of Sufism to nation-building and overcoming the spiritual drought (Hasan 2000).[24] The theme of the conference, meanwhile, was identified with the formula: "By popularizing the word *tawḥīd* (oneness of God), we will build a complete person (*insān kāmil*) who loves the unity and integrity of the nation in quest of a new Indonesia." (Muktamar IX JATMN 2000, 10)

Such high-minded sentiments are also conceived as being hot-wired to the nation in terms of the branch structure of the JATMN, which stretches (it seems) throughout Indonesia alongside the arteries of NU. Indeed, NU replicates the state at a certain level, with the progressive hierarchy of authority bound to these networks, and it is as an output of these nodes of authority that the fatwas of both NU and the JATMN are situated. But if the biannual council meeting (*shūrā*) convened by NU considers a wide range of issues connected with statements concerning Islamic orthodoxy in Indonesian society, the proper punishment to be meted out to corrupt politicians, or the validity of the suicide bomb as a means to combat oppression,[25] those issued by the JATMN in 2000—including the unusual headliner on lightning with which I began this discussion—seem located in much less nationalized realms.

Indeed, it is striking in the collection of 2000 that the fatwas are not entirely conforming to current NU practice. Whereas Aziz Masyhuri had made a decision to follow the advice of readers by presenting the early fatwas of the JATM in standard, roman-script Indonesian, these are given in Arabic-script Malay (*jawi*). At a certain level this seems rather artificial, as the effective use of *jawi* faded in Indonesia throughout the twentieth century. Perhaps this is deliberately designed to emphasize an image of traditionality, much as Habib Luthfi's (untranslated) opening address to the Congress was given in Arabic.[26]

I have already cited the longest, and most involved, fatwa of the Congress in my introduction, mainly to draw attention to the potentially other-worldly concerns of the Sufis that seem to pay no heed to scientific convention, or at least to play with the sort of fatwa that forms the lodestone for the attacks of anti-Sufi propagandists decried by Aziz Masyhuri as being the true ignorami of Islam. In a way this is somewhat misleading as the remaining nine fatwas of 2000 are much more down-to-earth, or at least out of the clouds. These discuss questions of: prayers for supplication (*ikhtiyār*) (no. 2); the meaning of the terms *bayʿa*, *Sharīʿa*, and *ḥaqīqa* (no. 3); visualizing the teacher while carrying out *dhikr* (no. 4),[27] the status of the obedience-pledge (*bayʿa*) of a tempted adept (no. 5); the possibility of the communal ritual of *tawajjuh* (no. 6),[28] the status of cooperative work done after obligatory prayers (no. 7); the ritual bathing of an aspirant disciple (*murīd*) of the Khālidiyya order (no. 8); the ramifications for an order if the shaykh supports a political party (no. 9); and the pledging of *bayʿa* by minors (no. 10). Several of these fatwas could easily have been found in earlier compilations—especially those on the mechanics of the Sufi concepts of *rābita* and *tawajjuh*—while the question of earthly temptations and the enrolling of juveniles in an order were often discussed, though usually to refute the accusations of irreligion made against the orders.[29] The fatwa on the definition of the terms *Sharīʿa* and *haqīqa* merely states that these have already been defined.

Even so, two of the fatwas, those on prayers of supplication (no. 2) and on politics (no. 9), betray the influence of modern ideas of the nation and the conflicts that can arise when the interests of mystical teacher and political party intersect or clash. The first questions the meaning of an act of supplication in part with reference to the formula "O Lord, strengthen Islam and make this Indonesia a land of goodness in which your laws and the Sunna of the Your messenger are enacted."[30] Rather unsurprisingly this is deemed to be a fitting prayer for aid. The matter of political loyalty, however, is more controversial. As the fatwa states:

> In every general election there are gurus and teachers (*murshid*) from orders whose political affiliation differs from that of some of their pupils (*murīd*) such that some of them force their pupils to follow the party they support with the [Arabic] instruction: "Dissension is the cause of parting" (*al-mukhālafa sabab al-firāq*). Moreover, there are some gurus who are even harsher. [They say things like]: "Whichever *murīd* does not enter the party of guru X, is considered to be cut off, or their obedience-pledge is invalid, or they will not attain the afterlife, etc."

> Q: (a) What is the ruling in regard to connecting an order with politics? (b) If a difference occurs such as that described above, must the pupil renew his pledge or [must he] make one to another guru? (c) To continue, what [is to become of] the pupil who has left his guru's order because of a difference in politics?

[Signed] Jember

> A: (a) According to the recommendation made by the JATM congress in Pasuruan, one cannot [mix an order with politics]. (b) At a time when the pupil has the right of refusal (*ikhtiyār*), the teacher should still continue to be revered and obeyed. But in times of emergency (*darūra*) it is obligatory to seek a new teacher (*murshid*). (c) See answer (b) above.[31]

On the one hand it would be easy enough here to make a connection with the popular *ḥadīth* in which the *'ulamā'* are urged to refrain from keeping company with rulers.[32] After all, the importance of the *kiais* and the number of votes that they can mobilize in a given election is no secret.[33] Despite attempts by the central board of NU to distance itself from direct party politics, it is a deeply political, and politicized, entity. It is no surprise therefore that the then chairman Hasyim Muzadi was entertaining overtures from various parties before the elections of 2004 to bring him on board as a potential vice president. Still, perhaps one should concentrate on the nub of fatwa no. 9 of 2000 rather than read it as a political statement. Politics has the unfortunate tendency to sever the all-important bond between Sufi master and pupil, and it is this bond, and the general welfare of the pupil and the order, that the JATMN wishes to safeguard above the links between NU and the political process. It is thus appropriate that after the exposition of sources in the above fatwa, a notation from the committee makes an appeal to the effect that: "It is mandated (*diamanatkan*) that all gurus in the order truly feel love for every single member of the Muslim people; and especially their male and female pupils. Let not a single guru abrogate the obedience-pledge of his pupils, nor abuse them."

What does this tell us?

From the brief coverage I have given to the fatwas of the JATM, it is clear that the range of issues is undeniably traditional, but in a highly specific frame, especially when it comes to matters related to the life of the orders and their representation as true inheritors to the less apparent practices of the Prophet and his successors. Even so, Indonesia appears in some of the later fatwas as a named entity and an expressed goal for cohesion of Muslims today, much as orders like the Chishtiyya in Pakistan have presented the nation as an important object of their activities (see Rozehnal 2004).

In a way this leads us to ask what it is that the JATM, if not Sufis in general, have to offer Indonesia's Muslims. Perhaps this is best answered by the former NU chairman, Sahal Mahfudh, who, in an interview published in the journal *Sufi*, urged that the JATM should not be regarded as an organization that managed Sufism, but rather as a "container" (*wadah*) to represent their (public) interests. Moreover, when asked for his opinion on internal criticisms from the younger generation of NU that the Jam'iyah

Ahlith Thoriqoh was "unable to develop intellectually or artistically," Mahfudh concentrated on what he regarded as "the real achievement of the Sufis," which he asserted was their "strengthening of the morality of the community" (*Sufi* 1–1 [April 2000]: 10). In this sense he was following in the respected footsteps of Saifuddin Zuhri with his calls for the JATM to provide the spiritual fibre for the modern nation, even if that nation is at times struck by lightning from unexpected quarters.

Part Two

ISLAMIC LAW AND INSTITUTIONS WITHIN THE
INDONESIAN LEGAL SYSTEM

Five

ISLAMIC LAW IN COURT DECISIONS AND FATWA INSTITUTIONS IN INDONESIA

Rifyal Ka'bah

In support of the characterization of Islamic law as a "jurists' law," this chapter examines two of the principal fora in which Islamic law has been produced within the context of the codified legal system of a modern nation state. Rather than through formal legislation, this takes place by way of authoritative decisions and by means of various mechanisms of case-dependent legal reasoning. The most prominent contexts for such work in contemporary Indonesia can be found in the nation-wide system of Islamic religious courts (*Pengadilan Agama*), as well as in the work of various fatwa-issuing organizations established over the course of the twentieth century. While both of these institutions purport to produce legal opinions based upon the Shari'a, their pronouncements have widely varied consequences, not to mention differentially demarcated legal status. Islamic religious court decisions in Indonesia have the force of law and can be enforced by the state, while fatwas are binding in a religious sense only, with the strength of their sanctions dependent upon individual obedience to religious teachings and to various degrees upon local perceptions of societal pressure. After a discussion of the production of Islamic law through religious court decisions, the remainder of this chapter will focus on legal opinions issued by the fatwa boards of Indonesia's two largest Muslim organizations, the Muhammadiyah and the Nahdlatul Ulama (NU), respectively.[1]

Fiqh as Islamic law

Islamic jurisprudence (*fiqh*) consists of the understanding of scholars (*fuqahā'*) of the legal stipulations (sg. *ḥukm*) found in the Qur'an and Sunna from the result of their own juristic reasoning (*ijtihād*), either where there is no explicit text on the subject or where there is a difference of opinion in understanding or interpreting the explicit text. The collective understanding of *fiqh* scholars regarding legal issues has continued to grow throughout history.

Although *fiqh* is often considered to be synonymous with Shariʿa, the scope of Shariʿa is broader than that of *fiqh*. The use of the word Shariʿa to indicate *fiqh* is based on the principle from Islamic legal theory of "mentioning a general term in order to indicate a special usage." This practice can be seen in the phrase "Islamic Shariʿa as a source of legislation" in the constitutions of Egypt and Syria (Abū Ṭālib 2001, 15–18 and n. 1). The same practice is also encountered in Indonesian laws that are connected with institutions such as "Shariʿa banks," "Shariʿa councils," and "Shariʿa-based transactions," as well as in the designation of the Shariʿa High Court in the Province of Nanggroe Aceh Darussalam and others. What is generally meant by Shariʿa in such cases is actually *fiqh*.

A judge can only apply the *fiqh* that is within the field of his competency or expertise. If there is more than one opinion on an issue, the judge looks for the strongest of several opinions (a method called *tarjīh*) from one particular school of law, or for the strongest opinion from several schools.[2] According to Ibn Taymiyya, the essence of *tarjīh* is the recognition of the basic validity of two opinions on the same issue; one of them is recommended while the other is neither faulted nor rejected as incorrect (as quoted in Kamali 1998, 144). Both opinions are in fact equally correct, but one of them more completely satisfies the judge's heart. Ibn Taymiyya holds that if the heart of the judge is filled with righteousness, then the *tarjīh* that he carries out is valid according to Islamic law. He adds: "If he discovers that what is in his person and in his heart indicates that a certain matter or statement is more pleasing to God and His Messenger, then that matter or statement is a *tarjīh* based on valid evidence (*dalīl sharʿī*)." (Ibn Taymiyya 2000, XX:42)

In addition to specific points of law, judges also decide cases based on broader conceptions of justice. The Qurʾan teaches that justice is a command from God that is to be upheld (Q 7:29), and that being just is nearer to piety (Q 5:8). Justice is an absence of favoritism, whether toward oneself, one's parents, one's close kin, the rich or the poor (Q 4:135), toward friend or foe, or those whom you like or dislike (Q 5:8). There are two understandings of justice at work in the formulation of legal decisions by Muslim scholars. The first is justice based upon divine command, which is itself inherently just because all of the commands of God contain truth and justice. He is the All-Hearer and the All-Knower (Q 6:115). The second, general sense of justice is discoverable through rational thought (Kaʿbah 1999, 33). Like the divine command, justice based on logic is also a gift from God, and is designed to guide mankind to the correct state of affairs.

ISLAMIC LAW IN COURT DECISIONS AND FATWA INSTITUTIONS   85

Legislation as Islamic law

Jurisprudence (*fiqh*) is the primary source of substantive and procedural law for Islamic courts. However, in light of the scarcity of judges who have attained an adequate mastery of Islamic jurisprudence, many judges are in need of a more streamlined system of Islamic laws that have been extracted from the jurisprudence. The need for legislation began to be felt in the Muslim world toward the end of the rule of the Ottoman Empire. Along with the adoption of European codes came the establishment of civil or Niẓāmiyya courts, which had the authority to hear cases that had previously fallen under the jurisdiction of the Shariʿa court, but whose judges were not specially trained in the *fiqh* tradition. It was at this point also that the civil law was codified as the Mecelle (*Majallat al-aḥkām al-ʿadliyya*), which was proclaimed the law of the land in regions under the control of the Ottoman Turks in 1876.

Another factor contributing to the need for legislation is the fact that many Muslim countries that had been colonized by European nations had come to employ codified systems of civil law. In Indonesia efforts to codify, or at least compile, Islamic law have been only partially successful for several reasons. When Indonesia achieved independence from the Dutch in 1945, the laws that had been in effect during the colonial era remained in force, largely in order to avoid a legal vacuum. Article II of the 1945 Constitution states that existing law shall remain in effect until revised or replaced. The slow pace of codification of Islamic law following independence was a result of many factors. One obstacle to codification was the colonial legacy that had been adopted by Indonesian legal experts and practitioners. A second factor has been a lack of consistency within the national legal system in efforts to replace existing laws with laws reflecting aspects of an Indonesian character. A third factor has been the lack of political will on the part of the legislature, both the low level of support for Islamic law from political parties in the Indonesian legislature (DPR) and within representative government in general. Last, but not least, the codification of Islamic law has been hampered by a shortage of academics and legal drafters capable of preparing laws based on *fiqh* in particular and on the Islamic Shariʿa in general. At a more basic level, this problem is related to the need to create a curriculum and to the process of Islamicizing the study of law in the existing Shariʿa and university law departments as well as in some think-tanks.

Despite these problems, Indonesia has a number of laws that contain Shariʿa principles. These laws are applied by a system of religious courts, which constitutes an Islamic judicature with a limited jurisdictional competency.

The existence of Islamic law as national legislation can be seen in a number of laws that have been implemented since the proclamation of Indonesian independence on August 17, 1945. For instance, there is Law No. 1 of 1974, which regulates marriage under Islamic religious law; Law No. 7 of 1989 regarding religious courts (meaning Islamic courts in Indonesia); Government Regulations (PP) Nos. 70 and 72 of 1992, which define and regulate profit-sharing banks as recognized in Law No. 7 of 1992 as banks based on Islamic law; Law No. 10 of 1998 regarding banking, which legitimizes Shari'a banking; Law No. 17 of 1999 regarding the performance of the annual pilgrimage; Law No. 23 of 1999 regarding the Bank of Indonesia, which provides a mandate for the formation of government Shari'a banks or bank branches; Law No. 38 of 1999 regarding *zakāt* or alms management; Law No. 44 of 1999 regarding the Implementation of Special Province Status for Aceh. The most recent is Law No. 18 of 2001 regarding Special Autonomy for the Special Region of Aceh as the Province of Aceh Nanggroe Darussalam (UU NAD), in connection with the implementation of Islamic law there as a part of the culture and religion of the people of Aceh. Finally, the Kompilasi Hukum Islam (KHI, Compilation of Islamic Law), which was drafted by representatives from the Department of Religion and the Supreme Court and promulgated by means of Presidential Instruction (InPres No. 1/1991) in 1991, contains detailed rules of marriage, inheritance, and charitable endowments, and has been designated as an authoritative reference for the Islamic courts.

Decisions of the religious courts as "Islamic law"

Another important source of Islamic law is the decisions or precedents of Religious Courts (*Pengadilan Agama*/PA). Religious Courts operating under various names have existed in the Indonesian archipelago since before independence. These courts, both at the first instance and appellate levels, have produced a substantial number of court decisions in the fields of marriage, inheritance, and Islamic endowments (*waqf*). However, this extensive body of jurisprudence has never been examined to evaluate the extent to which the decisions of the courts are in accord with the substance of Islamic law as formulated by the jurists, either past or present, and in accordance with the spirit of the law as contained in the primary sources—the Qur'an and Sunna. Such research would be of great value to assess whether Indonesian judges have performed *ijtihād* in fields that have not yet been formulated in *fiqh* or have engaged in a reconsideration of doctrines addressed in *fiqh* opinions taught in madrasas and other Islamic educational institutions. Such research would also be significant for what it reveals regarding the methods used in the formulation of law or the legal considerations used by judges in reaching their decisions, whether they more closely resemble the methods used by the jurists of the past, or are methods and considerations of the judges' own creation.

The most fundamental question faced by the PA is whether the judges in these special courts are limited to national laws alone, or may they take the opinions of certain past jurists of the broader Islamic tradition of *fiqh*? May the judges, as discussed above, perform *ijtihād*? Because they are tied to a civil law system, there is a great possibility that judges are restricted to national laws and can only refer to *fiqh* in matters that are not regulated by national law. If so, another question is, which sources of *fiqh* do these judges refer to, or do they only rely upon the articles of the Compilation of Islamic Law? A factor bearing on sources relied on by judges of the PA is the belief, prevalent among senior judges, that many of the younger judges in the PA are very weak in their command of Arabic and thus lack the necessary mastery of Islamic jurisprudential texts. While it is stated in both national law and the 1991 Indonesian Compilation of Islamic Law that judges in the PA decide cases based upon Islamic law,[3] Islamic law throughout the world ultimately finds its source in the Qur'an, Sunna and opinions of the jurists.

Relying on *fiqh* to decide matters not regulated in the Compilation raises concerns about assuring legal certainty. Many issues are not treated in the Compilation, which creates the possibility that different courts will reach different decisions on the same issue. One way to address that problem would be to follow the course taken in Egypt. The religious courts in Egypt, which are now called "Family Courts," possess their own law based on *fiqh* from the Hanafi school. For matters not treated in national law, Egyptian lawmakers have authorized judges to choose the strongest legal opinion within this school (El Alami and Hinchcliffe 1995, 51). This was done, first, because judges may not refuse to hear cases brought before them on the ground that the matter is not yet regulated by (national) law, and, second, to make it easier for the judge to reach a verdict because the Hanafi school has been predominant in Egypt for a long time. In the future, Islamic law in Indonesia could follow Egypt's lead. For instance, if no legal stipulations are found for problems faced by the court, then the Indonesian judges could perform *ijtihād* or take the strongest legal opinion of the Shafi'i school, which has long been a source of reference in Indonesia. If this course is taken, a consequence would be the necessity for PA judges to master the legal opinions of the Shafiʿi school, and thus also the need to incorporate the study of Shafiʿi jurisprudence in the country's Shariʿa and law faculties.

Another issue that arises within the framework of applying Islamic law in Indonesia concerns the judge's obligation to uphold law and justice with his decisions. What is the judge's duty if he or she determines that the application of national law will not produce a fair result, and that the national law is not representative of Islamic law as contained in the *fiqh* of past and present jurists? May judges then abandon established rulings based on existing state legislation? This is an important question because, in a system of Islamic law, judges decide cases based on Islamic law and their sense of right and wrong. If due legal consideration and good conscience indicate that there is a contradiction between prevailing national law and Islamic law, then the judge should decide according to Islamic law, the truth of which he is convinced. These decisions can then serve as precedents for the revision of the positive law of the Indonesian state.

Fatwas as "Islamic law"

During the lifetime of the Prophet Muḥammad, people frequently inquired about legal matters directly to him. There are many verses of the Qurʾan that begin with "They ask you [Muḥammad] regarding . . ." followed by a reply introduced with the words "[Muḥammad] Say that . . ." or "Know that. . . ." Muḥammad himself would often preface his speech with the phrase "Do you know . . .?" This question was usually answered with the phrase "God and His Messenger know best!" Only then would the Prophet mention the matter that he wanted to clarify. This indicates that many questions posed by the public and the answers given to those questions are preserved in the Qurʾan and Sunna. Some of these questions were about legal issues, broadly defined. As such, the Qurʾan and Sunna are the primary sources and models for the formulation of fatwas.

In Muḥammad's time, there was no separation between religious and state law. As a judge, Muḥammad decided cases that were presented to him and ordered his verdicts to be carried out. After Muḥammad's death, legal problems were presented to the caliphs and judges, who presided over public hearings. But as the territory of Islam expanded, resort to the caliph became impractical, and in many remote areas far from central and regional governments there was no court. When faced with legal issues, Muslims residing in these remote regions sought the assistance of public figures such as Muslim scholars (*ʿulamāʾ*) for answers to their questions. A legal opinion or fatwa issued in these circumstances is not binding but is provided to the requesting party to satisfy the individual's personal need. The person who gives such a fatwa is known as a mufti. In the past, these non-binding legal opinions were issued by individual scholars. Because of the scarcity of qualified muftis in modern times, however, the task of providing fatwas has been taken over by institutions whose members are ideally experts in *fiqh* and the methodology of *fiqh* (*uṣūl al-fiqh*). With the development of modern nation states, the post of mufti has become an official position in a number of Muslim countries. Indonesia does not have a single authoritative government-sanctioned fatwa institution which can serve as a national point of reference, whether for the executive, legislative or judicial branches of the government, or for the general public. The lack of an official fatwa institution carries a number of implications, including the existence of difference of opinion regarding the date of the major Islamic holidays of *ʿīd al-fiṭr* and *ʿīd al-aḍḥā*. Instead, there are a number of fatwa organizations representing several Islamic organizations in Indonesia.

Indonesian Muslims continue to seek guidance from muftis and *ʿulamāʾ* on a range of issues. Because marriage, inheritance, and the charitable trust are the only subjects regulated by the state-sanctioned Compilation of Islamic Law, there remains wide scope for other sources of information on legal questions. In recent years, the public has become increasingly inquisitive regarding Islamic law and Islamic issues in general. In the past, these questions were relegated to the mosques, small prayer houses or study forums. Today, however, inquiry into issues of Islamic law has become national in scope. This expansion has been fueled by the mass media, which have created religious programs and question-and-answer columns for the general public. The number and variety of the questions asked indicate an increasing level of public interest in religious law, as well as a growing awareness of Islamic law as a norm regulating daily life.

The general impression one takes from these question-and-answer sessions is that anyone and everyone can give their opinion in the form of a fatwa, whereas within the Islamic legal tradition the issuer of a fatwa is an authorized mufti or an imam known for his depth of knowledge and high level of understanding. People who are not religious scholars, such as psychologists and businessmen, and even actors, singers and models, give fatwas on television and radio. From one perspective this trend is cause for celebration since it shows that all elements of society are concerning themselves with issues of Islamic law. But from another perspective the trend is very alarming, since the party issuing the fatwas is no longer known as an expert in his field. For example, the Minister of Religious Affairs in the Sixth Presidential "Development" Cabinet, who is a medical doctor, often issued legal and political fatwas. Among the Minister's fatwas was one on the legality, under Islamic religious law, of killing instigators of social unrest. During the presidency of Abdurrahman Wahid, the public was frequently confused by the fatwas of the President, which were often the direct opposite of the fatwas of the Council of Religious Scholars (MUI), an institution that had been created by the government in part for the purpose of issuing fatwas.

Unlike in some Middle Eastern nations such as Egypt, Lebanon, and Saudi Arabia, as well as in Malaysia, Brunei, and Singapore, fatwas in Indonesia are not issued by authorized government institutions. Indonesia has the Fatwa Commission of the Majelis Ulama Indonesia (Council of Islamic Scholars) at the national level, and within the major Islamic organizations such fatwa institutions as the *Lajnah Tarjih* (LT) of the modernist-oriented Muhammadiyah and the *Lajnah Bahth al-Masāʾil* (LBM) of the traditionalist Nahdlatul Ulama. Although there are also government instances in Indonesia that issue official fatwas—the religious courts and the Ministry of Religious Affairs both issue fatwas on inheritance and the Supreme Court issues fatwas (known as *Fatwa Mahkamah Agung*)—the fatwas that are most well known are the fatwas of the *ʿulamāʾ* or their institutions. The remainder of this chapter will focus on the two most important Indonesian Islamic institutions mentioned above: Lajnah Tarjih Muhammadiyah, and Nahdlatul Ulama's Lajnah Bahth al-Masāʾil.

Lajnah Tarjih Muhammadiyah

The Muhammadiyah organization was founded in 1912 and functions primarily as a social welfare organization, operating a variety of social services, including education, health care, orphanages, information services, and benevolent societies. There are also a variety of autonomous organizations that are affiliated with Muhammadiyah and share its vision and goals.

The name of Muhammadiyah's fatwa-issuing institution, Lajnah Tarjih (LT), literally means "a committee seeking the strongest (juristic) opinion." The function of the LT is to determine the Islamic legal ruling (*hukm*) on questions about which there is disagreement within society. The LT's function extends both to matters that are within the traditional realm of *fiqh* as well as to more general questions. In keeping with its name, the LT Muhammadiyah is tasked with, among other things, studying the legal opinions of various classical legal scholars on disputed questions of law, and then selecting from among the existing views the opinion which is viewed as stronger in accordance with current ways of thinking and prevailing conditions. Prior to 1960 the LT frequently addressed questions bearing on issues of ritual and worship, such as prayer, fasting, and burial. But the LT also issued fatwas on questions that had not previously been discussed by the jurists, such as banking, modern finance, insurance, health, and woman's issues, among others.

In formulating its opinions the LT uses as supporting evidence the Qur'an and Prophetic reports (*ḥadīth*) considered reliable. In its evaluation of the authenticity of the Sunna, the LT relies on eleven (scholarly) principles (*Himpunan Putusan Tarjih* n.d., 300–01). Analogy is used as a method for extracting legal stipulations from primary sources only as a last resort; generally, as long as there is primary evidence from the Qur'an and Sunna, analogy is considered unnecessary. The same applies for other methods approved by legal methodology. Another notable feature of the LT is that decisions are reached through the "collective deliberation of legal experts . . ." (*Himpunan Putusan Tarjih* n.d., 240). LT sessions deliberate significant issues encountered by followers of the Muhammadiyah organization, or by its affiliated organizations or branch offices located in various regions, or by its own central leadership. Decisions taken in LT Muhammadiyah sessions usually take the form of a statement of the reasons why a particular action is judged allowable or unallowable, although a number of LT decisions have been presented in a modern format consisting of a forward, main body of the decision, evidence used, and conclusion. A unique characteristic of the decisions taken by the LT is their characterization of the practice of "discovering" (*istinbāt*) rulings in the texts of the Qur'an and Sunna. A number of particularly complex decisions, such as the decision regarding family planning, are, however, modeled after the decisions of modern bureaucratic organizations in Indonesia, like the legislature or a cabinet ministry. These decisions are organized in sections labeled "considering" (*menimbang*), "recalling" (*mengingat*), "deciding" (*memutuskan*), etc., and frequently refer to state law in addition to Islamic scriptural sources.

Despite the meaning of Lajnah Tarjih as "a committee seeking the strongest (juristic) opinion," the strongest opinion taken by the LT is generally not the opinion of another jurist, but its own legal opinion as extracted directly from the text of the Qur'an and the Sunna; evident in LT decisions is a desire to avoid what the Muhammadiyah defines as blind, unquestioning adherence to an opinion or school of law (*taqlīd*). (Various conceptions of *taqlīd* are practiced by some elements in Indonesia, which is generally viewed as following the school of Imam Shāfiʿi.)

The three types of independent reasoning (*ijtihād*) LT uses in making decisions are:

1. *ijtihād bayānī*, which is based on a clear text (*naṣṣ*) whose meaning may be less
   clear, or potentially understood in more than one way, or contains multiple
   meanings, or the understanding of the text is in a phrase whose context has a
   similar (*mutashābih*) meaning, or there are a number of contradictory evidences
   (*taʿāruḍ*). In the latter case *ijtihād* is made by using the *tarjīḥ* method.
2. *ijtihād qiyāsī*, which is extending a ruling based on a (primary) textual reference to a new problem which does not have a ruling based on a textual reference, because there is an equivalence of the underlying cause (*ʿilla*).
3. *ijtihād istiṣlāḥī*, which is based on matters that have no specific primary textual
   reference, and for which there are no primary textual references for problems
   with similar underlying causes. In these cases, the law is decided based on considerations of public interest.[4]

With the first method, *ijtihād bayānī*, the LT selects the interpretation
that it regards as the strongest among the several interpretations of the
text held by recognized experts in Islamic law. This method is used only
when the text is capable of multiple meanings. For this reason, what is
called *ijtihād bayānī* is actually *ijtihād tarjīḥī*.[5] The reasons for the choice of
one opinion over others are not explained. In general, however, the LT
gives preference to the text it regards as most authentic. Decisions on this
issue are not regarded as final. If a decision is later determined to be mistaken, the LT will revise the decision and inform readers of the change
(*Himpunan Putusan Tarjih* n.d., 371–71).

The formulation of legal decisions based on the Qurʾan and Sunna
directly is perhaps the most distinctive feature of LT decision-making. When
referring to the Qurʾan, a citation is included in the decision, but the LT's
decisions do not make reference to Sunna compilations when referring to
Prophetic reports. The LT's references to the Qurʾan are to the text of
the Qurʾan itself; no explicit use is made of Qurʾanic exegesis. The same
is true for Sunna commentary. The analogical method used by the LT is
similar to the practice recognized by al-Shāfiʿī. That is, even without a
direct ruling on the matter in question found in the text of the Qurʾan
and Sunna, the matter decided based upon the analogical method is in
actuality still based on those two sources through a process of extension
by analogy. As mentioned in Qurʾan 4:59 and explained by al-Shāfiʿī (1979,
81), the disputed question is referred back to God and His Messenger.

The use of analogy is evident in the decisions formulated by the LT
Congress in 1954/1955 in Yogyakarta (*Himpunan Putusan Tarjih* n.d., 278),
for example, the decision regarding the assessment of tax (*zakāt*) for live-
stock other than cattle, goats, and camels. The rates (*nisab*) and measures
(*qadar*) of these animals was analogized to the rate and measure of cattle,
goats and camels. Likewise, the *zakāt* for crops such as sugar cane, lum-

ber, rubber, coconut, cloves, pepper, and others was determined by analogy to wheat, rice, corn, and other staple foods. The *zakāt* of five or ten percent becomes obligatory once the quantity of these crops reaches five *wasak* (7.5 *kwintal*).

The third method, *ijtihād istiṣlāḥī*, functions according to the principle that God's purpose in revealing religion is to safeguard the public interest. Indeed, one of LT's principles states that "the channeling of differences of interpretation in religion in the direction of that which is more beneficial" is one of the primary functions of the organization. The theory of *ijtihād istiṣlāḥī* is faithful to the principle of *ijtihād tarjīḥī*, since the LT makes a selection regarding the legal opinion which, in its view, is more beneficial. The LT's use of the method of "finding good [in society]" (*istiṣlāḥ*) is illustrated by its ruling—reversing an earlier decision—that it is permissible for women to leave the home, provided they adhere to Islamic stipulations regarding the conduct of women outside of the home, based on the benefit of granting women freedom to move about in society. The LT selected the legal opinion that allows them to leave the home, because, as it happens, the text of the Qur'an and Sunna do not forbid women from performing public activities.

This reversal of the previous decision was made upon discovering that a *ḥadīth* that was cited as evidence for the earlier ruling did not have an authentic (*ṣaḥīḥ*) chain of transmission. This decision was the result of *ijtihād tarjīḥī*. Although the choice made was not between two or more opinions of individual scholars or schools of law, it cannot be said that the method that was used, i.e., choosing the "stronger" or "more authentic" report, was a departure from the *tarjīḥ* method. As with analogy, the *istiṣlāḥ* or public interest method is not used in matters of "pure worship" (Ind. *ibadah mahdhah*), or what is known in Muhammadiyah circles as *khāṣṣa* (particular worship). The use of these methods of *ijtihād* is only for worship that is "general" (*ʿāmma*), namely, all deeds that are allowed by God (*Himpunan Putusan Tarjih* n.d., 276).

Another category of decisions based on an evaluation of the public interest are those aimed at avoiding damage and destruction and fostering benefit. These decisions are based on the principle of "closing off the means that allow evil" (*sadd al-dharāʾiʿ*) (Nurdin 1996, 17), as, for example, the LT decision declaring games that direct one to immoral acts to be unlawful (Nurdin 1996, 382-83). The same principle was also a reason used by the LT's Twelfth Congress to declare interfaith marriage unlawful (*Keputusan Muktamar Tarjih Muhammadiyah XXII*, 8–10). The permissibility to sell endowed objects in danger of decay or damage in order to buy new objects or other

items that are useful, was decided upon by the LT based on public interest (*Himpunan Putusan Tarjih* n.d., 270, 274), while other examples are the
decision that it is permissible to attend events where there are bonfires, as
long as the gathering is deemed to have a useful function (*Himpunan Putusan
Tarjih* n.d., 283), and the decision stating the unlawfulness of buying lottery tickets (*Himpunan Putusan Tarjih* n.d., 292).

Upon closer inspection of the decisions made by the LT, it becomes evident that what is meant by "independent judgment" (*ijtihād*) in the practice of the LT is actually not *ijtihād* as understood by the jurists who founded
the various schools of law. In general, the LT formulates a number of legal
problems by piecing together selected Qur'anic verses or *hadīth* reports that
the LT deems fitting for the issue under discussion. In matters where no
reference is found in the Qur'an or Sunna, the LT deals with the matter
by culling from books of exegesis and *fiqh* that are familiar to the members involved in formulating the decision. These views are then taken by
the LT as its own. This understanding of *tarjīh* is the current prevailing
practice of the LT.

Based on an examination of both criticism of the LT and the efforts
undertaken by those sympathetic to the Muhammadiyah, it seems that
there is a definite desire on the part of Muhammadiyah supporters to
improve the quality of the LT in order to anticipate and meet the challenges of the future. It is also apparent that LT has the potential to develop
existing methods of *ijtihād* to encompass both its traditional sense—as understood by the jurists of the past—and its modern understanding, which
involves consulting experts from secular disciplines that bear on the topic
under consideration in order to adapt the law to current circumstances.

Criticism of the LT as well as the call for improvement have generally
come from the youth within the Muhammadiyah. The rarity of Muhammadiyah scholars who are capable of undertaking the kind of reasoning
that was done in the past and dwindling Arabic-language capabilities are
two of the main criticisms. The first generation of LT scholars (the generation of Ahmad Dahlan) has passed away, and the second generation of
scholars, whose strength is in their Arabic and their ability to understand
classical texts, is slowly dying. In the past, the LT's decisions were always
written in both Arabic and Indonesian, but the decisions of the recent congresses of the LT have generally been written in Indonesian only. In fact,
in the Muhammadiyah Congress in Banda Aceh (1995), the *Majlis Tarjīh*
changed its name to *Majlis Tarjih and Development of Islamic Thought*. With
the addition of the phrase "Development of Islamic Thought" we can dis-
cern a narrowing of the field of *tarjīh*, which was mostly focused upon matters of Islamic law.

The most pressing need now felt by the Muhammadiyah is the training of qualified scholars. According to an evaluation made by a Muhammadiyah activist, they should at the very least own and have mastery of the texts of Qur'anic exegesis and *ḥadīth* that are either required or recommended by university Shariʿa departments in various Muslim countries.[6] Among the steps taken to achieve this was the founding in 1982 of an educational institution in Surakarta by the name of Pondok Muhammadiyah Hajjah Nuriyah Shabran.[7] Other obstacles to improving the quality of the LT are an unwillingness to perform professional work on a full-time basis (the general impression now is that the LT conducts activities only for a short period before and after each congress, the months and years before the next congress being devoid of activity), and a shortage of managerial and administrative staff.

Overcoming the obstacle of professionalization will require organizational changes within the Muhammadiyah. Allocating sufficient funding to ensure that the function and duties of the LT are carried out properly will overcome the problem of staffing. The Muhammadiyah does have considerable resources, including masters and doctoral graduates from universities in Middle Eastern and Western countries, as well as from Indonesian institutions, including the State Islamic Studies Institutes (IAIN) and a number of other religious institutions of higher education. Although accurate data regarding the number of these graduates are not available, it is estimated that there are more than two hundred.[8] Muslim scholars who have acquired proper training in both old and new traditions of scholarship should be able to contribute their energies to enhance the quality of the future decisions of the LT.

The NU's Lajnah Bahth al-Masā'il

The Nahdlatul Ulama (NU), the largest Muslim organization in Indonesia, was founded in 1926. The organization is strongest in rural areas, especially on the islands of Java and Madura. As indicated by the name of the organization, which means the "Revival of Religious Scholars," the NU perceives its mission to be the preservation of the scholarly tradition of the past. Since the end of the caliphate, it has been the religious scholars who have been principally responsible for the preservation of the Shariʿa throughout the Muslim world; this is nowhere more true than in Indonesia where the state has never assumed responsibility for implementation of the Shariʿa. For that reason, the scholars have had a significant influence on views on Islam and Islamic law in society.

Clause 7, Art. 16, of the Nahdlatul Ulama (NU) organizational charter states: "The *Lajnah Bahth al-Masāʾil* (LBM) has the duty to compile, discuss, and solve problems that are *mawqūf* and *wāqiʿa* and that are in immediate need of legal certainty." (*Mawqūf* (lit. "stopped") problems have become stuck due to a lack of any clear legal stipulations, while those that are *wāqiʿa* are posed by present-day circumstances.) The LBM has performed this duty continually since the first NU Congress (*Muktamar*) in Surabaya in 1926. In the 80 years since the first Congress the LBM has met approximately 40 times. From this it can be seen how NU scholars are concerned to restore the stipulations of Islamic law decided by the jurists of the past, as well as to solve the new legal problems of the present.

The objective of the LBM meetings is to achieve certainty with respect to Islamic law as understood by the traditional treatment of *fiqh*. The focus is on "religious" (*diyānī*) Islamic law as embodied in fatwas, which are not binding under modern law. More specifically, Islamic law for the LBM is *aḥkām taklīfiyya*—religious law as applicable to those people, generally adults, with the capacity for moral answerability—concerning what is religiously lawful and unlawful (*ḥalāl* and *ḥarām*). The LBM has retained its exclusive focus on religious law despite growing interest among Indonesian Muslims in Islamic law that is justiciable or enforceable (*qaḍāʾī*). However, law in this second sense has not been discussed in any of the sessions of the LBM for decades, despite its recently having gained the attention of the Indonesian public. The question raised by the LBM's exclusive focus on *diyānī* law is whether the disregard of Islamic law of the justiciable type is characteristic of the NU religious mindset overall, or does it simply constitute the particular views of the scholars who are involved in the LBM sessions? This question is of particular importance because one wing of the NU, represented by Abdurrahman Wahid, has indicated that it does not want Islamic law to become a part of the formal Indonesian legal system.[9]

At an NU national congress held in the south Sumatran city of Bandar Lampung in 1992 the organization settled on a more uniform and systematic methodology for formulating legal rulings. The approach, which is referred to as the *Sistem Pengambilan Keputusan Hukum* (SPKH, "Legal Decision-Making System"), is oriented toward the objective of adhering to one of the four major Sunni schools of law and following the precepts and established rulings of that school. The procedure to handle issues has been formulated in the following order:

> In cases where a satisfactory answer can be provided by a textual precedent (*naṣṣ*) and where there is only one statement (*qawl*) or precept (*wajh*), then that will be used as explained in the precedent.

In cases where a satisfactory answer is obtained by a textual precedent and where there is more than one relevant statement or precept, then a collective determination (*taqrīr jamā'ī*) is conducted to select the one that is most appropriate.

In cases where there is no relevant statement or precept, the procedure of subjunction (*ilḥāq*) under a comparable ruling or a corresponding issue is undertaken by qualified scholars.

In cases where there is no relevant statement or precept and it is not possible to conduct *ilḥāq*, then a process of collective "discovery" of a new ruling (*istinbāṭ jamā'ī*) is carried out according to school methodology (*manhajī*) by qualified scholars.

The National NU Congress held at Bandar Lampung in 1992 acknowledged the complex nature of Islamic jurisprudence, including issues of diversity in the opinions of the various schools. However, in practice it is the tradition of the Shafi'i school that is almost always referred to. Moreover, while the LBM sometimes references the work of this school's eponymous founder, it more often refers to works by later scholars within one specific Shafi'i sub-tradition. In particular, the *pesantren*-trained scholars of the LBM most often work in the line of Shafi'i scholars associated with the *Muḥarrar* by Abū Qāsim al-Rāfi'ī (d. 1226), which was passed on to the work *Minhāj al-ṭālibīn* by Muḥyi al-Dīn Abū Zakariyyā Yaḥyā b. Sharaf al-Nawawī (d. 1227), which in turn was passed on through five major books: *Kanz al-rāghibīn* by al-Maḥallī (d. 1460); *Manhaj al-ṭullāb* by al-Anṣārī; *Tuḥfat al-muḥtāj* by Ibn Ḥajar (d. 1565); *Mughnī al-muḥtāj* by al-Sharbīnī (d. 1569); and *Nihāyat al-muḥtāj* by al-Ramlī (d. 1596). These five works were annotated (*sharḥ, ḥāshiya*) in turn by even later Shafi'i scholars, and a number of these were translated into Arabic-script forms of Javanese, Sundanese, Madurese, and Malay as well as into modern Indonesian (Van Bruinessen 1990).

NU has been criticized by some reformist Muslims for being overly constrained in its adherence to one established school of law, for clinging to its views (*taqlīd*), and for being reluctant to open the door to independent reasoning (*ijtihād*). In truth, this problem is not unique to the NU organization; many other traditional scholarly communities in the Muslim world grapple with it as well. Nevertheless, it can be contended that if the LBM relied more on the writings of al-Shāfi'ī himself, such as *al-Risāla* or *al-Umm*, then the door to "discovering the rules" (*istinbāṭ al-aḥkām*) might be opened more widely.

Ideally Islamic law is a divine law. In practice, however, it also involves man-made law which is understood to have been culled from divine law. For this reason, decisions on the lawfulness or unlawfulness of a certain practice do not originate from direct revelation alone, but also from the opinions of scholars who view certain matters as being such. The Qur'an enjoins Muslims to "refer any disputes back to Allah and His Messenger." Al-Shāfiʿī explains in the *Risāla* that this "referral" is done by employing formal analogy (*qiyās*) in making legal rulings that are not explicitly defined by clear textual statements in the Qurʾan and Sunna. Here, however, the analogies are drawn not from scriptural statements, but rather from the rulings of earlier jurists.

The fourth method, *istinbāṭ jamāʿī*, has been utilized in a limited manner since it was first embraced at NU's National Congress in Lampung in 1992. At that meeting the decision was made that matters of insurance and banking were to be addressed directly on the basis of scriptural texts, rather than on the rulings of classical scholars in the Shafiʿi school as had been the case in previous meetings of the LBM. After considering evidence from the Qurʾan and Sunna, adducing the opinions of scholars who had served as traditional references within NU, and discussing the matter in the meeting, the Congress arrived at its own opinion on the issues. This constituted a new model of "discovering the rules." This was also evidenced in the LBM meeting in Central Lombok in 1997, in which rulings on women's issues, leadership, and other matters were formulated after quoting not only established Shafiʿi opinions, but also referencing well-known books of Qurʾanic exegesis and *ḥadīth*, such as those by al-Ṭabarī, Ibn Kathīr, al-Qurṭubī, al-Bukharī, and Muslim, and the works of modern, non *madhhab*-affiliated writers, particularly from Egypt, such as ʿAbd al-Qādir Awdah, Yūsuf Mūsā, Sayyid Sābiq, Ḥusayn Makhlūf, and others, along with verses of the Qurʾan and the Sunna.

Conclusion

Through this examination of judicial processes of legal decision-making in Indonesia's system of Islamic religious courts (*Pengadilan Agama*), as well as the processes at work in the Lajnah Tarjih Muhammadiyah (LT) and the Lajnah Bahth al-Masāʾil Nahdlatul Ulama (LBM), this chapter has attempted to provide a sense of some of the major non-legislative dynamics of the development of Islamic law in modern Indonesia. Attention to the mechanisms of court rulings and the production of fatwas in non-state Muslim organizations can help to establish a more broadly representative view of Islamic law in the country than could be gained solely by a cataloging of existing and proposed legislation.

Six

ISLAMIC DIVORCE LAW AND PRACTICE IN INDONESIA

Mark E. Cammack, Helen Donovan, and Tim B. Heaton

In April of 1973 the government of Indonesia's then President Suharto presented a marriage reform proposal to the Indonesian legislature. The government's draft law proposed a single set of marriage rules for all Indonesians regardless of race or religion. In proposing a unified law of marriage the draft represented a significant change from the existing marriage law system, in which the law that governed a person's marriage depended on the person's race or religion.

The government's draft marriage law, which was apparently prepared without consulting the Department of Religion, also proposed significant changes to the substance of the law of marriage and divorce for Indonesian Muslims. In 1973 when the marriage legislation was put forward, the law governing the marriages of Indonesian Muslims was based on un-codified rules from the Shafi'i school of Islamic law. The government's proposed statute, however, differed from standard Indonesian interpretations of Shafi'i doctrine on several fundamental points. The proposal required a minimum marriage age, consent to marry, and state registration in order to contract a valid marriage. Marriage was defined in the draft as monogamous, and the requirements for divorce included proof of statutory grounds and a judicial order of divorce.

The government's proposal was adamantly opposed by Muslim parties inside the legislature and sparked an angry response from protesters outside the assembly. Tanks and soldiers were eventually dispatched to the parliament grounds to restore order. In an effort to find some middle ground, the military initiated compromise negotiations with representatives from Muslim parties that opposed the draft law. Those talks produced an agreement for revision of the draft stipulating that "all matters contrary to Islamic law" be removed from statute. In exchange for this concession, however, the agreement also required that the legislation include measures to reduce divorce, polygamy, and underage marriage. The proposal was revised according to the terms of the agreement, and on December 22, 1973, the date designated as "Mothers Day" in Indonesia, the legislature approved the revised statute. On January 2, 1974 President Suharto added his signature to the legislation, which became Law 1/1974 on Marriage.

At first blush the agreement that is the basis for the statute appears to promise the impossible. With respect to divorce, the subject of this chapter, standard Indonesian interpretations of Shafi'i doctrine at the time of the Marriage Act authorized a Muslim husband to terminate his marriage unilaterally and without grounds by simply uttering the repudiation or *talak* (Ar. *ṭalāq*). In insisting that the statute not deviate from Islamic doctrine the opponents of the government's original proposal unquestionably intended that the validity of the *talak* continue to be recognized. However, recognition of the husband's power of unilateral repudiation would appear to conflict with the government's demand for the implementation of mechanisms to limit divorce. The ease with which Muslim men could terminate their marriages was believed to encourage divorce, and eliminating or restricting the *talak* was considered necessary to address what was considered to be a significant social problem. The first prong of the agreement—that Islamic law not be changed—seems to stand in direct contradiction of the second prong—that the law be used to reduce divorce. This apparent contradiction is also present with respect to the other terms of the agreement regarding polygamy and underage marriage.

This chapter explores the tension between the demand that traditional divorce doctrines be held inviolate and the demand of government reformers that the law be changed to make divorce more difficult. We argue that the tension between these two positions was not resolved in the statute, but has continued to shape the development of Indonesian Islamic divorce law over the years since the Marriage Act was passed. As will be shown in the final section of the chapter, the tension is also reflected in divorce practice.

The first part of the chapter focuses on the interpretation of the Marriage Act. We trace the changing content of the law of divorce as applied by Indonesian Islamic courts since passage of the Act. It will be shown in this section that, since the passing of the Act, the law of divorce applied by Indonesian Islamic courts has been gradually and quietly transformed. The change has been most dramatic with respect to divorces initiated by men. Whereas prior law gave Muslim men the peremptory power of unilateral repudiation, a Muslim man wishing to terminate his marriage must now produce evidence in court of legal grounds for divorce. The changes to the law relating to divorces initiated by wives have been less far-reaching but nevertheless significant.

In the final section of the paper the focus shifts from law to practice. Comparing the results of survey data on the frequency of self-reported divorces against divorce statistics drawn from court records, we show that significant numbers of "divorces" occur outside of formal state processes. We next address the reasons for non-compliance with state divorce procedures. Although complete and reliable information regarding the reasons for non-compliance is not available, we conclude that practical considerations relating to cost and convenience explain much of the extra-judicial divorce behavior.

Ṭalāq in Islamic tradition

Common understandings of classical Islamic doctrine give Muslim men an unfettered power to dissolve their marriage at any time for any reason and without prior approval by either the wife or any other person or institution. A Muslim man can divorce his wife by simply declaring the termination of the marriage through the utterance of the performative repudiation formula known as the *ṭalāq*. Moreover, the law also grants the husband a limited power to change his mind after the divorce and re-institute the marriage. Like divorce, the revocation of divorce is accomplished by simply declaring it to be so—the husband simply decrees a reconciliation (*Ensiklopedi Hukum Islam* 1996, 1777).[1] There are strict limits, however, on the number of times and on the circumstances under which a man can divorce and then reconcile with the same woman.[2]

Although Islamic law imposes few strictly legal restrictions on divorce by men, divorce is thoroughly regulated by Islamic morals, which are regarded as an inseparable component of Islamic law. Notwithstanding that Muslim husbands have an unfettered right of divorce, in exercising that right they may nonetheless be committing an act that is sinful in the eyes of God. Within Islamic law all conduct is assigned a particular moral classification depending on whether its performance will attract reward or punishment when adjudged in the hereafter. Divorce occupies the full spectrum of moral categories from obligatory (*wājib*) to forbidden (*ḥarām*). The classification of divorce within this scheme depends on the circumstances that precede and motivate it. For example, because the purpose of marriage is to form a loving and harmonious relationship, divorce is considered obligatory where there is ongoing quarrelling which cannot be resolved by mediators. Divorce is forbidden in circumstances where the husband knows that his wife will commit unlawful sexual intercourse (*zinā*) if he repudiates her (*Ensiklopedi Hukum Islam* 1996, 1777).[3] Along the spectrum between the polar categories of obligatory and forbidden lie milder positive and negative assessments of "recommended" (*sunna*) and "reprehensible" (*makrūh*) and a neutral category (*ḥalāl/mubāḥ* "permissible") describing conduct that carries no eternal consequences. According to some authorities, one situation in which divorce is considered recommended is when a wife refuses to carry out her duties towards God (such as her daily prayers) or her husband (such as serving him). A divorce that is performed for no particular reason, however, is regarded as reprehensible. Thus, arbitrary repudiation can be efficacious in effecting a valid divorce, but its performance is morally disapproved.[4]

The Marriage Act seeks to reduce the number of divorces by Muslim men by regulating the use of the formula of repudiation (*talak*). Employing the generic Indonesian word for "divorce" (*cerai*), the Act provides that a marriage can only be terminated because of death, divorce, or a court decision (Art. 38). The Act further provides that divorce may only be carried out in the presence of a court, after the court has tried but failed to reconcile the two parties (Art. 39(1)). In order to carry out a divorce there must be sufficient grounds why the couple are unable to live harmoniously as husband and wife (Art. 39(2)).

The Marriage Act itself does not specify what constitutes "sufficient grounds" for divorce. However, a list of six grounds for divorce is set out in the official elucidation to the Act (Art. 4(e)).[5] Although the origin or explanation for these six reasons is nowhere specified, the grounds for divorce contained in the Marriage Act appear to have been adopted from a Dutch colonial enactment first implemented in 1933 for the regulation of the colony's Christian populations. The Act further states that a divorce suit must be filed with the court and foreshadows the enactment of future legislation containing procedures for the filing of divorce suits and for the performance of a divorce in the presence of the court (Art. 40, 39(3)).

The provisions of the Act regarding divorces initiated by Muslim men are brief and ambiguous such that the type of regulatory regime envisaged is not apparent. The word *talak* does not appear anywhere in the Act or Elucidation, and there is no apparent differentiation between divorces initiated by men or women or by people of different faiths. The legally significant act that would effect a divorce is not specified. The executive branch regulations designed to implement the Marriage Act (Gov. Reg. 9/1975) contain more detailed provisions on the initiation and conduct of divorce proceedings.[6] The implementing regulations, discussed in more detail below, establish two separate divorce procedures, one for men married according to Islamic law and a second for all others. The regulations provide that a Muslim husband who intends to divorce must notify the court of his intention and his reasons and request that the court convene a hearing to witness and certify the divorce. Furthermore, although the word *talak* does not appear in the text of the regulations, the accompanying elucidation describes the relevant procedures as "regulating *talak* divorce." Two procedural hurdles must be overcome before this can occur: the court must be of the opinion that there are grounds for divorce, as defined by the regulations, and that the couple cannot be reconciled.

The Marriage Act and implementing regulations therefore recognize and preserve the use of the *talak* as the means of effecting divorce in proceedings initiated by Muslim men. However, the circumstances of its use are restricted and made contingent on the prior approval of the court which, in theory, may be refused. The legal status of an extra-judicial pronouncement of the *talak* is a critical issue that is not addressed in either legislative instrument. The Act is framed in mandatory terms: divorce can *only* be carried out before a court and there *must* be sufficient grounds for divorce. Nonetheless, this does not preclude the validity of a *talak* recited out of court and in violation of the legislative procedures. The Act and regulations may be interpreted such that a failure to comply with the procedures prescribed would not and could not of itself invalidate a divorce, but rather would constitute a breach of the Act and potentially be subject to penalty (Art. 45). However, no penalty is specified for breach of the *talak* procedures.[7]

That this issue remains unresolved in the text of the Marriage Act and implementing regulations is highly significant. Islamic legal doctrine recognizes and sanctions state laws that create an administrative framework within which divine law can be applied. However, a law that denies a certain act the significance and consequence that God has deemed that act to have is an impossibility. Legislative attempts to interfere with the terms and substance of the divine law, the embodiment of God's immutable will, are not only regarded as impermissible but ineffectual. Based on the text of the Marriage Act, it is not clear whether it is intended that Muslim men have a right to divorce which may only be exercised in certain circumstances (a principle entirely compatible with the Islamic moral position on divorce) or that Muslim men only have a right to divorce in certain circumstances (a principle irreconcilable with common interpretations of classical Islamic doctrine). It is only in the application of the law by the courts that the nature of the regulatory regime introduced by the Marriage Act has taken shape. Even then, its application has not been uniform throughout the period of its operation and throughout the court hierarchy.

Early implementation of statutory talak divorce procedures

As initially practiced, the function of the court in a *talak* divorce was essentially administrative rather than judicial. Divorces by men were not generally treated as contentious actions requiring notice, proof, and adjudication, but rather as *ex parte* ministerial proceedings in which the court's role was to witness and certify the husband's action rather than weigh evidence and issue a decision.[8]

Such a view of the court's role in *talak* divorce proceedings was supported by the language and terms of the implementing regulations.[9] Firstly, the regulations provide that the mechanism by which a *talak* divorce proceeding is initiated is neither a complaint (*gugatan*), that is the mechanism for initiating a civil suit, nor a petition (*permohonan*), that is the mechanism for instituting an application for a legal decree, but rather a "letter of notification" stating the intention to divorce, the grounds for divorce, and a request for the court to convene a hearing for that purpose (Art. 14). This mechanism for initiating proceedings implied that what was sought from the court was primarily a forum within which to recite the *talak*.

Although the court is required to call the wife in order to request clarification in relation to any matter relevant to the intention to divorce (Art. 15), there are no procedures set out in the regulations prescribing the manner in which the wife must be notified and summoned. This is in contrast to the provisions dealing with general divorce proceedings, which contain detailed procedures governing when and how the parties must be summoned before each hearing and by whom (Arts. 26–29). Such procedures are characteristic of contested proceedings where both parties are afforded the right to be present and heard.

Neither the Marriage Act nor the implementing regulations expressly require proof of grounds for divorce in *talak* divorce proceedings. Article 16 of the implementing regulations states that the court may only convene a hearing to witness a *talak* divorce where there are grounds for divorce, as defined in Article 19 of the regulations. The elucidation to that Article states that "after careful examination and the formation of the opinion that there are grounds for divorce, and after unsuccessfully attempting to reconcile the couple," the court may witness the performance of a divorce by the husband.

Regulations promulgated by the Minister for Religion also require the court to "be of the opinion that there are grounds" before witnessing a divorce (Department of Religion Reg. 3/1975 Chapter X(4)). There are no provisions, however, that are framed in terms of proof or evidence or that require the court to call relevant witnesses. This again is in contrast to the provisions regulating general divorce proceedings, which prescribe the steps required to establish certain grounds for divorce. For example, if the ground for divorce relied upon is the existence of ongoing and irreconcilable differences between a couple, the implementing regulations require the court to hear from the families and others close to the couple before accepting the ground as established (Art. 22(2)). The manner in which the provisions on *talak* divorce proceedings are phrased suggests that the role of the court is limited to ensuring that grounds for divorce are properly cited and are consistent with the available grounds listed in the regulations.

A further significant distinction between *talak* divorce proceedings and general divorce proceedings, as governed by the regulations, is that the final outcome of a *talak* proceeding is neither a decision (*putusan*) nor a decree (*penetapan*) but a "Certificate Respecting the Occurrence of a *Talak*" (*Surat Keterangan tentang Terjadinya Talak*) or a certificate verifying that a *talak* divorce has occurred (Art. 17).

Early jurisprudence reflects the limited and largely passive role initially assumed by the Islamic courts in *talak* divorce proceedings.[10] In a case decided in 1977, the provincial appeals court for Medan found that a *Talak* Certificate could not be appealed, and subsequently refused a wife's request to nullify the certification of divorce issued by a lower court.[11] The appeal had been brought on the bases that there were no grounds for divorce and that the lower court's decision had failed to consider the husband's legal obligations towards his wife. The appeals court did not address the competing assertions of husband and wife as to whether the marriage had been harmonious and, therefore, did not review whether there were in fact grounds for divorce.[12] The court stated that the occurrence of a divorce as described in the Marriage Act and the implementing regulations is not a divorce that is effected by a decision or decree of a court, but rather occurs automatically on the declaration of the *talak* by the husband. Further, the court stated that provided the declaration of the *talak* is performed according to the procedures established by legislation, it is to be regarded as the exercise of the husband's right. For those reasons the court found that a *Talak* Certificate merely constitutes a certification of the divorce while the divorce itself is effected by the husband's recitation of the repudiation formula, to which there can be no appeal.[13]

Another indication of how the court perceived its role was the initial willingness of Islamic courts to give effect to repudiations pronounced out of court in violation of the Marriage Act. If the essential function of the courts was to verify and certify a husband's repudiation, then there was no obvious barrier to the court validating an extra-judicial *talak*, provided that its pronouncement could be proven. In one early case decided in 1977 both the first instance Islamic court in Pekanbaru[14] and the provincial level Islamic High Court in Padang unequivocally declared that a *talak* pronounced out of court in violation of statutory procedures was valid.[15] The court had been petitioned to issue a decree that a *talak*, pronounced ten days earlier, was valid. The relevant repudiation had allegedly been witnessed by four people and recorded in a written declaration. The declaration was signed by the four purported witnesses and attested by the thumbprint of the husband, who was paralyzed and unable to write. The validity of the *talak* was contested by the petitioner's wife on a number of grounds. She claimed that the testimony of the witnesses regarding the occurrence of the *talak* was false; that the *talak* was invalid because her husband suffered from a nervous condition and paralysis; and that the written repudiation was invalid because it was not issued by the court.

The court at first instance accepted the husband's petition and decreed the occurrence of a first revocable *talak* effective from the date of the extra-judicial pronouncement. The provincial level Islamic appeals court affirmed the decree of the lower court. At both first instance and on appeal, the court's decision focused exclusively on whether the pronouncement of the *talak* had been proven[16] and, if so, whether it might nonetheless be invalid owing to the husband's mental and physical condition. The court resolved these issues by reference to texts from classical Islamic sources. At both first instance and on appeal, the court cursorily cited the Marriage Act and implementing regulations as relevant factors in its deliberations. However, no mention was made of the statutory requirement that a repudiation be based on sufficient grounds and pronounced in the presence of the court to be valid.[17]

Other contemporaneous decisions reveal a similar approach.[18] In a number of the reported cases, women were the petitioning party seeking court validation of repudiations pronounced extra-judicially by their husbands.[19] In one case a first instance Islamic court accepted a wife's petition and decreed that a *talak* pronounced out of court more than one year earlier was valid and effective from the date of pronouncement, even though the petitioner's husband appeared in court and denied that he had repudiated her.[20] The exclusive focus of the court's inquiry in all the cases cited was whether the pronouncement of the *talak* could be proven. Issues pertaining to the validity of a particular pronouncement of the *talak* were discussed and resolved in the context of Islamic doctrine without reference to the requirements of the Marriage Act and implementing regulations.[21]

It is apparent from these early cases that, although the court may have promoted reconciliation and discouraged divorce, those tasks were discharged without challenging or derogating from, in any significant way, a Muslim husband's assumed unilateral right of divorce.[22] In operation, the requirement that a husband utter the repudiation in court in the presence of a judge was not fundamentally different from the requirement, in effect since 1946, that a husband report his repudiation to a marriage registrar.

The approach of the Supreme Court

Supreme Court precedents from the same period reveal a distinctly different understanding of the Marriage Act and implementing regulations. The Supreme Court approached compliance with the Act and regulations as an essential requirement of a valid divorce and regarded the existence of sufficient grounds for divorce as a matter to be proven, not merely asserted.

In a case decided in 1979 the Supreme Court emphasized the adversarial nature of *talak* divorce proceedings.[23] The court at first instance had rejected a husband's divorce petition on the basis that he was unable to prove the grounds for divorce cited in the petition, namely, a lack of harmony in his home life.[24] In both the originating petition and the final decree issued by the court, the husband was listed as the only party to the case. The decision at first instance was quashed by the provincial level Islamic appeals court in Banda Aceh.[25] The court found that the lower court had attempted but failed to reconcile the couple, demonstrating that reconciliation was not possible. The court also considered that the couple's inability to live together harmoniously was further demonstrated by the wife's indirect acknowledgment that her husband had already repudiated her, a fact asserted by him in his initial petition to the court. On the basis of those findings, the appeals court found that grounds for divorce had been established. The lower court was ordered to convene a hearing to witness the husband's repudiation.

The wife sought cassation in the Supreme Court. At its own initiative, the Court first addressed the question whether the wife was able to lodge an appeal. The Court stated that a divorce is in essence a contentious proceeding, irrespective of whether it is initiated by a husband or wife, and as such there must be two parties. The fact that a proceeding is styled as a "petition" does not necessarily mean that there is only one party, except in cases that are voluntary in nature. Moreover, it is a principle of court procedure that everyone has a right to present a defense, including in a divorce case, regardless of whether the proceedings are in the form of a petition. For that reason a husband or wife whose rights may be adversely affected by his or her spouse has the right to present a defense, and that requires standing as a party to the case, both at first instance and on appeal. On that basis, the Court concluded that the wife did have a right of appeal in this case. The Court then addressed the wife's application for cassation and found that the provincial level appeals court had reached its conclusion that the couple were unable to live together harmoniously without carefully examining the evidence. The Court quashed the appeals court decision and rejected the husband's initial petition.

In addition to establishing the contested nature of all divorce proceedings, Supreme Court jurisprudence has also unequivocally declared that an extra-judicial *talak* is invalid and ineffective. One early case establishing this rule originated in the Islamic court in Padang Panjang, West Sumatra.[26] The court at first instance refused to validate an unauthorized *talak* because grounds for divorce were not proven and it was not in accordance with relevant statutory requirements. The provincial level Islamic appeals court reversed the lower court decision.[27] The court explained that the act of reciting the *talak* outside the courtroom represented a contravention of the Marriage Act and implementing regulations, but that such a contravention was not within the authority or jurisdiction of the Islamic courts. However, the court found that the legal status of an unauthorized *talak* was a matter within the Islamic courts' jurisdiction. On that issue, the court observed that neither the Act nor implementing regulations directly address the legal status of a *talak* pronounced outside the courtroom. The court stated that extra-judicial *talak* continued to occur within the community and that there was a need for the status of such *talak* to be legally resolved. The court referred to Article 3 of the elucidation, which states that the Act incorporates elements and principles of religious law, and then quoted two classical Islamic texts to the effect that a *talak* "falls" (comes into effect) when it is pronounced. On that basis, the court decreed that the *talak* uttered by the petitioning husband was valid notwithstanding that it had occurred outside the presence and supervision of the court.

On cassation, the Supreme Court reversed the decision of the appeals court and reinstated the decision of the first instance court. The court dealt with the issue in succinct and stark terms finding that the appeals court had incorrectly applied the Marriage Act and implementing regulations. The court stated that from the date those legislative instruments came into effect, all *talak* divorces were required to be performed before the local Islamic court.[28]

Not content with the level of compliance with its precedents, in August 1985 the Supreme Court published a circular directed to the chairs of the Islamic courts and the Islamic high courts throughout the country (Sp. Ct. Cir. 13/1985).[29] The circular observed that some Islamic courts continued to handle cases of requests for permission to pronounce a *talak* in a way that is not in accordance with governing regulations and Supreme Court jurisprudence. Among other things, the Court wrote, some judges believe that a decree is unnecessary when the parties to a *talak* proceeding have agreed to divorce, and the judges proceed directly to the issuance of a Certificate Regarding the Occurrence of a *Talak*. The circular emphatically declared this view to be *KELIRU* (mistaken) (emphasis here and below as in the original), and instructed all Islamic court judges that every

> decision in a petition for pronouncement of a *talak* must take the form of a DECREE (*PENETAPAN*) to give the parties the opportunity to take an appeal or seek cassation.

The Court further declared that "only after the decree has become final [in the sense of having obtained the force of law] shall a hearing be held to witness the pronouncement of the *talak*." And only then should a *Talak* Certificate be issued.

The unmistakable purpose of this instruction was to promote the transformation of the *talak* procedure from an essentially ministerial process, in which the court simply verifies the husband's repudiation, to an essentially adversarial proceeding, in which the wife is a full party with the right to be notified, appear, be heard on the merits, and challenge the decision. Beyond this, the Court was also clearly concerned with the more serious matter of extra-judicial *talak*. That is the probable explanation for the Court's description of the lower courts' error as proceeding "directly to the issuance of a Certificate Respecting the Occurrence of a *Talak*," rather than describing the problem as one of proceeding directly to the pronouncement of the *talak*.

That the real evil addressed by the circular was the practice of Islamic courts certifying extra-judicial *talak* was made explicit in a letter by the chair of the Islamic High Court in the Province of West Nusa Tenggara. This letter was sent with the Supreme Court circular to all first instance court judges. The letter referenced the Supreme Court circular, and then stated that "in order to eliminate the practice of unauthorized *talak*, which is still common within the jurisdiction," all Islamic court judges are instructed to fully implement the circular, and also to "reject all requests to validate unauthorized *talak* (*talak liar*), that is, *talak* that does not comply with statutory requirements."[30]

The Religious Judicature Act of 1989 and beyond

The Religious Judicature Act (Law 7/1989), passed in 1989, addressed the procedures for *talak* divorce proceedings at greater length than any previous enactment. In many respects the Religious Judicature Act confirms the adversarial nature of *talak* divorce proceedings. According to the prescribed procedures (Art. 67), the wife must be named as respondent (*termohon*) in the divorce petition and formally summoned to appear.[31] Further, the wife must appear in person at the first hearing (Arts. 69, 82(1)(2))[32] and has an unequivocal right of appeal (Art. 70(2)). The Act also clarifies that the court must not proceed directly to witness the pronouncement of the *talak* but instead, in order to facilitate the opportunity for appeal, must first issue a decree declaring that grounds for divorce have been established and that the petition for divorce is granted. Only after that decree has the force of law may a hearing be convened, the *talak* pronounced, and a second decree issued stating that the marriage is dissolved. With respect to this second decree there is no right of appeal or cassation (Art. 71).

Despite all of the above, the legal terminology used in the Act to describe *talak* divorce proceedings and their outcome is not the language used in Indonesian procedural law to describe the procedures and product of a contested legal action. *Talak* divorce proceedings are initiated by "petition" (*permohonan*) and the final product ultimately issued by the court is described as a "decree" (*penetapan*) rather than a "decision" (*putusan*). These terms, "petition" and "decree," are understood in Indonesian law to denote an *ex parte* proceeding that, because of its *ex parte* character, binds only the petitioner. This common understanding of the legal significance of a decree corresponds with the view that the court in a *talak* proceeding simply verifies and provides legal proof of the husband's repudiation.[33]

Case law from the period following the implementation of the Religious Judicature Act reveals the extent to which *talak* divorce proceedings were being approached in practice as contentious proceedings in which the petitioning husband must prove the asserted grounds for divorce and in which the wife has comprehensive rights to challenge the case advanced by her husband. For example, in 1993 a provincial level Islamic appeals court in Manado overturned a lower court decision granting a *talak* divorce petition on the basis that the decision was infected by procedural flaws.[34] The court found that the wife had not been correctly summoned to many of the hearings and, as a result, had not been afforded the rights to which she was entitled. Furthermore, the court had not heard evidence from the close family of the wife as required by the implementing regulations. The evidence that the court had heard from witnesses for the husband was found to be tainted because the lower court had failed to enforce the requirement that witnesses be separated while testifying, and had not properly ascertained their familial relationship with the husband. On that basis, the appeals court found that the husband was unable to prove his case and therefore his petition must be rejected.[35]

In a 1993 case, the provincial level Islamic appeals court in Central Kalimantan overturned a decision of a lower court granting a husband's divorce petition on the basis that the lower court had not taken into account everything that was put forward by both parties and that there were indications of bias towards the husband.[36] Specifically, the appeals court found that bias was suggested by the ease with which the court had accepted the husband's petition. The appeals court noted that in its decision the lower court had not referenced any real evidence from either party. In addition, the appeals court observed that the lower court had not attempted to reconcile the testimony given by witnesses presented by both sides and had ignored, both in its decision and during the proceedings, a written statement from the wife's mother to the effect that there was interference in the household by a third party. The appeals court rejected the husband's petition.[37]

Since the Marriage Act and implementing regulations came into force, the courts—in particular the Supreme Court—have gradually shaped the ambiguity and unanswered questions of those legislative instruments into a regulatory regime which would certainly have met strong opposition if introduced transparently and directly in 1974. The unfettered right of Muslim husbands to repudiate their wives has, in practice, been transferred to the court. Husbands must petition and persuade the courts to allow them to divorce and in so doing may be opposed by their wives who have equal access and rights before the court. It is still the pronouncement of the *talak* that effects the divorce, but the force of that pronouncement lies in its prior endorsement by the court and not in any divine injunction.

Divorces initiated by wives

Although Muslim wives in Indonesia have never enjoyed a unilateral power of divorce of the type traditionally vested in their husbands, they have always had limited avenues for pursuing divorce at their own initiative. In particular, they could avail themselves of three divorce procedures with roots in established traditions of *fiqh*, including *taʿlīq al-ṭalāq* (Ind. *taklik talak*), *shiqāq* (Ind. *syiqaq*), and *faskh* (Ind. *fasakh*), all discussed in more detail below.[38] With respect to divorces initiated by Muslim wives then, Indonesian government attempts to exercise regulatory control have proved less controversial. This is primarily because Muslim wives have always required the intervention and authorization of third parties in order to effect divorce and, as such, divorces initiated by wives are more amenable to regulatory control and state intervention.

1. Taklik Talak

The most commonly used divorce option for wives prior to the implementation of the Marriage Act was the *taklik talak*, a "suspended" or "conditional" repudiation, whereby a husband declares at the time of marriage that a *talak* will automatically occur or "fall" upon his wife if certain specified events occur and are proven in court.[39] As the practice evolved in Indonesian readings of *fiqh*, the actions recited by the husband that would give rise to an automatic *talak* generally include desertion for a period of six months, failure to pay obligatory spousal support for three months, physical abuse, or neglect of the wife for a period of six months.

The practice of *taklik talak* divorce allowed women to escape from unsatisfactory marriages in circumstances where their husbands refused or were unavailable to repudiate them.[40] *Taklik talak* declarations became such an integral part of Muslim marriage in some parts of the archipelago that in the 1950s the Indonesian Department of Religion began printing on the back of all Muslim marriage certificates a standard *taklik talak* formula containing the four conditions set forth above.[41]

Neither the Marriage Act nor the implementing regulations refer to the practice of *taklik talak* divorce. It is apparent from the provisions of both instruments, however, that Muslim wives are entitled to commence an action for divorce at their own initiative (see Gov. Reg. 9/1975, Elucidation Art. 20(1)). In order to obtain a divorce, a Muslim wife must satisfy the court, in the context of contested proceedings, that at least one of six grounds for divorce exists. Breach of a *taklik talak* provision is not listed among the statutory grounds for divorce. Likewise, the legislation only requires a Muslim wife to demonstrate that grounds for divorce exist; she is not required to prove in addition that her husband has given an undertaking to repudiate her upon the occurrence of any specified set of circumstances. Notwithstanding the terms of the legislation, however, *taklik talak* has remained an important part of divorce proceedings initiated by Muslim wives.

The Islamic legal doctrine of suspended repudiation continued to be used by the courts after the implementation of the Marriage Act because the grounds for divorce contained in the statute were interpreted as codifications of the corresponding terms of the *taklik talak* formula. This is illustrated by the treatment of divorces based on desertion. As noted above, one of the standard *taklik talak* provisions printed on marriage certificates stated that if the husband deserted his wife for a period of six months, a repudiation would automatically "fall." The Marriage Act and implementing regulations also recognize desertion as a ground for a divorce. The statutory pro-

visions require, however, that the party seeking divorce must show desertion for a period of at least two years (Gov. Reg. 9/1975, Art. 19(b)).

In the initial period following the implementation of the Marriage Act,
Islamic courts, consistently with the terms of the standard *taklik talak* provision, continued to grant *taklik talak* divorces based on desertion of only
six months.[42] In 1979, however, the Supreme Court issued a decision
unequivocally declaring that, for marriages entered into after the effective
date of the Marriage Act, a desertion of six months no longer established
grounds for divorce, whatever the terms of the *taklik talak* recited by the
husband, and in order to obtain a divorce a wife must prove that her husband had deserted her for a minimum of two years.[43] The Court stated
that the *taklik talak* procedure could continue to be used as a part of the
marriage contract, but that Article 19 of the implementing regulations must
form the basis for divorce decisions.[44] Because Article 19 requires proof of
desertion for a period of two years, the court concluded that "for marriages contracted after 1 October 1975," the date on which the Marriage
Act went into effect, "the *taklik talak* must conform to the two year time
period."[45]

In order to conform Muslim practice to the requirements of the statute,
the standard *taklik talak* provisions relating to desertion were amended to
match the grounds for divorce listed in Article 19. Under the current version of the *taklik talak* formula, which was prescribed by a Department of
Religion Regulation in 1990 (Dep. Rel. Reg. 2/1990), the husband promises
or decrees that a *talak* will occur upon proof that he has deserted his wife
for a period of two years. This alteration to the standard provisions demonstrates a willingness to amend the terms of the Muslim practice so that
practice and statute appear complementary.[46] In principle, the *taklik talak*
divorce procedure has been rendered redundant by the Marriage Act and
implementing regulations. It is not capable of conferring a right of divorce
upon a Muslim wife beyond that granted to her by statute, nor is it capable of limiting her statutory right to seek divorce. However, provided that
the standard *taklik talak* provisions do not diverge greatly from the statutory provisions, the two can conveniently co-exist. Proof that *taklik talak*
provisions have been breached may simultaneously constitute proof of statutory grounds for divorce. And any subsequent grant of divorce issued by
the court will be imbued with the authority of a *taklik talak* divorce, irrespective of the fact that it is granted pursuant to the statutory provisions
alone.

2. Syiqaq

In Indonesia *syiqaq* is a mediation procedure that has evolved into a mechanism for obtaining a divorce.[47] The procedure is said to be based on Q 4:39 which provides for the appointment of "mediators" to represent the husband and wife in circumstances where there are serious and frequent disputes within a marriage that have escalated to a critical point. Under the procedure, the appointed mediators first try to reconcile the couple in dispute. If their reconciliation efforts are unsuccessful, the husband is offered the opportunity to repudiate his wife. If he declines, the mediator appointed to represent the husband pronounces a *talak* for him.[48]

The Marriage Act and implementing regulations do not explicitly incorporate the *syiqaq* procedure. Article 19(f) of the regulations permits divorce when there are ongoing differences between husband and wife and when there is no hope that the couple can be reconciled and live harmoniously in one household (Gov. Reg. 9/1975, Art. 19(f)). When this ground is relied upon in divorce proceedings, the court is instructed to hear from the families and those close to the couple as to the causes of disagreement within the marriage (Gov. Reg. 9/1975, Art. 22(2)). Likewise, the court is instructed to attempt to reconcile the couple, and may make repeated attempts at reconciliation throughout the proceedings (Gov. Reg. 9/1975, Art. 31). Although no reference is made to the appointment of mediators or to the delegation of authority to repudiate, from its implementation Article 19(f) was approached by many Islamic courts as the statutory embodiment of the *syiqaq* procedure.

The interpretation of the irreconcilable differences provision of the statute as simply a recognition or codification of existing divorce practice based on *syiqaq* is reflected in early jurisprudence. For example, in a case heard before the Islamic court in Probolinggo, the court appointed two mediators to help reconcile a couple who had already been separated for two years.[49] When the court finally resolved that it would be better for the parties to divorce, the mediator appointed for the husband was given the opportunity to recite the *talak* on his behalf. The ultimate decision issued by the court stated, firstly, that the court granted the plaintiff-wife's application and, secondly, that the court validated the defendant-husband's *talak*, which was recited by his appointed mediator and accepted by the mediator appointed for the wife.[50]

In cases that reached the Supreme Court, the Court emphasized that the requirements of the legislation were paramount. However, the Court did not disavow either the use of *syiqaq* procedure or its association with divorce proceedings founded on Article 19(f). In a 1979 divorce case,[51] the

Supreme Court overlooked a failure to strictly comply with the relevant statutory provisions—that is, a failure to hear from the parties' families and clarify the sources of disagreement within the marriage—and upheld a grant of divorce on the basis that the *syiqaq* procedure had at least been followed. The decision was based on a finding that compliance with the *syiqaq* divorce procedure in essence fulfilled the requirements of the Marriage Act and implementing regulations with respect to Article 19(f).[52]

In a decision the following year the Supreme Court emphasized that compliance with the legislation was of singular importance. Implicit in the Court's decision was the view that if the statutory requirements were fulfilled, it was purely incidental whether and how the *syiqaq* procedure had been employed.[53] The case involved a wife's application for divorce on the basis that she and her husband were engaged in constant quarrelling. The first instance court accepted the wife's application and annulled (*memfasakh*) the marriage. The provincial level appeals court overturned the decision on the basis that the *syiqaq* procedure should have been followed. The appeals court found that where quarrelling is given as the reason for divorce and where the quarrelling has escalated to a critical level, the *syiqaq* procedure must be followed rather than the annulment procedure (*fasakh*). On cassation, the Supreme Court stated that compliance with Islamic formalities was not critical provided that the court's decision was in accordance with Indonesian law. The Supreme Court found that the requirements of the Marriage Act had been satisfied and reinstated the divorce without discussing whether the *fasakh* or *syiqaq* procedure should have been followed.[54]

With the Religious Judicature Act of 1989, the assimilation of the irreconcilable differences grounds for divorce under the Marriage Act with the *syiqaq* procedure under Islamic law was formalized. Article 76 of the 1989 Act provides that when a claim for divorce is based on the grounds of *syiqaq*, the court may appoint mediators for the two parties after taking evidence regarding the nature of the dispute between husband and wife. That a divorce based on the grounds of *syiqaq* refers to a divorce based on Article 19(f) of the Marriage Act is made explicit in the standard form interlocutory decision prescribed by the Department of Religion to be issued by the court when appointing mediators.

Article 76 of the 1989 Religious Judicature Act does not alter the position enunciated by the Supreme Court in 1980. Islamic courts are not mandated to adhere to requirements of the *syiqaq* procedure and such adherence does not occur in practice. In divorce proceedings based on Article 19(f), the courts' only obligation is to comply with the statutory provisions. The courts retain complete discretion in relation to whether to appoint mediators, whom to appoint, and what role to give them. More importantly, authority to effect a divorce in practice remains vested in the court and is not delegated to the husband's appointed mediator to exercise on his behalf.[55] However, irrespective of whether or to what extent the *syiqaq* procedure is followed, a divorce obtained by a Muslim wife based on the grounds in Article 19(f) is styled as a divorce issued pursuant to the authority of the *syiqaq* procedure and, by implication, the authority of the Qur'an.

3. Fasakh

Fasakh is a mechanism for dissolving a marriage more akin to annulment than divorce. There is disagreement among Islamic scholars on the circumstances in which a wife may obtain a judicial declaration that a marriage is *fasakh*. The only basis for *fasakh* on which there is universal agreement is apostasy. Other grounds for a decree of *fasakh* recognized in classical *fiqh* include, among others, if the husband suffers from mental illness, suffers from leprosy, is impotent, is unable to pay spousal maintenance, or has deserted the wife.

The Marriage Act and implementing regulations include no reference to *fasakh* divorce. As with the *taklik talak* and the *syiqaq*, however, the Islamic courts have assimilated the *fasakh* grounds for divorce to the available statutory grounds and have continued to grant, pursuant to the Marriage Act, divorces or annulments that are styled as *fasakh* divorces. For example, Article 19(e) of the regulations implementing the Marriage Act cites physical defect or illness which renders a person incapable of performing his or her spousal duties as a ground for divorce. Referencing Article 19(e) and citing classical Islamic texts, the courts continued to grant *fasakh* divorces to Muslim wives in cases where their husbands suffered from leprosy[56] and mental illness.[57]

The provisions of the Marriage Act and implementing regulations enable Muslim wives to obtain a divorce upon proof of the existence of one among six statutory grounds. The grounds for divorce contained in the statute are framed without reference to *taklik talak*, *syiqaq* or *fasakh*. In theory those divorce procedures, rooted in the theory and practice of traditional Muslim jurisprudence, are no longer relevant to determining when a Muslim wife may or may not obtain a divorce. Those procedures are not capable of expanding or diminishing the right to divorce that a Muslim wife has under the statute.

The remarkable accomplishment of the Marriage Act provisions relating to divorces by Muslim women is that, without significantly compromising or corrupting the statutory scheme, divorce procedures that have their source in Islamic doctrine and carry the weight of religious endorsement have been grafted onto the legislation. The reported cases reveal that Muslim wives continue to be granted *taklik talak*, *syiqaq*, and *fasakh* divorces pursuant to the statute. The Supreme Court insists that compliance with the legislation is of paramount importance. As a consequence of the assimilation of the statutory grounds for divorce with Islamic divorce procedures, however, it is possible to couch compliance with the statute in terms that also suggest compliance with Islam.

Divorce practice

In May of 1985 the headlines of Jakarta's sensationalist "red press" announced that the country's best known entertainer, music and film sensation Rhoma Irama,[58] had secretly taken a second wife, 29-year old actress and co-star, Ricca Rahim.[59] The marriage between Rhoma and Ricca had actually been contracted more than a year earlier, in January of 1984, but came to light only after Rhoma's first wife, Veronika, revealed that Rhoma had divorced her. According to Rhoma's account, disputed by Veronika, Veronika had demanded the divorce when she learned of the secret marriage to Ricca. Rhoma said that he acceded to Veronika's request and repudiated her with a single *talak*. According to "Vero," however, the *talak* pronounced in May of 1985 was actually Rhoma's second. After the first repudiation the couple had reconciled "in the interest of their children and to preserve Rhoma's good name."[60]

In June of 1985 Rhoma and Veronika were again in the headlines. This time the focus was on Veronika who, it was reported, had married Erwin, one of Rhoma's employees, shortly after she was divorced by Rhoma.[61] Erwin's marriage to Veronika was his second; when he married Veronika, Erwin was still married to another woman. It was for that reason, perhaps, that the marriage between Veronika and Erwin, like Rhoma's marriage to Ricca, had not been attended by a marriage registrar and was without proper documentation.

Rhoma Irama's film and music credits guaranteed that his marriage to Ricca would be front page news. But the story of Rhoma Irama's polygamous marriage and unilateral divorce was more than just the usual gossip about the sexual adventures of the rich and famous. The extraordinary interest in Rhoma's marriage and divorce was based as much on his status as a Muslim figure as it was on his status as a performer. Rhoma Irama's musical success, which was the catalyst for his film career, was launched upon his having appropriated and redefined an obscure genre of

Indonesian music as a kind of Islamic pop (Frederick 1982). Rhoma Irama's music, onomatopoetically named *dangdut* in echo of its signature rhythms, was more than simply religiously-themed dance music; he considered it a form of Islamic propagation (*daʿwa*).[62]

The religious and legal angle on the story of Rhoma Irama's marriage was not neglected in either the press coverage or popular commentary. The *Pos Kota* article that broke the news observed that frequent marriage and divorce is common for "artists," but then quoted a dictum of the Prophet regarding the despicability of divorce, and queried whether Rhoma Irama, as a devout Muslim, should be held to higher standards than prevail "in Hollywood." The headline of a *Barata Minggu* story that ran the first week in July declared that "Rhoma Irama and Veronica Are Not Genuine Muslims," and proceeded to report the comments of critics that "the great preacher had failed utterly as a servant of God whose example should be followed."[63] Rhoma Irama and his supporters responded to such criticisms in various ways. Rhoma described his repudiation of Veronika as "God's will" and a "spiritual offering" to Veronika. In another interview he said that "polygamy and divorce are disapproved by some segments of society," but that "nothing he had done violated God's laws." A letter to the editor of the news weekly *Tempo* dismissed the magazine's characterization of Rhoma in a prior article as a "hypocrite" (*munafik*). The writer praised the self-proclaimed "King of Dangdut" as superior to the Prophet himself as a singer, and observed that a polygamous marriage did not require permission from existing wives or anyone else.[64]

While most of the controversy focused on whether the marriage of Rhoma to Ricca and his divorce of Veronika were actions becoming good Muslims, there was also some discussion about whether the marriages of Rhoma to Ricca and Veronika to Erwin were legally valid. The most substantial question related to the validity of Veronika's marriage to Erwin, since Veronika had married before the end of the required period of abstention from sexual relations (*ʿidda*) following the repudiation by Rhoma. It was reported that the religious official who witnessed the marriage had required that Veronika present a letter of permission from Rhoma to provide assurance that he would not exercise his right of reconciliation;[65] several papers printed facsimile copies of the letter of permission complete with the official seal of the Republic of Indonesia to reassure anxious fans.[66] The question of the validity of Rhoma's marriage to Ricca received less attention, probably because the matter was hardly in doubt. The fullest statement on the issue came from Rhoma Irama's spiritual advisor and martial arts teacher, who was also a Muslim scholar with the title of *ustadz* (honorific for religious teacher). The focus of the article was on a published rumor that Rhoma's unauthorized marriage to Ricca had destroyed his "spiritual powers," a defamatory allegation that the Ustadz firmly denied. In support of the contention that the marriage caused neither loss of spiritual potency nor other ill effects, Ustadz Bahruddin emphasized that the marriage between Rhoma and Ricca was perfectly valid even if in violation of statutory requirements. "One need not be an ustadz or a Muslim with a title," according to Bahruddin, "ordinary Muslims familiar with Islamic marriage rules can tell you that an unauthorized marriage is nevertheless valid."[67] The validity of the (also unauthorized) divorce was apparently never questioned.

The extent of extra-judicial divorce

Although Rhoma Irama's unregistered polygamous marriage and unauthorized repudiation were among the most high-profile examples of noncompliance with state marriage requirements, extra-legal marriage and divorce are not rare. In order to determine the prevalence of extra-judicial divorce we use the results of a large-scale family life survey conducted in 1993 to estimate the total number of divorces occurring in any single year. We then compare this number of self-reported divorces to the number of cases decided each year by the Islamic courts.[68] This comparison shows that a large percentage of self-reported divorces was not processed by the courts.

We estimated the number of divorces by years based on demographic results from the 1990 census and rates from the 1993 Indonesia Family Life Survey (IFLS). The IFLS is based on personal interviews from a probability sample of 7,224 households spread across 13 provinces. Together these provinces encompass about 83 percent of the national population. Persons were asked the dates of each marriage and divorce. Divorce rates are calculated as the number of divorces occurring in a given year divided by the married population for that year.

According to the 1990 Census, 40.6 percent of the total population was married. We also assume that 87 percent of the population is Muslim. Thus 35.3 percent of the total population is assumed to be married and Muslim. The formula for calculating the estimated number of divorces in any year is:

[no. of divorces = r × population × .353]

where r is the divorce rate for a given year and population is the total population for that year. These values have been calculated and entered in Table 1.

Table 1

Year	Divorce Rate:*	Estimated Muslim Divorces	Five Year Moving Average‡	Court Authorized Divorces	Court Divorces as % of Self-Reported Divorces
1971	1.1446	479,717			
1972	1.5522	668,771			
1973	1.4397	635,113	573,242		
1974	0.9970	450,322	553,826		
1975	1.3283	614,290	517,035	32,800	
1976	0.8461	400,635	510,268	133,419	
1977	0.9612	484,815	511,536	191,077	37.35
1978	1.2113	601,281	480,050	245,511	51.14
1979	0.8985	456,660	483,193	257,337	53.26
1980	0.8775	456,861	482,657	256,112	53.06
1981	0.7823	416,351	456,978	226,758	49.62
1982	0.8862	482,134	434,389	222,758	51.28
1983	0.8503	472,887	409,721	212,552	51.88
1984	0.6047	343,715	392,277	207,361	52.86
1985	0.5739	333,518	369,661	204,132	55.22
1986	0.5568	329,133	339,556	199,781	58.84
1987	0.6138	369,053	331,875	174,949	52.72
1988	0.5271	322,362		164,046	
1989	0.4908	305,312		162,063	

* where the rate is the number of persons reporting themselves divorced in that year expressed as a percentage of the married population. (In 1989, that rate was about 1 person in every 200 married persons or 1 couple in every 200 married couples existing in that year.)

‡ the "moving 5 year average" is the average of the figure for that year and those of the two years prior and following.

Our analysis of the survey data reveals two important facts. First, analysis of the survey indicates a substantial decline in both the divorce rate and the absolute number of divorces over the period studied (see also Cammack, Young, Heaton 2000). Second, and more to the point of the present study, a comparison of the estimated number of Muslim divorces occurring each year with the total number of cases decided by Islamic courts each year indicates that no more than about half of all Muslim divorces are processed through Islamic courts.

Reasons for lack of compliance

We are not aware of any systematic attempt to identify the various reasons for the failure or refusal to comply with statutory divorce requirements. Our general conclusion, which is based on an unsystematic investigation of the issue carried out over several trips to Indonesia and confirmed by comments of other observers, is that practical considerations of cost, convenience, and knowledge of the law's requirements are the principal reasons for non-compliance with statutory divorce procedures. While there is some evidence of principled defiance of the law's commands, the more common reason for non-compliance is a simple judgment that the costs of adherence in terms of expense and inconvenience outweigh the perceived benefits.

One factor that inhibits compliance is ignorance of the law's requirements. Communicating accurate information about changes in long-standing requirements for marrying and divorcing across Indonesia's large and far-flung population is a difficult task. The state has undertaken to publicize the Marriage Act in various ways. One frequently sees charts describing the procedures for marrying and divorcing at local government offices, such as the office of the *lurah* or village head, the local religious affairs office, and the Islamic courts. These charts provide a step-by-step depiction of the process of marrying and divorcing using simple visual illustrations of the various offices and officials whose cooperation and permission are required. Though we are not aware of specific programs, the government has certainly publicized the law through the nation-wide network of village level quasi-governmental women's groups known as the *Pembinaan Kesejahteraan Keluarga* (Family Welfare Movement or PKK). It is also likely that the government has used the machinery of its more aggressive family planning initiative to communicate information about the Marriage Act.

The government and other organizations supportive of marriage and divorce reform have also used popular forums to communicate information about the Marriage Act. The *Kongres Wanita Indonesia* (Indonesian Women's Congress or KOWANI), an association of women's groups with strong ties to the government, has published both guides to the Marriage Act and comic book-style pamphlets containing stories of characters facing divorce, polygamy, and underage marriage. The plots of these simple stories portray the characters processing their marital affairs through the courts and other governmental offices in accordance with statutory procedures. One of us observed a brief spot broadcast in a movie theatre before the beginning of the feature with a cartoon-style drawing of an elderly man covered by the type of shawl characteristic of Islamic clerics and bearing a written admonition that to be valid marriages must be registered.[69]

Not surprisingly, progress in the project of informing the public about the new requirements to marry and divorce has been slow and gradual. A series of studies on marriage and divorce commissioned by the Center for Demographic Studies at Gajah Mada University in the late 1970s found that a majority of the population of marriageable age was not aware of the requirements of the Marriage Act relating to minimum marriage age. Six of the seven studies we examined—carried out in Jakarta (Muliasakuauma 1982), Central Java (Kasto 1982), North Sumatra (Arian 1982), South Sumatra (Mahmud 1982), North Sulawesi (Inkiriwang 1983), South Sulawesi (Kassim and Idrus 1983), and South Kalimantan (Mahfudz 1982)—found that fewer than half of the respondents were aware of the existence of the marriage law, and in some areas awareness of the law was as low as fifteen percent. The level of awareness of the Act was generally higher among males than females, and higher among the married respondents than among the unmarried. The only location where the level of awareness of the Act was high was in one of the villages surveyed in Aceh. The researchers attributed the high level of awareness in that village, where more than 90 percent of the males reported familiarity with the Act, to the fortuitous presence in the village of a respected expert on local custom who had explained the changes wrought by the Act to the villagers.

The surveys used in these studies were completed in 1978 or 1979, only three or four years after the Marriage Act was implemented. Although we are not aware of any more recent attempt to measure awareness of the Act, knowledge of the statute has surely increased significantly since the late 1970s. This rising awareness has not, however, resulted in increasing rates of compliance. The ratio of all divorces to authorized divorces was almost exactly 2:1 in 1978, the year the surveys were conducted. That ratio varied little through the 1980s when awareness of the law was pre-sumably rising.

One reason for non-compliance with the divorce requirements of the Marriage Act is that Indonesian Muslims find compliance burdensome. The simplest divorce requires at least three court hearings. Additional hearings are necessary if either party opposes the divorce or if there are disagree-ments concerning property, spousal or child support, or child custody. The procedures for obtaining a divorce in an Islamic court are quite simple and generally adapted to the needs and abilities of the ordinary Indonesians who invoke them. But while divorcing in an Islamic court does not ordi-narily require the services of a legal advisor, it does entail a certain amount of paperwork and bureaucratic annoyance. The parties must obtain a letter of residence from the local village head (*lurah*), and must present an original state-issued marriage certificate. For most litigants, the court staff translates the couple's wishes into a cognizable legal claim or claims, and completes the forms that constitute the complaint or petition. Additional procedures are sometimes required to give notice to an absent spouse; the parties must secure the attendance of witnesses; and the court may require documentary evidence of the couple's property. While the process is simple and the courts comparatively comfortable and informal, the experience is probably confusing and somewhat intimidating for most rural folk and urban poor. Moreover, although Islamic courts are now located in almost every district (*kabupaten*) and municipality (*kotamadya*) throughout the country, and some courts conduct travelling hearings, attending court is nevertheless a considerable burden for many people, for whom ready means of transportation are not available. Furthermore, fees are assessed for obtaining documents from village heads, for filing the case, for every court hearing, and for registration of the divorce at the local Office of Religious Affairs. Additional informal payments must often be made to court clerks, village heads, and sometimes others whose services are required. Though obtaining a legally recognized divorce is comparatively quick and simple, it is always easier to terminate the marriage with an extra-judicial *talak*.

Thus, one reason for the frequency of unauthorized divorce is the cost and inconvenience of state divorce requirements as compared to a repudiation. Another, probably more common reason, is the unavailability of or inconvenience of obtaining an authorized marriage certificate. The saga of Rhoma, Ricca, Veronika, and Erwin illustrates one of the reasons for the contracting of unauthorized marriages. Polygamy, though not entirely forbidden by the Marriage Act, requires prior approval by a court. Men who wish to take a second wife but are unable or unwilling to obtain judicial authorization may go through an Islamic ceremony but never obtain the approval or documentation that is required by the state. Because documentary proof of the marriage is necessary for a court-authorized divorce, those who enter into unapproved marriages will invariably secure an unapproved divorce should the marriage fail.

A desire to enter into polygamy is only one of the reasons for contracting an undocumented or "secret" marriage (*kawin sirri*). Another, probably more common reason for secret marriages is that one (or both) of the parties is under age. The Marriage Act includes a minimum marriage age requirement—18 for males and 16 for females—and proof of age is required for a state-sanctioned marriage. Until relatively recently, early marriage was very common among many Indonesian ethnic groups, and marriages by persons who have not yet attained the legal age to marry continue to occur with some frequency even after the passage of the Act (see Jones 1994; Cammack, Young, Heaton 1996). In some cases parents pressure their children to go through an Islamic ceremony if they fear that the young couple is, or is likely to become, intimate. Other reasons for underage marriage include cultural attitudes that encourage parentally-arranged marriage of girls as soon as they achieve sexual maturity, and the economic burden on parents of non-productive children in school.[70] It is probably generally assumed that a legal marriage before a marriage registrar will soon follow, but it sometime happens that the union collapses and the marriage is terminated before the formal ceremony occurs. In addition to minimum age to marry, the statute also requires that marriage partners who have not yet reached the age of 21 have parental consent to marry. Early marriages are especially unstable. Because a court divorce requires an official marriage certificate, couples who marry below the minimum age without obtaining court approval and a marriage certificate have little choice, and little reason, to follow statutory procedures if they choose to divorce.

Finally, some couples fail or refuse to document their marriages for the same reasons of cost and convenience that inhibits compliance with state divorce requirements. These couples invariably divorce out-of-court. The association of unauthorized, "secret" marriage with extra-judicial divorce is sufficiently common that some marriage registrars take the view that there are essentially two marriage regimes, one for registered marriages and one for marriages that are not registered, and that compliance with court divorce procedures is required only for those marriages that are officially recognized.

When asked about non-compliance with the Marriage Act's divorce requirements, judges and other observers are often anxious to distinguish between non-compliance for benign or even honorable reasons, such as lack of awareness of the law or the need to arrange a quick marriage to prevent young lovers from sinning, and defiance of the Act's requirements, which most observers insist is rare. Most Indonesians probably do not have strong opinions about the Marriage Law and its relation to Islamic doctrine. The requirements of the Act are likely viewed with the same resigned acceptance as other bureaucratic inconveniences imposed by the state. On the other hand, judges and Religion Department officials sometimes offer apologetic interpretations of the Act as a mechanism for encouraging responsible marriage behavior. On this view, the requirements of establishing grounds for divorce and obtaining judicial approval to pronounce the *talak* promote the more perfect implementation of Islamic law. The Act's divorce provisions bring Islam's purely legal doctrines more nearly into line with its moral injunctions by requiring that divorce occur only under circumstances in accordance with Islamic morals.

While most Indonesians either accept or welcome the changes contained in the Marriage Act, there is also occasional evidence of pockets of resistance. Rejection of any state interference with Islamic law, together with a demand for wider state enforcement of Islamic doctrines generally, is a central tenet of scattered Islamist or neo-Wahhabi groups that exist around the country. In addition, some local Islamic elites who would not be considered "extreme" also reject any modification of Islamic marriage and divorce rules. Judges we interviewed on the island of Lombok, where the level of non-compliance is reportedly high, attributed the frequency of extra-judicial repudiation to the strong influence of Islamic scholars and teachers known locally as *tuan guru*. We also interviewed a marriage registrar in Lombok who insisted that Indonesians do not wish to be bound by the requirements of the Marriage Act, and boasted about the large number of unauthorized marriages and divorces in his village.

Thus, non-compliance with the divorce rules contained in the Marriage Act is primarily a result of neglect and avoidance rather than principled rejection and refusal. Nevertheless, disregarding state definitions of marriage and divorce would hardly be an option in the absence of some alternative set of rules for organizing intimate relationships. That alternative, of course, is Islam. And while Islamic procedures are appealing in part because of their simplicity, Indonesian Muslims continue to adhere to Islamic marriage doctrines because those doctrines continue to receive the endorsement of the mainstream of the Indonesian Islamic establishment. That fact is shown most clearly by an official legal opinion issued in 1989 at the annual congress of the country's largest Islamic organization, the Nahdlatul Ulama. The question before the Congress was:

> What is the status of a *talak* pronounced in court, and what is the relation between a court *talak* and one pronounced extra-judicially, in relation both to the number of *talak*s and the determination of the wife's waiting period? (Masykuri 1997, 343)

The legal opinion issued by the 1989 Congress in response to the inquiry made clear that an extra-judicial *talak* is given the same effect as a *talak* pronounced in court, and spelled out the consequences. If the husband has already pronounced a *talak* out of court and then utters a second *talak* in the presence of the court, the second judicial repudiation is counted as a second *talak*, and the wife's waiting period commences with the first *talak*. If the first *talak* has become final because of the expiration of the waiting period, or if the judicial repudiation is a fourth *talak*, then the *talak* pronounced in court is not counted. Nor is a *talak* pronounced in the presence of the court counted if it is uttered in response to force or simply for the purpose of repeating an earlier action. To be sure, the Nadhlatul Ulama does not speak for all Indonesians. But for Indonesian Muslims who find state-mandated divorce procedures irksome or expensive, a marriage blessed by Islamic principles alone offers a simple and appealing alternative.

Conclusion

Family life, no less than economic activity and other aspects of social life, is subject to the pressures for change incident to the increased level of interaction among the peoples of the world caused by vastly greater mobility of people and ideas. The Indonesian family in particular is subject to multiple global influences. These include global Islam, industrialization, images of family and gender projected in global media, and nationalism, the nation state, and the logic of purposive legal regulation. Moreover, the various forces impinging on the family are not necessarily in alignment. To complicate the issue further, when it comes to matters of intimate relationships and the family, global forces are especially apt to be deflected or transformed as they encounter stubborn local "folkways." Thus, while industrialization resulted in higher divorce rates in much of the world, the same forces have reduced the frequency of divorce in Indonesia. The forces of globalization are affecting family law and the conduct of family life, but not necessarily in the direction of a single global model.

Over the past quarter century the Indonesian state has attempted to implement uniform national marriage and divorce rules and to promote its model of family life predicated on stable, monogamous, free-choice marriage. The analysis presented here has demonstrated that this project has been only partially successful. On the one hand, the state has effected a remarkable transformation of official Indonesian Islamic marriage doctrine, especially as it relates to divorces initiated by men. Through a long, gradual process, the Muslim male's traditional power of unilateral divorce has been quietly if not covertly subjected to legal regulation. Moreover, whereas orthodox doctrine grants special divorce privileges to males, Islamic divorce in Indonesia is now available to husbands and wives on essentially equal terms.

The state's efforts to affect behavior have been less impressive. While the state bureaucracy now applies a uniform body of Islamic divorce rules, those rules have only limited purchase with ordinary Muslims. The law requires that all divorces receive judicial approval, but only about half of all divorces are processed through the courts. Nearly half of all divorcing couples continue to divorce on their own, confirming William Faulkner's observation that, in matters of family life as well, "the past is never dead; it's not even past."

Despite the widespread evasion of statutory divorce requirements, the significance of the government's accomplishments should not be underestimated. While it is generally easier to rewrite laws than to redirect behavior, Islamic legal doctrines, especially personal law, has enormous symbolic significance, and resistance to legislative interference with received doctrines is often intense. The fact that the law of divorce has been changed is itself highly significant, even if the reforms are not always obeyed. Moreover, while many Indonesians simply avoid state divorce rules, and while, as demonstrated elsewhere (Cammack, Young, Heaton 2000), legal rules restricting divorce have had little or no direct effect on divorce behavior, changes to the law that require reasons for divorce and grant increased rights to wives are undoubtedly changing popular attitudes, and new ideas about marriage and divorce are an important element in the complex of factors that are driving divorce rates down. Law is more than simply regulation. And while law competes with other systems of meaning in shaping social understanding, law is not insignificant simply because it is not entirely dominant.

Seven

TOWARD A JUST MARRIAGE LAW: EMPOWERING INDONESIAN WOMEN THROUGH A COUNTER LEGAL DRAFT TO THE INDONESIAN COMPILATION OF ISLAMIC LAW

Siti Musdah Mulia, with Mark E. Cammack

Family law is a matter of surpassing importance in Islam, and has been since the time of the Prophet. The law of marriage, divorce, and inheritance is treated more thoroughly and in greater detail in the Qur'an than other subjects of a strictly legal nature. One of the signal contributions of Islam to seventh-century Arabian society was a dramatic improvement in the status of women both within marriage and in society generally. While Islamic doctrines regarding crimes and civil transactions have been replaced in most of the Muslim world by laws based on models that first developed in Western Europe, family law continues to be governed by some form of Islamic law in many parts of the Muslim world, including Indonesia.

In contemporary conversations, the importance of family law within Islam is most often mentioned in connection with efforts to resist changes to established doctrines. Conservative rejection of proposals to limit male divorce and polygamy and to equalize male-female inheritance rights is frequently cited as evidence of the central place of family doctrine within Islamic jurisprudence. But concern with marriage and inheritance is not limited to conservative defenders of the received doctrine; family law is also vitally important to Muslims who are committed to reinterpreting or renewing the legal tradition in response to the needs and realities of contemporary life.

In this chapter we examine an Indonesian draft Islamic marriage code that is based on the principle that the Qur'anic ideal for the Muslim family is founded on the fundamental Islamic values of human equality and freedom. The Code, referred to as the Counter Legal Draft (CLD),[1] differs from previous Indonesian family law proposals in that the CLD embraces the implications of the Qur'anic commitment to equality and freedom in a thoroughgoing and uncompromising way. The Draft is constructed on the premise that the realization of the Qur'anic vision of the family can be achieved only if the values of equality and freedom are reflected in all aspects of the formation and regulation of marriage and family.

The CLD was drafted by a seven-member committee of Islamic legal scholars led by the first author of this chapter in her capacity as Special Assistant to the Minister of Religion.[2] It was prepared under the authority of the Minister of Religion with the intention of submitting the draft for consideration by the legislature. Although the proposal was withdrawn from formal consideration before it was acted upon, the preparation of the Code was more than simply an academic exercise. The release of the Code should be understood as a contribution and invitation to the ongoing quest to understand the meaning of Islamic family law for contemporary Indonesian Muslims.

The first section of this chapter will outline the history of family law reform in contemporary Indonesia leading to the preparation of the CLD. Section II examines the CLD itself, beginning with a brief discussion of the interpretive assumptions and methodology underlying the CLD, followed by an examination of the content of the Code. The chapter will conclude with a brief summary of popular reaction to the release of the CLD in October 2004.

Family law reform in Indonesia

Dutch legal policy for the East Indies was based on the principle that the law that governed a particular transaction depended on the ethnic and religious identity of the parties. For purposes of applying this system, the entire population was divided into three "law groups"—Europeans, "Foreign Orientals" (*vreemde Oosterlingen*), and indigenous Indonesians. The determination of the law governing a particular transaction depended on assigning the parties to one of these groups (Gautama 1991, 4–7).[3]

Replacement of the colonial legal structure with a national legal system was a major priority of the new government upon achieving independence. This goal applied to all areas of law, but family and inheritance were regarded as matters of particular urgency. The colonial system of ethnically- and religiously-based law groups was regarded as incompatible with a modern nation state. Enactment of a national marriage law was also viewed as a means of cultivating an Indonesian national consciousness. In addition to these nation-building goals, women's groups sought changes to existing Islamic doctrines that permitted child marriage, unilateral male divorce, and polygamy, while some Muslim groups advocated codification of established practices locally considered to be sanctioned by Islam.[4]

If marriage law reform was considered especially important, it was also unusually difficult. A variety of marriage law proposals was put forward during the first quarter century following independence, but none was enacted (see Lev 1972). Although there were many obstacles to marriage law reform, the principal impediment to passage of a marriage law was disagreement over whether there should be a single statute applicable to all Indonesians or separate statutes for different ethnic or religious communities.

Indonesia's first president, Soekarno, remained in power from 1945 to 1965. His successor, Suharto, was assisted in his rise to power by an anti-communist slaughter in which Muslim groups played a considerable role. Once he had consolidated control, however, Suharto set about to dismantle the structures of Muslim social and political power, including the formal implementation of various aspects of Islamic law. In July of 1973 the Suharto government introduced a draft marriage law in the Indonesian legislature that would have greatly reduced the role of Islamic doctrine in Indonesian family law. As explained in the chapter by Cammack, Donovan, and Heaton in this volume, the statute that was passed in early 1974 as the National Marriage Act (Law 1/1974) differed fundamentally from the original proposal, and had the effect of consolidating the position of Islamic doctrine in Indonesian law.

The compromise embodied in the Marriage Act is not the final statement on the law of marriage or the place of Islamic marriage doctrine within the Indonesian state. Over the 30 years since the Act was passed there has been an ongoing process of judicial interpretation and executive and legislative revision and clarification. Under the direction of the Supreme Court and the Department of Religion, the Islamic courts have generally interpreted the Marriage Act in a manner favorable to the rights of women. A 1989 statute ostensibly dealing with the organization and powers of the Islamic courts includes rules on procedures for divorce that amount to revisions of the substance of the law of marriage and divorce (Law 7/1989; Cammack 1989). The most important development, however, has been the promulgation of the Compilation of Islamic Law (*Kompilasi Hukum Islam*).

The Compilation of Islamic Law (Compilation) is a code of marriage, inheritance, and charitable foundation rules that was promulgated as a guide for Indonesia's Islamic courts in 1991. The Compilation was drafted by a committee made up of representatives from the Supreme Court and the Department of Religion, and ratified by an assembly of religious leaders convened by the government for that purpose. The preparation of the Compilation followed carefully planned procedures that included researching and compiling authorities from both classical and contemporary sources and interviewing a broad range of Indonesian Islamic leaders. Although the Compilation is in the form of a code, it was not enacted by the legislature, but was implemented through a Presidential Instruction (Inpres 1/1991).[5]

The necessity for a code of Islamic marriage rules was justified on the basis of the need for uniformity in the application of Islamic marriage doctrines. The effect of Article 2 of the Marriage Act, which states the requirements for marriage, has been interpreted as incorporating by reference the Islamic law of marriage as state law. But since the content of Islamic marriage law is nowhere definitively specified, the decisions of Islamic courts on issues not addressed in the Marriage Act relied on Arabic-language compendia of Islamic doctrine or *fiqh* texts.[6] The government defended the need for a code of Islamic rules on the basis that the lack of uniformity in the *fiqh* sources created an unacceptable level of uncertainty and inconsistency in the application of the law, and that inconsistency in the decisions of the Islamic courts had caused "turmoil" within the Muslim community. The Compilation was intended to quell this turmoil.

Thus, the drafting of the Compilation was the government's response to supposed popular dissatisfaction over the lack of uniformity in the decisions of the Islamic courts. The lack of consistency in the courts' decisions is the logical consequence of the diversity of opinion found in the *fiqh* texts. Diversity of opinion, moreover, is the essence of the *fiqh* literature and Islamic doctrine. None of the legal scholars (*'ulamā'*) who authored the texts ever claimed that his opinion on any subject was absolutely correct or that the opinions of others were wrong. And yet while freedom of opinion is highly valued and protected in Islam, the principal objective of the government's codification effort was precisely to eliminate difference of opinion through the creation of a definitive and uniform positive law.

In a certain sense the government was successful in its attempt to put an end to the situation in which different courts decide the same issue in different ways. The Compilation has simplified the task of judges, for whom a clear and instantaneous source of reference is now readily available for many issues. But the Compilation has also had significant negative consequences. The existence of a single uniform reference has stymied creativity and adaptation within the law. Because the answers to legal issues are readily available in the Compilation, judges no longer feel the need to engage with the rich literature of the Islamic legal tradition. This, in turn, has stultified the exercise of independent reasoning (*ijtihād*) and effectively imprisoned Muslims in a legal straightjacket. While dynamic social change generates a steady stream of novel legal problems, such as domestic violence,

human trafficking, short-term marriage, cohabitation, and interfaith marriage, the law remains stagnant. This, of course, creates its own set of problems for both judges and society generally.

In designating the work as a "Compilation" rather than a "Code" it was
suggested that the task of the drafting committee was merely to restate in
a more accessible format a set of already existing doctrines. But none of
those involved in the project suffered from the illusion that the process
could be accomplished that simply. Islamic marriage law is not a body of
known or knowable rules, and any purportedly authoritative statement of
Islamic marriage doctrine is almost certain to elicit disagreement and debate.
Part of the purpose of the Compilation may have been to give greater certainty to the law, but some of the drafters also wished to use the project
as a vehicle for promoting a novel and generally progressive interpretation
of Islamic family law. Mindful of the fate of the 1974 marriage law proposal, however, the drafting committee was careful to enlist the participation of religious scholars in the drafting process so as not to repeat the
experience with the failed draft marriage law. At the end of the day, however, many of the reforms favored by the committee were unacceptable to
the religious establishment, and the Compilation as finally approved and
promulgated, like the Marriage Act, clearly reflects the influence of reac-
tionary defenders of traditional marriage doctrines.

The Counter Legal Draft: Empowering women

The Compilation was intended from the outset as a temporary step toward
a more permanent and satisfactory statement of Indonesian Islamic family, inheritance, and charitable foundations law. The decision to formulate
the law as a Compilation rather than a legislative enactment was based
on pragmatic reasons, and it was anticipated that the legal status of the
law would eventually be upgraded through enactment by the legislature.
As mentioned, the Compilation was promulgated in 1991 through the
issuance of a presidential instruction and designated as a guide or reference for the courts. This approach was chosen because of concerns that
the legislative process might take years to complete, and that achieving legislative agreement on such highly sensitive issues would be extremely difficult
or impossible. But the form that was adopted in lieu of legislation presented its own difficulties. The novelty of the process created confusion
and uncertainty over the legal status of the Compilation, and many courts
simply ignored it for several years following its promulgation.

In order to address these problems and to provide a firmer legal foundation for the marriage law of the country's Muslim population, the Bureau for the Study and Development of Islamic Law within the Department of Religion undertook the drafting of a marriage law for Islamic courts based on the Compilation. In addition to strengthening the legal status of the law, the draft also proposed the addition of new sections providing penalties for violation of its provisions.[7] For example, failure to register one's marriage could result in a fine and prison sentence.[8] Work on the draft was completed in late 2003.

Meanwhile, in 2001 the Ministry for the Empowerment of Women had announced a national policy of "zero tolerance" for violence against women and issued a National Action Plan for the Elimination of Violence Against Women.[9] The Action Plan specified the eradication of the socio-cultural roots of gender discrimination as one of the means for accomplishing this objective. The Compilation was singled out for special consideration because some of its provisions reinforced social attitudes that contribute to violence against women, particularly domestic violence.[10] Pursuant to the mandate of the National Action Plan, the Minister of Religious Affairs appointed a "Working Group for Gender Mainstreaming," which then formed a ten-person committee with the assignment of undertaking a study of the Compilation. Siti Musdah Mulia was designated as Chair of the committee.

The decision to review the Compilation was also influenced by a number of other considerations. The decentralization of governmental power that has occurred in Indonesia since the fall of Suharto has resulted in demands for the implementation or formalization of "Islamic Shariʿa" in a number of localities including, among others, West Sumatra, South Sulawesi, Cianjur in West Java, and Madura. Unfortunately, however, those urging the application of Shariʿa lack a clear conception of precisely what the Shariʿa is. The Working Group believed that preparation of a revised version of the Compilation of Islamic Law that is adapted to the needs and cultural circumstances of the particular areas could serve a useful purpose in responding to these demands.

Beyond these external factors in forming the need for revision, there are also serious problems with the Compilation itself. A number of recent studies have concluded that the Compilation is inconsistent with other binding national and international laws. Among the domestic laws that conflict with the Compilation are the Human Rights Act passed in 1999 (Law 39/1999), which emphasizes the protection and strengthening of the rights of women, the 1999 Law on Regional Government (Law 22/1999), which stresses the equal participation of men and women in the process of decentralization, and the 2004 Law on Domestic Violence (Law 23/2004).

International and regional instruments containing provisions in conflict with the Compilation include the 1948 Universal Declaration on the Rights of Man, the Convention on the Rights of the Child, the Convention Against Racial Discrimination, and the Cairo Declaration of the Islamic Conference.

The Working Group was also influenced by the record of family law reform in other majority Muslim countries, such as Tunisia, Jordan, Syria, Iraq, and Egypt, countries that have revised their family law repeatedly in the modern period. The history of family law reform in these countries manifests two general tendencies. First, the reform or renewal of family law has consistently sought the improvement of the position and status of women and the protection of the rights of children. Second, family law legislation in these countries departs from the classical *fiqh* texts on many issues. For example, after enacting a number of family law reforms the Tunisian Family Law Act of 1959 imposed a requirement that divorce can only be obtained through a court and abolished polygamy.

Finally, interviews of judges and other religious leaders conducted by the Drafting Committee in the provinces of West Sumatra, West Java, South Sulawesi, and West Nusa Tenggara found that a majority of those interviewed favored changes to the Compilation.[11] The individuals interviewed cited three primary reasons for supporting revision of the Compilation: First, although the Compilation had been in use for 14 years, there had been no systematic effort to assess its effectiveness, to gauge popular attitudes toward the Compilation, or to evaluate its continued relevance. Meanwhile, the results of a number of empirical studies by students and others had called for a re-evaluation or revision of the Compilation on the ground that some of its provisions were no longer suitable to contemporary circumstances. Second, the respondents believed that the legal status of the Compilation should be clarified through enactment by the legislature. And third, they felt that the substance of the Compilation should be expanded and amended to enable it to meet the practical demands of Indonesia's increasingly complex society. Four specific reform proposals received nearly unanimous endorsement: making registration with a government marriage registrar a requirement for a valid marriage; increasing the minimum marriage age for girls to 19, thus raising it to the minimum age currently applicable to boys; applying the doctrine of disobedience (*nusyuz*) to husbands and wives equally; and requiring the consent of wives for reconciliation following divorce.

The Drafting Committee began its work by undertaking a critical review of all three sections of the Compilation. This evaluation identified a number of specific doctrines that have contributed to the continued social subordination of women.[12] Among the features of the Compilation deemed to be in particular need of revision were the absence of a registration requirement in the definition of a valid marriage, the rules regarding minimum age, polygamy, the role and status of husbands and wives within marriage, and the rights of husbands and wives upon divorce. These five issues were regarded as matters of particular concern. More fundamentally, however, these and other doctrines that harm women or perpetuate women's subordination to men are reflective of a deeper problem that permeates the Compilation as a whole. The problem with the Compilation is not simply that it incorporates many standard *fiqh* marriage doctrines. At a more basic level, the problem is that the Compilation as a whole is grounded in a worldview in which women are presumed to be inferior to men. This outlook has its source in an interpretive methodology that is excessively literal and insufficiently attentive to historical context.

An Islamic marriage law that is faithful to the spirit of Islam must find its source in the first principles of the faith. The first and most fundamental principle of Islam is *tawḥīd*, literally "making one." At its most basic level, *tawḥīd* denotes Islam's commitment to monotheism, and finds expression in the declaration of faith—"there is no God but God and Muhammad is the Messenger of God." But the full significance of *tawḥīd* goes beyond an affirmation of monotheism. "*Tawḥīd* means that God is Oneness. God is Unity: wholly indivisible, entirely unique, and utterly indefinable. God resembles nothing in either essence or attributes" (Aslan 2005, 150). God is beyond description or comparison: wholly other.

The primacy of *tawḥīd* as the foundation of Islam is universally acknowledged, but the full implications of divine unity are frequently overlooked. *Tawḥīd* is too often misunderstood as applicable solely to the vertical relationship between humans and their Creator—as a doctrine regarding the attributes of God, the pillars of the faith, and similar matters. But the true significance of *tawḥīd* is inseparable from the everyday concerns of social relations among humans, including the relationship between men and women. This is because understandings of the relationship between God and his human creations have direct implications for the structuring of inter-personal and social relations in Muslim societies. The conviction that there is only one God, that God is without equal, and that God has neither child nor personification, can be interpreted as implying the principle of the equality of human beings before God. No human is above any other; rather, all are essentially equal. Because God alone is Lord, no human may be deified or exalted as an object of awe, worship, or unconditional obedience. Kings are not lords of their people, husbands are not lords of their wives, the rich are not lords of the poor. Fear of or unconditional obedience to kings, leaders, superiors, or husbands that exceeds fear and obedience to God is a denial of *tawḥīd*.

A logical inference from the Prophet's message of the indivisibility of the divine is the fundamental equality of God's creatures. The doctrine of *tawḥīd* is also the foundation for human freedom. Since the time of Adam mankind has been subject to various forms of human tyranny and oppression, as most of humanity has lived under the domination of others. The rich and powerful have used their wealth and power to repress the weak and the powerless. Slaves, the poor, women, and children have generally been the most oppressed. In addition to tyranny imposed by others, humanity has also been subject to the domination of their own false beliefs, values, and traditions. The worship of idols and the glorification of the tribe and tribal values in the pre-Islamic "age of ignorance" (*jāhiliyya*) produced their own forms of subjugation. Discrimination against women, for example, was justified by a patriarchal gender ideology that was rooted in the tribal value structure. Shame over the birth of daughters led to the murder by parents of innocent baby girls.

Just as *tawḥīd* is the foundation of Islam, the denial of *tawḥīd—shirk—*is the greatest evil. The word *shirk* is conventionally translated into English as "polytheism," but the concept of *shirk* is deeper and more complex than the English term suggests. A more accurate definition of *shirk* is the association of anything with God (Aslan 2005, 151). The worship of other gods is *shirk*, but it is also *shirk* in any way to anthropomorphize God, since identifying God with human qualities implies limits to God's boundless majesty and power. In its broadest sense *shirk* includes anything that in any way detracts from God's absolute oneness or impedes complete devotion to God and God alone. The Qur'anic condemnation of *shirk* applies not only to worship but to every facet of human existence. In the context of social relations, the prohibition against *shirk* means that no individual or group may exalt itself over any other individual or group. *Tawḥīd* requires obedience to God over every other allegiance. Kings and rulers may not dominate or reign over their people; the strong may not oppress the weak; white-skinned races may not esteem themselves above people of color; men can no longer consider themselves proprietors of women. Likewise, traditionally disadvantaged groups, like the poor, the weak, and women, may not acquiesce in domination by others, since in doing so the purity of *tawḥīd* is inevitably tainted.

While the Qur'anic commitment to the values of equality and freedom is total and unqualified, practical considerations have made immediate implementation of those ideals difficult, and thus necessitated the adoption of a gradualist approach to their full realization. Slavery, for example, is plainly incompatible with the principle that all human beings are free and equal before God. But despite its evident inconsistency with the message of *tawḥīd*, slavery could not be immediately abolished, since it was accepted as legitimate in many parts of the world. Prudence required that the emancipation of slaves be accomplished in stages. This gradual approach to the eventual complete abolition of slavery is manifest in, inter alia, the admonition to free slaves as compensation for various types of legal infractions, such as unintentional killing.

For the same reasons the full emancipation of women could only be achieved gradually. In Arab society before Islam women were regarded as not fully human, and for that reason lacked the rights to have their own opinions, to work, and to own property. Women did not even own their own bodies. Islam gradually restored the rights of women as free individuals— to give voice to their own convictions, to work for themselves, and to own property so as to be acknowledged as full members of society. During the time of the Prophet women were pictured as active and free. The figure of the ideal Muslim woman in the Qur'an is represented as an individual active in the fields of politics (Q 60:12), like Queen Bilqis who headed a powerful kingdom (Q 27:23); and also involved in the fields of economics (Q 16:97) as women in the story of the Prophet Moses in Madyan (Q 28:23). In the Prophet's time women were free to form their own opinions contrary to the opinions of their fathers or husbands (Q 66:11), and free to oppose public opinion. The Qur'an extols the rights of women to oppose all forms of tyranny in support of truth (Q 9:17).

Qur'anic images of women possessed of broad freedom to participate in all forms of public life contrast sharply with the actual conditions faced by Muslim women today. Although Muḥammad's work can be seen in part as a struggle to establish gender equality, the Qur'anic ideal of emancipation was not realized during his lifetime. Islam has adopted a gradualist approach to the full liberation of women. A case in point is the treatment of the rights of women to inheritance. In the pre-Islamic era women were regarded as property and were themselves objects of inheritance; with the arrival of Islam women assumed their proper place as subjects having inheritance rights. But to avoid social upheaval and in recognition of the existing social structure in which men bore the full burden of providing for the physical needs of the family, the inheritance portion of women was fixed at half that of men.

It would be a mistake, however, if the rule declaring a 2:1 division of inheritance between men and women were to be interpreted as justifying discrimination against women. The moral message of the 2:1 division is the principle of justice and fairness, and not a pronouncement on the worth of women as half of that of men. Like other specific rulings rendered during the founding era of Islam, the Qur'anic inheritance rulings are properly understood as the application of timeless and universal moral values adapted to the needs and understanding of seventh-century Arab society. The ruling that grants males a double share in inheritance is not an end in itself but a means toward the eventual realization of full equality between men and women. The foundational texts of Islam, especially those pertaining to women's issues, have often come to be interpreted in a highly ahistorical and decontextualized manner. As the foregoing examples illustrate, however, the purpose and goal of Qur'anic texts that relate to the conduct of social life is the eventual emancipation of humanity from all forms of bondage and oppression. For that reason, adoption of a literal or strictly textualist approach to these texts can lead to interpretations supporting dominant patriarchal cultural norms. Through the application of a contextual interpretive methodology that is sensitive to the background and social circumstances in which the text was revealed, alternative readings of the implications of such Qur'anic stipulations can be developed.

In undertaking a revision of the Compilation the Working Group was guided by six basic precepts. First, a reactualization of Islamic law is possible and desirable in order to meet the demands of social change. The scope of permissible change is limited, however, as the second premise of the Working Group is that reactualization of Islamic law extends only to the "branches" (*furū'*) of the law—the positive law, or the results of the scholar's interpretation of the Shari'a—which are partial and temporal in nature; it does not apply to foundational principles (*uṣūl al-kulliyyāt*), which are universal. Third, changes to the law should conform to the principle "preserve what is relevant from the past; but offer new proposals that are superior to past achievements." Fourth, maintain a critical attitude, but also due respect and high regard for the heritage of the classical scholars. Fifth, rationalization and reactualization of Islamic law demands in-depth study and thorough mastery of the Islamic tradition. Qur'anic exegesis and study of the Sunna must be directed toward achieving moral, intellectual, and contextual understanding, and avoiding overly formalistic approaches that are inevitably partial and local. Sixth, the reactualization of Islamic law must be faithful to the essential objectives of Islamic law (*maqāṣid aḥkām al-sharī'a*) and the welfare of the Islamic community (*umma*).

Substance of the CLD

The CLD puts forward a number of novel interpretations of Islamic law of marriage and divorce. The proposed changes, however, are greater than the sum of the parts. Taken together, the proposals contained in the CLD reflect a fundamentally different conception of marriage and the rights of men and women within marriage than those embodied in the 1991 Compilation.

Article 2 of the CLD characterizes marriage as a "powerful bond between a man and a woman entered into with understanding for the purpose of creating a family and based on the assent and agreement of the parties." This emphasis on marriage as an institution founded on awareness and choice is in conscious contrast to the analogous provision of the Compilation, which stresses that marriage is commanded by God and its performance a religious obligation. The values of autonomy and choice in marriage are reflected throughout the CLD. The traditional requirement that the marriage be contracted through an offer by the male guardian of the bride and an acceptance by the prospective husband, which is also contained in the Compilation, is not recognized in the CLD. Whereas the Compilation lists the "marriage guardian" (*wali nikah*) as one of five requirements (*rukun*) for marriage, the CLD requires the use of a guardian only if the parties lack legal capacity to marry because one or both is not of age, of sound mind, and mature. Under the CLD each party contracts his or her own marriage personally. In contrast to *fiqh* doctrine, in which the prospective wife is always in the role of the offering party and the prospective husband the accepting party, the CLD authorizes either party to act in either role.

The most notable feature of the CLD that sets it apart from standard interpretations of the law of marriage in Islam is its uncompromising commitment to the principle that women and men are equal within marriage. The principle of equality of the sexes is stated unequivocally in Article 47, which provides:

> The status, rights, and responsibilities of husband and wife are equal (*setara*), both in family life and in their life together in society.

This affirmation of the equality of husbands and wives contrasts sharply with the gender ideology of the Compilation. The Compilation defines the role of the husband as "the head of the family" and that of the wife as "homemaker" (Art. 79(1)); it declares the rights and status of husbands and wives to be "equivalent" (literally, "balanced" [*seimbang*]) (Art. 79(2)). Moreover, the role and duties of men and women within marriage are defined in the Compilation in highly paternalistic terms.[13]

The principle that women are full equals within marriage permeates the CLD and is the basis for a variety of specific doctrines. With respect to the minimum age to marry, for example, the CLD establishes a single standard applicable to both sexes. While the Compilation specifies minimum marriage ages of 16 for girls and 19 for boys, the CLD makes 19 the minimum marriage age for both parties. According to traditional practice, the prospective husband is obliged to give a marriage gift (*mahar*) to the prospective wife. The Compilation preserves the traditional doctrine intact, but the CLD makes payment of *mahar* an equal obligation of both parties (Art. 16). The CLD also departs from the Compilation and traditional doctrine with respect to the doctrine of disobedience (*nusyuz*). The Compilation preserves the traditional rule that a disobedient wife is not entitled to the financial support of her husband (see Art. 80(4)(a)(b)). A wife is disobedient if she refuses to perform her obligations (under Art. 83(1)) without valid reason. The CLD states that *either* spouse can be considered disobedient for failing to perform his or her obligations to the marriage or for violating the rights of the other party. If the matter cannot be resolved by the parties and their families, the wronged party is entitled to file a claim in court.

The arena in which application of the principle of equality within marriage has arguably had the greatest impact is in the law of divorce. Common interpretations of Islamic law grant husbands significantly greater rights of divorce than is available to wives. Muslim men can terminate their marriages at any time and without grounds or judicial approval by simply reciting the formula of repudiation (*talak*). The law with respect to the circumstances in which wives can obtain a divorce varies significantly, but the divorce rights of women are far narrower than men, and women generally require court action to divorce.

Over the decades Indonesian judicial practice had come to recognize comparatively broad divorce rights for Muslim women. But while Muslim men possessed the power to terminate their marriages on their own, all divorce options available to women required the intervention of the court. A principal objective of the marriage reforms initiated in the mid-1970s was to limit arbitrary divorce by Muslim men. Conservative Muslim interests, however, objected to any legislation perceived as derogating from Islamic law or impairing the *talak*. The Marriage Act accommodated these seemingly contradictory demands by preserving the husband's *talak* as the mechanism for terminating the marriage, but requiring that repudiations receive prior judicial approval and be pronounced in the presence of the court.

The CLD departs from both the Marriage Act and the Compilation in prescribing a single divorce procedure applicable to both men and women. The procedures that govern all divorces under the CLD resemble the *talak* procedure under the Compilation in that once the divorce petition is granted the petitioner is authorized "to pronounce (*mengikrarkan*) the divorce (*perceraian*) in open court and in the presence of the other party." This approach, wherein the act of the parties is decisive in terminating the marriage, reflects the essentially contractual character of the marriage bond under Islamic law and the fundamental value of human autonomy exercised within the parameters of the divine law.

Although the CLD divorce procedures are patterned after the Compilation *talak* divorce, the recognized grounds for divorce in the CLD differ from the Compilation. The illness or disability of a spouse is not recognized as grounds for divorce under the CLD, and a spouse who changes religion or leaves Islam cannot for that reason be divorced. The CLD provision regarding divorce for abuse or cruelty is also broader than the analogous Compilation provision; the Compilation requirement that the abuse or cruelty be severe (*berat*) is eliminated, and language is added to recognize other types of violence that do not qualify as abuse or cruelty as grounds for divorce.

Under generally recognized Islamic doctrine a husband has a limited right to reconcile (Ind. *rujuk*) with his wife and reinstate his marriage following two of three repudiations. A man exercises this right and reinstates his marriage by simply declaring reconciliation. The Compilation follows conventional doctrine in granting the husband the privilege of reconciliation, after a first or second repudiation, during the wife's waiting period (*'idda*, whose purpose is twofold: to protect a wife against her marriage being reinstated months or even years after the divorce, and to determine the paternity of unborn children). However, it departs from traditional practice in requiring that the wife agree to the reconciliation. A husband wishing to exercise his right of reconciliation is required to appear before the marriage registrar *accompanied by his wife*. After the husband pronounces the reconciliation, both parties are required to sign the reconciliation registry. A reconciliation recorded over the wife's objection can be declared invalid by a court.

The CLD reconciliation provisions go beyond the reforms contained in the Compilation by making both the right of reconciliation and the requirement of a waiting period reciprocal. Both parties to the marriage observe a waiting period following divorce during which they may not marry or receive offers of marriage. The waiting period for the wife is measured as three menstrual periods or until the birth of any child that she may be carrying at the time of the divorce; the divorced husband's waiting period is declared to be equal to the waiting period of his former wife. Reconciliation is available to either spouse during the waiting period. As in the Compilation, the right of reconciliation must be exercised in the presence of the marriage registrar and two witnesses. The CLD includes an added protection against unwanted reconciliations by requiring an express statement of agreement at the time the reconciliation is pronounced.

Both the Compilation and the CLD have provisions on the *li'ān* procedure applicable in cases of unchastity. *Li'ān* is a criminal doctrine, but because it has the effect of dissolving marriage it has long been considered an avenue to divorce. As conventionally interpreted, a husband who believes his wife to have engaged in adultery is offered the opportunity to swear four oaths of accusation followed by an oath of self-imprecation if his accusation is false. The wife is then offered the opportunity to deny the accusation, followed by her own oath of imprecation. The Compilation recognizes the *li'ān* procedure and follows majority opinion in making the *li'ān* available exclusively to men. The CLD *li'ān* procedure is in all respects identical to the Compilation except that it is made available to either party.

One of the most controversial features of the Compilation and a point on which the Compilation takes an approach that is narrower than the majority opinion within Islamic jurisprudence is the rule regarding marriages across religious lines. The generally accepted view within the schools of Islamic law permitted a Muslim man to marry a Christian or a Jewish woman, but disallowed marriages between Muslim men and other non-Muslims, as well as all marriages between Muslim women and non-Muslim men. The Compilation takes the restriction on inter-religious marriage a step further, prohibiting all marriages between Muslims and non-Muslims. The CLD, by contrast, rejects all religious restrictions on marriage. Article 52 of the draft states that "the marriage of Muslims and non-Muslims is permitted," and that such marriages are "based on the principles of mutual respect and esteem for the right of free exercise of religion and belief."

Reception of the CLD: Praise and criticism

The CLD was officially made public in September of 2004. Predictably, the proposal provoked intense and sharply different responses from the Muslim community. Vocal and often strident groups of fundamentalists or Islamists were intensely critical of the proposal.[14] These critics derided the proposal as secular and un-Islamic, and suggested that it was supported by foreign money and influence in order to sow division within the Indonesian Muslim community. The leading representatives of this group included the Majelis Mujahidin Indonesia (Indonesian Council of Mujahids, MMI), the Front Pembela Islam (Islamic Defenders' Front, FPI), Hizbut Tahrir Indonesia (Freedom Party), and a conservative faction within the Majelis Ulama Indonesia (Council of Islamic Scholars). An article by Chairman of MMI's Executive Committee Irfan Awwas entitled "The Confused Methodology of the Draft Compilation of Islamic Law" condemned the CLD as a product of beliefs and approaches taken over from secular philosophy, literary criticism, and contemporary movements within Christianity.[15] The interpretive approach employed by the drafting committee, according to the article, is not the approach that developed in the Islamic tradition, but is the "hermeneutic methodology" of, among others, Paul Ricoeur, Michael Foucault, and Wilfred Cantwell Smith. In addition to its non-Islamic origins, an approach that looks beyond the language of the text to consider its historical and socio-cultural context is unacceptably flexible and subjective, and can be used to support any result the interpreter wishes. An article attributed to Hizbut Tahrir denounced the CLD as an example of a slavish acceptance of democracy and secular values rather than obedience to God.[16] Another Hizbut Tahrir article identified the CLD with "liberal Islam" which, according to the author, subordinates authentic principles of Islamic jurisprudence to the secular Western cultural values of gender, human rights, pluralism, and democracy.[17]

The CLD also drew a critical response from some more mainstream Muslim thinkers. While some critics fitting this description articulated suspicions of foreign support for the project and a covert agenda of dividing Indonesian Muslims,[18] the most common criticisms were that the CLD exceeds the limits of permissible reinterpretation or that it conflicts with accepted doctrine. The first objection is based on a distinction recognized by many scholars of Islamic law between texts whose meaning is certain ($qat^\varsigma\bar{\imath}$) and those that are uncertain ($zann\bar{\imath}$). While texts whose meaning is uncertain are subject to interpretation, according to this view, texts that are clear and certain are not. Because the CLD departs from texts that are regarded as certain, its conclusions are considered unsound.[19] Tahir Azhary, who then held the chair in Islamic Law at the University of Indonesia, cited the CLD provisions on the inheritance rights of the deceased's children and on marriage between Muslims and non-Muslims as examples of interpretations that conflict with Qur'anic texts regarded as clear and certain.[20] Tahir also objected to other aspects of the CLD, the provision that a woman can contract her own marriage without the use of a guardian (*wali*), for example, on the basis that the CLD provision does not conform to doctrines agreed upon by scholars. Another prominent scholar of Islamic law, Huzaemah Tahido Yanggo, professor at the prestigious Islamic State University in Jakarta and member of the Majelis Ulama Indonesia, expressed a broader disagreement with the proposal. Huzaemah criticized the approach used to produce the CLD, which she characterized as improperly focusing on the meanings (*maqāṣid*) rather than the letter of the text and affording too broad a scope for reason and considerations of public interest.[21]

Although critics of the proposal attracted the most attention, feelings were just as strong among supporters of the CLD. Prominent among groups supporting the CLD were the Lembaga Bantuan Hukum Apik (Legal Aid Society for Women), the Komnas Perempuan (National Commission on Violence against Women), Solidaritas Perempuan (Women's Solidarity for Human Rights), the two women's affiliates of the Nadhlahtul Ulama (Fatayat NU and Muslimat NU), and a range of NGOs working on issues relating to discrimination, human rights, and pluralism. In March of 2004, for example, Komnas Perempuan urged the government to rescind its decision shelving the proposal. In support of the appeal Komnas Perempuan Chairwoman, Kamala Chandrakirana, pointed out that reported cases of violence against women increased nearly 100 percent between 2003 and 2004, and argued that existing definitions of women's rights and a politicization of religious identity had contributed to the problem.[22] An alliance called the Network for Strengthening Civil Rights, consisting of about forty individuals representing mass organizations and NGOs, has been formed to campaign for the CLD and for amendment of the Marriage Act. The proposal is also widely supported among progressive academics. This is borne out by the fact that the CLD is being studied in almost all of the country's post-secondary Islamic institutions, and that the CLD is a popular thesis topic among students. Among the country's large Muslim organizations, Muhammadiya, Matlaul Anwar, and PERSIS took no position on the proposal, while the Nadhlahtul Ulama issued a statement rejecting the proposal.[23]

The two issues that emerged as the most contentious in public discussions of the CLD were inter-religious marriage and polygamy. That these doctrines should engender disagreement is not surprising, since these issues implicate sensitive questions about gender roles and group identity that have stirred controversy since before Indonesia achieved independence. In response to the mounting controversy, Minister of Religious Affairs Maftuh Basyuni announced in February 2005 that the CLD was being withdrawn from consideration.[24] In announcing the withdrawal of the CLD Basyuni offered little in the way of explanation beyond stating that the draft had created "unrest."

Conclusion

The controversy over the proposal for a revision of the Indonesian Compilation of Islamic Law replayed many of the same issues that had been debated 30 years earlier at the time of the enactment of the National Marriage Law. A number of the controversial features of the CLD had also been proposed in the initial draft of the 1974 Marriage Act. Like the CLD, the draft marriage law would have abolished polygamy, authorized inter-religious marriage, required registration for a valid marriage, and granted wives divorce rights equal to the divorce rights of husbands. Those proposals were objected to when the draft was presented for consideration in the legislature, and were removed from the bill before it was approved.

There are significant parallels between the experience with the Marriage Act in the mid-1970s and the proposed revision of the Compilation of Islamic Law in 2004. But there are also equally significant differences—differences that reflect major changes in Indonesia and Indonesian Islam in the three decades since the Marriage Law was proposed. The CLD grew out of Indonesia's vibrant women's movement and is based on the principles of freedom and equality. The reforms in the marriage law proposal, by contrast, were put forward by an authoritarian military regime, and were inspired by a conception of the ideal "modern" family and the supposed necessities of economic development. While the CLD is grounded in the Islamic legal tradition, the Suharto government's draft marriage law was an element of Suharto's program of suppressing Indonesian Islam.

The CLD did not secure legislative approval or even a hearing in its first outing. Stung by the intensity of feeling generated by the proposal, the Indonesian government withdrew the CLD from consideration and has distanced itself from the project. The CLD will not soon become law, but it continues to be an important stimulus to further debates on the reconceptualization of Islamic law in modern Indonesia, and thus represents a valuable contribution to a remarkably robust and diverse set of conversations among contemporary Muslim thinkers and activists there.

Eight

THE INDONESIAN ISLAMIC JUDICIARY

Mark E. Cammack

The role of Islamic doctrine in state law was perhaps the single most divisive issue at the time of the founding of the Indonesian state, and it has been a recurring source of controversy ever since. The original preamble to the draft constitution in 1945 contained language that would have obligated the state to "carry out Islamic law for adherents of Islam." Opposition to this preamble, referred to as the "Jakarta Charter," was so intense in some quarters that it threatened to derail the entire process. When the final version of the constitution was promulgated on August 18, 1945 the language regarding Islamic law had been removed. There have been a number of attempts to restore the Jakarta Charter to the constitution in the years since 1945, but none of those efforts has been successful.[1]

The debate over the Jakarta Charter excites passionate feelings on both sides of the issue. As a practical matter, however, constitutional language regarding Islam may be less important than the strength of the institutional structures that apply Islamic law. Unlike many countries with large Muslim populations, where state-sponsored Islamic legal institutions have been eliminated or absorbed into the secular legal system, the Indonesian Islamic legal system has expanded and grown stronger over the past half century. The backbone of Indonesia's Islamic legal apparatus is a nation-wide system of Islamic courts. The system consists of more than 340 first instance courts, called *Pengadilan Agama* (literally, Religious Courts), and an additional 25 Islamic appeals courts, called *Pengadilan Tinggi Agama* (Religious High Courts). The Islamic court system is staffed by some 2,700 judges and processes nearly 150,000 cases each year.

This chapter provides a broad overall view of the history and current composition and functioning of the Islamic judiciary. The first section traces the origins of the current system of Islamic courts to its creation by the Dutch in the nineteenth century, and outlines the expansion of the system to cover the entire country after independence. We then examine changes made to the Islamic courts to accommodate a dramatic increase in the courts' caseload following passage in 1974 of a national marriage law. The chapter concludes with a brief profile of the Islamic judiciary and a discussion of the operation of the courts in the performance of their principal function in processing divorce claims.

Colonial origins of Indonesia's Islamic legal system

Institutions for the implementation of Islamic law have operated in parts of island Southeast Asia since at least the seventeenth century. The origin of the current system of Islamic courts, however, is generally identified with a Dutch Royal Decree of 1882 that served as the principal legal basis for the Islamic court system for more than a century, and had a lasting effect on the character and composition of Islamic tribunals in Indonesia. The Decree authorized a system of Islamic tribunals called "Priests' Councils" (*priesterraden*) to function alongside the existing ordinary courts on the islands of Java and Madura. As the label indicates, these tribunals were collegial in nature, consisting of the chief religious official of the district (*penghulu*) and from three to eight member judges, who were chosen from the local religious elite. A minimum of three judges was required to make up a quorum. Although the *penghulu* received a small civil service salary in his capacity as religious advisor to the local civil court, the member judges were not civil servants and received no government compensation. Instead, they received a portion of the fees paid by litigants and a share of the estate in inheritance cases, which was also a principal source of remuneration for the chairman. Because the *priesterraden* had no enforcement powers, enforcement of the tribunals' decisions required an executory decree from the local civil court.

The next major government initiative relating to the administration of Islamic justice was in the 1930s. Regulations issued in 1937 changed the name of the *priesterraden* on Java and Madura to "*Penghulu* Courts" (*penghulu-gerecht*), and created new institutions, called "*Kerapatan-Qadi*," in South Kalimantan. In order to promote the independence of the courts and improve court management, the regulations provided for the payment of salaries to court chairmen and the addition of a salaried clerk. The regulations also established an Islamic appeals process with the creation of two appeals courts—one for Java and Madura, called the *Mahkamah Islam Tinggi*, and one for South Kalimantan, called the *Kerapatan Qadi Besar*.

The final element of the 1930s era reforms related to the courts' jurisdiction. Under the 1882 Decree the substantive competency of Islamic tribunals was limited to matters of marriage, divorce, and inheritance. A regulation issued in 1937 reduced the competency of the Islamic courts further by transferring inheritance jurisdiction to the civil courts. This change reflected the influence of the Dutch "*adat* law" school of jurisprudence, which held that the only authentic law in the Indies was indigenous customary law, and that Islamic rules were relevant only insofar as they had been "received" into the region's custom. The restriction of the jurisdiction of Islamic tribunals to matters of marriage and divorce was based on the results of ethnographic studies that purported to show that those issues were carried out according to Islamic legal prescriptions but inheritance practice was governed by custom.

Islamic courts after independence

The subordinate status of Islamic legal institutions was naturally blamed on Dutch hostility to Islam as long as the Dutch controlled the state. But as the outcome of the debate on the Jakarta Charter demonstrates, Indonesian Muslims are themselves divided on the question of state enforcement of Islamic law, and independence did not dramatically improve the prospects for wider application of Islamic law or greater powers for the Islamic courts. One important change that did occur at independence concerned administrative control of the courts. In a move intended to mollify Muslim interests for the removal of the Jakarta Charter from the constitution, the leaders of the new state created a Ministry of Religion as a part of the executive branch (Lev 1972, 43–5). The portfolio of the Ministry of Religion included administration of the Islamic courts. The effect of placing the Islamic courts under the authority of the Ministry (later Department) of Religion rather than with the civil courts under the Ministry of Justice was to ensure that Islamic institutions remained under the control of Islamic groups, rather than that of the more secular-minded nationalists who dominated the rest of the state bureaucracy. Also critical to the survival of the courts was the emergence of Islamic political parties, which were able to check to some degree the secularizing and modernizing tendencies of the executive. Thus, while Islamic leaders often disagreed over issues relating to Islamic law and some favored the eventual absorption of the Islamic courts into the civil judiciary, there was enough support for the continued existence of a separate Islamic court system to prevent the abolition of the courts or a further encroachment on their powers (Lev 1972, 63–75). When the nation's first law on judicial organization and procedure was enacted following the transfer of sovereignty (Law No. 1951), Islamic interests were able to marshal enough clout to secure recognition of the existence of Islamic tribunals as a part of the national legal system, even though the drafters of the statute in the Ministry of Justice clearly favored their abolition (Lev 1972, 65). The 1951 statute did not expressly authorize Islamic courts, but stated that provision for the administration of Islamic justice would be made through a separate government regulation. This language provided the basis for the eventual establishment of a nation-wide system of Islamic courts.

Following the passage of the 1951 statute the Ministry of Religion set about to unify, centralize, and, to the extent possible, expand the Islamic court system into those parts of the country where courts were not then formally established. The Ministry worked with local leaders to acquire control over existing Islamic tribunals and established a limited number of new courts by means of ministerial regulation. The Ministry was also able to use local Religious Affairs offices, which existed throughout the country, to assert some control over marriage and inheritance in areas without Islamic courts. Finally, in 1957 the cabinet approved a government regulation (*peraturan pemerintah*) authorizing the formation of Islamic courts everywhere in the outer islands where they did not already exist (PP 45/1957). Patterned after the Royal Decree of 1882, the 1957 regulation authorized the establishment of Islamic courts, styled *Pengadilan Agama* or *Mahkamah Syariah*, wherever there were civil courts, and granted the courts a territorial jurisdiction co-extensive with the civil courts (PP No. 1, 1957, Art. 1). The new tribunals were to have the same collegial organization as the courts created under the Dutch era regulations (Art. 2, 3). Unlike the existing courts, however, the substantive competence of the new courts included inheritance as well as marriage and divorce (Art. 4(1)), resulting in a disparity between the powers of the courts in Java, Madura, and South Kalimantan and those elsewhere in the country.

Thus, the Islamic court system was able to survive and even expand in independent Indonesia despite opposition from some segments of the bureaucracy, especially the Ministry of Justice, whose lawyers—trained in the civil law tradition—considered the existence of sectarian tribunals to be incompatible with a modern national state. But while defenders of Islamic courts had enough leverage to protect them against threats of abolition or absorption into the civil judiciary, the Islamic courts suffered from inadequate budgets and a general neglect that left them ill-housed and with staffs that were both too small and inadequately trained (Lev 1972). Many courts, especially those in the outer islands, did not have their own court buildings and court sessions were held in the back rooms of other government offices or the residence of the court chairman. All Islamic courts suffered from insufficient support staff. Some courts did not have a full-time court chairman, but relied exclusively on part-time member judges. By comparison to civil court judges, Islamic court judges were badly paid and poorly educated.

The 1974 National Marriage Law

The most significant development in the modern history of Indonesia's Islamic courts was the passage in 1974 of a National Marriage Act (Law 1/1974). The Act, which is applicable to all Indonesians regardless of religion, does not address the Islamic courts directly, but assigns significant new functions to Islamic tribunals in the regulation of underage marriage, polygamy, and divorce. The new functions granted to the Islamic courts in the implementation of the Marriage Act had the effect of greatly expanding the courts' caseload. This increase in the workload of the courts necessitated far-reaching changes in their organization and staffing.

The most significant change made by the Marriage Act as it relates to the Islamic courts concerns divorce. As explained above in the chapter by Cammack, Donovan, and Heaton, prior to the passage of the marriage law, a Muslim man could divorce his wife extra-judicially by simply pronouncing the repudiation (*talak*). The government's initial marriage law proposal would have banned the *talak* outright and required proof of grounds and a judicial order for a Muslim man to divorce. When some Muslim groups refused to go along with this scheme, a compromise was agreed upon whereby the *talak* was preserved as the mechanism for dissolving Muslim marriages, but the exercise of the *talak* was placed under the supervision of the Islamic courts. The law also requires that Muslim men wishing to repudiate their wives demonstrate statutory grounds for the divorce. Thus, a man wishing to divorce is required to file a petition with the court containing a statement of his reasons for divorce and requesting the court to convene for the purpose of witnessing his *talak*. The court is charged to examine the sufficiency of the petitioner's reasons against the grounds for divorce in the statute, and convene for the purpose of witnessing the husband's *talak* if the petition is found to be adequate. The Act also assigns the courts new powers in the supervision of child marriage and polygamy.

The new responsibilities assigned the Islamic courts under the Marriage Act resulted in an enormous increase in the courts' caseload. In 1974, the last full year before the Marriage Law was implemented, the Islamic courts nationwide processed a total of 23,758 cases.[2] In 1976, the first full year after the implementation of the Act, the courts processed 133,419 cases.

As awareness of the requirements of the Act became more widespread, the number of cases grew further. By 1979 the growth in the courts' caseload peaked at an impressive 257,337 cases, an increase of more than tenfold.

A tenfold increase in caseload over the space of five years could be expected to impose a significant strain on any court system. At the time the Marriage Act was implemented in 1975 the Islamic courts were in many respects particularly ill-equipped to absorb the increased caseload. The Indonesian Islamic courts of 1975 were in important respects little changed from the courts created nearly 100 years earlier by the Dutch. Each court consisted of one full-time judge who served as chair assisted by a panel of member or "honorary" judges who were chosen from the local religious elite. Only a small fraction of the judges had a university education; the overwhelming majority of judges—both full- and part-time— had training in traditional Islamic religious sciences only. There was little in the way of support staff, and the courts possessed few of the managerial skills or bureaucratic procedures needed for the efficient handling of large numbers of cases.

In response to the challenges presented by the Marriage Act the Department of Religion undertook an ambitious program of expansion, restructuring, and modernization to equip the courts to carry out their new functions. In 1976 two new branches of the Islamic appeals court for Java and Madura were established in Jakarta and Surabaya (the provincial capital for East Java). Regulations issued by the Minister of Religion in 1978 and 1982 regularized and rationalized the management and administrative structure of the courts. Thirty-four new first instance courts and five new appeals courts were created in 1982. Between 1974 and 1982 the budget authorization for Islamic courts increased thirteen-fold. These increases applied to both the routine operating budget and the development budget.

The most complete statement of the government's intentions for the future development of the Islamic judiciary was unveiled in 1983 when the Department of Religion produced a plan for the "standardization" of the courts (Departemen Agama 1983). The plan, outlined in an internal Department of Religion publication titled *Standarisasi Pengadilan Agama dan Pengadilan Tinggi Agama* (Standardization of Islamic Courts and Islamic High Courts), set forth a bold agenda for improvement in the facilities and staffing of the courts and called for major changes in the organization of the courts and significant tightening of central government controls. These goals are reflected in the stated objectives of the plan, which included the facilitation of the effective and efficient use of resources in order to provide simple, speedy, and inexpensive adjudication, creation of effective control mechanisms at every level of the system through the establishment of a fixed bureaucratic management structure, and cultivation of a proper sense of authority through improvements in the physical surroundings in which the courts operate.

The most striking feature of the Standardization Plan is the level of detail. The plan contains specific instructions concerning a range of facilities and staffing matters, from the provision of ashtrays and wastebaskets for office staff to the educational qualifications for appointment to the highest levels of the Islamic judiciary. A section of the plan dealing with court buildings states that Islamic courthouses should present both a "uniform appearance and a distinctive aspect in order properly to express and reinforce the courts' authority." With respect to first instance courts, these objectives are to be achieved through the construction of low front, single-story buildings distinguished by three large pillars in front of the entrance. Because the first instance courts serve the public directly, the plan also calls for an interior central garden in order to lend a "fresh" feel to the surroundings. Appeals courthouses are described in the plan as two-story affairs, also with large pillars. The plan stipulates the precise layout and dimensions for two different sizes of first instance court buildings and a single model for appeals courts, including instructions regarding the function and exact size and arrangement of the rooms.

Office furniture, equipment, and books are all specified and enumerated in elaborate detail. The style, dimensions, and number of desks, tables, chairs, and cabinets are precisely described and illustrated with diagrams. Office appointments are keyed to position and rank. Those with higher civil service rank receive larger desks and more elaborate furnishings. Offices of echelon II level employees, for example, are furnished with, i.a., a globe, wall map, photographs of the president and vice president, an elite font typewriter, and a teak desk chair. Advancement from echelon IV to echelon III is accompanied by the addition of a telephone and a wall clock. All employees assigned to a desk are outfitted with a pencil box, desk almanac, and ashtray.

A list of the different articles of furniture, furnishings, and equipment required by each court contains 87 separate items. Quantities for each of these items are specified for each of six categories of courts—four classes of first instance courts and two classes of appeals courts. Depending on the type and size of the court, the number of Indonesian flags, for example, ranges from four to seven, the number of fans from eight to 16, the number of staff chairs from 17 to 35, and the number of black caps (*peci*) worn in administering oaths from three to eight. The plan also contains a listing of the books that are to be included in the court library. The books are divided into seven categories as follows: Qur'anic exegesis (14 titles),

Prophetic reports (*hadīth*) (13 titles), Islamic jurisprudence (24 titles), statutes and regulations (20 titles), accounting (11 titles), administration and management (two titles), and dictionaries (four titles).

The most important element of the Standardization Plan is the section relating to staffing. The blueprint specifies the staffing needs for each of four classes of first instance courts and for the high courts of appeal. The qualifications for appointment to the various positions are also stated. Each court is to be staffed with from five to 11 full-time judges, including a court chair and deputy chair. In an important change from past practice, all judges are required to hold civil service status and must have either a law degree from a university or a Shariʿa degree from an Islamic institute.

The Standardization Plan made equally far-reaching changes to court support staff. The policy prescribes support staff of from 23 to 29 employees depending on the class of court. The staff are organized functionally under a head clerk, one clerk each for law and administration, and sub-clerks with responsibility for complaint filings, petition filings, personnel, budget, and Shariʿa. The balance of the staff is made up of additional administrative staff, drivers, and messengers. All employees to the level of sub-clerks are required to have some degree of post-secondary academic training. The final section of the blueprint describes more than 20 types of official documents or reports that are produced or issued by Islamic courts, and sets forth estimates of the number of blank forms needed annually by each of the nearly 300 tribunals.

The changes to the Islamic courts reflected in the court Standardization Plan and other post-Marriage Act reforms are consistent with prior Department of Religion policy for the Islamic judiciary. Expansion, modernization, and centralization had been Religion Department objectives for the courts from the time the Department assumed control. But the improvements and reorganization described in the Standardization Plan were far more ambitious than anything that had been contemplated previously, and the implementation of the plan signaled a fundamental change in government policy with respect to Islamic legal institutions and a watershed in the courts' history. Prior to the enactment of the Marriage Act the future of the Islamic courts remained in doubt. Indeed, the original version of the marriage law (which was apparently prepared without consulting the Department of Religion) would have transferred jurisdiction over Muslim marriages from the Islamic courts to the civil courts; if approved this change would have effectively put the Islamic courts out of business. When the plan to vest control over Muslim marriages in the civil courts proved politically unworkable, the strategy changed from one transferring the functions of the Islamic courts to the civil courts to one of transforming the Islamic judiciary based on the model of the civil courts.

Integration of the Islamic courts into national judiciary

During the same period in which the Islamic courts were being centralized and modernized under the court Standardization Plan they were also being integrated with the rest of the Indonesian legal system. Prior to the enactment of the Marriage Law the Islamic judiciary was almost completely independent of the system of secular civil courts. From the time Indonesia assumed control at independence, the Islamic courts had been under the administrative authority of the Department of Religion rather than with the civil courts under the Department of Justice. The appeals process for Islamic courts also operated separately from the civil courts, since the highest appellate authority within the Islamic system was the Islamic High Courts, and cases from the Islamic system were not reviewable by the Supreme Court. This administrative and judicial separation continued even after the enactment in 1970 of a basic law on the judiciary that designated the Supreme Court at the apex of a theoretically unified Indonesian judiciary which included the Islamic courts.

The monopoly over the management of the Islamic courts that had been exercised by the Department of Religion since 1946 began to crack following the passage of the Marriage Act. Beginning in the 1970s the Supreme Court gradually assumed a role in both the development of Islamic law and the administration of the Islamic judiciary. The Supreme Court first began to assert authority over the Islamic courts in 1977. In November of that year the Court issued a regulation setting forth procedures to be followed by parties seeking cassation review in the Supreme Court of decisions by Islamic courts (Sp. Ct. Reg. 1/1977). The Department of Religion initially resisted the Supreme Court's attempt to intervene in the administration of Islamic law. Judges from the Islamic High Courts meeting in West Java issued a statement strongly opposing Supreme Court review (Working Group Committee Rep. of 26–28 Dec., 1977), and the Department of Religion sent a circular letter to all chairmen of the Islamic courts throughout the country, expressing opposition to Supreme Court cassation review and, in effect, instructing courts not to cooperate with litigants seeking cassation (Dept. of Religion Circular 89/1978).

For the next year the question of Supreme Court review of Islamic court decisions was extensively debated in the public press. Then, in mid-1979, the Supreme Court effected a de facto resolution of the matter when it issued two decisions on cases originating in the Islamic courts. The following month the Court announced the appointment of six justices—five men and one woman—as a special panel to hear cases from the Islamic courts. All six judges assigned to the special panel were from the civil judiciary and all six had been educated in secular universities, though at least two had studied in *pesantren* and were able to read Arabic. Shortly thereafter the Department of Religion reversed its position, rescinded its earlier directive to oppose cassation review, and instructed the courts that henceforth all requests for cassation were to be honored.[3]

The direct impact of Supreme Court review on substantive law is relatively minor. Islamic court judges generally take the view that a decision by the Supreme Court in one case is not binding on a lower court facing a similar issue in a different case. Moreover, even if the courts did recognize a principle of precedent, Supreme Court decisions are not routinely published, which means that lower court judges could not follow the decisions of the Supreme Court even if they wanted to.[4] While cassation review gives the Supreme Court only a limited leverage to influence the law applied by the Islamic courts, the establishment of lines of appeal from the Islamic judiciary to the Supreme Court is symbolically significant as an indication of the status of the Islamic courts within the Indonesian legal system and the Indonesian state. For the Islamic judiciary, association with the Supreme Court has a dual aspect. On the one hand, secular judicial institutions have always enjoyed higher status than the Islamic judiciary, and integration of the Islamic courts with the rest of the Indonesian legal system implies an equivalence between the two systems that redounds to the benefit of Islamic judges. But integration also carries risks for the Islamic courts. There is an inherent tension in the existence of sectarian tribunals that apply non-state religious law within a national state. So long as the Islamic courts remained independent of the Supreme Court and under the exclusive control of the Department of Religion they were largely insulated from the pressures to conform to the imperatives of a national legal system. The initial resistance of the Islamic bureaucracy to Supreme Court review of decisions by Islamic courts was based on the fear that cassation review might set in motion a process that would eventually compromise the courts' fundamental religious character.

The Department of Religion's misgivings about Supreme Court review of Islamic court decisions were eventually resolved in favor of wholehearted cooperation. Whereas the Supreme Court's initial overture had been received with suspicion and hostility, the Department quickly came to embrace

Supreme Court involvement with the Islamic judiciary, and actively cooperated with the Court as it expanded its role and influence.[5] In 1982 the Supreme Court extended its involvement with the Islamic courts beyond review of cases and began to assist in the administrative management of the courts. The Court's administrative functions were initially carried out through joint working groups set up with the Department of Religion to address issues of Islamic court staffing, administration, and facilities. These ad hoc structures were later replaced by establishment of a permanent "Section on Islamic Courts" within the Supreme Court and the appointment of a new office of "Deputy Chief Justice for Islamic Courts" to head up the Section.

In the years since the Supreme Court became involved in the management of the Islamic courts the Islamic system has come increasingly to resemble the parallel civil court system. I have no specific information on how the 1983 Islamic court Standardization Plan was drafted, but it is likely that the Supreme Court had a hand in the process, since the plan contains many features also found in the civil system, and was completed the year after the Supreme Court first became involved in the administration of Islamic courts. Other significant practices from the civil system that have been carried over into the Islamic courts include the case management system and the policy of regular rotation of judges. The establishment of a Section on Islamic Courts within the Supreme Court also paved the way for the appointment of judges from the Islamic bench to the Supreme Court. Though never more than a small percentage of the 51 judges who make up the Supreme Court, the inclusion of a contingent of judges from the Islamic system seems to have been accepted as a permanent feature of the Supreme Court. An important milestone was reached in the late 1990s when Judge Taufik, whose career had been in the Islamic courts, was appointed to the powerful post of Deputy Chief Justice.

The final phase of Islamic court integration with the rest of the Indonesian legal system began in 1999 as part of a broad package of structural governmental reforms following the collapse of the Suharto regime. An amendment to the basic law on judicial power approved in 1999 did away with the so-called two-roof administrative structure for Indonesian courts, in which control over the judiciary was shared between the Supreme Court and the executive branch. Under the two-roof system the Supreme Court had responsibility for "technical juridical" matters while an executive agency—either the Department of Justice in the case of the civil courts or the Department of Religion in the case of the Islamic courts—was in charge of administrative matters. As part of a fundamental restructuring designed to establish a stricter separation of governmental powers, the 1999 amendment declared an end to executive control over the courts and mandated the consolidation of judicial administration in the Supreme Court. A deadline of five years was set for the transfer to the Supreme Court of the Department of Justice's administrative functions over the civil courts. The Department of Religion had initially lobbied for a total exemption for the Islamic courts from the restructuring. While that effort failed, opponents of the change succeeded in blocking the specification of a timetable for relinquishment of Department of Religion control. In the end, however, resistance to the restructuring plan proved futile, and in June of 2004 full responsibility for administration of the Islamic courts was transferred to the Supreme Court.

The Religious Judicature Act of 1989

The Dutch decree of 1882 remained the principal legal basis for Indonesian Islamic courts for more than a century. Through the years advocates for state enforcement of Islamic law had pressed the case for confirming a permanent role for Islamic legal institutions within the Indonesian legal system, but many policy makers outside the Department of Religion would have preferred to see the courts absorbed into the civil courts or simply abolished. As mentioned, the initial version of the government's national marriage law proposal in 1973 would have effectively closed down the Islamic courts by transferring most of their powers to the civil courts. In 1983, however, the prospects for statutory recognition of the Islamic courts received a big boost when the Office of the State Secretariat, the powerful arm of the presidency that served as the clearinghouse for all legislation during the Suharto era, gave final authorization for the preparation of two bills relating to the Islamic courts—one bill on the organization and powers of the courts and another bill on the law of procedure (Departemen Agama 2001, 38). Busthanul Arifin, the Deputy Chair for Islamic Courts on the Supreme Court and an untiring supporter of Islamic legal institutions, was assigned as chair of the drafting committee. During the preparation of the legislation the two original bills were combined into a single consolidated proposal addressing both the courts and the law of procedure. In December of 1988 the Minister of Religion presented the proposal to the Indonesian legislature, and it was approved and signed into law a year later (Law 7/1989).

The Islamic courts bill generated substantial interest and controversy during consideration of the proposal in the legislature. Debate focused primarily on the broad question whether a system of sectarian courts was proper in an officially secular nation. For the most part, however, the statute as proposed and enacted simply ratified the status quo. The Act provides for the existence of first instance courts, called *Pengadilan Agama*, in every district (*kabupaten*) and municipality (*kotamadya*) throughout the country. Appeals courts, called *Pengadilan Tinggi Agama*, are established at the provincial level. Together these courts exercise judicial power for Muslim litigants in civil matters specified in the Act.

The statute's provisions regarding the organization and staffing of the courts conform to the Department of Religion's 1983 Standardization Plan. The Act states that the Islamic courts are comprised of court leadership, consisting of the court chair and deputy chair, member judges, clerks, secretaries, and bailiffs. The qualifications for appointment as a judge require, among other things, that the candidate hold civil service status and have completed either a law degree or a Shari'a degree (Art. 13(1)). Judges are eligible for appointment as chair or deputy chair after having completed at least ten years service as a judge (Art. 13(2)). With the exception of the bailiff, all statutory employees are required to have some post-secondary education. None need be civil servants.

The Act specifies the powers of the Islamic courts as including the power to hear and decide cases between Muslims in three broad areas: marriage; inheritance, testaments, and gifts performed according to Islamic law; and charitable foundations (*waqf*) (Art. 49(1)). The courts' marriage law jurisdiction is further defined as extending to all matters treated in the 1974 Marriage Act (Art. 49(1)). Twenty-two specific subject areas relating to marriage that fall within the courts' powers are listed in the elucidation of the statute.

The granting to the Islamic courts of full authority to apply the Marriage Act resulted in a significant extension of the courts' powers. Prior to the passage of the Religious Judicature Act, the courts' marriage jurisdiction extended only to matters addressed in regulations promulgated by the government implementing the Marriage Act. While regulations had been issued on the courts' powers to decide issues relating to the validity of marriage, including dispensation from minimum age requirements and granting permission for polygamy, and to suits for divorce (PP 9/1975), the courts lacked the authority to decide questions relating to the consequences of divorce, including child custody, division of property, and post-divorce support obligations. The listing of these matters in the elucidation to the 1989 statute has been interpreted as providing the necessary authorization for their exercise.

The provision granting inheritance jurisdiction to Islamic courts throughout the country is a change from prior law, since the Islamic courts for

Java, Madura, and South Kalimantan had lost their power to decide inheritance cases in the 1930s. The Act defines the courts' inheritance jurisdiction as including "designation of heirs, designation of the estate, designation of individual shares, and distribution of the estate" (Art. 49(3)). The courts' inheritance powers are subject to two limitations, however. The Islamic courts' inheritance jurisdiction is voluntary rather than compulsory, and resolution of disputes over ownership of property remain under the jurisdiction of the civil courts.

The committee charged with drafting the law on Islamic courts favored restoration of full inheritance powers to the Islamic courts throughout the country.[6] Opposition to vesting compulsory inheritance jurisdiction in the Islamic courts surfaced early on, however, expressed first by the Supreme Court during discussions of the draft legislation in 1984 (Departemen Agama 2001, 51), and then by the nationalist-oriented Indonesian Democratic Party (PDI) when the bill was debated in the legislature in 1989. In its formal response to the government's proposal, the PDI faction expressed the opinion that litigants should be granted the broadest possible choice of fora in the resolution of inheritance cases (Departemen Agama 2001, 110). Representatives of the government argued in response that a choice of law principle was implicit in the language of Article 49(1)(b), which empowers the Islamic courts to decide "cases relating to inheritance, wills, and gifts *that are carried out according to Islamic law*" (Departemen Agama 2001, 112). In response to PDI's demand that the choice of law principle be stated explicitly, the Armed Forces Faction suggested that, because the choice of law question was fundamentally a "sociological and philosophical matter," the issue should be addressed in the general elucidation rather than in either the statute itself or the elucidation of a particular article (Departemen Agama 2001, 113). This compromise won general acceptance, and language was added to the general elucidation stating that "prior to the [initiation of the] case the parties can choose which body of law shall be used in the division of the estate." If the parties elect to have the estate decided according to Islamic rules, the matter falls under the jurisdiction of the Islamic courts; if the parties choose either *adat* law or Dutch private law, the case is decided by the civil court.

Another apparently significant limitation on the inheritance powers of Islamic courts is contained in Article 50 of the statute. That article appears to deny to Islamic courts the power to resolve disputes over the ownership of property in cases falling within the courts' jurisdiction. In the event that such disputes arise, according to Article 50, the question of ownership must be decided by a civil court as a preliminary matter, after which the Islamic court may proceed to address the merits of the inheritance claim.

The prohibition against decision of questions of ownership, which is rooted in the historical status of Indonesian Islamic tribunals as essentially advisory bodies without real judicial power, would appear to impose significant limitations on the exercise of the courts' powers, since disputes concerning ownership of property at the time of death are common. In practice, however, the courts have largely if not entirely ignored the limitation, at least in cases in which all of those claiming ownership to the disputed property are parties before the court. In cases not requiring the joinder of additional parties, Islamic courts routinely decide ownership issues in a single proceeding with the underlying inheritance claim. The justification for this approach, which effectively reads Article 50 out of the statute, is based on the view that to halt proceedings in the Islamic court pending filing, decision, and appeal of claims relating to the ownership of property in the civil court would undermine the fundamental principle that justice be provided expeditiously and without delay.

Section Five of the Islamic Judicature Act addresses the law of procedure. Article 54 of that Section states that procedure in the Islamic courts is governed by the general civil procedure law except with respect to those matters specifically treated in the Act. The special procedural rules contained in the Act all relate to suits for divorce. The Act prescribes different procedures for divorces filed by husbands and divorces filed by wives. There is also a section setting forth a special procedure for "Divorces on Grounds of Adultery." This section codifies a version of the traditional *li'ān* doctrine, which permits a party who is unable to adduce proof of an alleged adultery to perfect his claim by swearing four solemn oaths in support of his suspicions. The most notable difference between the procedure set forth in the Act and the traditional *li'ān* doctrine is that the opportunity to prove a spouse's adultery by means of oath is made available to both husbands and wives.

Changing profile of Islamic courts

The reforms outlined in the Department of Religion's 1983 Standardization Plan and subsequently mandated by the 1989 Religious Judicature Act called for nothing short of wholesale transformation of the Islamic judiciary. Before the 1980s the structure of the Islamic courts was based on colonial legislation that prescribed a single full-time judge assisted by local religious notables. In 1977 there were a total of 225 full-time civil service judges in the entire system, fewer than one judge per court. Only a fraction of existing judges satisfied the educational requirements under the statute; the overwhelming majority of judges, both permanent and part-time, had been educated exclusively in traditional religious sciences. The reorganization plan called for the elimination of the use of part-time judges and their replacement by judges with civil service status and college degrees.

Immediate implementation of the reorganization plan was manifestly impossible. The blueprint required an estimated 2,372 judges. Because the process of hiring additional judges had commenced soon after the passage of the Marriage Act, by 1983 the number of permanent judges nationwide had reached 680, and of that number 401 had academic degrees (Departemen Agama 1984, 33). In order to achieve the targets contained in the restructuring plan the Department of Religion and the Supreme Court launched an aggressive program of recruitment with a goal of hiring 100 new judges each year. In the late 1980s the use of part-time judges was discontinued and benches were staffed entirely by regular judges. Because some courts, especially courts outside of Java, did not have enough judges to function without part-time staff, the Supreme Court authorized the temporary use of single-judge courts.[7] By 1989 when the statute on Islamic courts was approved the number of judges had reached 1,200. At that point the use of part-time judges was discontinued, and any remaining judges who did not have academic degrees were retired. Thereafter all court sessions were staffed entirely by full-time judges with qualifications required by the statute.

In 2004 the Department of Religion reported a total of 2,741 Islamic court judges—2,521 judges on first instance courts and 220 High Court judges (Departemen Agama 2004). The vast majority of judges on Islamic courts—almost 90 percent—have degrees from one of Indonesia's State Islamic Institutes (IAIN). Notably, however, nearly one-third of the judges (817) have university degrees (Departement Agama 2000).[8] Approximately eight percent of all judges (229) have advanced degrees—the rough equivalent of a Masters Degree (Departemen Agama 2004). The number of judges with both university training and post-baccalaureate education is likely to increase in the future, since additional education is a reliable avenue to promotion.

Judges appointed under the new standards have very different training and backgrounds from their predecessors. In the past the principal qualification for appointment to an Islamic court was an ability to read Arabic and some mastery of the *fiqh* literature. Academically educated judges, by contrast, have been exposed to a broader range of disciplines, including some degree of training in state law. The new cadre of judges also has different allegiances from their predecessors. In the past the part-time judges, and frequently the court chairmen as well, were recruited locally, and were individuals with strong ties to the community who spoke the local language and were familiar with local customs and values. Under the current system judges are hired through a nationwide recruitment and undergo a process of training and socialization in Jakarta before being sent into the field. Assignments are in principle based on considerations of administrative need rather than regional origin or ethnic identity. Additionally, the Department of Religion adheres to the policy followed within the civil courts of transferring judges to a new posting every five years. The purpose of the program of periodic reassignment is to prevent judges from becoming too rooted in a particular locality. In the past a judge serving as chair of a local court had no real prospect of promotion within the system. As employees within a theoretically homologous nationwide judiciary, today's judges expect to rise through the ranks. The career ladder for Islamic court judges now reaches from the humble member judge on a first instance court in a remote part of the country to a seat on the Supreme Court. While most judges cannot hope to get to Jakarta, virtually all judges can reasonably expect to advance to the position of court chair. Promotion within the system depends on performance as measured by bureaucratic standards prescribed in Jakarta.

The changes contained in the Religious Judicature Act have altered the demographic profile of the Indonesian Islamic judiciary. The professionalization of the judiciary placed younger judges on the bench since the part-time judges who made up two-thirds of most panels were typically older than their civil service counterparts. In 1983, for example, the median age of civil service judges was 41, while the median age of non-civil service judges was 59. Today nearly 60 percent of all judges are under the age of 45. The new qualifications also favor the appointment of ethnic groups, particularly the Javanese, which have greater access to formal education (Departemen Agama 2000).

The new recruiting standards have increased the number of female judges. Women have served as Islamic court judges in Indonesia since at least 1964 (Lev 1972, 110). In 1976 an assembly of religious scholars was convened to consider the legality of the practice. The assembly concluded that Islamic law permits women to serve as judges in all but criminal cases, and since Indonesian Islamic courts do not exercise criminal jurisdiction there is no legal obstacle to the appointment of women as judges. By 1983, among all full-time judges, 34 (five percent) were women (Departemen Agama 1984, 32–3). Over the next 20 years the proportion of women more than tripled. As of 2004 there were 461 women, 17 percent of the entire judiciary. The representation of women in the less desirable positions on support staffs is much higher.

Though not as dramatic as the changes to the judiciary, the support staffs of Islamic courts have also been thoroughly reconstructed. In 1974 the support staff for the Islamic courts totaled fewer than 2,000 (Departemen Agama 1984, 27). By 1982 the number had nearly doubled to 3,782 (ibid., 29). As of 2003 the Department of Religion reported a total of nearly 7,000 staff, 24 percent of whom had college degrees (Departemen Agama 2004).

The notion that the Islamic courts are understaffed and under-resourced is so well rehearsed that it is now uncritically repeated without apparent recognition of the enormous changes of the past quarter century. An assessment of the adequacy of the current staffing of the courts would require a more careful evaluation of the actual workload of the courts than has so far been attempted. In some respects, however, the physical provisioning of the courts has not kept pace with the increase in personnel. The Department of Religion reported in 2000 that all but nine of the Islamic courts have their own building. Most of these structures were built in the late 1970s or early 1980s when the push to accommodate the increased demands on the courts under the Marriage Act was greatest. Islamic courthouses are smaller, dingier, and less imposing than the civil courts. They are also likely to be located inside the *kampung* rather than on a major street. But family law institutions, which traffic in the concerns of ordinary people rather than the problems of the rich and powerful, are everywhere inferior to courts of general jurisdiction, and many of those who invoke the services of the Islamic courts probably appreciate the relative informality of the surroundings.

The courts do not appear to suffer for want of sufficient desks, chairs, and ashtrays. The appointments, however, are simple. Hearing rooms are rectangular spaces with a large, raised judges' table draped in green in the front of the room. The clerk assigned to serve as court reporter sits at a separate table one-half step below the three judges. Litigants or witnesses are seated on chairs facing the bench in the middle of the room. Chairs or occasionally simple, backless wooden benches line the back wall for use by family and supporters. Hearing rooms vary somewhat in size, but none of the hearing rooms I have seen is large enough to require the use of a microphone for the judges and witnesses to make themselves heard. Air conditioning is rare, and one cannot help but admire the fortitude of judges who sit for hours under heavy black robes in the stifling tropical heat.

The court chair and the chief clerk usually have separate offices. Member judges are accommodated in a single large room. A common area that is open to the public contains tables and desks for clerks and other support staff. Benches and a separate space are typically provided for litigants and witnesses waiting for their case to be called.

One area in which complaints about lack of resources appear to be well founded concerns office equipment. The courts often lack typewriters, much less computers. In 2000 the Department of Religion reported 2,207 Latin-script typewriters but only 252 typewriters with Arabic script for use by more than 300 courts (Departemen Agama 2000). Photocopy machines are rare or non-existent outside of the appeals courts, and carbon paper is still much in evidence. Office vehicles are also in short supply. As of 2003 there were 177 automobiles and 407 motorcycles for use by the 378 courts (Departemen Agama 2004).

The salaries and other remuneration of Islamic court judges have increased as the judges' educational attainment and civil service rank have risen. Judges holding certain leadership positions are also entitled to an official residence, but the number of houses allocated to the Islamic courts is not nearly sufficient to fill the need.

The work of the courts

The Islamic judiciary has jurisdiction over marriage, inheritance, and charitable foundations. In practice, however, the Islamic courts are primarily divorce courts. According to Department of Religion statistics, more than 90% of the cases decided by Islamic courts in any given year are suits for divorce. The next largest category of cases after divorce is requests for validation of marriage, followed typically by permission to enter into polygamy and requests for dispensation from minimum age requirements. The balance of the courts' caseloads is made up of issues relating to the obligations of the spouses and guardianship of brides and children. Inheritance cases comprise less than one percent of the total number of cases decided each year.

In addition to being large in relative terms, the absolute number of divorce cases decided each year by Islamic courts is also substantial. In 2003, the most recent year for which I have statistics, the Islamic courts decided a total of 145,593 cases. In the mid 1980s the numbers were significantly larger; in 1983, for example, Islamic courts decided an impressive 191,750 cases.

The Islamic courts process a large number of cases each year, but the majority of those cases present few complications, either legal or factual. Indeed, in many cases the court's function is more administrative than adjudicatory, since the court's only real role is to formally terminate a marriage that both parties have agreed to dissolve. Uncontested divorces can often be resolved in two or three short hearings, and require little in the way of evidence beyond proof of identity, residence, and the existence of the marriage. Cases that include claims for property, support, or custody of children are somewhat more complicated, but even these cases are typically resolved fairly quickly. The use of lawyers in Islamic courts is rare and in general not welcomed by judges. Apart from the usual complaint that lawyers prolong and complicate the proceedings, Islamic court judges emphasize the importance of addressing the parties personally in order to hear their stories and observe their demeanor and attitude. Court personnel assist the parties in formulating the claim and complying with procedures. Apart from necessary documentary evidence, such as marriage and birth certificates, the presentation of the case is generally completely oral.

The handling of divorce cases is sufficiently standardized that the course of a divorce suit can be described with some precision. When an individual or couple arrives at court seeking a divorce they are directed first to "Table 1." There a clerk questions the couple about the facts of the case and draws up either a petition if the claimant is the husband or a complaint if the divorce is being sought by the wife. Once the pleadings are complete the parties are sent to another clerk for payment of fees. The clerks then create a file for the case and forward the case file to the court chair. The chair assigns a panel of three judges to hear the case, and designates one of the judges to serve as chair of the panel. The panel chair then schedules the date for the first court hearing.

Under Indonesia's outdated and cumbersome civil procedure law the processing of a civil suit proceeds inchmeal through a drawn-out series of weekly or biweekly hearings. The first hearing of the case is devoted to the reading of the complaint. There then follows a succession of hearings for the reading of the answer and a series of replies (*replik*) and rejoinders (*duplik*) until at last the issues have been sufficiently narrowed to permit the taking of proof. The presentation of evidence is followed by more hearings for more formal submissions until in the final hearing of the case the court reads out the judgment.

To their credit, Islamic courts take a pragmatic approach to these requirements, and divorce proceedings in Islamic courts proceed more expeditiously than in the parallel civil courts. Hearings are typically scheduled for 9:00 a.m. and continue until all cases scheduled for that day have been completed. Most hearings are brief, generally no longer than three-quarters of an hour in duration. On the days when court proceedings are being held, parties congregate in the waiting area with friends and supporters waiting for their case to be called. At the first hearing of a case the parties are summoned to the hearing room and questioned about their name, age, residence, religion, and marital status. Answers are checked against the parties' identity cards to verify identity and confirm the court's jurisdiction. This is followed by a ritual inquiry from the judge regarding the parties' purpose in coming to court. After eliciting that the couple or one of them wishes to divorce, the court is required to counsel the couple with the aim of achieving a reconciliation. This counseling function is mandated by statute as a means of reducing the frequency of divorce, but in practice the courts' reconciliation efforts are directed primarily toward confirming the seriousness of the moving party's intentions. After delivering mild warnings about the negative consequences of divorce and securing an unequivocal declaration that the marriage is beyond repair, courts typically undertake to provide the couple with what they want.

After discharging its counseling function the court proceeds to address the merits of the case. The hearing is then closed to the public for the reading of the complaint or the petition. Because all divorce actions are in principle adversarial, the defendant is required to present a formal answer to the allegations, and is offered the choice of delivering an immediate oral response or submitting a written statement at the next hearing. Most defendants choose to speak. The plaintiff is then invited to reply to the defendant's response, whereupon there typically follows an informal and largely unrestricted give-and-take that enables the judges to discover the relevant facts, clarify the issues, and acquire a sense of the parties and their attitudes toward the case and each other.

The next hearing is for the purpose of proof. The general rule under the civil procedure code is that proof of any fact requires at least two items of evidence. An admission by an opposing party is evidence of the fact admitted, but must be supported by additional evidence to be legally sufficient. Islamic courts, however, generally take the view that an admission is sufficient in itself, and if the responding party admits the allegations of the complaint no further proof is required. The effect of this rule is to permit what amounts to divorce by consent of the parties. When the facts are disputed and proof is required, the usual rule from the civil code regarding two forms of proof applies. In another departure from standard practice, however, a party who is unable to muster two forms of evidence may take the oath and act as a witness in support of his or her claim. No distinction is made in the weight attached to male and female witnesses.

The courts' lenient and occasionally loose application of the law of procedure eases the burden of litigants seeking a divorce. This leniency is partially offset, however, by a special procedural rule applicable only in divorce suits requiring the moving party to secure the attendance of family members with knowledge of the facts. These "family witnesses" (*saksi keluarga*) function essentially as witnesses for the court, enabling the judges to seek confirmation of the facts. Though not explained in the legislation, this rule is apparently based on a recognition that the members of the couple's family are the persons most likely to be familiar with the relevant facts, but are disqualified from serving as witnesses because of the privilege rules. The statements of family witnesses are typically unsworn.

It is only relatively recently that the jurisdiction over the division of marital property and other incidents of divorce was added to the courts' powers. But Indonesian Islamic tribunals have a long tradition of exercising extra-legal jurisdiction, and many judges did not hesitate to decide property or custody issues before 1989, either because the parties requested the courts to act or because the judges' view of the circumstances seemed to call for intervention. Enforcement of decisions regarding property was typically achieved by withholding the divorce until the division decreed by the court had been carried out. While the absence of formal authority did not prevent the courts from addressing the consequences of divorce, most such questions were resolved privately in the past and continue to be resolved privately even after the courts' powers have been expanded.

Restoration of inheritance jurisdiction to Islamic courts has long been a priority among Indonesian advocates for state enforcement of Islamic law, and the achievement of that objective with the 1989 Religious Judicature Act was celebrated as the overdue rectification of a longstanding colonial wrong. Based on available statistics, however, the passage of the 1989 Act did not increase the number of inheritance filings in Islamic courts, and the total number of inheritance cases remains very small. Since 1990, the first year after the Religious Judicature Act went into effect, Islamic courts nationwide decided fewer than 1,000 cases per year in each of the five years for which I have statistics.[9] The frequency of inheritance litigation varies considerably around the country, and no doubt constitutes a larger proportion of the caseload for some courts than for others.

Since the inheritance jurisdiction of the Islamic courts is not mandatory it is possible that Muslims are exercising their option under the choice of law rule to have their cases decided by the civil courts. While some Muslims may be choosing the civil courts their numbers are small. The inheritance caseload of the civil courts is more than twice the inheritance caseload of the Islamic courts, but is nevertheless small in absolute terms; Department of Justice statistics report that the civil courts decide between 1,000 and 2,000 cases per year. The significant implication from these numbers is that inheritance litigation in either court is very rare.

The assistance of the courts in inheritance cases is sometimes requested even though there is no dispute among the heirs. This can occur for at least two reasons. Parties who wish to have an estate divided according to Islamic law but lack expertise in Islamic doctrine may request a judicial decree identifying the heirs and their respective portions. Parties sometimes also seek judicial decrees as legal proof required for transfer of title to land or to gain access to property in the possession of third persons—bank accounts, for example. The Religious Judicature Act specifically authorizes the Islamic courts to issue these ex-parte inheritance decrees as an exception to the general principle that Indonesian courts are prohibited from accepting non-contentious filings (Art. 107). According to Department of Religion statistics, non-contentious inheritance filings, referred to as Requests for Assistance in the Division of an Estate (P3HP), make up about one-fourth of the courts' inheritance cases. Other sources, however, have found that non-contentious filings comprise the majority of the Islamic courts' inheritance caseload.[10]

While most of the work of the Islamic courts is routine and uncompli-cated, that is not invariably the case. Difficult questions of law or fact arise more often in inheritance disputes than in divorce cases.[11] Disputes over ownership of property often present difficult factual questions both because of the absence of regularized land titles and because the courts are often called upon to determine the effect of attempted or purported property transfers that are not evidenced by convincing documentation. Identification of the deceased's relatives and the extent of the deceased's property are also complicated, particularly when, as often happens, the court action is not filed until years after the deceased died. Much of the evidence in inher-itance cases is in the form of witness testimony, since family and property records are often not available. When an estate is divided many years after the deceased died, the relationships among people and property will have changed from the time of the death, and witnesses with knowledge of the relevant facts will be even harder to come by.[12]

Conclusion

Over the past three decades Indonesia's Islamic courts have experienced a remarkable transformation. In the 1970s the courts were essentially informal, non-professional institutions subject to relatively loose controls by the state. In order to enable the courts to fulfill their new functions under the 1974 Marriage Act the Islamic courts were restaffed with an entirely new cadre of academically trained judges and the Islamic judiciary was thoroughly integrated into the national legal system. Whereas the courts had previously based their decisions on religious texts, judges now look almost exclusively to legal authorities promulgated by the state.

The post-Marriage Act restructuring of the Islamic courts was designed to enable the courts to manage an enormous increase in cases. The question arises, however, whether the changes to the courts have had the effect of alienating them from their clientele. Despite their shortcomings (or perhaps because of those shortcomings) the unrestructured Islamic courts were generally successful in addressing the needs of those who used them. It might be asked whether in the process of becoming more efficient the courts have sacrificed the qualities that made them effective.

It is my sense that the professionalization and bureaucratization of the Islamic judiciary has not fundamentally altered the essential institutional culture of the courts. A 2002 survey of public perceptions of justice sector institutions by the Asia Foundation found that the courts were regarded as generally trustworthy and capable (Asia Foundation 2002). While not without weaknesses, Indonesia's Islamic courts are a relative success story within Indonesia's otherwise dysfunctional legal system.

Nine

FAIRNESS AND LAW IN AN INDONESIAN COURT

John R. Bowen*

Introduction

Recently, historians, sociologists, and anthropologists (Dupret 2000; Libson 1997; Moors 1995; Powers 1994; Tucker 1998) have addressed the ways in which Islamic court judges draw on broad social norms in making their decisions. In the general spirit of this enterprise, in previous works (Bowen 1998, 2000, 2003) I sought to identify the social norms underlying legal reasoning by Indonesian judges. Here I shall focus on the language of justification employed by judges in deciding inheritance cases, taking as my examples several recent decisions from the Islamic court of Central Aceh, in the highlands of Sumatra.

Indonesia has a nationwide system of Islamic courts that runs parallel to its system of civil courts. In each of these two legal systems, one may appeal from a court of first instance to the provincial appellate court. The Supreme Court may review cases from either an Islamic or a civil appellate court. The jurisdiction of the Islamic courts is limited to matters of marriage, divorce, and inheritance in cases involving Muslims. Jurisdictional conflicts in cases involving mixed-religion couples do arise and have not been definitively resolved. To a great extent, the organization, procedures, and the language of decisions in the Islamic courts are modeled after Western-style civil courts (Lev 1972).

The judges who serve on the Islamic courts are appointed by the Indonesian government, and they are rotated from one post to another during their careers. Most current judges graduated from one of Indonesia's State Islamic Institutes, the IAIN (Institut Agama Islam Negeri), where they specialized in Shari'a. Some judges also obtained a law degree from a general university, and all chief judges now are required to have done so. At the IAIN, they learn the basics of the legal method (*uṣūl al-fiqh*), details of the substantive law areas in which they will be ruling (marriage, divorce, and inheritance law), legal procedures, and relevant bodies of Indonesian state law. Since the mid-1990s they also have studied the state Compilation of Islamic Law in Indonesia. Until a new arrangement took hold in 2005, they were responsible to two distinct bodies: as civil servants they worked for the Ministry of Religion, but the Supreme Court oversaw their competence as judges. Since 2005 the Court has responsibility for both administrative and juridical matters.

As with many other Indonesian courts, the Islamic court in the town of Takèngën, Central Aceh, developed out of older Islamic legal institutions. During the Sukarno years (1945–1965), the court was staffed by local men, some of whom had no formal legal training. Some of these early judges served on the court for decades. Under President Suharto (1966–1998), efforts were made to rotate judges more frequently and to demand a more uniform legal training. In the 1980s and 1990s, the province-level appellate court in Aceh exercised increasing degrees of control over local courts by overturning decisions and by summoning local judges for frequent "upgrading" sessions, where they were informed of new legal developments and sometimes upbraided for incorrect judicial decisions.

The legal and political situation has changed rapidly, and often violently, since the early 1990s. In 1991, Suharto proclaimed that a newly-written Compilation of Islamic Law was to be the sole source of law for judges serving on the Islamic courts (as well as for other civil servants). Since 1991, judges have justified their decisions in terms of that Compilation. In Aceh, the escalation of violence in the 1990s and early 2000s led many judges to flee the province. In 2001, a new set of laws for Aceh province, now renamed *Nanggroe Aceh Darussalam* (The State of Aceh, the Abode of Peace) to capture resonances of its past as an Islamic sultanate, promised that "Syariah" would be the basis for laws and that the courts would now be called "Mahkamah Syariah." By 2006 a peace agreement appeared to have taken hold, permitting the provincial courts, the provincial administration, and Jakarta to negotiate and broker a new working relationship.

A sketch of the Islamic court

The court hears cases from throughout the district of Central Aceh, an area with about 200,000 people. Takèngën is the largest town both in the district and in the Gayo highlands, a larger area comprising Central and Southeast Aceh districts. Although the majority of highlands residents speak the Gayo language, considerable numbers of Acehnese (the majority people in the province) and Javanese also live there—the Acehnese mainly as traders, the Javanese as farmers, brought to the area through the government resettlement program called transmigration. Acehnese domination in provincial politics and economics long has been an irritant to many in the highlands, and at present there is considerable support in the highlands for the creation of a separate province, to consist of the non-Achehnese areas.

Takèngën has a civil court and an Islamic court. Since the 1970s, civil court judges have come from outside the province, and have looked at Takèngën as a way-station in a series of short-term appointments. Many of the Islamic court judges, however, were born in the highlands, speak the Gayo language, and are knowledgeable about Gayo social norms (*adat*). In court these judges play the role of the wise counselor, and often correct witnesses who mistakenly describe a rule of Gayo *adat*. Many Islamic judges served for long periods because the Indonesian government had trouble recruiting enough judges to staff the court. The court should have nine judges, but at the very least it must have three judges in order to hear cases involving disputes over property transfers (inheritance, gifts, and bequests). In order to reach even that minimum number, the provincial government approved the appointment as judge of a local man, Aman Arlis, who had served as chief clerk in the 1950s and 1960s and did not have a law degree. By the late 1990s, the court had been fully staffed with three Gayo judges, two Achehnese judges, one Malay man from the city of Medan who had lived for a long time in North Aceh, and three Javanese judges. (The three Javanese judges fled the highlands in 1999 to escape violence that was directed against Javanese settlers.) For a period of a few months in 1988, a woman judge (from West Sumatra) had served on the bench.

The court meets in a one-story wooden structure on a quiet residential street in the center of town. The court is near shops, primary schools, the mosque, and the district administrative offices. Two large buildings are joined by an open walkway. During court hours people mill about in the front courtyard, most of them relatives or supporters of someone appearing before the court that day. The scene is chatty and informal; people sit and openly discuss the cases at hand with much less animosity than I expected to find. Even in 2000, as violence was increasing in the highlands, the court was busy.

A man or woman coming to the court for any reason first visits the clerks' building, which in the 1990s housed about a dozen male and female court clerks. Some clerks already have their law degrees and are waiting for judicial appointments; others have completed only high school. A clerk will interview the petitioner, usually in an effort to persuade him or her to settle the matter privately. Failing that, the clerk will help prepare the paperwork for the case and often give advice about how the petitioner should present his or her case, for example, suggesting which of many possible complaints about marital life are legitimate grounds for divorce.

An informal division of labor operates among the clerks. Some clerks do most of the initial interviewing, while others travel to villages to survey land under dispute. In the mid-1990s, three men shared duties as court reporter, sharing also a single dark sport coat that they would don before entering the courtroom. One clerk usually is charged with filing current cases, law books, and copies of the official Ministry of Religion journal *Mimbar Hukum*, and another with trundling older cases into the archives, a small back room with dusty, nearly forgotten files dating back to the 1940s.

Next to their large, shared work area is the office of the chief clerk, the *panitera*, who supervises the stream of paperwork flowing between clerks and judges. There is also a small, one-judge courtroom. The second court building contains a larger courtroom, in which all cases tried by a panel of judges are heard, and two judges' offices: one for the chief judge and another shared by the remaining judges. Each office has a back door, which permits the judges to enter the larger courtroom without first exiting the courthouse.

Most of the clerks who had been working at the court in the early 1990s were still at their jobs in mid-2000 when I next visited the highlands. In one room three clerks were typing up documents on resounding manual typewriters. One woman had become the informal leader of the clerks, and it was to her that most court visitors first addressed themselves. Dressed in a white headscarf and a long print dress worn over trousers, she addressed everyone, judge, supplicant, or colleague, in the same friendly and direct manner. On a June day in 2000 she was busy typing up divorce papers for a Javanese couple in their late teens, lamenting to all who could hear, "Oh, you're so young and you're divorcing! Well, I guess you're no longer meant to be together (*tidak jodoh lagi*)." She asked them if they had children, and if the wife was pregnant, maintaining an informal tone with the couple. In another room a senior clerk was dealing with a large group involved in an inheritance case. A young man was visibly fuming about the fact that his adversary was occupying the house and selling goods from it even while the suit was in progress. The clerk kept urging him not to take matters into his own hands (*main hakim sendiri*), i.e., not to turn a civil suit into a criminal matter.[1]

The jurisdiction of the Islamic court is strictly limited to certain types of cases; all others are heard at the civil court. The Islamic court hears cases regarding marriage or divorce, as well as matters directly related to marriage and divorce, such as the reconciliation of a couple or the custody of children. As in all provinces of Indonesia, marriage and divorce cases involving Muslims may be brought only to the religious court. The court also hears demands to determine the rightful heirs to an estate, to adjudicate disputes over a gift or bequest of property, and to divide marital property as part of (or following) a divorce. In theory, disputes heard by the Islamic court may involve non-Muslims, if, for example, the heirs to an estate include people of more than one religion, or if a wife has converted to Christianity and then is sued for custody of her child. Such cases rarely if ever arise in Aceh, where all Acehnese or Gayo are Muslim, but they sometimes receive considerable popular attention when they arise elsewhere in Indonesia.

The frequencies of different types of cases have changed markedly through the years. In its first few decades (1945–1970s), the Islamic court in Takèngën heard a relatively small number of cases per year. Most of these cases involved either a request to register a marriage, or a dispute over the ownership of land. By the 1980s and 1990s the court heard a large number of divorce cases each year and fewer cases in other categories. The divorce cases involved requests for permission to take a second wife, demands that a husband meet his obligations to support his wife, petitions for divorce, requests that the court formalize the reconciliation of a divorced couple, and requests to determine the proper division of an estate. Table 1 lists the cases decided in the calendar years 1992 and 1993, and during the first half of 1999.

Type of case	Number of cases decided in:		
	1992	1993	Jan–July 1999
Marriage			
Validation of marriage	28	25	0
Petition for polygamy	11	4	1
Petition for husband's support	3	2	0
Divorce			
Husband's petition	110	99	80
Wife's petition	95	102	91
Child custody	2	0	0
Property division			
After divorce[2]	0	3	4
Inheritance	12	5	3

Table 1. Number of cases decided in the Central Aceh Islamic court, 1992, 1993, and January–July 1999, by type. (Source: court records)

Cases involving marriage occupy a small part of the court's time. People may request a marriage certificate if they either lost the original or were married before such certificates were routinely issued. These cases were numerous in periods of social upheaval, and again in the years after the passage of the 1974 Marriage Law, but there were no such requests in early 1999. Few requests were made for the court to approve taking a second wife. Divorce cases are the most numerous, and the number of such cases doubled during the 1990s. Inheritance cases are far fewer in number, but because they often require numerous witnesses (some of whom fail to appear the first time they are called), as well as trips to measure disputed plots of land, these cases usually stretch out over weeks or months. About half of the inheritance hearings I attended in 1994 lasted less than a quarter of an hour because a witness had failed to appear or one of the parties had failed to produce a document required for the hearing.

The cases are spread evenly throughout the year (including the fasting month of Ramadan). The court hears cases each Monday through Thursday, from about 9:00 in the morning until about 2:00 in the afternoon. A black-board lists the cases scheduled for each day, along with the judges and clerk assigned to each. The court usually hears inheritance cases on Mondays, after each judge has finished hearing his assigned divorce cases and when three judges are free to make up the judicial panel. No hearings are held on Fridays, when the judges and staff spend a few hours catching up on paperwork, and then drift off to play badminton. Clerks set up ping-pong tables in the large courtroom and play until it is time to attend noontime congregational worship in the town mosque.

One judge suffices to hear a divorce case or to legalize a marriage (although by 2000, with what in theory was a larger staff, three judges had begun to hear divorce cases). Three judges must sit as a panel to hear an inheritance case. In 1994, twenty to thirty people would show up for the inheritance cases, fewer for divorce cases. Farmers for the most part, they dress up for the occasion. The women wear long batik wrap-around skirts (rather than the everyday India-cloth kind), dressy shirts called *kebayas*, and headscarves. The men wear good shirts, trousers, decent sandals, and black caps. One or two men don sport coats.

The larger courtroom can hold forty people if they sit close together on the long wooden benches. Witnesses sit on folding chairs, toward the front of the room, facing the judges. The three judges sit behind a table on a raised dais, with the court reporter to their right and slightly behind them. The judges wear robes with maroon fronts and black sleeves, with a white ascot tied around their necks. They wear the same black caps worn by all other local men. Although the court has a permanent chief judge, in the courtroom the judges take turns presiding.

When a case is ready for hearing, the presiding judge rings a bell, and a clerk calls for the parties to enter the courtroom. The judge calls the session to order by pronouncing the *basmala* formula ("In the Name of God, the Merciful, the Compassionate"), and proceeds to business. When the session is over he says so, pounding his gavel once to emphasize closure. The inheritance hearings are entirely open to all visitors, as are the initial hearings in divorce cases, when the judge tries to reconcile the parties. If, however, efforts to reconcile fail, then the judge continues in closed session.

Plaintiffs always sit to the judges' right and defendants to their left. The witnesses are asked to leave at the beginning of the session so as not to be influenced by others' testimony. They are then called in one by one to testify. After giving testimony, each witness joins the others on the long benches.

Between sessions each judge sits in an office, reads new or pending cases, listens to the radio, and fields requests from petitioners. As I sat in the chief judge's office one day in 1994, a steady stream of people knocked on his door and entered. One woman came to request a divorce. The judge posed some questions to determine the grounds for her claim (her husband had taken her to her parents and not returned for 14 months) and then gave her the right form to fill out. Other people came with various bits of paperwork to be filled out by the judge.

Judicial procedure follows a colonial-era version of European civil law. Plaintiffs and defendants introduce written statements, replies, and counter-replies, which are handed to the judges and entered into the court record. Attorneys rarely are involved in any way. After questioning the parties and their witnesses, judges write a decision in which they outline the arguments and testimonies offered by each side, and present the legal considerations relevant to the case, followed by their decision.

At the appellate level, the judges reiterate lower court proceedings and then issue a judgment. Generally they work only from the documents forwarded to them. The appellate court might overturn, affirm, or send back the case for further evidentiary hearings at the first-instance level. From time to time it will set aside the lower court's decision, and issue a new ruling. The Supreme Court has the same options, but it generally restricts itself to the question of whether or not the lower court interpreted the law correctly, and avoids weighing claims about evidence, or considering arguments not already introduced at a lower level. A published account of a case that has been heard by the Supreme Court includes the decisions of the first-instance and appellate courts, and thus allows the reader to follow the arguments and legal reasoning presented at all stages.

Two types of family property cases showed up most frequently in a sample of cases drawn from the court's archives: requests to divide estates and marital property suits.[3] In the first type of case, a plaintiff asks the court to divide an estate according to Islamic law. The defendant is a sibling, cousin, or other close relative who has refused to divide the property. In some of these cases, the defendant does not contest the request, and the court divides the property. In other cases the defendant makes the counter-claim that he or she had received some of the estate as a gift (*hiba*) from the deceased. The court either accepts or rejects the counter-claim, according to the proof offered by the defendant and the burden of proof required by the court. Marital property suits first were brought to the court in the 1970s. In these cases, the plaintiff, an ex-wife, asks for her share of marital property.

Women have benefited more from the court's actions than have men. For the 49 cases for which I have complete information concerning the litigants, women were the plaintiffs in 31 cases, usually against men, and they won significantly more frequently than did male plaintiffs. As has been reported elsewhere (Hirsch 1998; Tucker 1998), women often perceive Islamic courts to work in their interest, not because the substantive rules constitute an improvement over traditional rules, but because the courts can offer property divisions relatively quickly. In the case of the Central Aceh Islamic court, moreover, judges increasingly have added purported gifts and testaments back into the estate pool, thereby increasing the absolute size of the shares received by daughters (Bowen 1998, 2000).

The form of court decisions

Islamic court documents are almost identical to documents produced in the local civil court. Each case has a number indicating the year it was introduced. Each time a court decides a case it issues a document called a "Decision" (*putusan*). It is written in Latin-script Indonesian; quotations from the Qur'an or Prophetic reports (*ḥadīth*) are written in Arabic and then translated into Indonesian.

In a typical inheritance dispute, the Decision consists of three major sections. In the first section, called *Tentang duduk perkaranya* ("Concerning the dispute in question"), the judges summarize the statements and testimony presented by the two sides during the course of the trial. The judges first list all plaintiffs and defendants in the case; when needed, they assign each a number (e.g., "Plaintiff 3"). The substance of the case is presented as a list of propositions claimed by one side or the other, and findings of fact by the court, all written as a series of clauses of the form "Considering that x. Considering that y." These clauses are grammatically subordinate to the final section in which the judges reveal their decision. This series of claims extends over most of the Decision, including the presentation of both parties' positions and replies, the evidence introduced by each side, any findings of fact by the court (such as the size of land parcels under dispute), and the testimony of witnesses. The court may also cite a verse of the Qur'an or a Prophetic report as one such "consideration."

In the second major section of the Decision, *Tentang Hukumnya* ("Concerning the law"), the judges restate the problem before them, evaluate each piece of evidence as strong or weak, make additional findings, most commonly concerning the identity of legitimate heirs to the estate, and cite the relevant Qur'anic verses, Prophetic reports, or articles from the Compilation of Islamic Law. Sometimes the court will also specify the amount of land or money due each heir according to Islamic law. It is, however, in the third and final section, entitled *Mengadili* ("Judges" or "to Judge"), where the court declares its judgment, including the division of land and other objects, the payment of court costs, and the names of the judges presiding in the case. (I will label the three sections "Claims," "Law" and "Judgment.")

The Decision, then, is a long statement, conceptually a single sentence, collectively authored by a panel of judges, which presents a smooth, continuous process of legal reasoning. The court presents all the evidence as grammatically and logically subordinate to a main clause, containing its finding, which comes only at the very end of the document. The form of the Decision represents the legal process as one of, first, evaluating the evidence and, second, deducing the judgment from the relevant laws.

These formal representations of the legal process derive from the European civil law tradition, as transformed by the Dutch colonial administration, applied in the colonial civil courts, and then adopted for the new, postindependence civil and Islamic courts. This resemblance between Islamic and civil court processes probably will increase, as Islamic court judges more frequently graduate from law faculties as well as from the State Islamic Institutes (IAINs). In parallel fashion, the sources cited by Islamic court judges in their decisions increasingly resemble those cited by their civil court counterparts. Islamic court decisions written in the 1950s and 1960s referred to Arabic-language books of Islamic jurisprudence as well as to the Qur'an, but never to state law. The 1974 Marriage Law significantly modified the content of marriage law and expanded the competence of the courts. Judges began to cite this law shortly after it was signed into law. By the early 1990s, the Compilation of Islamic Law, declared binding on judges by then President Suharto, began to appear as a major and sometimes sole justification for a decision (Bowen 1999), although some judges continued to cite the older books of *fiqh*.

In the ways in which they represent their processes of legal reasoning, then, Islamic court judges in Indonesia highlight processes of deductive reasoning, and rely increasingly on positive law. Even if they hold dissenting views on the matter, the appellate process and the top-down supervision of judges together have compelled judges to publicly reason following a civil law tradition model of law. Elsewhere (Bowen 1999), I consider difficulties with the state's efforts to make *fiqh* and state law appear as perfectly compatible, particularly with regard to agency in divorce (who makes a *ṭalāq* happen?) and legality of marriage (which acts constitute marriage?). Here I wish to look at the way judges bring other norms to bear in their decision-making.

Was there an agreement? The anatomy of an inheritance case

I present here a case decided in 1998 involving a disputed inheritance division. The case is one of many in which the court has had to sort out conflicting claims made by the parties concerning bequests (*wasiat*), consensual agreements (*musyawarah*), and division according to Islamic law (*fara'id*). In this case, as well as in others heard during the 1990s, the judges drew on non-legal social norms to make up their minds, but couched their decision in terms of such issues as the burden of proof, state law, and the rules of Islam governing the division of an estate. In these cases, the two parties do not differ on the relevant substantive Islamic law. The major issues facing the court have to do with the intentions of the parties and the fairness of any prior divisions of an estate.

The case at hand, which for convenience I shall call *Inen Maryam v Aman Mas* (there were, in fact, four plaintiffs and three defendants), is representative of inheritance disputes heard in Takèngën during the past two decades with respect both to the form of the case itself and to the direction of the legal reasoning carried out by the judges. At issue was not how to interpret the law, whether it be *fiqh* or state law, but whether agreements made by the parties superseded legal rules.

In the case, four of six sisters asked the court to redivide their parents' estate. These sisters were daughters of Abdul Kadir Aman Siti Esah (Abdul Kadir, Father of Siti Esah), and his wife Letifah Inen Siti Esah (Letifah, Mother of Siti Esah). The father had died in 1971, the mother in 1986. The estate consisted of several plots of land, a house, and other property, and most of it was in the hands of the only son, Aman Mas. The plaintiffs claimed that there never had been a meeting (*musyawarah*) to decide how to divide the land. Aman Mas said there had been such a meeting and that it had led to an agreement about the division. The two remaining daughters, who were listed as codefendants in the case, agreed with his version of the events. In 1998 the Court ruled in favor of the plaintiffs and ordered the land divided among all the heirs. The defendants appealed to the Islamic High Court in Banda Aceh, which affirmed the decision in August 1999. In January 2000, the defendants asked the Supreme Court to quash the decision; as of June 2000 the case was awaiting a hearing.

Claims

In their arguments, the plaintiffs claimed that Aman Mas had held on to more than his share of the estate. They said that their father had instructed Aman Mas to give a particular plot of rice land to one of the plaintiffs, Halimah, because she had been the one initially to clear the land. In their Decision the court quoted (in Gayo, without translation) the plaintiffs' version of the father's oral commission (*manat*) on this matter to Aman Mas, which included the threat to haunt him from beyond the grave if he did not comply. The plaintiffs said that Aman Mas had promised to give his sisters some land, but that he had added that they should take it or leave it, because as the son he was the one who could rightfully determine what happened to their parents' estate.

In his reply to these charges, Aman Mas stated that after their parents' deaths each of the children had enjoyed use-rights over portions of the land. In 1986 they had held a meeting governed by the norms of consensus, a *musyawarah mufakat*, and at this meeting all the children agreed that Aman Mas had rightfully received some land as a bequest (*wasiat*).[4] According to him, the heirs agreed that they would divide the remaining land by lottery, and that they were all satisfied "and would not demand anything more." Although the subsequent division of the wealth was done by lottery, in his testimony Aman Mas frequently used the verbal form *difara'id* ("to be divided according to Islamic rules") to refer to the division, seeking to suggest that it was in accord with Islam. The two co-defendant sisters sided with Aman Mas regarding his claim that their father had bequeathed him a plot. When asked their opinion by the presiding judges, they agreed that there had been a consensual agreement among all the heirs.

After each side had presented its initial position statements, each had the opportunity, after a delay of some weeks, to submit replies: a *duplik* from the defendants, followed by a *replik* from the plaintiffs. At this point the two sisters who had sided with Aman Mas played an important role. Because they had not received large portions of the estate, one would have expected them to join their sisters in calling for the land to be redivided. However, they agreed with their brother that all the land had been divided, 42 days after their father's death, using the term *difara'id*. With this term, the sisters meant to say that the land had been divided in a way that gave to each party ownership of a share. They did not imply that the land had been divided according to the Islamic rules of division. Indeed, they went on to say that the division had been carried out according to a lottery.

In their reply to the initial statement of the defendants, the plaintiffs conceded that there had been a lottery, but complained about how it had been carried out. They explained that Aman Mas had first selected which plot was to be his own, and then held the lottery on his own. Only afterwards did he call them to his house and point out to each sister her plot. Each side offered witnesses. Among them was the village headman, who said that the division indeed had taken place in 1986, but that several years later two of the plaintiffs had come to him, saying it was not fair. At that time, he reported, Aman Mas had given them a house in return for "a promise that they would not ask for any more" from the estate.

Law

The judges then presented their analysis of the issues and the relevant law. First, they enumerated those claims that had not been rebutted. The two parties agreed that the disputed land plots were part of their father's estate, and that there had been a lottery to divide the land. These claims could be set aside for the moment. They then considered claims that were yet to be resolved. For each such claim they focused on the credibility of the claim and the appropriate burden of proof.

The matter of allocating the burden of proof is of considerable importance in these cases. Very often the testimony offered by one side is countered by rebuttals from the other. Even written documents attesting to an estate division can be said to have been produced under duress or without

all signers fully understanding the meaning of the document, as in a case
discussed below. As a result, if the burden of proving the case falls squarely
on one side, that side is highly likely to lose. The effect of assuming the
burden of proof increased during the 1990s, as the court began to demand
higher standards of proof.

The judges do have a certain room to maneuver with regard to the burden of proof. They can assign the overall burden to the plaintiffs, on
grounds that the plaintiffs have made a claim that has been denied by the
defendants. They can rely on a notion of the preponderance of the evidence, handing the decision to the party whose proof is stronger with
respect to a particular factual claim, such as the date when a plot of land
was purchased. (This fact may be relevant to deciding whether land is part
of the family estate or the property of one party.) In cases such as the one
at hand, in which the plaintiffs request a division of the estate, and the
defendants counter-claim that a division already had taken place, the judges
might rule differently. They can claim that it is up to the defendants to
prove the case, because they are the party making a "positive claim," i.e.,
a claim about an event that took place in the past. My conversations with
judges have led me to believe that sometimes they first decide who is telling
the truth about a key matter of fact in the case, and then they assign the
burden of proof to the other party.

The case involving Aman Mas fits into the third category of proof, that
in which the burden falls on the defendants. The judges cited an article
of the colonial-era civil law code stating that whoever makes a positive
claim thereby assumes the burden of proof. In this case the defendants
had claimed that the land already had been properly divided among the
heirs. The burden of proof therefore fell on them to show that the land
had indeed been divided in accordance with Islamic law. The key passage
begins as follows (pp. 20–21):

> Considering, that in court the Plaintiffs stated that the wealth left by the deceased
> had not yet been divided. It is true that by means of a lottery the female heirs
> were allotted shares, but the Defendant had already taken his share beforehand,
> and in any case the daughters were given shares not through a division, but by
> the Defendant designating plots as he wished.
>
> Considering, that according to article 283 of the civil code, the burden of proof
> follows the system of positive proof. In this case, because the Plaintiff claims that
> the disputed items had never been divided among all the heirs, it is the Defendants,
> not the Plaintiff, who assume the burden of proving that the disputed wealth had
> been divided (difara'id) among all the heirs.
>
> Considering, that the Defendants have offered witnesses, and we find that the
> second witness's testimony may be heard even though he is the husband of the
> second co-defendant.

Considering, that the second witness just referred to explained that before the division of wealth among the six female heirs, the Defendant took out his share. This testimony corroborates the admission of the Defendant. The Court (*Majelis*) is of the opinion that the division by lottery should have been held for all the heirs, male as well as female. However, this lottery was only used to distribute shares to the female heirs, such that there arose dissatisfaction among the heirs, and the Defendant later gave two of them, Plaintiffs III and IV, additional wealth in the form of a house.

Considering, that in these facts clear indications can be seen that the Defendant's share was much larger than the share he should have received, a point strengthened in the Defendant's own conclusions by his statement that the daughters each received 15 bamboo measures of land, plus a house to share among them, whereas the Defendant received 6 1/2 *kaleng* measures of land.

Considering, that despite the testimony of the Defendant's first and second witnesses that the disputed items had been divided following a *musyawarah*, the witnesses (supported by the Defendants) also stated that after the division there arose dissatisfaction among the Plaintiffs because the gap between their shares and that of the Defendant was too great and unbalanced, such that from the Defendant's share an additional house was given to Plaintiffs III and IV. These events were confirmed by the third defense witness.

Now, the division of the estate clearly had not been along the lines stipulated by the Islamic "science of shares": the son had taken much more than twice the share awarded each daughter. His claim that the court ought to ratify the earlier division rested on the claim that all the heirs had agreed both to the lottery and to the bequest of land to him by their father. The court does indeed regularly affirm agreements reached by parties and considers such findings to be a matter of Islamic law, a proposition strengthened by the Compilation of Islamic Law (Article 183). The court could have restricted their findings to an assessment of the evidence offered by the defendants that all parties had agreed to the division and to the bequest.

But the judges did not so restrict themselves. Instead, they made claims about the fairness of the division and the probable states of mind of the daughters. Although they did not object to a lottery qua lottery, they stated that the lottery should have been held for all the heirs rather than only for the daughters. Thus, the court did not object to the manner of division per se, to the absence of a reference to Islamic law, but to the control exercised by the son over the process. The fact that the son later added a house to the daughters' shares only confirmed in their minds that the daughters had been dissatisfied and that the son had recognized, if not the legitimacy of their complaint, at least its potential strength.

The judges then addressed the claims that the division had been made according to a *musyawarah*. In the Indonesian political-cultural context, the

term *musyawarah* indicates more than a meeting; it implies that the participants reached a consensus on their topic of deliberation. The term is part
of the state ideology, *Pancasila*, and its cognates appear in local ways of
talking about dispute resolution in many parts of the country (Bowen 2000).
To the defendants' claims that a *musyawarah* had settled the division, the
court replied that witnesses had testified to the effect that the plaintiffs subsequently were unhappy with the division because of its unfairness. The
judges concluded on the basis of the testimony that the defendant had
failed to prove his case and that the *musyawarah* had not obtained the free
agreement of the daughters.

> Considering, that from the facts presented at the hearing, the court (*Majelis*) is of
> the opinion that the division of the disputed wealth carried out by the Defendant
> on the 44th day after the death of the deceased Letifah was not based on agree-
> ment and consensus (*kata sepakat dan mufakat bulat*) among all the heirs, but was
> dictated by the Defendant's own desires, this division therefore has no legal value
> and must be put aside (p. 22).

The court then took up the Defendant's claim that their father had left to
him by bequest (*wasiat*) a plot of land.

> The Defendant did not offer any proof in the matter, and according to the
> Compilation of Islamic Law, article 195 (3), bequests to heirs are valid [only] if
> they are agreed upon by all the heirs. In this case, however, the Plaintiffs said
> that they did not agree to it, and the court is therefore of the opinion that this
> *wasiat* never took place, and that it must be stated that the disputed objects are
> part of the deceased's estate and must be divided among the heirs (p. 22).

Here, too, the court reached a conclusion about the state of mind of the
daughters at the time of the bequest based on their current testimony in
court.

Judgment

Most of the decisive judgments, in fact, had been made in the Law section, leaving to the final judgment only the statement of the heirs and their
shares.

> Considering, that the heirs are the Plaintiffs and the Defendants, consisting of six
> daughters and one son. Because there are no other heirs with rights to receive
> the deceased's wealth, the division of the deceased's estate is based on the stipu-
> lation in the Qur'an [Q 4:11].

Written below this statement in longhand is the Arabic of the verse followed by its Indonesian translation as: "God has ruled (*mensyari'atkan*) that the share of a son is twice the share of a daughter" (p. 23).[5] Article 176 of the Compilation of Islamic Law is cited as the second basis for the decision; this article restates the ratio of shares to sons and daughters.

The plaintiffs had presented the court with estimates of the monetary value of each plot of land, and because these estimates were not contested by the defendants, they were accepted. The values were added up to produce an estimate of the total monetary value of the estate, and the shares awarded to each heir were stated in rupiah. Typically, the court would stop at that point in its calculations, but in the mid-1990s the appellate court began to insist that it also specify which plots each heir would receive. Accordingly, the court assigned a certain area to each heir in this case, awarding, for example, Siti Esah and Saunah each 4,479 square meters of plot 1. (The judges told me that they did not expect the siblings to take control of the land exactly as prescribed, because it made more sense for one party to sell to another.)

The court concluded by assigning court costs to the defendants and identifying themselves. The judge who presided over the case also wrote the decision: a Gayo judge, Drs. M. Anshary, SH (Sarjana Hukum, degree only awarded by law faculties). Judge Anshary, who studied at an Islamic Institute (IAIN) as well as at a law school, had been acting as Chief Judge of the court for much of the previous three years. Two other judges sat on the panel, Drs. Jumaidi (from Java) and Drs. M. Ihsan (from Medan), both of whom graduated from an IAIN, where they specialized in Shari'a, not from a law faculty.

Appeal

Later that year, Aman Mas, dissatisfied with the decision, appealed to the higher Islamic court in Banda Aceh, the provincial capital. The estate had been divided by *musyawarah mufakat* in 1986, he complained, "such that the defendant/appellant is surprised and startled that after more than ten years, suddenly there arrives a lawsuit." The Takèngën court's decision was wrong, he added, because it had overturned a *musyawarah mufakat*, and so doing "clearly invites social conflict, and it upsets our deceased parents (*Almarhum dan Almarhuma*) in the otherworld (*alam barzah*)." Furthermore, he continued, property divisions carried out through *musyawarah mufakat* have a firm foundation in Islamic law because God said, "Consult among yourselves in all your affairs (*Bermusyawaralah dalam segala urusan*)." After the appellate court affirmed the earlier decision, Aman Mas and the two daughters requested cassation from the Supreme Court. In each of these appeals, the original defendants, now called "the party requesting review/cassation," submitted a *memorie* outlining their argument, to which the original plaintiffs, now "respondents," submitted a *kontramemorie*. In these and other cases, both sides sometimes make strategic use of the original court's arguments and rhetoric when formulating their memoranda. In this case, the four sisters, now in the position of respondents, quoted the husband of one of their opponents as admitting that Aman Mas had taken his share out of the estate before the lottery was conducted. To this quotation, which had been cited in the original testimony before the Takèngën court, the authors of the memorandum now added that "he did this without *musyawarah*," emphasizing the point made by the court.

When do people really agree?

In June 2000, as I sat in the courtroom reading through the typescript Decision of this case, Judge Anshary, its author, walked up to me and peered over my shoulder. I asked him how the judges had decided that the heirs had not freely consented to the division at the *musyawarah*. His answer linked the inequality of the division to the intentions of the heirs:

> In that case, when we went to inspect the plots of land, we saw that the daughters had small plots of land, maybe one-half hectare for all six daughters, while the son had two hectares all to himself. We asked about each parcel, whether it had been bought, and for each they said no, that it had been left by their father for them. The difference in the size of the parcels assigned to the brother and the sisters was so great that it was clear that they had not agreed on the division. At that time people would divide by just pointing to parcels, but that is not valid. The men dominated and the women could not say anything, although as soon as there was an opportunity to go to the court, they would do so.

In other words, a true *musyawarah* had not been held.

The judge distinguished between overt acts of agreement to a division of property, and true, sincere agreement. Yes, there had been a meeting at which all parties had come to a conclusion, and there was no evidence that anyone objected to the meeting at the time. It was only several years later, according to the village headman, that some daughters had complained that the division was unfair, and twelve years passed before they brought suit. Did their earlier participation in the meeting mean that they had once agreed and later changed their minds? And, regardless of the answer to that question, could they contest the earlier division on the grounds that it did not correspond to the Islamic "science of shares"?

In the 1960s and early 1970s, the Takèngën court routinely said "yes" to the first question and "no" to the second question. In cases adjudicated in the 1960s, the court said, "We should not keep redividing property": Once a settlement had been reached, the court was reluctant to change it. Indeed, the civil court—to which, until the rules of jurisdiction in Aceh changed in 1970, one could also bring inheritance cases—invented a legal category of "elapsed claims" and used it to disallow such requests to redivide property. The judges treated as irrelevant the objection that sons had coerced daughters into agreeing to the settlement, on the grounds that a settlement had been reached, and Islam supported agreements among heirs. In some cases the judges also accepted defendants' arguments that according to Gayo social norms (*adat*), once a daughter married out of her natal village, she lost her right to make future claims on the family estate.

By the early 1990s the court had changed its position on this issue. It now could do so because it was politically stronger than before—it had a firmer foundation in statutory law, it had the backing of an authoritarian government, and it now operated under conditions of relative stability (which were, however, to change). Moreover, the judges had changed their views on what women and men thought about rights and rules. Judges now assumed that all daughters, regardless of where they married, considered themselves to have rights under Islamic law.

Even in cases in which a purported *musyawarah* had led to the signing of an agreement, the objective inequality of the division sometimes led the judges to declare that the daughters could not have freely consented to the arrangement. In the 1987 case *Samadiah v Hasan Ali*, for example, a daughter who had received nothing from her parents' estate demanded the share due her according to Islamic law. The other children acknowledged that they had all quarreled over the disposition of these lands in 1969, but said that they had settled the dispute in a large village meeting that same year. They also said that their father had left a bequest stipulating that whoever took care of him would get certain lands, and that it was one of the sons, a man named Egem, who had done so. They noted that the bequest and the transfer of those lands to Egem had been made publicly at a meeting and had been approved by all the children. They produced a document attesting to the bequest that had been declared valid by the Takèngën civil court in 1970.

The practice of leaving land to the child who cares for his or her parents is widely followed in the Gayo highlands. Such bequests, called *pematang*, are generally considered to be the privilege of the parents. A parent's bequest is ipso facto valid; its authority comes from the right of the owner to dispose of the wealth, not from the consent of the other children. Bequests can be, and indeed are, challenged as contrary to Islamic law ("no bequest to an heir" unless all heirs agree to it). Indeed, the Compilation of Islamic Law, Article 195 (3), follows general Indonesian interpretations of *fiqh* in allowing bequests to heirs only if such agreement is produced (a rule cited by the court in the case described earlier).

In *Samadiah*, the Islamic court ruled that despite the document, the very fact that some heirs now contested the case was a sign of the absence of consensus. (Although the judges made no mention of this to me, they may have disregarded the general court's finding as having been tainted by bribery.) Furthermore, the judges argued that even according to Gayo *adat*, bequests must be agreed to by all the heirs. "*Pematang*, according to the Gayo *adat* that is still held to and approved of by the people, is considered valid only if all Wahab's children accept and approve of the declaration [of the agreement]," explained one of the judges who ruled in the case (interview, 1994). The judges ruled that because the plaintiff and two of the defendants said they knew of no such declaration, the bequest could not be approved. The judges ordered all the wealth divided.

The defendants appealed the case to the Aceh appellate court, insisting that the document proved that all the heirs had agreed to the division. The higher court, which heard the case in 1990, returned the case to the Takèngèn court, ordering them to take a second look at the document. The lower court did as they were told. "We still thought the daughters were pressured, but we followed instructions," Judge Kasim commented to me. In 1992 they sent the case back up, unchanged, to the court in Banda Aceh, which set aside the decision and ruled in favor of the plaintiffs. (The case was appealed to Jakarta, and has yet to be settled.)

On what grounds did the judges determine that consensus had not been reached despite the existence of a document attesting to the contrary? Judges Hasan and Kasim explained to me in 1994 that the other heirs, principally the two daughters, could have sincerely accepted the 1969 agreement only if it had been in accord with their Islamic rights. That agreement clearly was in contradiction with the contents of the Qur'an, however, because it did not award them their rightful shares. It therefore could not have been the product of consensus. Judge Kasim stated that he and the other judges had felt that the two daughters had been pressured into signing the 1969 document, even though such pressure could not be proven.

Because no daughter would freely sign such an agreement if it were clearly against her interests, he reasoned, there must have been pressure.

Judge Kasim's statement also helps clarify the first case above, *Inen Maryam v Aman Mas*. In both cases, the judges concluded from the objective unfairness of an earlier settlement that the plaintiffs could not have sincerely accepted the settlement, a conclusion based on the assumption that all parties knew and accepted the social norm that estates ought to be divided according to Islamic law, and not according to Gayo *adat* or any other arrangement. This assumption concerns the normative knowledge of the population, and not the law itself.

In this case, however, the judges went one step further. Not only did they find the bequest invalid because Islamic law requires a true consensus to have been reached, but they also claimed that Gayo *adat* requires such a consensus. In years of work in Takèngën and nearby villages I have never heard anyone characterize the rule concerning bequests in this way. The court in effect recategorized the Islamic rule regarding bequests as "local custom." They did not need to do so in order to rule as they did, because the Islamic law on the matter is clear. Their invention made it possible for them to base their ruling not only on an Islamic rule, but also on an agreed-upon local social norm. This claim made the decision not a matter of enforcing *adat* over Islam, but of enforcing a rule found in both *adat* and Islam.

In 1994, Judge Kasim discussed with me a similar case that was awaiting review by the Supreme Court, *Syamsiah binti Mudali v M. Aji Aman Sarana*. "A father had a son and four daughters," he explained:

> The father gave a lot of his rice land to the son and the son's wife; the son also received a large bequest. He gave very little to the daughters. In the 1970s, he drew up a document and had everyone sign. He even sent one of his grandchildren to persuade a daughter who had been reluctant to sign, and she signed. She was not satisfied, though. Later a second document, probably drawn up by the son, but written as if it were from the father, stipulated that the bequest was made officially to the son, and the son's portion of the remaining lands was increased! Each daughter, who should have received 2.5 *tem* measures of land [under a hectare], received only 0.5 *tem*!
>
> This was going too far, it deviated too far from justice. There is a *ḥadīth* that says that, although gifts should be given fairly, they can still be valid even if they are not fair. But this is going too far. Finally, after the father died, the daughter petitioned the court. She was joined by his other daughters, but at least one daughter sided with the son. The defendant based his case on the first document, but we said it was going too far. They appealed and lost, and the case is now with

the Supreme Court. We are very interested in seeing whether the Court can support our judgment, because it introduces a sense of justice (*rasa keadilan*) into the court. Now, no one is totally fair—just look at the fingers on one hand: they work together but are all different lengths. And so it is with children: some will taste sweet, some rich, some bitter. But there are limits.

Observe in this case how easy it would have been for the judge to say that the agreement was valid. After all, all the interested parties had signed the letter of agreement, and no proof of coercion was offered. But the judges said that they disbelieved these documents. Here again the judges contrasted sincere (*ikhlas*) agreement, which could only be obtained if the division had been fair, with mere procedural correctness.

In 2000 I was able to see the case in the court files. The Takèngën court's ruling had indeed been appealed to the Supreme Court.[6] The father's document had stipulated that the daughters could not sell the land they had received to anyone but their brother, the defendant, because the land was *tanah pusaka*, "heirloom land"; this was their father's "final *wasiat*" to them.[7] The land was divided at a meeting held in the presence of the village headman. However, the headman announced at the meeting that the division was conditional, saying to the recipients that "if you sell the rice land, then one-half of your land will go to the defendant."

In their written decision the Court, with Judge Kasim presiding, stated that they doubted the validity of the letter, adding that "the division is far from being just, and is 'tied' (*mukhait*, referring to the restrictions on selling the land), leaving the rights of the heirs unclear; therefore this exhibit [the document] is not accepted." Unfairness both in the division and in the power wielded by men over women rendered the settlement invalid despite the presence of a contract.

Conclusion

In all three cases, the judges found in favor of daughters who had demanded that estate divisions be redone to give them their rightful shares. The judges drew on two kinds of social norms to reach their decision: their own ideas of equality and fairness, and their assumptions about ideas held by the daughters at the time of the earlier division. In the course of developing a mode of reasoning that would support their conclusions, the judges rejected a written agreement that had been validated by the civil court, and they invented a rule of Gayo *adat* that would correspond both to their own norms and to Islamic law.

The judges might have reasoned otherwise within an Islamic legal frame-work. Indeed, their predecessors had done so (Bowen 2000). In two of the cases, *Samadiah* and *Syamsiah*, they might have fallen back on the strength of the written agreement as a contract binding on all parties. In *Inen Maryam*, even without a written agreement, the testimony of the village headman could have served as a basis for a ruling that the heirs had, in fact, reached an agreement. In all three cases, the judges might have argued that unless the plaintiffs could prove that they had been coerced (thereby shifting the burden of proof), there was no compelling reason to place that agreement in question.

That they found as they did, then, is illustrative both of the capacity of judges to reach a range of decisions in what is formally and substantively "the same" judicial framework, and of the importance of their moral and social ideas in shaping their decisions. From where did the judges derive these ideas of equality and fairness? One can find such ideas in the tra-ditions of Islamic jurisprudence, in norms of Gayo *adat*, and in the gen-eral values of gender equality that have served as a ground for a number of Indonesian reinterpretations of Islamic law (Bowen 1999). Moreover, the Indonesian Supreme Court long has urged lower courts to overturn prop-erty settlements when those settlements disproportionally favor men (Lev 1972). In other words, the judges may have drawn on one or more of several distinct normative frameworks in arriving at the conclusions they did.

The judges themselves did not justify their stance in legal terms; they did not refer to Islamic sources, to specific rules of *adat*, or to Indonesian statutes or court decisions. Instead, they referred to what we might call a common sense version of *adat*: not a body of law-like rules (the *adatrecht* constructed by the Dutch and taken over into Indonesian jurisprudence), but a set of everyday principles. In the explanation quoted above, Judge Kasim referred to the kind of equality that we can see in the fingers of the hand, with each finger performing different functions, but just as impor-tant as the others. This and other concrete images of equality draw from the Gayo poetic tradition of *didong* (Bowen 1991), in which concrete images are described at length as ways of talking about social life.

In its appeal to common sense and mundane life, this language has much in common with a style of reasoning about Islamic law that I frequently encounter in Takèngèn and Jakarta, in which everyday social practices pro-vide a normative ground for rethinking law (Bowen 1998). That village men and women work together in the fields, equally sharing the burdens and the fruits of their manual labor, offers concrete proof that equality and fairness are socially appropriate bases for choosing among alternative interpretations of the law. Takèngën judges (and, I would argue, most Indonesian Islamic judges and jurists) reason much as do judges and jurists everywhere, in striving to make the law fit with the norms of social life, and social life with the norms of the law.

Ten

THE POLITICS OF SHARI'ATIZATION: CENTRAL GOVERNMENTAL AND REGIONAL DISCOURSES OF SHARI'A IMPLEMENTATION IN ACEH

Moch. Nur Ichwan*

Adat bak Poteumeureuhom,
Hukom bak Syiah Kuala,
Qanun bak Putro Phang,
Reusam bak Laksamana.[1]

Introduction

One consequence of the greater political openness that followed the resignation of Indonesia's long-time dictator Suharto in 1998 was the demand in several localities for implementation of Shari'a.[2] The region that has experienced the greatest change is Aceh where the provincial government has been granted broad authority to establish Shari'a Courts (*Mahkamah Syariah*), to implement Shari'a legislation, and to have its own Shari'a police and enforcement mechanisms (*wilayatul hisbah*).[3] The Department of Religion officially inaugurated the new system on March 4, 2003, a date chosen to coincide with the Islamic New Year (Muharram 1, 1423 AH). On that date the existing Religious Courts (*Pengadilan Agama*) in Aceh were transformed into Shari'a Courts and vested with new powers in the fields of Islamic belief (*'aqīda*), religious practice (*'ibādāt*), and symbolism (Ind. *syiar* < Ar. *shi'ār*).

This chapter examines the significance of the discourse on implementation of a "comprehensive Shari'a" (*Syariat Islam yang Kaffah*) for Acehnese society. It will be argued that in the first years of the twenty-first century Shari'a discourse has come to serve as a "master signifier" in Aceh, and that other social signifiers, such as politics, law, education, and the economy increasingly refer to and are defined by reference to the Shari'a.[4] The chapter focuses on the discourse on the establishment of Shari'a Courts and implementation of Islamic law at two levels within the government—at the

level of the central government in Jakarta and at the provincial level in
Aceh.[5] The discourse of the religious establishment in Aceh will also be
considered. The analysis will seek to go beyond official accounts of the
process to grasp the power relations between central and regional governments on the one hand and between the regional government and the
local religious establishment on the other. I will argue that the regional
government has attempted to position itself in the middle between the central government and the religious establishment, and that this has enabled
the regional government to play the two sides off against each other. Thus,
instead of seeing Shari'a in Aceh purely in terms of a legal discourse, I
will emphasize its political dimensions as well.

The Aceh problem and the politics of the "religious approach"

The Indonesian government's plans for implementation of Shari'a in Aceh
cannot be divorced from the long history of political turbulence in the
region and the attempts by successive Indonesian governments to impose
a military-security solution to the problem. Aceh has been perceived as a
problem by central government authorities since the Dutch colonial era.
During the New Order regime of President Suharto (1965–1998) thousands
of Indonesian troops were sent to Aceh to suppress the separatist Free Aceh
Movement (*Gerakan Aceh Merdeka*, GAM).[6] The region was then considered
a special "military operation zone" (DOM), and fighting between GAM
and the Indonesian military resulted in the death of many innocent civilians. Human rights abuses by the Indonesian military drew criticism from
both national and international communities.

The regime's repressive actions in Aceh became increasingly unpopular
following Suharto's resignation and the declaration of a new era of *Reformasi*
(reform) in 1998. The transitional administration of B.J. Habibie, which
held power from May 1998 to October 1999, made no significant effort
to address the problem. The subsequent governments led by Abdurrahman
Wahid and Megawati Sukarnoputri changed the policy on Aceh from an
exclusive reliance on military force to more comprehensive strategies. One
aspect of this new policy was a "religious approach" that included allowing Aceh to establish Shari'a Courts and to implement Shari'a.

On April 11, 2001, President Abdurrahman Wahid issued Presidential
Instruction No. 4/2001 on the Special Treatment of the Situation in Aceh.[7]
Six months later, on October 11, Megawati, who had since replaced Wahid,
issued a repeat of this order as Presidential Instruction No. 7/2001.[8] Both

presidential instructions describe the problems in Aceh in terms of "social discontent" (*ketidakpuasan masyarakat*) and an "armed separatist movement" (*gerakan separatis bersenjata*). In addition to their common definition of the problem, both presidential instructions also employ the same framework in describing the solution to Acehnese separatism. In both instructions the centrality of the discourse of *Negara Kesatuan Republik Indonesia* (NKRI, Unitary State of the Republic of Indonesia) is emphasized. Both the separatist issue and the problem of social discontent are to be addressed in a "wise, accurate, comprehensive, and integrated manner." It is also stated that these issues are to be accorded "special treatment" (*penanggulangan secara khusus*), although what is meant by "special treatment" is not made clear.

Furthermore, the instructions express pessimism about the chances of achieving a resolution through the use of "persuasion and dialogue" in negotiations with the armed separatist movement, regardless of whether those negotiations are carried out within Indonesia or in another country under the auspices of a third party. They also emphasize that "security and order" are at stake and that social disharmony could disturb the effectiveness of both governance and the development process. Both instructions—approved by cabinet meetings, the Council of People's Representatives (*Dewan Perwakilan Rakyat*, DPR), and the Supreme Advisory Council (*Dewan Perwakilan Agung*, DPA)—suggest the need for more comprehensive steps in the fields of politics, economics, law, social order, security, and information and communications.[9]

Notably, religion is not specifically mentioned in the instructions as a problem. This is perhaps because GAM did not rely on religion (Islam) as the basis or ideological motivation for its actions, and the formation of an Islamic state was not part of its formal platform. GAM aimed to create a secular, monarchical state in Aceh, not a religious republic. The presidential instructions, however, instruct the Minister of Religion "to promote the initiative for creating security through a religious approach." It is now clear that the use of a religious approach, to be defined and implemented by the Department of Religion, was intended as a means of ensuring security for Indonesian national interests. (See Diagram 1)

As the conflict between GAM and the government escalated in the first half of 2002, President Megawati issued Presidential Instruction No. 1/2002 on the Enhancement of the Special Treatment of the Situation in Aceh.[10] As with the previous instructions, this instruction mandates use of a religious approach as one of the steps to be taken to create security in Aceh. The reference to religion in the instruction, which speaks of "maintaining the unity of the Republic of Indonesia through [the] *religious approach*" (emphasis added), suggests that the Department of Religion's program for Aceh was to serve as a means of discouraging separatist efforts and preserving Aceh as part of a unified Indonesia.

Although a religious approach was central to the government's plans for resolving the conflict with Aceh, precisely what this was to entail was not clear. During the New Order, the term "religious approach" was usually associated with gatherings for religious instruction (*pengajian*), religious ceremonies, meetings (*silaturrahmi*) between religious scholars and government officials, public prayers (*doa bersama*), and *safari Ramadan*, in which government officials travelled from one mosque to another during the month of Ramadan to participate in *tarāwīḥ* prayers. But these were not the activities envisaged by the instructions, since such measures had been in use in Aceh long before the instructions were issued. The meaning of this apparently critical phrase became clear only after the passing on July 19, 2001 of Law No. 18/2001 on Special Autonomy for the Privileged Province of Aceh as the Nanggroe Aceh Darussalam.[11] That statute provided for establishment of the Shariʿa Courts and the implementation of Shariʿa in the Province.

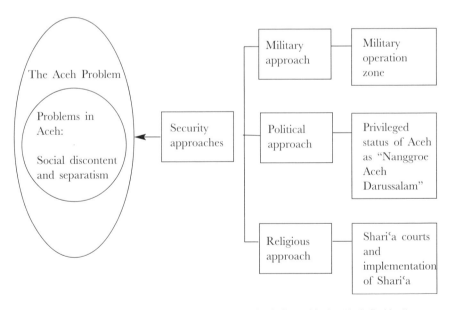

Diagram 1. The central government's approaches in dealing with the "Aceh Problem"

Islamic law in Aceh in the pre-Reformasi era

The discourses on the newly established Shari'a Courts that emanate from the central government in Jakarta and the regional government in Banda Aceh appeal to different aspects of Acehnese history. The central government envisions the new Shari'a Courts as a modified version of the region's pre-existing Religious Courts (*Pengadilan Agama*), which are part of the Indonesian national legal system.[12] Legislation enacted by the regional government in the form of Qanuns refers to earlier parts of the nation's legal tradition. These Qanuns imagine the roots of the current courts in Islamic tribunals recognized in 1946 (which bore the title "Mahkamah Syariah") and are viewed as having an "absolute authority" (Qanuns Nos. 10 and 11/2002). The state legislation also indicates that the implementation of Shari'a is not new for the Acehnese, arguing that Shari'a was part of the legal and judicial system of the pre-colonial Acehnese sultanates.[13]

Prior to Dutch colonization Shari'a Courts exercised a broad jurisdiction in Aceh. During the period of colonial rule, the Dutch administration had direct control in only some areas (such as Aceh Besar, South Aceh (Singkil), and Sabang). Regions not under direct Dutch control were governed indirectly based on the *Plakat Panjang* (Dutch East India Company, *Vereenigde Oost-Indische Compagnie*, VOC) charter.[14] After independence, the operation of the Islamic tribunals in Aceh was initially based on local authority. On August 1, 1946 the Acehnese religious establishment, represented by the Association of Acehnese 'Ulamā' (*Persatuan Ulama Seluruh Aceh*, PUSA)[15] under the guidance of Muhammad Daud Beureueh, established Shari'a Courts throughout Aceh. These courts dealt not only with family law (marriage, divorce, inheritance) but also with *waqf* (religious endowments), gifts (*hiba*), and the public treasury (*bayt al-māl*). In December of 1947 the Acehnese People's Representative Assembly (*Dewan Perwakilan Rakyat*) gave formal legal recognition to the Shari'a Courts with the promulgation of Decree No. 35/1947 (Lev 1972, 80–1). Aceh's leaders demanded that the Department of Religion in Jakarta grant legal recognition to the Shari'a Courts. While these demands ultimately led to the payment of salaries to judges in Aceh, the Department of Religion rejected the demand for legal recognition of the Acehnese courts on the grounds that the Acehnese Shari'a Courts did not have sufficient basis in Indonesian law. According to at least one writer, the Department's reluctance to embrace the Acehnese courts was based at least in part on a concern that the judges who staffed the courts did not share the nationalist views of Jakarta (Lev 1972, 83).

In 1953 Daud Beureueh led a revolt against the central government under the banner of Darul Islam. Needless to say, this complicated efforts to obtain central government recognition of the Shariʿa Courts. Nevertheless, as a result of enormous pressure from Acehnese religious and political leaders, working in collaboration with a small number of officials in the Department of Religion's Bureau of Religious Justice, the Acehnese Shariʿa Courts were formally established through Government Regulation No. 29/1957. This Regulation, which dealt specifically with Aceh, was subsequently confirmed and superceded by Regulation No. 45/1957 on Pengadilan Agama/Mahkamah Syariah, which served as the legal basis for all Islamic tribunals outside of Java and Madura (Lev 1972, 83–4, 89).[16]

Daud Beureueh was not inclined to trust Jakarta. He demanded an explicit and substantive statement on the implementation of Shariʿa in Aceh. After long, hard negotiations, Colonel Jasin (in his capacity of regional martial law administrator) issued an official decision on April 7, 1962 that provided for "the orderly and proper implementation of elements of Shariʿa for adherents of Islam in the Special Region of Aceh with consideration being given to extant national statutes and regulations."[17] The statement also stipulated that further regulations concerning the meaning and intent of the decision would become the responsibility of the Acehnese provincial government. Beureueh then called off the revolt. Colonel Jasin's decision proved to be meaningless, however. The statement itself was qualified, providing only that some "elements" (unsur-unsur) of Shariʿa were to be implemented. More importantly, there was no explicit devolution of power to Aceh from the central government. Jakarta's promises of Shariʿa for Aceh in the 1960s were not carried out, but lived on in Acehnese memory. In response to Jasin's decision, Beureueh issued a statement expressing his own vision of the applicability of Shariʿa to all aspects of human life.[18] This vision survived and was later embraced by the religious establishment in Aceh nearly four decades later in the Reformasi era.

Meanwhile, the Acehnese Shariʿa Courts were integrated into the Indonesian national legal system. Law No. 14/1970 on Judicial Authority placed the Acehnese Mahkamah Syariah under the administrative rubric of the national system of Religious Courts (Pengadilan Agama). With the passage of the Religious Judicature Act in 1989, the Acehnese courts were renamed Pengadilan Agama to bring them into conformity with the rest of the Islamic judiciary (Law No. 7/1989). The 1989 Act also limited the jurisdiction of the courts in Aceh to matters of marriage, divorce, and inheritance in line with the other nationally established Religious Courts.[19]

The Law on Nanggroe Aceh Darussalam

The enactment of Law No. 18/2001 granting special autonomy for Aceh (hereafter, Law on Nanggroe Aceh Darussalam or "Law on NAD") should be viewed in light of the history of Aceh and the efforts of the Wahid and Megawati governments to address the situation inherited from the Suharto era. The elucidation of the law attributes the social discontent in Aceh and Acehnese separatism to the centralized policies of previous regimes and the resulting injustices to the Acehnese people.[20] Instead of characterizing the Acehnese as "rebellious," the law describes them in a positive and heroic way, and as the embodiment of Indonesian nationalist ideals:

> One special characteristic manifest in the history of the struggle of the people of Aceh is the great resilience and fighting spirit derived from their worldview and sense of community infused with Islamic ideals, so much so that the region of Aceh has become an inspiration for those striving to achieve and preserve the independence of the Republic of Indonesia.[21]

The Acehnese character that makes the region a model for Indonesian nationalism becomes a reason for granting Aceh privileged autonomy and permitting the region to bear the name "Nanggroe Aceh Darussalam." The Indonesian form of the Qur'anic phrase *dār al-salām* (literally, "the abode of peace") is attached to Aceh to represent its strong Islamic culture. Peace, however, has historically been hard to come by in the region.

A comparison of the treatments of Islamic law and the Shari'a Courts in the initial draft and in the final versions of the Law on Nanggroe Aceh Darussalam reveals several important differences.[22] First, the draft of the Law begins with the phrase: "With the blessing of God (*Allah*) the Most Powerful," whereas the revised text begins with: "With the blessing of the One and Only God (*Tuhan*)." The former seems to be more "Islamic" by its use of Allah rather than the general Indonesian-language term for God found in the preamble to most Indonesian legislation. Second, it is surprising that there is no mention of either the Shari'a Courts or Islamic law in the draft. The draft also makes no reference to "Religious Courts" although they were already established in Aceh prior to this legislation. The word *mahkamah* is used in its secular sense to refer to *Mahkamah Tinggi* (High Courts) and *Mahkamah Rendah* (Low Courts), which are envisaged as exercising jurisdiction over all legal matters, including those under the jurisdiction of Islamic Religious Courts. The only specific mention of Islamic law in the draft is contained in Article 12, which states:

1. The judicial power in the Nanggroe shall be exercised by an independent and impartial judiciary.
2. The judiciary referred to in subsection (1) has jurisdiction over all civil, criminal, administrative, religious, and customary matters, as well as other matters in the Nanggroe that are regulated in the Qanuns based on Shari'a.

In contrast to the draft, the Shari'a Courts have a prominent place in the final Act. The Shari'a itself and the Shari'a Courts are central features of Chapter XII of the Law on NAD, and that chapter has become the basis for further executive branch regulation of Islamic law in Aceh.

It bears mention that both the draft and the Act use the term *qanun* (including the variant spelling, *kanun*) in a secular rather than a religious sense. In the draft *qanun* is defined as "legislation (*peraturan perundang-undang-an*) that regulates the affairs of the Nanggroe" and that is "formulated by the Wali Nanggroe and the People's Council of Aceh (*Dewan Rakyat Aceh*)." The definition in the statute is to the same effect: *qanun* is defined as "regional regulations (*peraturan daerah, perda*) intended for the implementation of the Law on Special Autonomy for the Privileged Province of Aceh as the Nanggroe Aceh Darussalam." In both texts the term *qanun* is no more than an Arabicized label for regional regulations that serves to cast them in a more "Islamic" hue. It appears then that with respect to Islamic law the central government actually gave more than the regional government requested. As we shall see, however, a new dynamic gradually emerged after the Law on NAD had been enacted. Responding to demands from the Acehnese religious establishment, the regional government came to find itself asking for more than the central government had offered.

From Religious Courts to Shari'a Courts

In March 2003 President Megawati Sukarnoputri issued Presidential Decision No. 11/2003 implementing the provisions of the Law on NAD relating to the Shari'a Courts.[23] The Decision effectuates the transformation of the existing Religious Courts to the new institution of Shari'a Courts.[24] The issues covered in the Decision include the name, territorial jurisdiction, and powers of the courts, as well as the status of the employees, infrastructure, and financial resources. The most important difference between the Religious Courts and the new Shari'a Courts is the broadening of the Courts' powers. Sofyan Saleh, Chair of the Religious High Court for Aceh, described the change as involving the addition of authority over public and criminal law to the Courts' existing jurisdiction over family law.[25] The Decision also extends the Courts' powers beyond the strictly legal to include "matters of worship" (*ʿibādāt*) and "Islamic symbolism" (*syiar*). Article 3:1 of the Decision states:

> The powers and authority (*kekuasaan dan kewenangan*) of the Mahkamah Syariah and Provincial Mahkamah Syariah consist of the powers and authority of the Religious Courts and Religious High Court, *augmented with further powers and authority related to social life in the fields of worship (ʿibādāt) and Islamic symbolism (syiar)* as shall be provided for in the Qanun. (Emphasis added)

Several features of this Decision are noteworthy. First, it is apparent that the Decision was issued as a transitional measure and without sufficient prior preparation. This is clear from the initial "Considerations" for the Decision where it is vaguely suggested that implementation of the Decision will be carried out in stages because critical regulations had not been finalized. Secondly, the Decision fails to clarify what is meant by "Shariʿa." Nor does the Decision indicate the extent to which the Qanuns mentioned in the Decision are intended to serve as codifications of the Shariʿa. This ambiguity has become a primary locus of struggle as the central government, the regional government, and the local religious establishment have all attempted to impose their preferred view of the scope of the Courts' powers.

Finally, other actions by the Indonesian government during the same time frame undermined the goals of the Decision. The Presidential Decision on the Shariʿa Courts was part of the government's strategy for gaining the trust and sympathy of the Acehnese people. Shortly after the Decision was issued, however, the government began escalating its military rhetoric, and two months later President Megawati formally declared a state of military emergency in Aceh.[26]

There is a significant disconnect between the discourses on Shariʿa for Aceh at the level of the central government and locally in Aceh. For the central government, Shariʿa is principally a matter of changing the name of the Courts. The grant of new powers to the Courts over worship and symbolism seems to be based on an assumption that the matters over which the Courts have been given authority are already practiced as part of Acehnese daily life. Because the Courts' new powers relate to enforcement of norms that are already followed, those powers are, as a practical matter, insignificant. The Acehnese regional government and the local religious establishment view the steps taken by the central government very differently. For them it is not simply a matter of a change in terminology but involves the addition of significant new powers.

Shari‘a Courts as part of the national judicial system

The creation of the Shari‘a Courts with authority over worship and symbolism replayed some of the same conversations that had occurred at the
time of the enactment of the Religious Judicature Act (Law No. 7/1989).
As was then the case, nationalists, non-Muslims, and progressive/liberal
Muslims criticized the policy of state enforcement of religious laws both in
newspapers and other public fora and inside the legislature. On both occasions the objections to the policies focused on three points: 1) the creation
of special courts for discrete segments of the population is contrary to the
principle of legal uniformity; 2) the enforcement of Islamic law would revive
the "Jakarta Charter," a reference to language contained in an early draft
of the 1945 Constitution obligating the state to implement Shari‘a for
Muslims; and 3) the enforcement of Islamic doctrine would lead to the
establishment of an Islamic state. Related to these points, a question was
also raised as to the position of Shari‘a Courts within the national legal
and judicial systems, which are officially described as based on the non-
sectarian national ideology of Pancasila rather than on Islam.

The relationship between the Shari‘a Courts and the rest of the Indonesian
legal system has proven to be a major point of disagreement between
Jakarta and Aceh. Indonesia's Basic Law on the Judiciary (Law No. 14/1970)
provides for a unified national judiciary consisting of four systems of courts
operating under a single Supreme Court. The four court systems that comprise the judiciary are the Civil Courts, Religious Courts, Military Courts,
and Administrative Courts. The Supreme Court administers the four court
systems and also has ultimate authority over the law that is applied in each
system through its power to decide appeals in cassation.

As discussed above, the Shari‘a Courts were created as part of a law
that purported to grant a degree of autonomy to the provincial government in Aceh. The Law on NAD, however, conceives of the Courts and
the law as part of the national legal and judicial system. This has been a
non-negotiable point for the central government, and the language of the
statute is unequivocal. Article 25 states that "the Shari‘a Courts (*Pengadilan
Syariat Islam*) in the Nanggroe Aceh Darussalam Province are part of the
national judicial system," and that the authority of the Courts "is based
on Shari‘a in the framework of the national legal system, as shall be regulated by the Qanun of the Nanggroe Aceh Darussalam Province." Moreover,
it is the Supreme Court that has the authority to resolve questions relating to the scope of the Shari‘a Courts' powers (Article 27). As an additional measure to ensure that the Shari‘a Courts conform to the national

judicial system, the Supreme Court, along with the Departments of Religion, Home Affairs, and Justice and Human Rights, established a "support team" (*tim asistensi*) to formulate the organization and competence standards of the Shari'a Courts.[27]

The Shari'a Courts and "comprehensive Shari'a"

The Law on NAD was ratified in August 2001 during the Presidency of Megawati Sukarnoputri. Prior to the passage of the special autonomy law, however, the regional government in Aceh initiated the application of Shari'a through the promulgation of Regional Regulation (*Peraturan Daerah, Perda*) No. 5/2000 on the Implementation of Islamic Shari'a (the "Regional Regulation").[28] Issued on July 25, 2000, during the Abdurrahman Wahid presidency, this Regulation designates the Qur'an and the Prophetic tradition as the highest legal authorities in the Province—above the 1945 Constitution—and requires the regional government to develop, guide, and monitor the implementation of Shari'a (Article 3). It also declares that individual Muslims are obliged to obey and practice Shari'a in its totality (*kaffah*) and in a precise and orderly manner in their daily lives (Article 4). The Regulation specifies punishments (Chap. V) including imprisonment, fines, and *adat* sanctions (Article 19) for violations, but *ḥudūd* penalties are not specifically mentioned.

Following the enactment of the Law on NAD and the issuance of the Presidential Instruction on Shari'a Courts in 2003, the Acehnese authorities undertook a revision of the Regulation to conform to the new framework. The Shari'a Office (*Dinas Syariat Islam*), the regional government office charged with producing Shari'a regulations, drafted legislation (*qanun*) on Shari'a Courts and the implementation of Shari'a in the fields of creed, worship, and symbolism. The drafts were circulated in academic circles, such as the Faculties of Law and Economics at Syah Kuala University, the Faculty of Shari'a at the IAIN Ar-Raniry, and among Islamic NGOs, including Forka (*Forum Kereta*, the Aceh CARE Forum) and Yayasan Ukhuwa. The regional legislative assembly discussed the drafts in September of 2002. During these discussions representatives of the regional assembly consulted with the Supreme Court, the Minister of Justice and Human Rights, and the Minister of Religion in Jakarta. The regional assembly completed its deliberations in early October. The draft was ratified (*disahkan*) by the Council of People's Representatives (*Dewan Perwakilan Rakyat*, DPR) on October 14, 2002, and enacted (*diundangkan*) by the President on January 6, 2003.

Shortly after approval by the DPR, a team of regional government officials met with representatives of the central government to discuss establishment of the Shari'a Courts. Five points were agreed on at this meeting: (1) Shari'a in Aceh was to be implemented in a comprehensive way (*kaffah*); (2) Shari'a should be implemented gradually; (3) investigation and prosecution in the Shari'a Courts were to be in the hands of the police and attorneys; (4) there was a need for the formation of a central governmental working group on Shari'a Courts, to be coordinated by the Department of Home Affairs, that would be headed by a general secretary and include representatives from the Indonesian police and Supreme Court, as well as the Departments of Home Affairs, Justice and Human Rights, and Religion; and (5) the formal creation of Shari'a Courts would take place on or before 1 Muharram 1424 A.H. (March 4, 2003).[29]

The discourse on implementation of Shari'a in Aceh has given rise to a social and religious ideal of "comprehensive (*kaffah*) implementation of Shari'a" or "comprehensive Shari'a" that has assumed the status of master signifier in Acehnese society. The Shari'a Courts and Shari'a have been promoted by the Acehnese religious establishment, but they have also been "socialized" (*disosializasikan*) by local governments from the village level to the provincial government in Banda Aceh.[30] This socialization process includes a mixture of publicity, education, indoctrination, and enforcement with a goal of enlisting public support and putting the policy into effect. Local authorities throughout the province have mounted socialization campaigns through the formation of special bodies such as the "Team for the Socialization of Shari'a" created in the district of Singkil in May 2002. As explained by the Singkil Team, these campaigns often target non-Muslims as well as Muslims to avoid misunderstandings among non-Muslims and to allay fears that the implementation of Shari'a will threaten their continuing to live peacefully in the region (*Serambi Indonesia*, May 28, 2002).

Institutions within Aceh engaged in the implementation of Shari'a have promoted an interpretation of Shari'a in line with contemporary normative conceptions of Sunni orthodoxy. The Shari'a Office, the government office with direct responsibility for Shari'a regulations, has worked closely with the religious establishment represented principally by the *Majelis Permusyawaratan Ulama* (MPU, Consultative Assembly of Ulama). Other social, religious, and political groups involved in Shari'a development and enforcement include the Mosque-Based Muslim Youth Organization (*Badan Komunikasi Pemuda Remaja Masjid Indonesia*, BKPRMI), the local State Institute of Islamic Studies (IAIN Ar-Raniry), *Badan Kontak Majelis Taklim* (The Coordinating Board for the Council of Islamic Learning, BKMT), and several national

Islamic political parties, including the Crescent Moon and Star Party (*Partai Bintang Bulan*, PBB), the United Development Party (*Partai Persatuan Pembangunan*, PPP), and the Justice and Prosperity Party (*Partai Keadilan Sejahtera*, PKS).[31] These institutions have assumed the role of society-based "watchdogs" of the regional government's efforts at implementation of comprehensive Shari'a.

The former Governor of Aceh, Abdullah Puteh, issued several major pieces of legislation on Shari'a and its implementation. Two pieces were issued on October 14, one on Shari'a Courts (*Pengadilan Syariat Islam*) (Qanun No. 10/2002),[32] and one on the implementation of the Islamic creed (*'aqīda*), worship (*'ibādāt*), and symbolism (*syiar*) (Qanun No. 11/2002).[33] An additional three Qanuns on intoxicants (*khamr*) (Qanun No. 12/2003), gambling (*maysir*) (Qanun No. 13/2003), and improper relations between the sexes (*khalwat*, Ar. *khalwa*) (Qanun No. 14) were issued on July 16, 2003.[34]

Islamic creed, worship, and symbolism

The current legal basis for realization of the "comprehensive Shari'a" is contained in Qanun No. 11/2002. This Qanun provides for implementation of Shari'a in three areas: creed, worship, and symbolism. The regulation of these subjects in the Qanun will be dealt with below. It bears mention, however, that these comprise only a part of the vision of comprehensive Shari'a contemplated by Qanun 11/2002. Article 1:6 anticipates the promulgation of further regulations in the future providing for the enforcement of "Islamic teachings concerning all aspects of life."

State enforcement of Islamic doctrine inevitably presents thorny political and religious questions. Apart from the status of non-Muslims, which will be discussed later, problems arise as to which concept of creed, worship, and symbolism are to be implemented, and according to which theological and legal schools of Islam. Qanun No. 11/2002 defines creed (*'aqīda*) in an exclusive and normative way: "*'Aqīda* is Islamic *'aqīda* according to the *Ahl al-Sunna wa l-Jama'a* [Sunnis]" (Article 1:7). Other theological schools, such as the Shi'a, Mu'tazila, and Ahmadiyya, are all lumped into the basket of "deviant beliefs and currents" and not allowed to exist in Aceh (Arts. 4, 5, and 6).[35] It seems likely that other non-orthodox liberal-progressive strains of Islamic thought will be relegated to the same category.

Qanun No. 11/2002 requires individual Muslims (Article 5:1), families (Article 4:2), social institutions, and local Acehnese government offices (Article 4:1) to protect and build up the creed. Individuals are "forbidden to disseminate deviant beliefs and currents [of thought]" (Article 5:2).

Violation of this prohibition is punishable by "a discretionary punishment (*ta'zīr*) of two years in jail or 12 strokes of the cane applied in a public caning" (Article 20:1). Religious conversion and blasphemy are also prohibited: "It is forbidden for any individual to convert deliberately from the [Islamic] creed and/or to condemn and/or blaspheme Islamic religion" (Article 5:3). The authority to determine which beliefs or currents deviate from Islamic orthodoxy is assigned to the *Majelis Permusyawaratan Ulama* (MPU) (Article 6). When requested by the Shari'a Courts, the MPU is required to provide fatwas on issues of creed. These pronouncements are then binding on the court. Qanun No. 11 does not specify punishments for religious conversion and blasphemy. It is stated that those matters are to be regulated in future regulations (Article 20:2).

The regulation of worship in Qanun No. 11/2002 is limited in scope—worship is defined as prayer (*salāt*) and fasting during Ramadan (Article 1:8)—but it nevertheless has the potential for enormous impact on public life. Government offices and social institutions are required to provide facilities for and to create an environment conducive to worship (Article 7:1). Parents are obliged to guide the worship of their children and all family members (Article 7:2). Attendance at Friday congregational prayers is mandatory for all Muslim males who do not have a legally recognized excuse (*udzur syar'i*). Government offices and social and educational institutions are obligated to suspend activities that interfere with congregational prayers (Article 8:1–2), to provide space and other facilities for Friday prayers, and to actively encourage individuals to pray. Neighborhood (*gampong*) leaders are responsible for mobilizing residents for congregational prayers and mass religious gatherings (*pengajian agama*). Operators of public transportation facilities are required to provide facilities for obligatory prayers and to allow passengers to perform the prayers (Article 9:1–3).

The provisions of Qanun No. 11/2002 concerning the Ramadan fast forbid both business enterprises and individuals from actions that create opportunities for violating or avoiding the fast. The Qanun does not explicitly require Muslims to fast, but states that any Muslim who does not have a "legally recognized Shari'a excuse" is forbidden to eat and drink publicly in the daytime during Ramadan. It also encourages performance of the special prayer during Ramadan known as *tarāwīh* and other practices that are recommended (*sunna*) during Ramadan (Article 10:1–3).

Qanun No. 11/2002 defines *syiar* as "all activities containing worship-related values for supporting and glorifying the implementation of Islamic tenets" (Article 1:5). *Syiar* is not, however, limited to "activities." In other parts of the Qanun it refers to Islamic symbols such as the Malay-Arabic script (*jawi*), the Muslim calendar and "Islamic dress." The Qanun enjoins provincial and local government as well as social institutions to commemorate Islamic festivals.[36] It is also suggested that government offices, private institutions, and individuals use Malay-Arabic script in addition to Roman script, and use both the Muslim and Western calendars in official letters. In certain official documents, the use of the Muslim calendar is mandatory (Article 12:1–4).

Article 13:1 of Qanun No. 11/2002 requires that "Every Muslim must dress in Islamic clothing." Islamic clothing (*busana Islami*) in this context includes the *jilbab* for women and clothing that covers at least that part of the body from navel to knee for men. Government offices, educational institutions, businesses, and other social institutions are made responsible for making the use of "Islamic dress" customary in their surroundings. These regulations on religious practice and orthodoxy have had the result of extending the power of the state over the personal life of Acehnese men and women. Prayer, fasting, and wearing the *jilbab* are no longer private choices, but rather subject to government regulation and official enforcement.

Intoxicants, gambling, and unchaperoned activities

Qanun No. 12/2003 defines intoxicants (*khamr*) as all kinds of drinks that are destructive to health, consciousness, and clear thinking. It prohibits not only the drinks themselves but also "all activities related to *khamr* and the like." The catalogue of banned *khamr*-related activities is exhaustive, including "producing, preparing, selling, pouring, distributing, carrying away, storing, hoarding, trading, offering, and promoting" (Article 6). The prohibition applies broadly to hotels, restaurants, cafés, and bars, as well as foreign institutions and the premises of foreign companies or those with foreign employees (Articles 7 and 8). Punishments for violations of this regulation have also been specified: anyone who drinks an intoxicant is threatened with the *ḥudūd* punishment of 40 strokes with a cane.[37] Individuals or institutions found to have performed activities related to *khamr* are subject to discretionary punishments, namely, imprisonment (maximum one year, minimum three months), and/or fines (maximum Rp. 75 million, minimum Rp. 25 million) (Article 26).

Qanun No. 13/2003 prohibits all forms of gambling (*maysir*) and associated activities. In this legislation *maysir* is defined as "betting activities and/or actions between two or more individuals or parties in which the winner receives some payment." Every individual and institution is prohibited to provide the means for or facilitate gambling (Articles 5–8). The punishment for gambling is either the discretionary punishment of caning (six to 12 times) in public, or fines of Rp. 15–35 million (Article 23).

Khalwat, as prohibited by Qanun No. 14/2003, is defined as "actions involving two or more non-marriageable and non-married, mature (*mukallaf*) men and women in isolated places." Persons who engage in *khalwat* are threatened with the discretionary punishment of caning (maximum nine times, minimum three times) and/or fines of Rp. 2.5–10 million (Article 22:1). The regulation also prohibits individuals and institutions from facilitating or protecting activities leading to *khalwat* (Articles 5–7). Those who facilitate or protect *khalwat* are punishable with imprisonment (two to six months), and/or fines of Rp. 5–15 million (Article 22:2). As with the other legislative measures, enforcement of this Qanun is overseen by the Wilayatul Hisbah.

Wilayatul Hisbah and Shari'a police

Oversight of Shari'a enforcement is assigned to the Wilayatul Hisbah, which is under the administrative authority of the Shari'a Office and tasked with "protecting public order and morality and providing expeditious resolution of minor offences" (Muhammad 2003, 102). According to the Qanun, Wilayatul Hisbah offices are to be established at the provincial, municipal, village, and even lower administrative levels (Qanun No. 11/2002, Article 14:1). The Wilayatul Hisbah does not have judicial authority. It may, however, issue warnings to those who commit minor infractions, such as unveiling for women or wearing too short trousers for men. If necessary, Wilayatul Hisbah may bring the offender before an investigating officer (*pejabat penyidik*). Investigating officers include Shari'a police and certain civil servants who have been granted specific authority to investigate such matters (Article 15:1). Current regulations require the appointment of about 2,500 Shari'a police officers whose duties are to include serving as investigating officers for the Shari'a Courts and overseeing the implementation of Shari'a generally.[38]

Women and non-Muslims

One of the most significant impacts of the implementation of the Shari'a in Aceh has been the formal obligation for women to wear the *jilbab*, and "jilbabization" has become a central issue in the implementation of the comprehensive Shari'a. Local police officers have distributed *jilbab* head-scarves to unveiled women on the street as part of the campaign to "social-ize" Shari'a and "enhance the image (*citra*) of women."[39]

The Shari'a apparatus has used the enforcement of rules regarding Islamic dress to hegemonize both the meaning of *jilbab* and the definition of female gender. According to Teungku Lembong Misbah, head of the Wilayatul Hisbah of the Shari'a Office, the *jilbab* should cover all parts of a woman's body considered to be "shameful" (*aurat*), should be loose, not transparent and not show the shape of the body. Tight fitting sports clothing, for exam-ple, is not allowed. Beyond these requirements the form of the *jilbab* is flexible.[40]

Professor Al Yasa' Abubakar, the head of the Shari'a Office, has stated that the purpose of covering the *aurat* is to honor women and protect their dignity, as well as to symbolize their Islamic identity. Women who cover their *aurat* are considered to be good and respectable women.[41] It is the responsibility of the Wilayatul Hisbah to conduct "raids" (*razia*) upon women who do not wear the appropriate *jilbab*. Though much less stringently enforced, the Wilayatul Hisbah are also charged to ensure that clothing worn by men fits the criteria for Islamic dress.[42]

The implementation of Shari'a in Aceh does not restrict women to house-hold activities, as is the case in some other countries where "Islamic law" is enforced. Aceh has a long history of women's involvement in the pub-lic sphere. Four of Aceh's rulers in the seventeenth century were women (*sultana*). Aceh also has a history of local Muslim heroines such as Tjut Nja' Dien and Tjut Nja' Meutia who fought against Dutch colonialism. In 2003 the Governor of Aceh, Abdullah Puteh, issued an assurance that the implementation of the Shari'a "would not reduce the rights and freedoms of women to education, work, protection, political involvement, and par-ticipation in public life. Women are allowed to become legislators and civil servants."[43]

The regional government has taken the position that the implementa-tion of Shari'a does not apply to non-Muslims. Governor Puteh has stated that Shari'a requires that "non-Muslims be respected, honored, protected, given the freedom to express their religious tenets, to worship peacefully, and to build places of worship according to their needs."[44] It is undeni-able, however, that the implementation of Shari'a has affected the lives of Aceh's non-Muslim communities. Most Acehnese believe that all Acehnese people are Muslims, and that most of the non-Muslims in the region are "immigrants."[45] As mentioned earlier, the socialization of Shari'a has been directed at non-Muslim citizens as well as Muslims in order to reassure them and avoid misunderstanding (*Serambi Indonesia*, May 28, 2002). While in principle the religious freedom of the minority is to be respected (Muhammad 2003, 63), non-Muslims, like other citizens, are obliged formally at least to respect Islamic worship practices according to existing Shari'a legislation in Aceh (Qanun No. 11/2002, Article 11).

The Acehnese regional government has avoided describing the region's non-Muslims as a protected community (*ahl al-dhimma*), and this is probably deliberate. The Islamic legal concept of *ahl al-dhimma* is very sensitive, and its use might be understood to mean that there exists a "protected, dominated minority" and a "protecting, ruling majority" and that the former is obliged to pay poll tax (*jizya*) to the latter. Although the government has refrained from describing non-Muslims as *ahl al-dhimma*, the concept of poll tax is being discussed in some Islamic scholarly circles in the region.[46]

How far will implementation of "comprehensive Shari'a" proceed in Aceh?

The understanding of Shari'a reflected in central government discourse differs from the understanding that exists in Aceh. For the central government, the Shari'a to be implemented in Aceh consists of matters currently applied in the rest of Indonesia, that is, Islamic family law, with the addition of creed, worship and symbolism. The impression, moreover, is that the addition of authority over these three areas to the powers of the Shari'a Courts will entail little if any coercion or public enforcement, since the new powers assigned to the Courts relate to matters that are already practiced spontaneously by Acehnese Muslims.

The regulatory Qanuns promulgated in Aceh have translated the central government discourse into the concept of comprehensive Shari'a. "Shari'a is Islamic guidance in all aspects of life" (*Syariat Islam adalah tuntunan ajaran Islam dalam semua aspek kehidupan*). As this statement makes clear, Shari'a is not to be "partially" implemented (*unsur-unsur syariat Islam*), as was stipulated by the 1962 decision of Aceh's martial law administration and in the 1989 Religious Judicature Act, but its implementation is to be "comprehensive" (*kaffah*). It is also clear that the implementation of Islamic legal doctrines in Aceh differs from that which occurs in the rest of Indonesia.

Over the course of these developments the idea of the "comprehensive Shari'a" (*syariat Islam yang kaffah*) has become a master signifier in public discourses about law and society in Aceh. By this I mean that it is not only part of religious establishment discourse, but has also become part of regional government discourses, from provincial to village levels. This has significant implications for the Islamization of both the private and the public spheres. As noted above, the use of Arabic script (*jawi*) alongside Roman script for the names of shops, markets, and government offices, the inclusion of *basmallah* in Arabic in official letters, the use of the Islamic calendar, and the "jilbabization" of the region's women are only some examples of the effects of implementation of Shari'a in the field of Islamic symbolism. All elements of Acehnese society have been mobilized to support the Shari'atization programs. Furthermore, all legislation produced in Aceh, including those concerning secular matters, must not contradict the government's conception of Shari'a.

To measure the extent of the implementation of "comprehensive Shari'a" in Aceh, it is useful here to adopt David E. Price's categorization of its reach into five legal spheres:

1. Issues of personal status, such as marriage and divorce;
2. The regulations of economic matters, such as banking and business practices;
3. Prescribed religious practices, such as restrictions on women's clothing, alcohol, and other practices that are considered against Islam;
4. The use of Islamic criminal law and punishment;
5. The use of Islam as a guide for governance. (Price 1999, 145)

Unlike the implementation of Shari'a in Indonesia in general, which is mostly restricted to the first and second of these levels,[47] the implementation of Shari'a in Aceh has also extended to the third level and partly to the fourth level. As in other regions, the law concerning marriage, divorce, inheritance, and *waqf* has long been under the jurisdiction of the Religious Courts. During the Reformasi period, *zakāt* institutions and Shari'a banks were established in Aceh.[48] In 2002, for instance, the Regional Development Bank established four Shari'a banks in Banda Aceh, Lhokseumawe, Langsa, and Meulaboh.[49] As discussed above, the state apparatus in Aceh has become involved in imposing religious duties on Muslim citizens.

Despite the prevailing rhetoric of "comprehensiveness" (*kaffah*), however, implementation of Islamic penal law has so far been partial and tentative. The Qanuns provide for discretionary punishments (caning, fines, and imprisonment) and "light *ḥudūd*" (caning for consumption of intoxicants and narcotics).[50] Harsh penalties in the form of amputations, stoning, and retaliation (*qiṣāṣ*) are not yet authorized.[51] There are several possible reasons

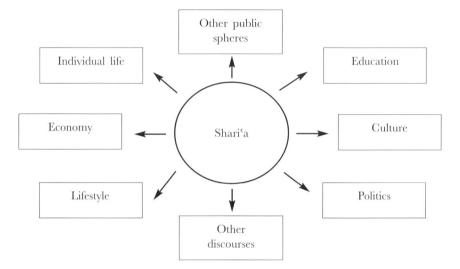

Diagram 2. The Shariʿa as "Master Signifier" in contemporary Aceh

for delay in their implementation. First, these punishments are seen by many as violating positive national law. Secondly, there are concerns that harsh penal sanctions might contribute to "unexpected," pejorative images of Islamic law. This concern is evident in a statement by Governor Puteh at the time of the inauguration of the Shariʿa Courts, who said that the implementation of Shariʿa by the Court would proceed "moderately and gradually." Puteh also said that the government had no desire to violate human rights or gender justice with the implementation of Shariʿa, which is sometimes associated with controversial punishments and religious radicalism.[52]

This does not mean, however, that the harsher penalties will not be authorized in the future. The elucidation of Article 49:c of Qanun No. 10/2002 states that the sanctions to be adopted for violations of the criminal law (*jināya*) include: (1) *ḥudūd*, (2) *qiṣāṣ/diya*, and (3) *taʿzīr*. Applying a "gradualist" approach, it is stated that *ḥudūd* for apostasy and blasphemy will "be regulated in separate legislation" (Qanun 10/2002, Article 20:2). Gradualism is also to be used with *qiṣāṣ*. To date, however, these penalties are not part of comprehensive Shariʿa in Aceh.

The comprehensive implementation of Shariʿa in Aceh is based on the legal principle of *lex specialis derogat lex generalis*.[53] Under this principle, the more specific regulations for Aceh take precedence over the generally applicable law that applies elsewhere in Indonesia. At the same time, however, it is also stipulated that the Shariʿa implemented in Aceh is in the framework of Indonesian national law. In this context, the Supreme Court is authorized to examine the substance of the Qanun. The status of Acehnese Shariʿa law as both comprehensive and at the same time part of the national legal system has resulted in considerable uncertainty and ambiguity (Qanun No. 10/2002, Article 1:2). First, although the Qurʾan and *ḥadīth* are not explicitly mentioned in the above two Qanuns as the basic principles of the Shariʿa Courts, they are mentioned along with "secular," national legal authorities as references or sources for Qanun Nos. 10/2002, 11/2002, 12/2003, 13/2003, and 14/2003. Second, the status and loyalties of Shariʿa Court judges and other personnel is ambiguous. In addition to being Muslim, judges and other personnel of the Shariʿa Court must be civil servants and loyal to the Pancasila and the 1945 Constitution (Qanun No. 10, Articles 12:1; 13:1; 14). The oath of office prescribed for Shariʿa Court judges states: "*Wallahi* [by God, I am taking an oath] that I will be loyal to the Shariʿa, the Pancasila and the 1945 Constitution, and to all other laws and regulations prevailing in Nanggroe Aceh Darussalam" (Qanun No. 10/2002,

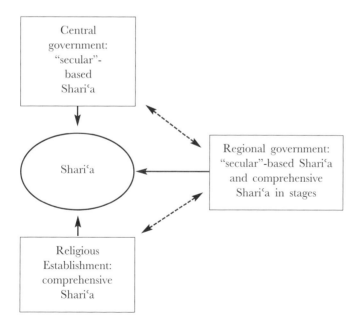

Diagram 3. Shariʿa contested in Aceh

Article 16:1). Third, since June of 2004 the Shari'a Courts have been under
the exclusive control of the secular Supreme Court.[54] This is a change from
the situation that had prevailed prior to 2004 in which the administrative
regulation of the Shari'a Court was under the authority of the Department
of Religion and the Governor (Qanun No. 10/2002, Article 5:1 and 2).
Finally, regulation of the protocol status of the judges is assigned to the
provincial governor (Qanun No. 10, Article 24:1).

As a practical matter, the Shari'a Courts began functioning only in
October 2004 when the government issued Law 4/2004 on the transfer of
commercial and criminal cases from the Civil Courts to the Shari'a Courts.
Prior to the enactment of that law, most litigation in Aceh continued to
be dealt with in the Civil Courts, and the docket of the Shari'a Courts was
limited to matters that had previously been under the jurisdiction of the
Religious Courts. The passage of the legislation paved the way for exercise of the Courts' new powers, and on October 11, 2004 the Chief Justice
of the Supreme Court, Bagir Manan, formally inaugurated the Shari'a
Court. Through these measures, the Shari'a Courts have begun in earnest
to take up their new charges with regard to implementing Shari'a in Aceh.

Concluding remarks

The establishment of the Shari'a Courts and the implementation of a particular conception of Shari'a in Aceh cannot be dissociated from the central government's efforts to develop a "religious approach" to resolve the
status of Aceh within Indonesia. The adoption of this approach was in
some sense intended to advance the agenda of protecting the unity of
Indonesia against the separatist aims of GAM, which was waging an armed
struggle to establish a secular monarchical Acehnese state. The government's encouragement of programs for the implementation of Shari'a was
calculated to convince the people of Aceh of the seriousness of the central
government's intention to deal with the crisis in a peaceful way through
responding positively to Acehnese demands. This approach, together with
military and political initiatives, has apparently proven successful. Nevertheless,
Aceh's experimentation with the implementation of Shari'a under secular
law on a regional level is seen by many as a pilot project that could possibly be followed by other regions of Indonesia.

The ideal of comprehensive Shari'a has thus become a master signifier
that has hegemonized both public and private life in Aceh. As shown above,
however, the implementation of this ideal has so far been less than com-

plete. Nevertheless, the goal of comprehensive implementation could be achieved in two steps: completing the implementation of the fixed (*ḥadd*) punishments and of retaliation, and using Islam as a comprehensive guide for governance. The central Indonesian government regards both of these steps to be contradictory to the national legal system and the *Pancasila* ideology, which is why comprehensive Shari'a has not been fully implemented in Aceh. All of these developments reflect the limits of the politics of Shari'atization exercised by both central and regional government in Aceh.

Eleven

SHARI'A REVIVAL IN ACEH

Tim Lindsey and M.B. Hooker
with Ross Clarke and Jeremy Kingsley

Shari'a has historically been influential in the creation of a distinct Acehnese Islamic identity (Salim 2004). A form of Shari'a was implemented by the Sultanate of Aceh in the late sixteenth or early seventeenth century. Since then, Shari'a has been far more evident in Aceh than in most other parts of Indonesia (Salim 2004; Hooker 1986, 394–405).

Under the pluralist legal system imposed by Dutch colonial rule, Shari'a was not formally recognized as an independent source of law, but was given legal effect to the extent it was accepted by the government or courts as having been absorbed by, or received into local customary law (*adat*) by members of the community in question (Hooker 1984, 244). This principle is known as the "reception theory" or, to the proponents of Shari'a, the devil's theory—*teori iblis*—(Lev 1972), because it conflicts with their conception of Islam as *dīn wa-dawla*, both religion and state. Despite this, the Dutch applied reception theory across Indonesia to marginalize Shari'a within the secularized legal system (Hooker 1984). In Aceh, however, a long tradition of Shari'a combined with the region's history of Muslim kingdoms and its relative isolation at the northern tip of Sumatra to create an Acehnese Islamic identity seen by most Indonesians as distinguishable from other manifestations of Islam elsewhere in the country (Bowen 2003). One result of this has been that in recent times Shari'a has become inextricably bound up with Acehnese identity. Attempts to secularize or displace Shari'a have never been successful in completely removing it from the local political agenda.

The resurgence of Shari'a, and its proponents' desire to privilege it over traditions that originate from sources other than Islamic doctrine (in Aceh, these are often referred to as *adat* or traditional customary law),[1] must be seen within the context of Aceh's desire to move on from its current social and economic problems and return to its past prosperity. For them, the seventeenth to mid-nineteenth centuries are imagined as Aceh's "golden age," a period when it was an independent power in the region, excelling, in relative terms, in the fields of science, law, economics, and politics. For many Acehnese, this period of affluence and progress is, rightly or, more often, wrongly, now linked to a perception of a holistic implementation of Shari‘a.

For a range of reasons, largely to do with the secularizing politics of Indonesian centralist nationalism, Shari‘a had become relatively marginalized as a point of reference in Aceh's public life since the peak of Dutch colonialism in the early 1900s, up to the end of Suharto's New Order in 1998. The recently-elected legislators of the new autonomous Province of Nanggroe Aceh Darussalam (Nation of Aceh, Home of Peace), have made their dissatisfaction with this clear in the text of recent Islamic regulations or Qanuns—laws for Muslims—passed by the Acehnese DPRD[2] or local legislature, pursuant to powers granted post-Suharto as part of a national process of decentralization (discussed below). In their eyes, the marginalizing of Shari‘a is the cause of a perceived corresponding reduction in quality of life and a degradation of Acehnese society and its regional influence (Qanun 11/2002, general elucidation). In this light, the resurgence of Shari‘a can be seen not only as an assertion of Acehnese identity but also as a means of re-emphasizing perceived traditional Acehnese values and thereby, it is hoped, regaining past prosperity.

The implementation of Shari‘a in Aceh and the province's conservative religious outlook more generally, have historically been sources of conflict, both among Acehnese and—more famously—between the Acehnese and outsiders. Aceh's sense of Islamic identity was, for example, an important rallying point for resistance against Dutch colonial forces (Ricklefs 1993) and has been a central aspect of Aceh's differences with the Indonesian central government (Salim 2004). Although Islamic discourse has been marginalized in the region's recent armed conflict with Jakarta, with tension over sovereignty for Aceh, natural resource profits, and human rights violations by the Indonesian military more prominent, the implementation of Shari‘a still remains an important political issue.

The post-Suharto resurgence of this idea of a localized Acehnese Islam has given the province's *‘ulamā’* (religious leaders, hereafter ulama) increased authority in the power struggle resulting from recent attempts to re-establish Shari‘a as a central part of Aceh's legal system. The ulama have benefited through both the Qanuns and a range of new religious institutions, including the MPU or Deliberative Assembly of Ulama (*Majelis Permusyawaratan Ulama*), the latest incarnation of similar bodies that existed in the past. Newer administrative institutions established in the same period, such as the Shari‘a Office (*Dinas Syariat Islam*) or the Wilayatul Hisbah (religious "police") have also benefited from these changes but they arguably lack a local historical and religious heritage of equal resonance and authority. The result is therefore that their influence in the process of implementing Shari'a is constantly tested by the MPU, albeit usually not overtly.

The tension between local and national interests and between religious and other authority is most apparent in Aceh's demands for independence, or, at the very least, significant regional autonomy. A pervasive theme throughout the debate—one that is still prevalent today despite the 2005 Helsinki peace agreement between Jakarta and rebels in Aceh—is the Jakarta bureaucracy's concern to devolve as little power as possible from itself and the secular regional bureaucracy in Aceh to Aceh's ulama. As a result, the process of implementation of a new, expanded version of Shari'a in Aceh has been marked by intense competition for control of the new Shari'a Courts (*Mahkamah Syariah*) established under the Qanuns between, on the one hand, the bureaucratic institutions established by Jakarta and, on the other, the new institutions through which the ulama exercise author- ity. This political competition is understood among Acehnese ulama explic- itly in terms of the "reception theory" debate, with Shari'a being seen as represented by the ulama and the non-Islamic parts of *adat* being repre- sented by the local secular authorities. The general elucidation to Qanun 5/2000 makes this quite clear:

> *Adat* is alive and developed in the life of the community, and is accumulated and summarised in the statement: *Adat bak Poteumeureuhom, Hukum bak Syiah Kuala, Kanun bak Putro Phang, Reusam bak Laksamana*, which means, "*Adat* law is in the hands of the government and Shari'a law is in the hands of the *ulama*." This expression constitutes a reflection of the manifestation of Islamic Shari'a in the practices of daily life.

This tension between secular authorities and the ulama, and the implica- tions of that tension for attempts to implement Shari'a in Aceh, will be examined in more detail shortly. First, however, it is useful to outline the regional autonomy process, as it provides the context within which this contest for power should be understood.

Regional autonomy

Under the newly formed Republic of Indonesia, Aceh enjoyed a five-year period of de facto autonomy from 1945 to 1950, following which it was merged into the larger province of North Sumatra (United Nations Development Program 2003, 23). An armed rebellion led by Daud Beureueh commenced in 1953 and continued until 1959 when a central government resolution granted Aceh "special region" status in a bid to end the rebellion. Under this agreement, the Sukarno government granted Aceh wide autonomy in the fields of religion, education, and custom. Salim (2004) argues that the grant of these powers was effectively meaningless, as Law No. 1 of 1957 on Fundamental Rules of Regional Government, which regulated all of Indonesia's regional governments, continued to apply to Aceh.

Beureueh insisted on legal protection of Aceh's right to implement Shari'a as a prerequisite for acceptance of any regional autonomy offer. The rebellion therefore continued until a compromise was reached in 1962, with the issuance of a decree by military authorities that recognized the application of Islamic law in Aceh (Salim 2004). This settlement, however, was not upheld by the Suharto administration after it took power in 1966, and hope for the implementation of Shari'a seemed dashed when Law 5/1974 on Regional Government effectively abolished Aceh's hard-won special provincial status.

After the fall of Suharto in 1998, regional autonomy became a central aspect of governmental reform, and the Habibie administration that succeeded Suharto granted Indonesia's regional governments significant legislative authority (International Crisis Group 2001, 3). In an effort to prevent further separatist conflict between the armed Acehnese independence movement known as GAM (*Gerakhan Aceh Merdeka* or Free Aceh Movement) and the Indonesian armed forces, Aceh was allowed special regional status.

Law 44/1999 on the Special Status of the Province of Aceh formally granted the Acehnese authority to govern their religious, cultural, and educational life (United Nations Development Program 2003, 1). This meant that the province could implement Shari'a in social life, enact policies to empower and preserve customary institutions, include Shari'a within the education system, and establish a body of ulama to advise on regional policy (United Nations Development Program 2003, 8). Accordingly, regulations relating to Islamic dress, gambling, and alcohol were passed but, because there were minimal enforcement procedures, the new regulations had little effect on day-to-day life (International Crisis Group 2001, 13) for much of the next half-decade. Aside from this, Law 44/1999 did not contain any significant economic or political rights not already granted to other regions in the decentralization legislation (International Crisis Group 2001, 3). Nevertheless, as in other provinces, a Regional Legislative Council (Dewan Perwakilan Rakyat Daerah) was established and a governor was appointed to exercise executive power (International Crisis Group 2001, 8).

Special autonomy

As tension between GAM and the Indonesian armed forces intensified and anxieties grew in Jakarta about the potential for disintegration of the multi-ethnic Indonesian state, Jakarta was pressured to grant further concessions. This culminated in the grant of a new special autonomy package pursuant to Law 18/2001. This statute formally created the province of Nanggroe Aceh Darussalam and granted Aceh a more extensive form of self-government and a larger share of the profits from its natural resources (International Crisis Group 2001, 12). The Preamble to this Law reflects the Indonesian Government's intention to recognize Aceh's unique situation, but it also manifests an intention to limit the accommodation granted to Aceh within the confines of a unitary, republican state:

> One special characteristic manifest in the history of the struggle of the people of Aceh is the great resilience and fighting spirit derived from their worldview and sense of community infused with Islamic ideals, so much so that the region of Aceh has become an inspiration for those striving to achieve and preserve the independence of the Republic of Indonesia.

Since then, the Helsinki Agreement has been signed, which has further confirmed Aceh's autonomy and, in particular, its capacity to create a local system of governance derived from Islamic norms. In January 2006, President Bambang Susilo Yudhoyono submitted the Bill on Governance in Aceh to the National Legislature (*Dewan Perwakilan Rakyat*, DPR) for consideration. The Bill contained provisions that gave new legitimacy to Aceh's Islamic laws and institutions. Debate was scheduled for February and March 2006 but was continuing still in May 2006, amid some controversy. The balance of this chapter will therefore focus principally on the situation in Aceh prior to the Helsinki Agreement pursuant to Law 18/2001, much of the substance of which is likely to be basically confirmed in any future legislative regime.[3]

Law 18/2001 gave Aceh the power to create formal symbols of autonomous government. In particular, under Article 10 a *Wali Nanggroe* (symbolic head of state) and *Tuha Nanggroe* (council of elders) can be appointed. These positions are intended to be symbolic, rather than political, and were created to assist in the conservation of "traditional and cultural life." They have had little impact on the Acehnese political structure (International Crisis Group 2001, 12).

The Special Autonomy Law differs from the previous regional autonomy laws in that the primary locus of power in Aceh is at the provincial, rather than district, level (International Crisis Group 2001, 12). Thus, under

Law 18/2001 the province of Aceh has substantial control over areas such as revenue and law and order matters (including policing). More importantly for the purposes of this paper, the Special Autonomy Law also allowed locally-made laws to be based on Shari'a (International Crisis Group 2001, 13). The Law is thus, to this extent at least, a realization of the demands made by Daud Beureueh almost 50 years earlier (Salim 2004).

The primary advance in the implementation of Shari'a from the regional autonomy legislation of 1999 was the power to establish Shari'a Courts. Thus, Article 25 of Law 18/2001 establishes the Shari'a Court of the Province of Nanggroe Aceh Darussalam. Under Article 25(2), the authority of the Court is based on Shari'a as found "within the system of national law" which is "further regulated by Qanuns" of Aceh. These instruments will be discussed in detail below. It is important to note here, however, that under the Special Autonomy legislation the Acehnese Shari'a Court can only apply Shari'a when it is consistent with national law. As will be seen, this has been a highly significant and very restrictive qualification.

Aside from making its jurisdiction consistent with national law, the central government sought further control over the Shari'a Court by granting the Supreme Court (*Mahkamah Agung*) in Jakarta ultimate appeal authority (Art. 26(2) of Law 18/2001; International Crisis Group 2001, 12). The Supreme Court can thereby place considerable constraint on the actions of the Shari'a Court and effectively retains the discretion to overrule any decisions that it thinks depart from national secularist standards. The central government can further influence the Shari'a Court through the exercise of its role in the selection of judges. The Head of State has the power to appoint and dismiss judges on the proposal of the Minister for Justice who, in putting forward a candidate, must take into account the advice of the Governor of Aceh and the Chairman of the Supreme Court (Article 26(3) of Law 18/2001).

As indicated above, Law 18/2001 left most of the detail on the implementation of Shari'a to be determined by legislation to be produced by Aceh's DPRD at a later stage. However, there are aspects of the broad framework established under the special autonomy legislation that deserve comment.

First, the provision of Shari'a Courts, although a significant political symbol in granting autonomy, is severely limited by the Supreme Court's appellate jurisdiction. Clearly, Jakarta wanted to be seen as making significant concessions in regard to Shari'a but intended to retain ultimate authority.

Second, many Acehnese do not see Shari'a as directly relevant to the grievances behind the recent armed conflict, although the opposite has sometimes been true in the past (International Crisis Group 2001, 10), as,

for example, under Daud Beureueh. Shari'a and the hostilities between
GAM and the Indonesian military are, of course, linked because they both
relate to Acehnese self-identity. Today's conflict, however, seems primarily
concerned with Aceh's relationship with the central government, particularly the abstract question of political sovereignty and the much less abstract
questions of revenue from natural resource exploitation and human rights
violations (International Crisis Group 2001, 10). In this light, the allowance
of a broader if still limited implementation of Shari'a under the new regulatory regime can be seen as a political tool used by Jakarta to make
regional autonomy more palatable to the Acehnese and thereby to fend
off demands for complete independence. This strategy has had some success. The important place of Shari'a in Aceh's fight for self-determination
is not to be discounted, but it must be acknowledged that the central government has very successfully manipulated Shari'a for political purposes,
to the extent that the implementation of Shari'a has now been largely
detached from the idea of independence (Salim 2004). The flipside of this,
however, is that demands for implementation of Shari'a are unlikely to
cease, whatever the outcome of hostilities in the future.

Third, although the framework for the implementation of Shari'a was
laid down in autonomy legislation emanating from Jakarta, the substance
and detail of how the new court system would operate was left to be determined by Qanun. Aceh's regional legislature, the DPRD, which produces
the Qanuns, was thus the driving force behind defining how Shari'a, once
allowed, would be defined and applied. It has also been instrumental in
creating new institutions to oversee the putative transition to a Shari'a-
based legal system. It is important, therefore, to review the Qanuns to
determine the scope of Shari'a in Aceh. This will be the focus for the balance of this paper. It will look first at the structure of new Shari'a institutions, before turning to the substance of Shari'a in Aceh as set out in
the Qanuns themselves.

Institutions

The implementation of Shari'a in Aceh will primarily be overseen by three
institutions. These institutions take over functions previously exercised by
the national judiciary and the secular bureaucracy run from Jakarta, and
represent a meaningful devolution of power from the national to the regional
level. The first is the *Mahkamah Syariah* or Shari'a Court, originally envisaged
in the Special Autonomy Law of 2001. It is essentially Aceh's pre-existing

local branch of the national Religious Court (*Pengadilan Agama*) system, renamed and with a broader jurisdiction to hear cases. It is the symbolic centerpiece of the new Shariʿa system. Although, as will be seen, it is relatively weak, it was, prior to the tsunami of December 2004 at least, resistant to attempts to increase its authority by making it an active proponent of Shariʿa law. Post-tsunami, this has changed. The Court and its trajectory will be considered in more detail in the next section.

The two other Islamic institutions recently created by Aceh's provincial legislature are intended to sit alongside the state administration of Nanggroe Aceh Darussalam and are charged with overseeing the religious aspects of governance in Aceh. These have so far been far more significant players than the Court, at least as regards the process of creating an Acehnese Islamic legal system. The first is the Consultative Assembly of Ulama (MPU). Established under Qanun 3/2000, the MPU is a body comprised of ulama from across Aceh. The MPU must be consulted on laws passed by the regional government and has become heavily involved in both policy formation and the drafting process. The second is the Shariʿa Office, a section within the Governor's Office that has the general role of overseeing Islamic law in the province. The Shariʿa Office has taken a lead role in drafting Qanun bills and claims a leading voice in Shariʿa policy.

As discussed below, there is political competition between these three institutions, and this threatens to aggravate pre-existing divisions between Islamic authority and the state within Aceh. This inter-agency competition is also one of the reasons why implementation of a radical Shariʿa agenda in Aceh moved slowly prior to the tsunami.

Consultative Assembly of Ulama (Majelis Permusyawaratan Ulama or MPU)

Qanun 3/2000, promulgated on June 22, 2000, establishes the Consultative Assembly of Ulama, a new institution that must be consulted on all laws passed by the regional government. Ulama have historically held a central role in Acehnese society as religious and political leaders, and this has been recognized by a series of different representative institutions in the past. The influential position of ulama within Acehnese society now receives formal state recognition in the form of the MPU which, under Article 4 of Qanun 3/2000:

> has the task of providing input, opinions, guidance, advice, and suggestions in the determination of regional policy from the aspect of Islamic Shariʿa, both to the Regional Government and to the people of the Region.

Importantly, the MPU has no formal power to initiate legislation. Yet, it is not a mere advisory body. Under Article 3(2) the MPU is specifically designated as an "equal partner to the Regional Government and the DPRD." Its consultative role thus reflects both the ulama's traditional position of providing guidance on religious issues and their historical involvement in local politics. A further illustration of the way in which the MPU formalizes the traditional role of ulama is the body's power to issue fatwas[4] and "to provide their considered opinion, *whether requested or not*, particularly in the fields of governing, developing, and improving society, and Islamic economic ordering" (Art. 5, italics added). Using these provisions as justification, the MPU has asserted a de facto right to veto legislation it considers "un-Islamic." It now claims, with some justification, that bills will not, in fact, be passed by the provincial legislature if the MPU opposes them.[5]

The MPU is a regional body that has separate councils in each of Aceh's regencies (*kabupaten*) or cities (*kota*) (Art. 3(4)). These regional MPUs are overseen by the central MPU located in Banda Aceh. In terms of organization, the MPU is made up of a Leadership, Secretariat, Plenary Council of Ulama (*Dewan Paripurna Ulama* or DPU), and eight Commissions responsible for "planning and implementing operational programs that relate to their task fields" (Art. 7, 17). The Leadership of the MPU is comprised of one Head and two Vice-Heads who are charged with the important task of "unifying the opinions of the ulama in determining regional policies" (Art. 9(a)). The DPU is the main body of the MPU and is comprised of 27 members who are ulama and "Muslim intellectuals" (Art. 15). The eight Commissions are divided by subject matter, and cover areas such as "Shari'a and Legal Fatwa," "Empowerment of Women and Families," and "Community Harmony and Political Studies" (Art. 18). The MPU must sit at least three times a year and special sessions can be called for urgent matters (Art. 16). The standard term of the MPU is five years, but this may be extended by an additional term (Art. 21).

Qanun 3/2000 establishing the MPU was amended by passage of Qanun 43/2001 some 14 months after it was initially enacted. Two issues were addressed by the amendment. First, because the founding Qanuns did not sufficiently provide for regional representation of ulama, the maximum membership of the DPU was increased from 18 to 27 and the grammar of Article 15 was changed to clarify that ulama, rather than Muslim intellectuals, must be from the "provincial, *kabupaten*, and *kota* levels." Secondly, the powers of the DPU were not explicitly defined in Qanun 3/2000 and were presumed to be encompassed within the general powers of the MPU. This uncertainty was resolved through the insertion of Article 16A, which essentially allows the DPU to exercise those powers attributed to the MPU more generally. Subsequent to the amendment, the DPU explicitly has the power to produce fatwas, give considered opinions, submit suggestions, and request clarification from the Regional Government, as well as ensure general compliance with Shariʿa. The rights of individual ulama are also defined. Under Article 16B they can, among other things, express opinions, submit suggestions, and carry out consultation with Regional Offices and Institutions, all in a personal capacity. Qanun 43/2001 gives the impression of an intention to strengthen and clarify the role of the DPU and, indeed, as a practical matter, the DPU is now, for all intents and purposes, the MPU.

As to Islamic law, the MPU has an instrumental role in ensuring that governance in Aceh is consistent with Shariʿa. The MPU has thus effectively promoted its Islamization agenda through informal means, including persuasion and pressuring other institutions, particularly the provincial legislature. Given the high degree of moral authority of MPU opinions, it is not impossible that the MPU could perhaps become the rival branch of government that it aspires to be, at least so far as policy is concerned, although this has not yet happened and, indeed, the MPU was not particularly successful in asserting a leading role in reconstruction efforts post-tsunami. Nonetheless, the MPU is, in itself, certainly an alternative and thus a competing, albeit informal, source of authority to all of the Shariʿa Courts, the Shariʿa Office, and the Qanuns, at least so far as the implementation of Shariʿa is concerned. The result is that tension between the ulama and the Shariʿa Courts, and even the Shariʿa Office, is inevitable. It should not be assumed, however, that the ulama will always speak with a single united voice in these contests or in Acehnese affairs more generally. The MPU has its own internal tensions, the most significant of which is a long-running contest between more conservative members, usually referred to as "rural" (although many may be based in towns) and more modernist members, the so-called "urban"group. At present, the MPU has been largely captured by the "rural" group, and some "urban" ulama instead look to the Shariʿa Office for leadership. This may, however, change in the future and the division is not, and never has been, clear-cut.

Legal thinking of the MPU

As indicated, the MPU, as the successor to the Aceh Majelis Ulama (1982–2000), itself the successor to variously named ulama councils dating from the 1960s, is a not new idea. In all their various incarnations, however, the ulama councils have produced traditions of fatwas that are important to understanding Islam in Aceh today.

While form and structure has changed over the past half century, we can identify through fatwas a remarkably consistent exposition of Shari'a from the 1970s to the present. A key collection of 102 fatwas dating from 1965 to 1999 is contained in the *Kumpulan Fatwa-Fatwa Majelis Ulama Daerah Istimewa Aceh* (Compilation of Fatwas of the Ulama Council of the Special Region of Aceh), published in 2000 by the *Komisi Fatwa Hukum Majelis Daerah Istimewa Aceh*. The approach to Shari'a reflected in these fatwas differs in certain important respects from that of other parts of Indonesia.

The first point that should be made is that although the sources and methods of Acehnese fatwas have much in common with what most other fatwa-giving bodies in Indonesia issue, especially the MUI (Majelis Ulama Indonesia) in Jakarta, there are significant local differences. More than half of the Acehnese fatwas are given based only on Qur'an and Sunna. Consensus (*ijmā'*) is very restrictively defined (as in the case of Nahdlatul Ulama), while the use of analogical reasoning (*qiyās*) is confused and uncertain, so much so that only five fatwas actually even mention it.

The most unusual thing about the collection, however, is the breakdown by subject. The relative representation of topics among the 102 fatwas contained in the compilation is as follows:

> ritual: 18%
> offences against religion (alcohol, illicit sexual relations, etc.): 17%
> family: 14%
> deviant sects: 13%
> Islam and the state: 6%
> money: 5%
> miscellaneous topics: 10%

The surprising figure here is the 13% of fatwas on deviant sects. This compares to a general Indonesian average of only about 1% (Hooker 2003b). Obviously Acehnese Islam is both doctrinally contested and debated, despite the common assumption that Acehnese Islam is conservative and uniform. Interestingly, all of the fatwas on deviance (apart from those on Darul Arqam and the Ahmadiyya, which occur everywhere) are on gnosis (*wujūdiyya*). From a preliminary reading, this suggests that the sixteenth-century mystic Ḥamza Fanṣūrī still resonates in Aceh, or at least in northeast Sumatra. It is significant also in this regard that only about 30% of the Acehnese fatwas refer back to the standard *fiqh* texts of the Shafi'i school. Are these reasons, perhaps, for why "*Islam-Aceh*" is so often seen as special and distinct?

Finally, given local traditions of hostility to Jakarta, the proportion of the fatwas (about 12%) that make reference to Indonesian state or government authorities, including the 1945 Constitution and some nine national and provincial regulations dating back to the period 1956 to 1970, is surprisingly large. It is difficult to know whether citation of these regulations is simply intended to give formal authority to the predecessors of the MPU or whether these authorities are actually considered binding, since the language is not specific or clear on this point. Given the otherwise often distinctly local content of Acehnese fatwas, we are inclined to the former but do not insist on it.

Shari'a Office

The Shari'a Office is a section of the governor's office that has general oversight of Islamic law in the province. It drafted the new Qanuns that regulate Shari'a in Aceh and has responsibility for coordinating the regional government's activities in relation to instilling the Islamic faith within the community (Qanun 5/2000, Art. 6). Additionally, the Shari'a Office is involved with "preventing and eradicating heretical acts" (Qanun 5/2000, Art. 7), reflecting, again, the strong focus in local fatwas on the prohibition of deviant sects.

The Shari'a Office is a secular body but its responsibilities appear to overlap with those of the MPU. Intense competition between the ulama and Aceh's other power-holders, the *uleebalang* or local nobility, is a relic of the colonial period that is still influential today. Generally considered less powerful, the *uleebalang* were co-opted by the Dutch to divide the population and assist the colonial administration. They are often referred to by Acehnese as predecessors of the current secular provincial government authority in Aceh which answers, ultimately, to Jakarta. More precisely, the current central and provincial governments are seen as inheriting the role of the *uleebalang* in Acehnese politics (Salim 2004).

The favorable treatment they received under the Dutch included the initial grant of self-governing authority in their respective territories and a role in the colonial justice system. The influence of the ulama suffered accordingly, so much so that they were largely marginalized as a political force during the late colonial period. This shift in power resulted in the rise of a group of radicalized, reformist ulama in the late 1930s. They sought to challenge the dominance of the *uleebalang* and to counteract the pervading disaffection with perceived neglect of traditional Acehnese Islamic values (Salim 2004).

At the heart of the conflict between ulama and *uleebalang* were divergent views on the role of Islam in Aceh. The *uleebalang* favored "territorial particularism," that is, the predominance of local cultures and traditions over religion. They viewed Islam more as an aspect of local culture than a distinct, strictly-applied religion, let alone a legal system. Their views were thus effectively those of the Dutch "reception theory." The ulama, on the other hand, condemned the "corruption" of Islam under colonial rule and sought a return to more strict interpretations of Islamic doctrine with less influence from local cultural traditions. This approach, sometimes referred to as *receptio a contrario*, is the opposite of the Dutch reception theory, and holds that *adat* applies only insofar as permitted by Shari'a. The ulama opposition to dominance by the *uleebalang* was therefore based on a desire for religious integrity, as much as political dissatisfaction, but the distinction ultimately became moot, as religious difference led to political confrontation. The tension between the two groups turned violent during Indonesia's war of independence, and it was the ulama who initially gained the political ascendancy in the post-colonial period.

There is thus a long-standing historical cleavage between the religious and secular elements of Acehnese society. Secular government in Aceh has been associated with "foreigners" in a sense that embraces both the Dutch and, from the late 1940s, the Jakarta-based Republic and its regional representative, the provincial bureaucracy. The place of the "secular" Shari'a Office as a section of the governor's office in a new legal system based on Islam led by the ulama of the MPU is therefore suggestive of these old cleavages and potentially undermines the reassertion of the authority of the MPU implicit in a Shari'a "revival." We say "suggestive" because, although this cleavage is one identified by the Acehnese who, as in the Qanun cited above, expressly describe their institutions in its terms, it might well be an overstated dichotomy, and there must be real doubt as to whether these social groupings are, in fact, so simple, either now or in the past.

The Shari'a Office, under the leadership of Dr. Al Yasa' Abubakar, himself a religious scholar of some standing, has indicated that it favors "moderate" Islam. Abubakar envisages a "cultural" and distinctly "Acehnese," rather than "legalistic," version of Shari'a to be implemented slowly at first and "ratcheting up," perhaps over several decades. The view of Islamic morality put forward by the Shari'a Office may thus find itself from time to time in some tension with the MPU, which seeks a far more rapid and far more coercive implementation of Islamic law, although the attitudes of the two institutions appear to have become more aligned as implementation of the Qanuns accelerated in the wake of the tsunami. In any case, divergence of views from time to time will most likely reinforce historical divisions between ulama and secular political authorities in Aceh, and means that the precise direction of Islamic legal revival in Aceh is likely to remain somewhat unpredictable for some time.

Shari'a Courts

Although it is the MPU and the Shari'a Office that will determine the policy regarding the implementation of Shari'a, their role primarily concerns the framework of the Shari'a system. In practice, it is the Shari'a Courts that have the task of enforcing substantive Shari'a in Aceh.

As mentioned above, Aceh's Shari'a Courts are essentially the pre-existing Religious Courts under a new name. They sit in each of Aceh's regencies and cities, and appeals are heard by the Provincial Shari'a Court (*Mahkamah Syariah Propinsi*) located in Banda Aceh (Qanun 10/2002, Art. 4). The court buildings, budget, equipment, ongoing cases, and especially the judges remained unchanged, at least until the tsunami of December 2004. The Shari'a Court's annual report for 2004 states, however, that, tragically, the losses of personnel suffered by the new Islamic courts of Aceh totalled 85, including 5 judges, 13 administrative staff, and a further 657 family members, while its few computers, its entire library and archives, its vehicles, and the whole ground floor of the appeal court building in Banda Aceh were completely ruined. Similar losses, including complete destruction of archives, were experienced by the Banda Aceh first instance Shari'a Court and those in Calang and Meulaboh. The recovery process has had some success in terms of recreating a functioning judiciary and, according to anecdotal evidence, most courts now seem to function reasonably well in handling day-to-day business, although it will be some time before physical infrastructure is fully repaired and the courts can return to the levels of productivity they achieved before the tsunami. Both the Shari'a and secular court buildings were, for example, still under repair at the time of writing in mid-2006.

The "new" Shari'a Courts, notwithstanding the minimal change they initially represented from the pre-existing Religious Courts, were officially established by Presidential Decision 11/2003.[6] Promulgated on March 3, 2003, this Decision details the structure, authority, and role of the Shari'a Courts, which were lacking under the Special Autonomy legislation. Thus, a primary aim of this Decision is, as stated in its preamble, to address the need for "careful and detailed preparations that include the necessary laws and regulations, human resources, and supporting infrastructure."

The most important aspect of Decision 11/2003 is that it appears to contradict Qanun No. 10 on the Shari'a Court produced by Aceh's DPRD. This Qanun envisaged a broad jurisdiction for the Shari'a Courts, including criminal and family matters, while the Presidential Decision purported to limit the jurisdiction of the Courts to circumstances involving religious duties in "social life." The terminology in dispute is generally vague and, at best, the conflict between the two instruments leaves the jurisdiction of the Courts unclear. This is certain to be a major obstacle to any attempt to create a broad, formal Islamic legal system in Aceh that could challenge, and eventually even displace, the pre-existing, Jakarta-focused system.

The pre-existing Religious Court system

Across Indonesia today there are 339 Religious Courts, comprising 343 Religious Courts of first instance (Pengadilan Agama), including 19 Shari'a Courts in Aceh; and 25 High Religious Courts (Pengadilan Tinggi Agama) covering 29 provinces (including the Shari'a Appeal Court in Aceh). A further four new appellate courts will open in April 2006, catching up with the formation of new provinces in addition to the 25 that existed when Suharto resigned in 1998.[7] From the High Religious Court, appeal proceeds to the Supreme Court (*Mahkamah Agung*) in Jakarta. In 2005, these courts between them decided a total of 154,310 cases at first instance, of which 1,395 went on appeal to the provincial level and 536 (none from Aceh) made it as far as the Supreme Court in Jakarta and 53 even to the final PK (*peninjauan kembali*, judicial "return" review) stage in that court.

The 2,815 judges of the national Religious Court system, assisted by some 7,000 administrative staff across the archipelago, administer a highly secular version of Islamic law, embodied in the Compilation of Islamic Laws or *Kompilasi Hukum Islam*. Approved by Suharto by a Presidential Instruction in 1991, this Jakarta revision of Islamic law is a mixture of different schools of Islamic legal thinking (*madhhabs*), designed to create a version of Islamic law that sat well with the secularizing, developmentalist ambitions of the New Order. Although drawn from classical *fiqh*, the Compilation is a short and highly idiosyncratic document that presents conclusions rather than reasoning. It bears scant resemblance to the form of Shari'a envisaged by the Qanuns (United Nations Development Program 2003, 3; Hooker and Lindsey 2003, 44–50).

The jurisdiction of Indonesian Religious Courts was, and outside Aceh remains, clear. Since 1989, they have been restricted to marriage and divorce, wills, inheritance, and charitable trusts under Islamic Law (Law 7/1989, Art. 49).[8] Of these, the first category disproportionately dominates business. The Religious Courts have become, in effect, a divorce court, applying a bureaucratic form of on-demand divorce, largely for women plaintiffs (Hooker and Lindsey 2003).

These Courts have now applied the Compilation for more than a decade to deal with routine divorce, property settlement, and custody cases. The Compilation has come to dominate their jurisprudence to the extent that virtually no contemporary judgments of these Courts make any reference to the classical *fiqh*. Rather, the Courts' decisions are mechanistic—if efficient and generally fair—implementations of the complimentary rules in the Compilation and in the Marriage Law (Asia Foundation Survey 2001). For most litigants this is a very satisfactory state of affairs, with a recent survey (Asia Foundation 2001) rating the Religious Courts as regarded by the Indonesian public as the most honest and effective government institutions in the country. They were rated far more highly than the new democratic legislature and executive and all other courts and Commissions, notwithstanding their poor facilities, lack of funding, and general neglect by the government for decades (Hooker and Lindsey 2003).

Jurisdiction of the new Shari‘a Court in Aceh

At present there is no definitive answer to the question of how far the scope of the Shari‘a Courts' new jurisdiction extends. Significant uncertainty exists due to a central government law, a regional regulation, and a presidential decision, all of which place different limitations on the new Courts' jurisdiction. Contradictions between the regulation of Shari‘a at the regional and national level illustrate not only the divergent views on the place of Shari‘a as between Jakarta and Aceh, but also within Aceh, across the different branches of government. There is no agreement in Aceh as to which of these three legislative instruments takes precedence, despite a central *Majelis Permusyawaratan Rakyat* (MPR, Peoples Consultative Assembly) Decree (No. III of 2000) and a statute (the Law on Lawmaking No. 10 of 2004) that detail a hierarchy of legislation in Indonesia that is intended to resolve just such conflicts. The result is legal chaos, regulatory confusion, and political uncertainty. The relevant provisions of each of these regulations—the Special Autonomy Laws, the Qanuns, and the Presidential Decision—will now be discussed in turn.

Law 18/2001 on Special Autonomy for the Province of Nanggroe Aceh Darussalam

As mentioned above, the framework for the Shariʿa Courts was laid down in the Special Autonomy package of 2001. Under Article 25 of Law 18/2001:

> The jurisdiction of the Shariʿa Courts is based on Islamic Shariʿa as found within the system of national laws, which is further regulated by Qanuns, as it applies to the followers of Islam.

Observers generally interpret this phrase as granting authority only to enforce Shariʿa as codified by the Indonesian government and legislature and, further, by the Aceh Provincial DPRD Parliament (United Nations Development Program 2003, 2). Thus, the Shariʿa Courts cannot base their decisions directly on traditional sources of Islamic law, such as Qurʾan, *ḥadīth*, or classical texts, but can only apply a version of Shariʿa that has been translated into national laws and local legislation, that is, in most cases, the national Marriage Law and the Compilation.

  The key to this interpretation is the important limitation on the Acehnese legislature stating that any Qanun regulating Shariʿa must be consistent with Shariʿa as it exists under "national law" pursuant to Art. 25 of Law 18/2001. Accordingly, this jurisdiction, if interpreted literally, constitutes no real expansion on that previously exercised by Aceh's Religious Courts, that is, it limits jurisdiction to family law (marriage, divorce, custody, and related issues), some aspects of inheritance, and a few other related areas.[9]

Qanuns

As already mentioned, the Acehnese regional legislature, the DPRD, has issued Qanuns specifically defining the scope and content of Shariʿa in Aceh. Qanun 11/2002 provides the substance of Shariʿa in Aceh and details matters such as correct belief (*ʿaqīda*), ritual worship (*ʿibādāt*), and "increasing the greatness of Islam" (*syiar Islam*). Substantive elements of Shariʿa in Aceh will be considered in detail below, but the most important provisions dealing with the jurisdiction of the Shariʿa courts are found in Qanun 10/2002, which deals with their procedural framework. In particular, this Qanun envisages a wide jurisdiction for the Shariʿa Courts, with Shariʿa being applicable to most areas of life. It is therefore implicitly inconsistent with Article 25 of the Special Autonomy Law.

  Article 49 of Qanun 10/2002 states that the Shariʿa Court "has the duty and the authority to examine, decide, and determine proceedings at first instance, in the fields of *aḥwāl shakhṣiyya*, *muʿāmalāt*, and *jināya*," which, loosely translated, means personal status, civil, and penal matters.[10] Such an interpretation is, however, overly simplistic, as it does not fully take account of the nuances and intricacies of Shari'a. After all, Shari'a is a legal tradition based on religious scriptural texts, and known through more than 1,000 years of classical scholarship—the *fiqh* texts. It cannot easily be understood in terms of common law legal classifications, such as civil, family, and criminal law.

Taking each of the three areas of jurisdiction in turn, *aḥwāl shakhṣiyya* implies more than just family law, covering aspects of personal life as well. According to the general elucidation (*penjelasan*) of Article 49 of Qanun 10/2002, *aḥwāl shakhṣiyya* includes matters regulated in Article 49 of Law 7/1989 on the Religious Courts, that is, the pre-existing jurisdiction for the Religious Courts, except for charitable trusts (Ar. *waqf*), donations (Ar. *hiba*) and charitable alms (Ar. *ṣadaqa*). Presumably these now fall within the ambit of *muʿāmalāt*.

Muʿāmalāt cover mainly commerce and trade matters, but include everything that does not fall under the category of ritual worship. Examples given in the elucidation to Qanun 10/2002 include buying and selling, loans and debts, partnerships, seizure of goods, mining, banking, and insurance and labor. This is a significantly different jurisdiction to that exercised by civil courts in a common law system, as it is primarily commercial and does not encompass areas such as personal injury. It does, however, have similarities with the ambit of civil law in continental civil law systems, such as that of Indonesia's Dutch-derived general courts. *Muʿāmalāt* are therefore an entirely new jurisdiction for the Religious Courts and a radical expansion into the jurisdiction of the secular state courts.

Finally, *jināya* refers to Islamic criminal law, again a new area for the Religious Courts. According to the elucidation to Qanun 10/2002, this includes the Qur'anic *ḥudūd* crimes of sexual intercourse out of wedlock (*zinā*), accusation of *zinā*, and drinking alcohol, as well as murder, physical abuse, gambling, and the breach of prayer and fasting requirements. This category cannot, therefore, be simply understood as "criminal law" in the sense the term is understood in most secular legal systems.

The implications of these Islamic legal terms are difficult to comprehend for lawyers trained outside of the Islamic scholarly tradition. They are, however, long-established and well-traversed categories of Islamic jurisprudence. The key conclusion here is, however, that Article 49—in principle at least—establishes a wide new jurisdiction for Shari'a in Aceh: one that could be considered radical or "fundamentalist" in its aspirations, and one that is clearly inconsistent with the simplistic jurisprudence outlined in the Compilation and currently applied by Indonesia's Religious Courts.

It is questionable, however, whether the Shari'a Court system as defined by the Qanuns and discussed above can, in fact, extend beyond the narrow range authorized by the Special Autonomy legislation, whatever the ambitions of the Qanuns' drafters. The problem is that the phrase "system of national laws" includes other regulations, some of a higher status, that contradict much of what is provided in the Qanuns. On a plain reading of this phrase, its effect would be that, to the extent consistent with the national (Jakarta) interpretation of Shari'a, the Qanun is of no effect. To interpret the jurisdiction established under the Special Autonomy Law in this manner is, however, to render the establishment of the Shari'a Courts and much of the Qanuns meaningless, as the end result would be virtually no change from the jurisdiction of the pre-existing Religious Courts. Accordingly, although it is clear that the Acehnese regional legislature has the authority to implement Shari'a through Qanuns, the extent to which they can actually do so is unclear, because the definition of Shari'a differs between applicable regulatory instruments.

This apparent contradiction has not been formally resolved by legislation at the level of the Special Autonomy Law or by judicial decision. This may be because either process would have to take place at the national level in Jakarta and, from a central government perspective, the solution to this conflict of laws is straightforward. Under Article 2 of MPR Decree III/2000 on The Sources of Law and the Hierarchy of Laws and Regulations, it is clear that the Law on Special Autonomy, a law passed by the national legislature, the DPR, takes precedence over a regional regulation of a provincial legislature. Under Article 4 of this Decree "an inferior legal instrument must not conflict with a superior legal instrument." Accordingly, any attempt by Jakarta to clearly resolve the issue—for example, through the bills to implement the Helsinki Agreement currently being debated in the DPR—might well be counter-productive for the ulama.

Despite the apparent clarity of MPR Decree III/2000, uncertainty nevertheless remains, in Aceh at least, where the issue is hotly contested (as will be seen below). Does the Special Autonomy Law, with its tightly restricted Shari'a jurisdiction, or Qanun 10/2002, with its broader scope, apply? The debate is further complicated by Presidential Decision 11/2003, promulgated by the then President, Megawati Sukarnoputri, on March 3, 2003, which appears to be an attempt by Jakarta to decisively restate its narrow view on the preferred jurisdiction of the Shari'a Courts.

Presidential Decision 11/2003

The 2003 Presidential Decision officially renamed Aceh's pre-existing Religious Court as the *Mahkamah Syariah* or Shari'a Court, although the title had already been in use since at least 2002. It also includes important provisions regarding the Courts' jurisdiction. As mentioned above, since 1989 the jurisdiction of the Religious Courts across Indonesia has been restricted to areas such as marriage, wills, inheritance, and charitable trusts (*wakaf*) under Islamic law (Art. 49, Law 7/1989).[11] Under Article 3 of the Presidential Decision, the Aceh Shari'a Courts have the same authority and jurisdiction as the old Religious Courts but with additional jurisdiction over "the life of the people in religious worship and the greater good of Islam as provided for in the Qanuns" (Art. 3). The exact interpretation of this phrase is unclear, however. A United Nations Development Program (UNDP) report cites Acehnese Muslim leaders as interpreting it to permit the expansion of the Shari'a Courts' jurisdiction by Qanun, so long as it does not extend beyond "religious duties in social life," although no explanation of "social life" is given (United Nations Development Program 2003, 3).

If this is accurate, the limitation of the Shari'a Courts' jurisdiction over the "life of the people in religious worship" to "social life" represents a very significant restriction of the scope of Shari'a compared to that claimed by Article 49 of Qanun 10/2002, which includes such matters as mining and banking, insurance and labor regulation, clearly going beyond the "social life" restriction provided for in the Presidential Decision. By purporting to limit the Courts' jurisdiction to "social life," the Presidential Decision can therefore be seen as Jakarta reaffirming its "in principle" support for the implementation of a form of Shari'a in Aceh, but only given strict limitations as to the scope of its application so as to ensure that it does not go much further than what was available to the predecessor Religious Courts. The support offered by the Decision for Shari'a in Aceh is thus little more than minimalist symbolism.

Unsurprisingly, the Decision has been strongly rejected by both the Shari'a Office and the MPU. This raises the issue of which instrument prevails in Aceh—the Qanun or the Presidential Decision? The answer is, if anything, even more vexed than the problem of the conflict between the Qanuns and the Special Autonomy Law.

Resolving the inconsistency

It is clear that under the hierarchy of legal instruments fixed by MPR Decree III/2000, statutes (*undang-undang*) are higher than presidential decisions. Presidential decisions, in turn, are higher than regional regulations such as Qanuns. Thus, the Special Autonomy Law, an *undang-undang*, provides the most authoritative definition of the Shari'a Courts' jurisdiction, and takes precedence over both the Presidential Decision and the Qanuns. According to this formal perspective, based in the Republic's (secular) legal framework, the jurisdiction of the Shari'a Courts is that established under the Special Autonomy Law. On this reading, the "social life" restriction in the Presidential Decision must apply.

This would seem to settle the matter, but there is some dispute in Aceh as to whether the President has, in the first place, authority to issue a Decision limiting the jurisdiction of the Shari'a Courts. If the President lacks such authority, then the hierarchy issue never even arises, as the Decision is invalid in the first place. In particular, the Shari'a Office strongly opposes the limitation of the Shari'a Courts' jurisdiction as set out in the Presidential Decision. This is to be expected, given that the Courts still fall under the supervisory authority of the executive and are thus within the reach of the Shari'a Office. This Office designed Qanun 10/2002 and would be reluctant to see the ambit of the Courts' jurisdiction restricted, as it is an important part of its capacity to exert authority over Islamic issues vis-à-vis the MPU (United Nations Development Program 2003, 3).

The Shari'a Office therefore argues that the Decision encroaches on the framework established under the Special Autonomy Law which devolves the authority to regulate the Shari'a Courts to the regional level. As Presidential decisions are lower than statutes in the legal hierarchy, and as the attempt by President Megawati to limit Shari'a to "social life" seeks to arrogate a power already divested by the national legislature to the Acehnese regional legislature through the Special Autonomy Law (which is, of course, an *undang-undang*), the Decision is, to that extent, invalid. On this reading, the real issue is not whether a presidential decision trumps the Qanun (it does), but whether this Decision was properly made in the first place, because the Special Autonomy Law can be seen as already covering the field, thus leaving the President no space to issue such a Decision over the jurisdiction of the Shari'a Court. The better answer to this is probably that the Special Autonomy Law does not, in fact, cover the field; it sets the jurisdiction as "Islamic Shari'a *within the system of national laws*." The Decision is clearly part of that (broader) national system, and so too are Qanuns. Both are therefore valid and, because the Decision outranks the Qanun, its "social life" restriction applies.

Supporters of the Qanuns are thus forced into a corner. The only way the broad Qanun jurisdiction they advocate can apply is if they can somehow demonstrate that the hierarchy of laws does not rank the Decision above the Qanun. It is therefore not surprising that, according to a UNDP project on the judicial system in Aceh, this is precisely the argument now adopted by some DPRD members, the Shari'a Office, and some Acehnese lawyers.[12] They argue that Qanuns are a "special type" of regional regulation, and are therefore more authoritative, or in a special "higher" category, than other regulations. Proponents of this argument point to the general elucidation of Law 18/2001 on Special Autonomy, which states:

> The Qanuns of the Province of Nanggroe Darussalam are regional regulations of the Province of Nanggroe Aceh Darussalam, which can set aside other regulations by following the principle of lex specialis derogat lex generalis,[13] and the Supreme Court has the authority to conduct judicial review.

The principle that "special purpose laws overrule general laws" is a long-established and fundamental principle of Indonesian law. It relates to statutory interpretation and is used to resolve conflicts between laws at the same level in the hierarchy of laws. To our knowledge, however, it has never been understood as allowing a law of lower standing in the hierarchy to overrule a higher law. In any case, as a general jurisprudential principle of interpretation, regional regulations clearly cannot overrule a clear decree of the MPR, Indonesia's highest legislative body and at the time the highest source of law in Indonesia after the Constitution.

The argument put forth by Acehnese lawyers also has alternative grounds: since Qanuns can be reviewed by the Supreme Court, while DPRD regulations from other regions can only be reviewed by the bureaucracy, Qanuns are therefore "special." They are, the argument goes, more like statutes (*undang-undang*) passed by the national legislature, the DPR, because these too are only reviewable in a court (although only by the new Constitutional Court).[14] According to the Acehnese position, the fact that Qanuns must be reviewed by the judiciary, like *undang-undang*, and not by the executive, like other regional regulations, makes them a sort of hybrid of regional regulation and statute. This unique status give them a higher position in the legal hierarchy than other provincial-level regulations—presumably below laws, but certainly above regulations. Unfortunately for this argument, however, there is no provision in Law 18/2001 granting the Supreme Court exclusive jurisdiction over the review of Qanuns. The Elucidation to this Law does confirm the Supreme Court's right to review regulations (which has existed since Law 14/1970) but nowhere mentions that this power is exclusive. In other words, the Elucidation leaves open the possibility that Acehnese Qanuns are, in theory, still reviewable by the bureaucracy (the Department of Internal Affairs—*Departemen Dalam Negeri*— for example), just like other regional regulations.

The third argument raised to support the contention that Qanuns have a special, higher status than other regional regulations is the fact that they are, in practice apparently, not sent by the Acehnese DPRD to the Department of Internal Affairs for review.[15] Rather, they are implemented of their own accord. In that few regional regulations from other provinces have been reviewed either, this is not unusual. The absence of bureaucratic review to date may be simply political, a reflection of the sensitivities associated with Aceh's special autonomy, but the absence of the grant of a jurisdiction for review to the Supreme Court that is expressly exclusive leaves open the possibility that in future the executive may well reassert a right of review.

It is certainly true, therefore, that there are arguments for the proposition that Qanuns are more authoritative than other regional regulations. This is, however, highly unlikely to be sufficient to allow Qanuns to override the Presidential Decision that regulates the same matter, in that this would be inconsistent with the specific and unequivocal provisions of MPR Decree III/2000. The weak arguments for according special status to the DPRD regulations in Aceh would, therefore, be very unlikely to survive any test by an Indonesian court. They are, nevertheless, widely accepted within Aceh and are certainly consistent with the aspirations of the Acehnese proponents of special autonomy because, if effective, they would exclude the Jakarta bureaucracy from the regional legislative process.

Like so much else in this debate, these issues remain unresolved, not least because (at time of writing) no appeals from a decision on Qanun 10/2002 had reached the Supreme Court in Jakarta. In Aceh, the continuing uncertainty of the status of Qanuns is doubtless because of the enormous implications the issue has for emerging Islamic institutions and their leadership. As could be expected, neither the Presidency nor the Acehnese regional legislature is willing to accept that its attempts to regulate the jurisdiction of the Shari'a Courts are invalid due to purported inconsistency with the Special Autonomy legislation, or with each other. Having three legislative instruments claiming to regulate the Courts' jurisdiction has, however, created considerable confusion and legal uncertainty. Interviews conducted with local legal experts indicate that none of the parties involved at any level is likely to back down of their own accord (see also United Nations Development Program 2003). The question therefore is how to resolve this problem. At present it is unclear how a resolution can be achieved, even at the national level, because as will now be explained, it is not clear that any national court has sufficient authority to resolve the question, even if it were litigated as far as Jakarta.

Judicial authority and conflict of laws

The Supreme Court has jurisdiction to hear disputes over the hierarchy of legislation through a rarely-used power to exercise judicial review over "regulations inferior to laws (*undang-undang*) in the hierarchy" (Art. 5(2) MPR Decree III/2000 on The Sources of Law and the Hierarchy of Laws and Regulations). Accordingly, the Supreme Court could determine whether Qanun 10/2002 or the Presidential Decision should take precedence over the other, and to what extent, if any, either instrument is inconsistent with the Special Autonomy Law. The Supreme Court, however, has no power to judicially amend or strike out either Qanuns or Presidential Decisions, although under this limited form of judicial review its determination is "binding" (Art. 5(3), MPR Decree III/2000 on The Sources of Law and the Hierarchy of Laws and Regulations).

In theory, this Article 5 power should allow the Supreme Court to review the Acehnese Qanuns without the precondition of an appeal case. But given the Court's failure to exercise this power in the past, it must be considered unlikely that it would do so now (Millie 1999). In any case, even if a case were brought before the Supreme Court, it would likely take considerable time before being finalized. Thus a resolution to the uncertainty over the Shari'a Courts' jurisdiction will probably only be achieved by the Supreme Court if a case reaches the Court and it gives a decision that has the effect either of the regional parliament amending the Qanun or the President's Office amending its Decision (United Nations Development Program 2003, 3). This assumes, of course, that the matter would be handled in a competent and transparent fashion—and that would be to ignore the Supreme Court's well-documented problems of incompetence and corruption. These have been widely canvassed (Lev 1999; Lev 2000; Lindsey 1999; Butt 1999) and need not be covered in any detail here, other than by observing that there must remain a concern that even if this legal dispute reached the Supreme Court it might well not be dealt with on its merits.

A further option for judicial resolution of this complex problem is the new Constitutional Court. This Court has the power to solve disputes between organs of state and it is the final authority on constitutional issues, including, under Article 24 of the Constitution, review of the constitu-

tionality of *undang-undang*. Pursuant to Article 29 of Law 24/2003 on the
Constitutional Court, a written application can be made to the Court to
determine a constitutional issue, and there is no precondition of an appeal
case—the Court can deal with these issues at first instance. Argument
regarding the constitutionality of the Special Autonomy Law, an *undang-
undang*, could therefore be brought directly before the Constitutional Court.
Unfortunately, however, the constitutionality of that Law is not what is in
dispute here, as all seem to accept that it is constitutionally valid. The issue
is rather the validity of subordinate regulations made under or by reference to that Law—the Qanun and the Presidential Instruction.

For these reasons a high degree of uncertainty regarding the jurisdiction
of the Shari'a Courts is likely to remain for some time. Certainly, if passed,
the new Bill on governance in Aceh currently before the DPR in Jakarta
would rank over, and would overrule, both the contentious Presidential
Decree on Shari'a in Aceh and the Qanuns. It might therefore bring some
clarity to this issue. This is important because if either of the jurisdictions
as regulated by the Acehnese Qanuns or the Presidential Decision is eventually accepted in Aceh as binding and exclusive, that will have a significant
bearing on the version of Shari'a that is implemented in the province. Will
the application of Shari'a in Aceh be the more comprehensive form of
Shari'a favored in the Qanun? If so, it would apply to areas such as family, civil, and criminal matters and the Shari'a Court would become a general court of almost unlimited jurisdiction. This is certainly the direction
in which most of Aceh's Islamic institutions have been moving for some
time and, post-tsunami, it appears the Court is finally moving to join them.

Substantive Shari'a provisions of the Qanuns

A further indicator of the form that Shari'a may eventually take in Aceh
is, of course, the substantive provisions of the Qanuns passed to date,
assuming the Shari'a Courts have jurisdiction to hear such cases.

Crimes as defined in the Qanuns extend far beyond the family law issues
that formed the primary jurisdiction of the Religious Courts. Their enactment
formally introduces into Aceh a "conservative" form of Shari'a, but not
anywhere near as radical or hardline as some draft codes produced elsewhere
in Indonesia, such as the "Proposal for a Criminal Code for the Republic
of Indonesia Adjusted to Accord with the Syariah of Islam" (the MMI
Code), produced by *Majelis Mujahidin Indonesia* (MMI), a militant Islamic
religious movement whose spiritual leader is Abu Bakar Ba'asyir (Behrend
2003), allegedly also the spiritual leader of Jemaah Islamiyah (JI).[16]

The substance of Shari'a, as it applies officially in Nanggroe Aceh Darussalam is determined by Qanun 5/2000 and Qanun 11/2002. These regulations are the basic reference for determining what aspects of Shari'a are codified in Aceh, and legally speaking, the extent to which Shari'a applies on a day-to-day basis. Qanun 5/2000 provides for the implementation of Shari'a in 13 broad aspects of life. Each provision is generally worded and provides little detail. Qanun 11/2002, on the other hand, is more specific and provides greater detail on three of the 13 areas: correct belief ('aqīda),[17] ritual worship ('ibādāt),[18] and "increasing the greatness of Islam" (syiar Islam).[19] It is important to note that there is substantial overlap between Qanun 5/2000 and Qanun 11/2002. Since it is currently unclear how inconsistencies between the Qanuns will be resolved, no conclusion can be made as to which provision takes precedence. We will, however, speculate on the reasons behind the existence of two Qanuns that purport to regulate the same matters.

Correct belief ('aqīda)

Article 6 of Qanun 5/2000 declares that "Every Muslim is obliged to strengthen and to fulfil Islamic 'aqīda based on [the doctrine of] *ahl al-Sunna wa l-jamā'a*"[20] and obligates the Regional Government and community institutions "to instill faith and God-consciousness in every Muslim from childhood to adulthood."

Article 7 further states that the Regional Government and the community are obliged to protect against anything that may conflict with Islamic correct belief, specifically including disbelief in Islam as the religion of God; polytheism; belief in superstitions (which includes the excessive veneration of saints); atheism; and "other symptoms leading in that direction." The intention behind these provisions is to ensure the purity of Islam in Aceh and to protect against influence from sources seen as non-standard. Similar requirements are set under Article 4(1) of Qanun 11/2002.

The primary difference between the two Qanuns is that the latter gives the MPU the power to determine the interpretations and or sects of Islam that are misguided, where previously the procedure to determine this was left undefined. Pursuant to Article 6 of Qanun 11/2002, the MPU can effectively "outlaw" an interpretation of Islam by issuing a fatwa. This substantially increases the MPU's power from that established under Qanun 5/2000, and, in principle, at least, it effectively gives ulama, through the MPU, legal control over the practice of Islam in Aceh.

Ritual worship ('ibādāt)

Articles 8 and 9 of Qanun 5/2000 require every Muslim to perform the ritual of Islamic law such as prayer, pilgrimage, giving alms, and fasting, and prohibit actions that may disturb and obstruct the performance of ritual worship. Aside from these vaguely worded provisions, however, the precise meaning of *'ibādāt* is left undefined. It is envisaged that their specific times and forms would be determined by a decision of the Governor at a later stage (Art. 8(3)). The Governor has since issued relevant regulations, but in any case, Qanun 11/2002 provides the detail lacking in Qanun 5/2000 on the specific obligations required in their performance.

The DPRD therefore appears to have largely arrogated a power that it had previously given to the Governor. In particular, Qanun 11/2002 defines *'ibādāt* under the general interpretation provision as the prayers[21] and the fast of Ramadan (Art. 1). Parents and family members who are responsible for children are obliged to ensure that an environment conducive to prayer is available (Art. 7(2)). This Qanun further requires the performance of congregational midday Friday prayers unless an individual has an excuse (allowed by Shari'a, *uzur syar'i*)[22] and requires people, governments, businesses, and community organizations to "cease activities that may obstruct (or disturb) Muslims who are performing the congregational prayer" (Art. 8). Similar principles apply in regard to non-congregational prayer.

The fast during the month of Ramadan is given particular emphasis: people and businesses are prohibited from providing facilities or giving opportunities for Muslims to not fast, except for those who have a legitimate excuse (Art. 10(1)), and every Muslim who does not have a legitimate excuse is prohibited from eating or drinking in public during the daytime.

Qanun 11/2002 is not inconsistent with its predecessor but it provides more detail, is more practical, and is better suited for use as a basis for prosecution. To that extent, Qanun 11/2002 leaves the realm of symbolism in order to regulate Acehnese Islam and impose sanctions if its provisions are breached. This does not necessarily suggest that the version of Islam established in the *'ibādāt* provisions of this Qanun is "hard-line" (*garis keras*) or "radical." Rather, although the aspects of Shari'a contained in these provisions can now be formally enforced in Aceh (in theory, at least), the provisions themselves equally reflect long-standing local religious customs and are usually observed in the terms set out in the new regulations in any case. By contrast, the MMI Code—which is certainly both "hard-line" and "radical" in Indonesian terms—has a broad discretionary "catch-all" provision (Art. 28) to the effect that any actions contrary to the

MMI version of the Islamic faith are punishable by death, or, if repentance is undertaken by the accused, by *ta'zīr* (discretionary) punishment.

Increasing the greatness of Islam (syiar Islam)

The provisions regarding *syiar Islam* follow a similar pattern to those regarding ritual. Qanun 5/2000 imposes a general obligation on the Regional Government to arrange the implementation of *syiar Islam*, such as the Celebration of the Holy Days of Islam (Art. 16(1)), and then grants the Governor the power to further regulate the "types and forms of implementation of *syiar Islam*" (Art. 16(2)). As with the provisions on ritual, the Acehnese legislature appears to have changed its position in relation to *syiar Islam* and the DPRD has now assumed this power through Qanun 11/2002. The most striking provision is the obligation of every Muslim "to wear Islamic dress" (Art. 13(1)). Alongside this provision is the requirement of government, educational institutions, businesses, and community organizations to "promote a culture of Islamic dress in their environments" (Art. 13(2)). Other measures intended to spread the "greatness" of Islam are the observance of Islamic holidays (Art. 12(1)), and the use of the Malay Arab script (*jawi*)[23] (Art. 12(2)) and the Islamic calendar (Art. 12(3)).

Although on its face the provision requiring every Muslim to wear "Islamic dress" conjures up images of a hard-line Islamic society, Al Yasa' Abubakar of the Shari'a Office, who was involved in drafting this Qanun, explained the intention of the provision as nothing more than to ensure modesty and symbolic respect for Islam:

> We do not want to force women to wear the *jilbab* [the head scarf favored in Aceh], but we do encourage people to dress modestly out of respect for Islam. We're not going to force people, but if someone wants to run naked down the street, then we can use the law to stop them. That's no different to your country, is it?[24]

On this reading, the obligation to wear Islamic dress and to contribute to "the greatness of Islam" more generally amounts to not much more than a reflection of the DPRD's intention to preserve a perceived "Acehnese Islamic" culture. Indeed, for the first few years, Article 13 had little impact on how the vast majority of Acehnese dress, which is in the normal, polite Indonesian manner, albeit more conservatively than Jakarta and with a more-or-less uniform use of head-coverings by women. Post-tsunami, however, attitudes on Islamic dress for women appear to have hardened hugely as a result of a perception that the tsunami was a punishment sent by God and, in particular, that it "happened because women ignored religion,"[25] or, in the reported words of one religious scholar, "the Holy Qur'an says that if women are good then the country is good."[26]

This reflects a recent, somewhat aggressive, focus by Acehnese religious authorities and, especially, the religious police on the public role of women.[27] The results of this new approach have ranged from oppressive religious police raids on beauty salons[28] and cafes looking for "prostitutes" to pressuring women to wear the *jilbab* and cover up visible skin other than face and hands, which has led, in one case at least, to the parading in public of women with their hair "lopped off" as punishment for failure to wear the *jilbab*.[29] There have also been recent reports of prohibitions on women traveling unaccompanied on *ojek*, motorcycle taxis, driven by men, as almost all are.[30] The implications of these developments are obviously harsh for women, as they severely restrict capacity for individual expression. Their impact goes well beyond this, however. In a poor province where most women rely on public transport, they could well exclude many women from a role in public life and access to employment.

Why did the Acehnese DPRD appear to change its tack, first granting the Governor authority to further define some aspects of *syiar Islam* in Qanun 5/2000 and then reclaiming these powers two years later, through Qanun 11/2002? As the implementation of Shari'a has progressed, subsequent amendments to the Qanuns suggest a trend of ulama dissatisfaction with the process. At the outset of regional autonomy in 1999, the implementation of Shari'a appeared purely symbolic. The only apparent concrete development was the establishment of the Shari'a Courts in 2001, a formality that, prior to the tsunami, resulted in no perceptible change to the Religious Courts' existing functions in Aceh. The development of a Shari'a system occurred at a slow pace and did not, at first, result in substantial change to daily life. As a result, the ulama may have become frustrated. We speculate that, in response, their vision of Shari'a in Aceh has become gradually more conservative and, over the course of 2005, their view has increasingly influenced Islamic institutions in the province.

Despite this shift towards a more conservative position, the Qanuns remain relatively moderate on the issues of morality. This is clear from a comparison with the MMI Code, which, by contrast to the Qanuns' broad and general wording, is very direct and specific. This different approach goes beyond merely a stylistic differentiation. The influences of the MMI Code are more radical and its approach to Shari'a more prescriptive.

With respect to sexual offences, for example, the MMI Code is much more detailed than the Qanuns and its language uses a highly moralistic tone. The drafter's choice of pejorative terminology aims not only to allow for prosecution of sexual offences, but also to stigmatize those accused of these offences. In this light, the account of Shari'a morality in Qanun 11/2002 is both minimalist and reticent and, by contrast to the MMI Code, appears as much about symbolism as proscription. The Qanuns may create important new legal institutions and a hortatory framework for a system that pays much more attention to Islamic legal ideas, but they do not, in themselves, contain a strict Islamic moral code. That would require significant clarification and a much higher degree of detail. These Qanuns are therefore better characterized as a symbolic affirmation of a conservative but often vague perception of Islamic morality intended to strengthen the place of Islam (and ulama) within Acehnese society, accompanied by a group of key institutions intended to promote that vision.[31]

Punishment

This argument that Shari'a in Aceh is, to a large extent, symbolic is qualified somewhat by the punishments enacted for contravention of these provisions. Although these provisions are essentially a sign of respect towards religion, and are far from the blanket death penalty imposed by the MMI Code, the punishment regime outlined below suggests that the Qanuns at least create a framework that could conceivably allow a more "hard-line" application at a future time. Some indication of this began to emerge post-tsunami when, as mentioned, the Courts at last began to show a willingness to explore their new—if uncertain—criminal jurisdiction. Under Qanun 11/2002 two different sentencing options are generally available: imprisonment and public caning.[32] The first official caning (*cambok*) by the Bireuen Shari'a Court in coastal Aceh took place in mid-2005[33] and followed some 17 convictions (all for gambling) across Aceh (six in Bireuen and the rest in another regional center, but none in the capital, Banda Aceh) in the period from late December 2004 to April 2005. The "Islamic" punishments provided for in the Qanuns, such as public caning, are based on discretionary punishment (*ta'zīr*), and there is wide scope for judges to modify the sentence to take into account individual circumstances. The Qanuns only set a maximum punishment, so judges are free to issue lesser, or even nominal or no, sentences. In relation to Islamic costume, a warning system even applies.[34]

If caning does become a common penalty in Aceh, this should not, on its own, necessarily be seen as indicator of religious radicalism or conservatism. In Southeast Asia, caning as punishment sits as well with non-Muslim traditions as it does with a "hardline" Islamist approach. It already exists in neighboring secular states: Malaysia, which has a majority Muslim population, and Singapore, which has a majority ethnic Chinese, non-Muslim population. In contrast to the highly condemnatory language of the MMI Code, the Aceh Qanuns stress the point that the discretionary punishment system, in particular public caning, is intended to allow for the "education" and "guidance" of both the offender and the community at large, while the Shari'a Office has stated that caning will be introduced slowly, "over a 10-year period," because it is a "discretionary punishment that judges should be reluctant to impose without wide social education beforehand."[35] This is not to say that the application of Islamic legal norms is not becoming more conservative in Aceh—it is—but caning is not per se necessarily an indicator of Islamic values.

These factors may explain why when the first caning was conducted in the east coast town of Bireuen in June 2005 it met with little public opposition and did not result in an appeal to the Jakarta Supreme Court by the 15 convicted offenders.[36] Hundreds attended and the head of the Shari'a Office even commented that he "hadn't thought there would be so much enthusiasm."[37] There are, however, now reports that such appeals may well be lodged in the near future, as NGO leaders in Aceh increasingly take the view that the new punishments breach human rights protections introduced post-Suharto, pursuant to Chapter XA of the amended Constitution.

Significantly, no mention of caning is made in Qanun 5/2000, which allows only a maximum three-month prison sentence or a maximum fine of Rp2 million (approximately US$220 in 2005) as sentencing options (Art. 19(1)). The different penalties for contravention of similar provisions in the two Qanuns, combined with the fact that caning is not a sentencing option under Qanun 5/2000, re-emphasizes that Qanun 11/2002 constitutes a "toughening up" of Acehnese Islamic law and is thus probably an expression of dissatisfaction with the slow implementation of Shari'a. It can be seen as an attempt by ulama to indoctrinate their more socially conservative attitudes, at the expense of the more symbolic, secular-influenced Islam found in Aceh prior to special autonomy.

The Qanuns promulgated thus far make no attempt to expressly introduce the Qur'anic criminal punishments known as ḥudūd which include punishments such as stoning, amputation of limbs, execution, decapitation, and so on. The general elucidation to Qanun 11/2002 states that a separate Qanun concerning ḥudūd is a future possibility and some members of the MPU strongly support this.

This approach to ḥudūd offers another stark difference between the Qanuns and the MMI Code—one that highlights a dichotomy between local and foreign interpretations of Shari'a. The Qanuns are expressly sensitive to the local context, which is believed by Acehnese ulama to not be currently amenable to the harshness of the *ḥudūd*.[38] This reflects an implicit acceptance of the notion shared by many scholars that even if there is a "divine imperative" for *ḥudūd*, its implementation should be tempered to accord with society's expectations of criminal punishment (Hooker 2003c). The MMI, however, seems to take its lead from radical influences from Saudi Arabia, and would consequently seek to implement the *ḥudūd* regardless of their lack of general acceptance in Indonesia.

Shari'a "Police"

A body to control and supervise the implementation of Shari'a was first envisaged in Article 20 of Qanun 5/2000. Known as the Wilayatul Hisbah, the role of this body was left largely undefined. The general elucidation of Qanun 11/2002, however, provides more detail. It states:

> The Wilayatul Hisbah as a supervisory institution is granted the role of warning, guiding, and advising, so that the cases of contravention of this Qanun that are submitted to the investigators to be followed up and forwarded on to the courts are cases that have been through a process of warning and guidance towards the offender.

This makes it clear that a "police" force of sorts is intended, at least in terms of patrolling and reporting contraventions of the Qanun provisions. The supervisors under the authority of the Wilayatul Hisbah are comprised of two different groups: ordinary police who are given duties in the enforcement of Shari'a, and civil government employee investigators (Art. 15). These Shari'a supervisors are given two broadly defined powers under Qanun 11/2002. First, where there is sufficient reason to suspect there has been a contravention of a provision of the Qanuns, the supervising officer of Wilayatul Hisbah "is endowed with the authority to rebuke the offender" (Art. 14(3)). Secondly, after attempts to rebuke the offender have been carried out and his/her behavior has not changed, "the supervising officer" shall turn over the case of contravention to an investigating officer (Art. 14(4)). Aside from these two powers, the specific responsibilities and functions of the new police force are to be determined by the Governor.

It is clear, however, that the tasks of the Wilayatul Hisbah will not extend to prosecutions, which fall within the authority of a new Shari'a Prosecution Office that, at the time of writing, was not yet fully operational.[39] Prosecutions to date have therefore depended on assistance from the state prosecutors or *jaksa*, which was generally not forthcoming until 2005, when the personal intervention of the then Prosecutor General, Abdul Rahman Saleh, finally led to improved cooperation. This was probably another key factor in the sudden application of the criminal provisions of the Qanuns in the post-tsunami period. It is significant that this dramatic improvement in Jakarta's support for the enforcement of Islamic legal norms in Aceh took place during the post-tsunami emergency period and in the lead-up to the signing of the Helsinki Agreement, when its role in devastated Aceh was under great scrutiny. Media reports have shed further light on the potential make-up of the Shari'a police force. The *Antara* news agency has quoted the provincial secretary, Tanthawi Ishaq, as stating that it will consist of 2,500 people,[40] while *The Jakarta Post* reported that it will be recruited from among religious students (*talib*) and will enforce Shari'a provisions including the prohibition of extra-marital affairs (International Crisis Group 2002a, 13).

Of particular importance in the implementation of Shari'a is the use of government employees as civil investigators. These civil investigators can, among others things, receive reports regarding breaches of Shari'a law, seize items, take fingerprints and photographs, and arrange witnesses and experts for trial. While Qanuns 5/2000 and 11/2002 outline the powers of the civil investigators in similar terms, one important difference is that Qanun 11/2002 does not include the power to "order a suspect to stop and to examine the suspect's identification papers" (Qanun 5/2000, Art. 20(3c)). Presumably this power was considered too oppressive.

Granting civil employees the right to investigate contraventions of Shari'a raises some significant issues. First, why is this taking place? It is, to some extent at least, probably a matter of resources, with the police already over-burdened with little likelihood of an increase in police numbers. Likewise, the police, formally members of the armed forces under Suharto's New Order, have long institutionally supported *Pancasila* secularism and have become a notoriously corrupt, rent-seeking bureaucracy. There is thus little incentive for them to abandon their basic loyalty to Jakarta in favor of a relatively weak, local authority seeking to institute more rigorous, religiously-motivated standards that would, at the least, threaten rent-seeking. The police would thus be at best a highly unreliable instrument of policy enforcement for the ulama.

By contrast, the investigators appear to be under the authority of the Governor (Qanun 11/2002, Art. 15), which in practice, means the Shari'a Office. While the ulama may not be happy with this arrangement, they would certainly prefer control by the Shari'a Office (over which they could hope to exercise some influence) to control from Jakarta, which has always been largely beyond their reach. The Shari'a Office thus seems to have effectively used the drafting process to grant itself a potential "private"

police force. This may come to have real significance for future competition between the provincial executive and the MPU.

Until such time as the new Shariʿa police force—comprising the civil
investigators and police with authority in Shariʿa matters—is fully up and
running, however, the enforcement of Shariʿa has been in the hands of
Aceh's existing police. At first not much was done about enforcing any of
the criminal provisions of the Qanuns, except (as indicated above) as regards
gambling (International Crisis Group 2002a, 13). There have been media
reports of raids on nightclubs and entertainment venues intent on stamp-
ing out "immorality" in the province.[41] Of particular concern for authorities is the consumption of alcohol, which has been officially prohibited
across the province since the introduction of Shariʿa (see, for example,
Circular Letter of the Governor, No 536/20976 of July 10, 2002). Reports
note that offenders are often simply given a warning, have their identities
recorded, and are then sent away from the venue.[42] In one case, accompanied by the Governor "riding shotgun," police stormed a bar, smelled
drinks to confirm they were alcoholic, and physically removed a cigarette
from the mouth of a young man in order to smell it and determine whether
it contained marijuana.[43] Despite this, beer was certainly available, if dis-
creetly, in most of Banda Aceh's hotels and some of its restaurants in
February 2003 and even in late 2005, although by 2006 it was largely
unobtainable.

Prostitution, on the other hand, is treated more strictly, as seen in regulations such as Governor's Instruction No. 05/INSTR/2002. In 2003, for
example, at least five women were detained by authorities in the Pidie
Regency for visiting an "improper place" at which they were allegedly pros-
tituting themselves.[44] This, when read with the issues outlined above about
the enforcement of rules regarding the wearing of Islamic costume and
limiting women's rights to travel on public transport, may well be part of
an increasing post-tsunami focus on restricting the rights of women.

The conclusion to be drawn here is that the Governor and the police
were intent at first on making an example of a few relatively minor cases,
thereby highlighting the new powers gained through the introduction of
Shariʿa, probably as much for purposes of political demonstration as anything else. This seems to be true also of the first public caning in 2005,
where gamblers were punished for cases involving betting the equivalent
of only a few dollars.[45] Their punishment seemed to be mainly in the form
of public humiliation, rather then physical injury, which was reportedly
very light.[46] In practice, it appears that day-to-day life in Aceh continues
much as before—insofar as it can in the wake of the physical devastation
wrought by the tsunami of December 2004—but now with the stronger

conservative (although not necessarily radical) flavor imparted by the new Shari'a institutions, increasingly directed at women.

Judicial independence

Under Article 25(1) of Law 18/2001, the Shari'a Court is intended to be "free of the influence of other parties," but this is contradicted by Article 26, which expressly gives the Supreme Court jurisdiction over appeals from the Shari'a Court of Appeal in Banda Aceh. It also gives Indonesia's head of state the power to appoint and dismiss judges of the Shari'a Courts after taking into account the opinions of the Governor of Aceh and the chairman of the Supreme Court. The MPU here has no role, but can give fatwas on suitability. There is also no requirement that the head of state must follow the advice given, and therefore appointments to the Shari'a Courts are open to significant political manipulation by the central government.

Further, Article 25(1) of Law 18/2001 makes it explicitly clear that the Shari'a Courts are "part of the national judicature." Although there is no settled interpretation of this phrase, it is generally understood as granting the Supreme Court the general power to supervise and oversee the Shari'a Court. Such an interpretation is consistent with the Supreme Court's appellate jurisdiction over Acehnese Shari'a cases and reflects the constitutional framework of Indonesia's judicature, which at present places the Supreme Court at the apex of the legal hierarchy.[47]

The Acehnese Qanuns further jeopardize the independence of the Shari'a Courts. Under Article 4(2) of Qanun 10/2002 the "organization, administrative and financial management shall be carried out by the Minister [for Religious Affairs] and/or the Governor." This power of the Minister and Governor is further extended to the "management and general supervision of the Judges" (Art. 11(1)). The Governor can exercise further control of the Shari'a Courts through the power, exercised jointly with the President, to regulate the promotion and bonuses of the Shari'a Court judges, subject to the agreement of the DPRD (Art. 24(3)).

Qanun 10/2002 does attempt to protect against undue influence from Jakarta by stipulating that management "must not reduce the independence of judges in examining and deciding cases" (Art. 5(3)). It seems, however, that a provision such as this is more a rhetorical reference to the courts' independence than one that has any practical weight. In all likelihood, this safeguard provision will be meaningless given the multiple avenues available to the central government to influence the Shari'a Courts. The Supreme Court and Aceh's Governor can all exert substantial pressure over the

Shari'a Courts through the appointment and promotion of judges, while the Supreme Court's appellate jurisdiction also remains a direct check on the Shari'a law—and one that would certainly be used if and when an appeal from Aceh eventually reaches that court. And all this is, of course, in addition to the fact that the Shari'a Courts are still almost entirely dependent on funding from the central government.

Funding

The influential role of the Jakarta executive in the management of the Shari'a Courts is clear from Presidential Decision 11/2003. Under Article 6, funding for the Shari'a Courts is to come directly from the Department of Religious Affairs, which receives funds through the national budget. This maintained the position of the earlier Religious Courts, which received finances and supervision from the central executive. It has become redundant, however, because the organizational, administrative, and financial management of the Religious Courts across Indonesia has been transferred, after some years of delay, to the Supreme Court, pursuant to Law No. 5/1999, the so-called *Satu Atap* or "one roof" Law. At the time of writing, this transfer has been completed on paper, but the bureaucrats responsible for the Religious Courts were still the same, sitting in the same offices, although now answerable nominally to different institutions. The result is that despite the changes, the Shari'a Courts are still tightly controlled by the *beamtenstaat* (bureaucratic state) in Jakarta.

This continues to allow Jakarta substantial, albeit indirect, influence over the decisions made, and penalties given, in Aceh. Although concerned not to alienate the Aceh courts, the Supreme Court is, ultimately, strongly aligned with Jakarta and will continue to exert pressure to ensure that the Shari'a Courts do not diverge too far from the central government's (mainly secular nationalist) viewpoint. Accordingly, it is only by applying a version of Islamic law that does not offend the Jakarta-based bureaucrats that the Shari'a Courts can hope to receive the funding and administrative support they need so badly—a need that has only increased since the tsunami destroyed many courts and killed court staff. So long as funding and resources still emanate from Jakarta it seems only natural for the Shari'a Court judges to look to the central government, and not to Aceh, for guidance.

The independence of the Shari'a Courts is crucial to their success as the key to legal manifestation of a local Islamic identity in Aceh, for like all institutions that exercise judicial authority, ensuring independence and the ability to decide a case without fear of reprisal are preconditions to the dispensing of justice. Interference, pressure or manipulation by the central government has the potential to undermine the Courts' integrity and thus their place in the new system contemplated by the Qanuns. Possible areas of tension apparent at this stage include Jakarta's control over the appointment and promotion of judges, the possible restriction of funding if Jakarta disapproves of Shari'a Court decisions, and the overturning of appeal cases in which the Acehnese courts have applied a version of Shari'a considered too "hardline" by the Supreme Court.

Conclusion: A rhetorical commitment to Islamic values

Nanggroe Aceh Darussalam's Qanuns are potentially the most radical Islamic laws anywhere in Indonesia since colonial times. Until the tsunami struck in the last days of 2004, judges presiding over the Shari'a Courts were reluctant, however, to accept the expanded jurisdiction granted them by the Qanuns. They felt they lacked the expertise or resources to handle new and unfamiliar areas of law and preferred to stick to previous, well-established practice (United Nations Development Program 2003, 3). These judges were essentially career bureaucrats who were uncertain about the extent of their new authority, did not have experience in dealing with Shari'a, had routinely relied on the secularized Compilation, and remained dependent on Jakarta—not Banda Aceh—for funding and career path.

In the face of judicial recusance, neither the Acehnese government nor the MPU sought either to force the judges to implement the Qanuns or to take the implementation of Shari'a into their own hands, beyond a few limited incidents. The Qanuns therefore remained largely aspirational until December 2004. Since then, a significant shift has taken place, with the courts more willing to exercise their new, broader jurisdiction, including as regards the hitherto avoided new area of criminal law (*jināya*), slowly and cautiously testing their new authority by trying a small number of minor criminal cases, mainly gambling, such as those that resulted in the caning punishments described above. It is hard to explain precisely why this shift occurred, although a range of possible reasons have been identified, including a change of leadership within the Court as a result of deaths in the tsunami; an increased sense of religiosity among tsunami survivors; the likelihood of a huge number of inheritance cases being lodged with the court and a consequent perceived need to strengthen the Court's capacity and prestige in Acehnese eyes; and pressure from local institutions, including the Shari'a Office and the MPU. So far the Courts have not, however, delivered an Islamic revolution in Aceh.

Most Acehnese thus consider the implementation of Shari'a symbolic, rather than a move to what they call a "hardline" interpretation of Islam of the sort found in the proposed MMI Code. Encapsulated in this symbolism is the province's desire to assert its independence from Jakarta through formal recognition of its conservative, uniquely Acehnese, brand of Islam. The new Qanuns are, nevertheless, broad enough in principle to allow the creation of a far more "hardline" Islamic legal system in Aceh in the future, if the will for such a transformation existed, as increasingly seems to be possible, especially as regards the position of women: the Qanuns do contain what could be a subtle foundation for a more radical system. This would constitute a direct challenge to Indonesia's secular judicial system, of which the Shari'a Court still remains a part. It would also threaten to re-ignite the longstanding debate over the place of religion within Indonesia, a secular state promoting a moderate brand of Islam, but one which has always had to deal with acts of terrorism committed by radical Islamic groups committed to creating an Islamic state (Hooker and Lindsey 2003) and now must respond to increasing attempts across Indonesia to introduce Islamic norms through regional regulations, for example, in South Sulawesi, West Sumatra, and West Java.

It remains to be seen what impact the implementation of the Qanuns will have on daily life in the long term. Current practice suggests that the answer may be "very little." Judges of the Shari'a Court are still essentially unwilling to break with the secularized and bureaucratic version of Islamic law that has previously been applied and which they personally seem to respect. Further, while corporal punishments are now being introduced, albeit currently on small scale, there is no push for *ḥudūd* punishments, which are spoken of even by proponents as likely to remain inappropriate for decades to come.

Aceh is not a Wahhabi-oriented Islamic society. Its ulama are not presently demanding a strict application of the Qur'an or the Sunna, nor do they seem to aim to emulate the Islamic states of the Middle East, although they do see Malaysia as a model. Rather, Aceh is an isolated and rural province with a history of once-powerful, if long-gone, Muslim kingdoms and years of isolation or warfare. Since the 1970s Aceh has effectively been cut off from the rest of Indonesia for all but about a decade. Aceh was considered a "military operations zone" (DOM) from 1989 to the demise of Suharto's New Order regime in 1998 and more recently with the recommencement of military action in the province by the Jakarta military prior to the Helsinki settlement (Tapol 2002, 1). This isolation has contributed to underdevelopment, a severe lack of education, a damaged infrastructure, and a traumatized society and, importantly, has resulted in reduced contact with both more moderate, progressive Islamic movements and more "hardline" Islamist groups from elsewhere in the archipelago.

The result is that Aceh has developed a regional form of religious conservatism closely entwined with its local identity and distinguishable from other parts of Indonesia, even those mentioned above where some groups seek to implement more conservative interpretations of Islam. Aceh's Shariʿa revival is thus a local tradition that is now being developed, albeit in a gradual, piecemeal, and cautious fashion by ulama, eager to increase their traditional authority as against a weakened post-Suharto Indonesian state, but cautious about recommencing traditional rivalry with both Jakarta and local secular leaders—contests they have always lost in the past.

Aceh's ulama are not presently seeking to—and indeed probably could not—build an Islamic Shariʿa system that would completely displace secular bureaucracy or laws. They are, nonetheless, strongly committed to cementing images of Islamic legal culture in its own regional system and creating a public, symbolic rule for Shariʿa, one that is increasingly morally conservative and assertive. This will inevitably lead to conflict with the secular bureaucracy and national laws at some point. Shariʿa in Aceh is thus an old theme but very new as a legal system. It is also deeply riddled with uncertainties, regulatory confusion, and institutional tensions. The question now is how will it develop? One thing seems clear: it will have to do so without much enthusiam or real support from Jakarta.

Part Three

APPENDIX

Twelve

ISLAMIC LEGAL EDUCATION IN MODERN INDONESIA

Azyumardi Azra

The study of Islamic jurisprudence (*fiqh*) has arguably been one of the most important subjects in the history of Islamic educational institutions. The precedent for this was established at an early date by the Niẓāmiyya madrasa in Baghdad, which made Sunni jurisprudence the most important subject for students to learn. Thanks to its prominent position in the madrasa curriculum, the study of jurisprudence played a crucial role in the rise of Sunni orthodoxy from the twelfth century onward.

The study of Islamic law gained momentum in the Malay-Indonesian archipelago from the seventeenth century, when prominent Muslim scholars (*'ulamā'*) in the region began to produce books of Islamic jurisprudence in Malay. The most important among them were Nūr al-Dīn al-Rānīrī's *Ṣirāṭ al-Mustaqīm* on law relating to religious observances (*fiqh 'ibādāt*), and 'Abd al-Ra'ūf al-Sinkīlī's *Mir'āt al-Ṭullāb* on law relating to commercial transactions (*fiqh mu'āmalāt*). In the eighteenth century, Muḥammad Arshad al-Banjārī produced his masterpiece in *fiqh 'ibādāt* entitled *Sabīl al-Muhtadīn*, which is still studied today in some parts of Indonesia. These local works drew upon standard works of Shafi'i jurisprudence and in doing so they contributed substantially to the consolidation of that school of jurisprudence (*madhhab*) in the Malay-Indonesian archipelago as a whole (Azra 2004; 2002). Such works produced in Malay and other regional languages came to be studied in addition to Arabic works that were increasingly circulating among the *'ulamā'* in the archipelago.

The study of Islamic law was a central feature of the curricula of traditional Islamic educational institutions in the Malay-Indonesian archipelago. Although some local Islamic educational institutions had been in existence since the earliest history of Islam in the archipelago, it was in the nineteenth century that *pesantren*s most firmly took root. As Mastuhu (2004) and Van Bruinessen (1995) have observed, the study of Shari'a and *fiqh* occupied an important position in the *pesantren* curriculum.

The study of Islamic law also came to occupy a special place in Islamic

higher educational institutions that began to be established in Indonesia
after independence in 1945. The discriminatory policies of the Dutch toward
native educational institutions, or more precisely, toward Islamic educational institutions, had marginalized the *pesantren*s and given little room for
the development of Islamic higher education. It is not surprising, therefore, that the long-held aspiration of Indonesian Muslims to establish Islamic
higher educational institutions could be realized only after Indonesia gained
its independence.

This chapter will discuss Islamic higher educational institutions in Indonesia
and the place of legal education in those schools. It will be shown that
Islamic legal education has progressed through a number of stages and has
grown stronger both intellectually and institutionally. These developments
are closely linked to wider social, cultural, and political changes in Indonesia.
As Hooker and Lindsey also conclude, the last twenty-five years have seen
a revolution in Shariʿa education in Indonesia (Hooker and Lindsey 2003, 50).

Development of IAIN/STAIN/UIN

The study of Islamic law at higher educational institutions in Indonesia is
provided by at least two major types of schools. The first is Islamic higher
educational institutions. This includes the Institut Agama Islam Negeri
(IAIN) or State Institute for Islamic Studies, and the Sekolah Tinggi Agama
Islam Negeri (STAIN) or State College for Islamic Studies, and more
recently the Universitas Islam Negeri (UIN) or State Islamic University. In
addition to these state institutions there are also private schools, including
the Institut Agama Islam Swasta (IAIS) or Private Institute for Islamic
Studies and Sekolah Tinggi Agama Islam Swasta (STAIS) or Private College
for Islamic Studies. In terms of institutional structure and curricula, these
private Islamic institutions generally follow the IAIN and STAIN models.

The second type of higher educational institutions involved in Islamic
legal education is comprised of public (or "secular") universities, such as
the Universitas Indonesia (UI) in Jakarta and Universitas Airlangga in
Surabaya. At Universitas Indonesia, Islamic legal education was introduced
within the Faculty of Law at least as early as the 1970s under the tute-
lage of Prof. Muhammad Rasjidi, the first Minister of Religious Affairs of
the Republic of Indonesia. The program in Islamic law at UI has produced a number of doctorate graduates, including Muhammad Daud Ali,
Muhammad Tahir Azhary, and, more recently, Rifyal Kaʿbah, who later
became prominent scholars of Islamic law in Indonesia.

The rise of a number of "Shari'a institutions" in the 1990s that offer "Islamic" banking services, such as the Muamalat Bank, has ignited a growing interest in the study of "Islamic economics" (*ekonomi Islam*) and laws relating to financial transactions. This has led a number of public universities, such as Universitas Airlangga and Universitas Indonesia, to introduce programs in Islamic economics. The introduction of these programs has eroded the established "monopoly" of the Faculty of Syariah (Shari'a) at IAIN—which will be discussed below—on Indonesian academic discourse on Islamic economics under the rubric of commercial transactions (*mu'āmalāt*).

Beyond these sorts of specialized programs, other forms of Islamic legal education are also provided by private Islamic universities, like Universitas Islam Indonesia (UII) in Yogyakarta, Universitas Islam Jakarta (UID), Universitas Islam Bandung (Unisba), and at a number of Universitas Muhammadiyah campuses (in Jakarta, Surakarta, Yogyakarta, Malang, and other cities throughout Indonesia), as well as at many other private Islamic universities. Islamic legal education in these private Islamic universities can be found in the Department of Syariah of the Fakultas Agama Islam (FAI or Faculty of Islamic Religion). The curricula of such Departments of Syariah (*Jurusan Syariah*) are modeled after the Faculty of Syariah at the IAIN and UIN or the Department of Syariah at the STAIN. Some of these programs implement exactly the same curriculum, but some others make certain adaptations. Because of the important role they play in Indonesian Islamic legal education as a whole, we now turn to the IAIN/STAIN and the UIN.

There are at present 15 IAINs, 34 STAINs and three UINs throughout Indonesia. The three UINs are: UIN Syarif Hidayatullah, Jakarta; UIN Sunan Kalijaga, Yogyakarta; and UIN Malang (East Java). All of the IAINs are located in provincial capitals. They include IAIN ar-Raniry, Banda Aceh (Nanggroe Aceh Darussalam Special Province); IAIN Sumatera Utara, Medan (North Sumatra Province); IAIN Sultan Syarif Qasim, Pekanbaru (Riau Province); IAIN Imam Bonjol, Padang (West Sumatra Province); IAIN Sultan Taha Saifuddin, Jambi (Jambi Province); IAIN Raden Patah Palembang (South Sumatra Province); IAIN Raden Intan, Bandar Lampung (Lampung Province); IAIN Sunan Gunung Jati, Bandung (West Java Province); IAIN Walisongo, Semarang (Central Java Province); IAIN Sunan Ampel, Surabaya (East Java Province); IAIN Antasari, Banjarmasin (South Kalimantan Province); IAIN Alauddin, Makassar (South Sulawesi Province); IAIN Gorontalo (North Sulawesi); IAIN Mataram (Nusa Tenggara Barat Province); and IAIN Serang (Banten Province).

For many Muslim leaders and scholars the existence of the IAIN represents the realization of long-held aspirations among Muslim communities to have their own Islamic higher educational institutions. It has long been recognized that the *pesantren* are at best capable of providing pre-university education, and that there is a need for Islamic tertiary educational institutions in Indonesia where graduates of senior secondary level *pesantren* could continue their studies. Since the seventeenth century some *pesantren* graduates as well as graduates of other traditional Islamic institutions, like *surau* in West Sumatra, *dayah* in Aceh and *pondok* elsewhere in the Malay-Indonesian archipelago, have continued their education in Mecca and Medina (Azra 2004; Laffan 2003; Abaza 1993; 1994). From the early twentieth century, students from the region have also continued their studies at al-Azhar University in Cairo. Because of financial constraints and other reasons, however, opportunities to study in the Middle East have always been very limited. The desire to enable larger numbers of graduates from *pesantren*, *surau*, *pondok*, and *dayah* to pursue advanced studies has fueled the aspiration of Indonesian Muslims to found their own Islamic tertiary educational institutions.

Toward the end of the Dutch colonial period, a group of Muslim leaders, intellectuals, and scholars under the leadership of Dr. Satiman Wirjosandjojo attempted to found what they called "Higher Pesantren" (*pesantren luhur*) at the level of university. This early effort failed, mostly because of the unsupportive attitude of the Dutch colonial rulers, but in 1940 the Association of Muslim Teachers (Persatuan Guru-guru Agama Islam/PGAI) successfully founded the Sekolah Islam Tinggi (SIT/Islamic College) in West Sumatra. This Islamic College was short-lived, however; it ceased to exist with the coming of Japanese wartime occupation in 1942.

Efforts to establish an Islamic tertiary educational institution continued through the period of Japanese occupation. In contrast to the Dutch, who in one way or another suppressed Islamic education, the Japanese showed a more conciliatory approach to the Muslim community. In early 1945, the Japanese government made a promise to Muslim leaders to allow and support efforts to have their own Islamic higher educational institution. As a result, in April 1945, a group of Muslim leaders met in Jakarta to set up a preparatory committee for the establishment of an Islamic college. This committee was chaired by Mohammad Hatta, who became Indonesia's first Vice President after independence on August 17, 1945. Muhammad Natsir—who later held the position of Prime Minister—served as secretary (*Kiprah* 1999, 3; Mudzhar 2003, 179).

On July 8, 1945 the preparatory committee was finally able to found the Sekolah Tinggi Islam (STI) in Jakarta. The STI was a private college led by Abdul Kahar Mudzakir, a graduate of al-Azhar University. Because of the armed revolution that erupted following the return of the Dutch in the aftermath of the declaration of national independence, the STI was moved to Yogyakarta, the capital city of revolutionary Indonesia. The STI began functioning in Yogyakarta on April 10, 1946, and on March 10, 1948, the STI was transformed into Universitas Islam Indonesia (UII/ Indonesian Islamic University). The UII consisted of four faculties: Islamic Studies, [Indonesian "secular"/positive] Law, Economics, and Education (*Kiprah* 1999, 3; Mudzhar 2003, 179).

The further development of the UII and other Islamic and secular pub- lic educational institutions was heavily influenced by politics. This is appar- ent in the terms of a decree issued by President Sukarno in 1950 stating that the government had created the Universitas Gadjah Mada for "nation- alists." To balance this decision, in 1951 the government awarded the Perguruan Tinggi Agama Islam Negri (PTAIN/State College of Islamic Studies) to Muslims (*kaum agama*). The PTAIN was created from the Faculty of Islamic Studies of the UII. In the new college this faculty was divided into four departments: the Departments of Da'wa (religious propagation), Qadha (*qaḍāʾ*, which later became the Faculty of Syariah), Tarbiyah (Islamic education) and Ushuluddin (*uṣūl al-dīn*, religious sciences). The PTAIN offered two levels of study: a four-year baccalaureate program (culminat- ing in a BA degree), and a two-year post-graduate program (awarding the degree of doctorandus). Six years after the founding of PTAIN the Akademi Dinas Ilmu Agama (ADIA/Academy of Islamic Sciences) was established in Jakarta with the special mission of preparing future civil servants for the Ministry of Religious Affairs. Founded on June 1, 1957, the ADIA con- sisted of three departments: the Department of Islamic Religious Instruction; the Department of Arabic Language; and the Department of Military Chaplaincy. The program of study was five years.

Another important milestone in the development of the Islamic higher education system occurred on August 24, 1960 with the issuance of Presidential Decree No. 11/1960 integrating the PTAIN in Yogyakarta and ADIA in Jakarta into a new institution—the Institut Agama Islam Negeri (IAIN). The new IAIN consisted of four faculties: two in Yogyakarta—the Faculties of Ushuluddin and Syariah—and two in Jakarta—the Faculties of Tarbiyah and Adab (humanities). In the early 1960s the Temporary Peoples Consultative Assembly issued a special decree providing for the creation of additional IAIN faculties (MPRS No. I/RIS/MPRS/1963, enclosure A ad. 5), and new faculties were established in a number of provincial capitals. On February 25, 1963, the original IAIN in Yogyakarta was divided into two separate institutions—IAIN Sunan Kalijaga in Yogyakarta and IAIN Syarif Hidayatullah in Jakarta, each of which had branches in other provinces. The IAIN Yogyakarta was assigned to coordinate all branch faculties in

Central Java, East Java, Kalimantan, Sulawesi, Nusa Tenggara and Maluku, while the IAIN Jakarta was responsible for coordinating all branch faculties in Jakarta, West Java and Sumatra.

The expansion of the system of state Islamic institutes continued in late 1963 with the formation of additional IAIN outside of Java. Based on Presidential Decree No. 27/1963, five new IAIN were formed in Banda Aceh, Palembang, Padang, Jambi, and Pekanbaru on December 5, 1965. By the end of the following decade there were a total of 14 IAIN throughout Indonesia. Another important phase in the development of Islamic tertiary education occurred toward the end of the Suharto regime with the formation in 1997 of 34 STAINs from the faculties of IAINs located in smaller cities outside of the provincial capitals. These new STAINs were structurally independent from any IAIN. In terms of academic content, STAINs are similar to IAINs, but with smaller numbers of students. As a result, the STAINs are often referred to as "mini-IAINs."

Since the 1970s a growing number of academics and administrators in the IAIN system have come to believe that the most significant constraint on the further development of the IAIN is their official status as *instituts*. As an *institut*, the IAIN curriculum is confined to "religious sciences," which hampers the ability of IAINs to respond to the demands of the rapid social and cultural change that has accompanied Indonesia's economic development. As stated in the Indonesian Educational Act of 1989, while an *institut* is allowed to provide education and training in one particular discipline only, a *universitas* (university) is able to work in all the various disciplines of knowledge and sciences. During the Suharto period, political and legal constraints stood in the way of efforts to transform the *instituts* into full-fledged universities and move beyond the traditional boundaries of religious sciences. These barriers began to come down, however, after the Suharto regime collapsed in May 1998, and on May 20, 2002, IAIN Jakarta was transformed into Syarif Hidayatullah State Islamic University (UIN Jakarta). Two years later in June 2004 IAIN Yogyakarta and STAIN Malang were also converted to UIN. With their transformation into full-fledged universities, all three UIN are now able to provide training in the humanities and social and natural sciences, in addition to traditional Islamic religious studies.

The Faculty of Syariah; Institutional and curriculum development

The institutional development of the IAIN has had important implications for the Faculties and Departments of Syariah where Islamic law and jurispru-

dence are taught. As one of the core faculties in all IAIN, the Syariah
Faculties have not only been maintained but have been improved and
strengthened. Prior to the formation of the STAIN, Syariah Faculties made
up 25 out of approximately 90 faculties in the 14 IAIN throughout Indonesia.
With the establishment of the STAIN, there are now 34 Departments of
Syariah in all STAINs. The number of Syariah Faculties/Departments is,
of course, even greater if we include those existing in private Institutes for
Islamic Studies (IAIS), private Colleges of Islamic Studies (STAIS), and in
Faculties of Islamic Religion in private Islamic Universities. As mentioned
earlier, in recent years a number of public universities, like Universitas
Indonesia in Jakarta and Universitas Airlangga, have also introduced or
expanded academic programs related to Shari'a or Islamic law.

The Syariah Faculties of the IAIN generally consist of four departments:
the Department of Islamic Courts (*qaḍā'*), which sometimes includes a concentration or specialty in personal and family law (*aḥwāl al-shakhṣiyya*), and
the departments of comparative studies of Islamic legal schools (*muqāranat
al-madhāhib*), Islamic penal law and governance law (*jināya, siyāsa*), and commercial law (*mu'āmalāt*). The last of these is now effectively equated with
Islamic economics, Islamic banking, and Islamic "insurance" (*takāful*). It
bears mention that most of these departments in the IAIN Faculties of
Syariah also exist in the STAIN, where they are designated concentrations
or specialties within the Department of Syariah.

What, then, are the objectives of the IAIN Faculty of Syariah? The aims
of this faculty have been outlined in a Decree of the Minister of Religious
Affairs (No. 1/1972). Based on Article 2 of the Decree and statements produced at the second Workshop on the Improvement of IAIN (Jakarta)
Curriculum in 1979, the aims of Syariah Faculties have been formulated
as follows: "To produce Muslim scholars with noble God-fearing character who are experts in Islamic religious sciences, particularly in the field
of Syariah" (*Kiprah* 1999, 10–11).

This statement makes clear that the training of students in the Faculty
of Syariah is intended as more than simply an academic exercise or advancement of students' religious knowledge. In addition to transferring knowledge, the mission of the Syariah Faculty also includes the formation of
character and religiosity. Combining these two objectives is not always easy,
and there is occasionally some tension between them. The same tension
exists to some extent within the IAIN more broadly. On the one hand,
the IAIN (and particularly the Syariah Faculty) is expected to play the role
of fostering religious values and character formation, which is basically a
missionary (*da'wa*) expectation. At the same time, however, the IAIN are
also expected to achieve excellence in academic fields. The existence of

tension between religious and academic goals is neither new nor unique in religious-based academic institutions, and there has been a lively discussion of the issue among Western academics as it relates to Western universities.

The Ministry of Religious Affairs began prescribing the curricula for the Faculty of Syariah from the time of its founding. The task of formulating the Syariah curriculum has been assigned to experts from within the Faculties themselves together with other experts in Islamic law. Prior to the fall of the Suharto regime in 1998 the curriculum was set to national standards and implemented, with only minor adjustments and modifications, by all IAIN Syariah Faculties, and later also by Departments of Syariah at all STAINs. In other words, the curriculum was by and large uniform and monolithic. This reflects the New Order emphasis on centralized authority and uniformity in virtually all walks of life, including in higher education.

Within this framework of centralized control, there has, however, been a process of incremental change in the curriculum of the Syariah Faculty. Change has been most frequent since the 1980s and in the post-Suharto period. The curricular modifications that have been made reflect the response of the Ministry of Religious Affairs and officials within the IAINs and Syariah Faculties to the demands of rapid social, cultural, and political change in Indonesian society. Confronting an ever-changing situation in the wider world, there has always been a need to change—or, more appropriately, to renew—the existing curriculum. This is, of course, not unique to the curriculum of IAIN or the Syariah Faculty; the curricula of Indonesian schools in general are constantly changing. However, the particularities of Indonesian politics have added another dimension to this process. That reality is reflected in the adage, well known in Indonesian society: *ganti Menteri, ganti kurikulum* or "the Minister (of Education) changes, and so does the curriculum."

According to the 1997 IAIN curriculum, all courses are divided into three groupings. The first grouping is called the Mata Kuliah Dasar Umum (MKDU), which consists of General Basic Courses that must be taken by every IAIN and STAIN student, including those studying in the Faculties or Departments of Syariah. Included in this category are courses on *Pancasila* State Ideology, *Kewiraan* (National Defense and Security), Arabic, English, and Indonesian language courses, Introduction to Humanities, and the Methodology of Islamic Studies. The second grouping is called the Mata Kuliah Dasar Keahlian (MKDK) or Courses on Basic Expertise. The courses in this group include Islamic legal theory (*uṣūl al-fiqh*), the science of traditions (*ʿulūm al-ḥadīth*), the Qurʾanic sciences (*ʿulūm al-Qurʾān*), theology (*kalām*), Sufism, philosophy, research methodology, Islamic jurisprudence (*fiqh*), Prophetic tradition (*ḥadīth*), Qurʾanic exegesis, and history of Islamic civilization. The last grouping of courses is called Mata Kuliah Keahlian (MKK) or Courses on Specific Expertise. Most of these courses are detailed expositions of certain subjects in the field of Syariah, such as the Islamic penal law, etc. (Mudzhar 2003, 181; Bustaman-Ahmad 2002, 77–82).

All courses, furthermore, can be classified into other categories as well. For example, courses on the Qur'an would include the Qur'anic sciences, Qur'anic exegesis, history of Qur'anic exegesis, meanings of the Qur'an, philosophy of the Qur'an, and the science of Qur'anic recitation. Likewise, courses on the Prophetic tradition would include an introduction to the sciences of ḥadīth, selections of ḥadīth, ḥadīth related to law, the history of ḥadīth transmitters, and meanings of ḥadīth (Mudzhar 2003, 181). The courses in these two categories can be regarded as the foundation of Islamic religious sciences with a particular emphasis on Islamic law.

Core courses in Shari'a or fiqh are aimed at developing the expertise of students in classical Islamic law. According to the 1982 curriculum, this category includes an introduction to Islamic jurisprudence and legal methodology, ritual law, the law of commercial relations and Islamic economics (mu'āmalāt), family law, inheritance law, penal law, law of governance (siyāsa), comparative legal methodology, history of Shari'a legislation, and Islamic judicial decision-making.

When further modifications were made in 1995, a number of new courses were introduced. They were contemporary issues of law (masā'il al-fiqhiyya), regulating principles of law (qawā'id al-fiqhiyya), comparative positive law (muqāranat al-qawānīn), law of Islamic banking, and philosophy of Islamic law. Again, when further modifications were made in 1997, courses on the fatwa, institutions of Islamic economics (according to Islamic law), and research methodology in legal studies were also added (Kurikulum 1995; Mudzhar 2003, 181; Hooker and Lindsey 2003, 52–2). In addition to these offerings, there are other subject categories of courses covering Indonesian secular law and various aspects of the national legal system, Islamic history and civilization, general introductions to social sciences and the humanities as well as Arabic and English language studies.

In the years following the fall of President Suharto in 1998, the Ministry of Education granted greater autonomy—together with greater accountability and greater quality assurance—to universities in general. Education Minister Prof. A. Malik Fadjar decided in 2001, for instance, that there will be no uniform "national curriculum," thus giving each university freedom to formulate its own curriculum within the parameters of an outline of basic principles set forth by the Ministry. Ministry of Education policies for universities have also affected UINs, IAINs and STAINs, despite the fact that these institutions are officially under the supervision of the Ministry

of Religious Affairs. As a result, the Ministry of Religious Affairs has given
the UIN, IAIN, and STAIN greater autonomy to formulate their own curriculum as well.

The trend toward greater curricular autonomy for UIN/IAIN Syariah
Faculties is reflected in the introduction of more flexibility to incorporate
"local content" into the curriculum. As the proportion of locally-designed
curricula increases, the scope of the "national curriculum" is gradually
being reduced to a kind of "core curriculum." As has been shown by
Hooker and Lindsey (2003, 52–4), the local content of the Syariah Faculty
curriculum is not only becoming greater but also more diverse. The Syariah
Faculty of IAIN Surabaya, for instance, offers 56 *lokal* courses out of a
total of 90. The local content is even greater in the Syariah Faculty of
IAIN Palembang. The same trend is also occurring in the Syariah Faculty
of UIN Jakarta, which has been in the forefront of the introduction of
modifications and revisions of Syariah curriculum since at least 1999. The
present curriculum introduces new local content courses in at least four
fields: (1) aspects of Indonesian secular (positive) law, such as legal procedure, structure of judicial system, land law, criminal law, family law, and
so on; (2) certain aspects of customary law (*adat*); (3) various subjects related
to Islamic economics, such as accounting, and management; and (4) certain supplementary subjects such as sociology of law, politics of law, and
the like.

The latest development in the Syariah Faculty curriculum is the introduction in 2003 of *Kurikulum Berbasis Kompetensi* (KBK/Competency-Based
Curriculum). In line with current policy, all courses have been reassessed
and re-evaluated in order to ensure that all students achieve a certain
degree of competency prior to graduation. For purposes of implementing
the new competency standards, all courses now are divided into three
groupings: First, courses aimed at forming "primary" competency, which
consist of general courses on Islamic jurisprudence and Indonesian secular
law. Second, courses for "supporting" competencies that include courses
offering detailed and in-depth discussions of Islamic jurisprudence and
Indonesian secular law, Indonesian, Arabic, and English language courses,
sociology of law, and so on. These are further complemented by course
offerings designed to develop "other" competencies, such as Qur'anic recitation as well as components of *Kuliah Kerja Sosial* (KKS/Social Service Units),
and the *skripsi* or academic writing exercise (*Pedoman 2003/2004*, 2004,
39–40).

Despite these modifications and revisions, the number of credits that students must take in order to complete their undergraduate degree has
remained essentially constant since the introduction of the Semester Credit

System in the 1980s. The minimum number of credits required for graduation is 160. From 1997 to the recent introduction of KBK (Competence-Based Curricula), all of these credits have been spread across the three basic course groupings mentioned above: roughly one-fourth in the MKDU (General Basic Courses); one-half in the MKDK (Courses on Basic Expertise); and one-fourth in the MKK (Courses on Specific Expertise). With the introduction of the KBK, the number of credits within the three competencies is generally as follows: primary competencies, 60 credits; supporting competencies, 90 credits; and other competencies, 10 credits (*Pedoman 2003/2004*, 2004, 47–55). It typically takes four years for students to complete their undergraduate degree under these requirements.

An examination of the existing IAIN/UIN Syariah Faculty curricula demonstrates that the range of courses available to students is very broad, covering not only classical and medieval Islamic law, but also contemporary discourses on Islamic law with all of its attendant problems. Nevertheless, it is assumed by some that students in the Syariah Faculties study mostly classical law, and that their studies thus have little relevance to contemporary issues. It is often asserted, moreover, that the study of Islamic law in the Syariah Faculty differs little from its study in the *pesantren*, which deals only with traditional Islamic jurisprudence or *fiqh* (Bustaman-Ahmad 2002, 82, 87). The common assumption that the study of Islamic law in the Syariah Faculty is only a repetition of the students' *pesantren* experience is based mainly on the fact that some of the same *fiqh* books used in the *pesantren* are also studied in the Syariah Faculty. It is important to point out, however, that the study of these books in the Syariah Faculty differs significantly from that in the *pesantren* in terms of depth, approach, and methodology. The study of classical and medieval Islamic law in the *pesantren* is primarily for didactic or missionary purposes. Students in these schools are expected both to know the injunctions of Islamic law and also to practice them. Furthermore, the study of Islamic law in many *pesantren* is basically a process of rote-learning, while in the Syariah Faculty, generally speaking, the study of Islamic law is more academic and scientific, despite the use of some of the same materials. Also, the study of Islamic jurisprudence in the Syariah Faculty employs historical and comparative approaches. Thus, Islamic law is studied at the UIN/IAIN not only as Islamic legal doctrine, but also as a historical phenomenon in the context of the broader development of Islam.

The students in the Syariah Faculty also study subjects relating to contemporary debates, developments, and issues in Islamic law. In doing so they learn how Islamic law has been continually contextualized in response to modern and contemporary social, cultural, and political change. This is important not least because it gives students insight into the ways in which modern and contemporary Muslim jurists reexamine, reinterpret and reformulate *fiqh* in a rapidly changing world.

The comparative approach is one of the most distinctive characteristics of the study of Islamic law at the UIN/IAIN Syariah Faculty. A comparative approach is employed not only in the study of different schools of Islamic law (*madhhab*s), but also in connection with Indonesian secular and customary law. With regard to the former, the comparative approach provides a valuable perspective on the historical evolution of the legal schools in different Muslim societies from their founding to the present. The broader comparative approach, moreover, helps students learn how Islamic jurisprudence has interacted with both Indonesian secular and customary law and how further mutual interaction and accommodation might be conceptualized. The comparative approach within the Syariah Faculty as well as in IAIN more generally is non-*madhhab*-oriented. In other words, the study of the various schools of Islamic law is not for the purpose of orienting students or influencing them to choose or take sides with a particular school. By and large, all major schools of Islamic law—including the Twelver Shi'i school—are treated in an objective and fair manner without prejudice on the part of faculty lecturers.

Another important feature of the study of Islamic law in the Syariah Faculty is the increasing use of historical and sociological approaches. The historical approach to Islamic law—in fact to Islam as a whole—was perhaps initially introduced by the influential Harun Nasution, a graduate of al-Azhar and McGill Universities, and Rector of IAIN Jakarta in the 1970s and early 1980s. In his lectures, Nasution strongly criticized members of the Syariah Faculty for being too legalistic and normative in their approach. At the same time he appealed for greater use of historically contextualized approaches and independent reasoning (*ijtihād*) in the study of Islamic law.

The sociological approach to Islamic law is a more recent phenomenon in UIN/IAIN Syariah Faculties. Notable in this regard is Muhammad Atho Mudzhar, a graduate of IAIN Jakarta and the University of California, Los Angeles, who served as rector of IAIN Yogyakarta from 1997 to 2001. Mudzhar divides the study of Islamic law into three categories: the study of Islamic law as a fundamental doctrine of Islam; the study of Islamic law as a body of norms and regulations; and the study of Islamic law as a social and cultural phenomenon. Mudzhar emphasizes the importance of studying Islamic law as a sociological phenomenon, whereby Islamic law has been influenced by, and in turn served to inform, social, cultural, and political dynamics of Muslim societies (Mudzhar 2002, 244–46).

Having researched the study of Islamic law at the IAINs, Hooker and Lindsey conclude that the current curricula of Syariah Faculties are remarkable for their breadth and integration of modern theory and secular subjects. According to them, the past quarter-century of Islamic education in Indonesia has seen a revolution in Shariʿa education (Hooker and Lindsey 2003, 50, 51). Thanks primarily to the distinctive nature of Islamic legal education at UIN/IAINs, it is now increasingly possible to conceptualize a *mazhab fiqh Indonesia*—an Indonesian school of Islamic law—an idea that has circulated among Indonesian Muslim thinkers for fifty years. This Indonesian school of law is conceived as deeply involved in the social, cultural, and political realities of Indonesian life engaging with significant features of local historical contexts (Hooker and Lindsey 2003, 26; Feener 2001, 109, 115).

Conclusion

Islamic legal education in Indonesia has progressed significantly since the early 1980s when both IAIN Jakarta and IAIN Yogyakarta opened a Faculty of Graduate Studies (Fakultas Pasca-Sarjana/FPS). At IAIN Jakarta, the FPS concentrated primarily on general Islamic studies, while the FPS in Yogyakarta had a concentration in Islamic education. Thus, in the early development of these FPSs, there was no particular emphasis on the study of Islamic law, although a number of students in these faculties, who were in fact senior lecturers at IAINs, focused on Islamic law in their research.

Most of these early students also took additional courses and conducted dissertation research in Western countries, particularly the Netherlands. As a result, they were able to produce excellent dissertations such as those by Peunoh Daly, Amir Syarifuddin, Muardi Chatib, and others who played important roles in the further development of the IAIN Syariah Faculties. During this early period, the FPSs adopted what was essentially a "continental" model of post-graduate study, in which students conducted limited course work and devoted the bulk of their time to conducting research and writing their dissertations.

Later, the continental model was replaced by an "American system," in which students at the Masters level take courses for at least two years, followed by a period devoted to writing a thesis. When students continue in a doctoral program they are required to spend one or two additional years taking courses—depending on the academic background at the Masters level—before they are allowed to sit for a comprehensive doctoral examination and begin research towards a dissertation. In the 1990s the Post-Graduate Program (Program Pasca-Sarjana/PPS) at IAIN Jakarta began to introduce a more established and well-designed concentration or specialty in Islamic law. This concentration has proven to be one of the most popular concentrations in the PPS at both the MA and PhD levels. Although no systematic study has yet been done on the impact of these developments, there is little doubt that the graduates of these programs at both the Masters and doctoral level have played an important role in the further progress of Islamic legal education at UINs, IAINs and STAINs. They have also played an increasingly important role in the development of Shariʿa discourse in such prominent national institutions as Majelis Tarjih (fatwa body of Muhammadiyah), Bahtsul Masaʾil (fatwa body of NU), Majelis Fatwa MUI (Indonesian Council of ʿUlamāʾ), and the like.

Rapid social, cultural, and political changes since the 1990s have provided greater momentum for ongoing development of Islamic legal education in Indonesia. The rise of the Bank Muamalat and the enactment of Law No 7/1989 on Islamic Courts have led the Faculties of Syariah to open new departments and admit a greater number of students. With the greater accommodation of the Islamic banking system by the Indonesian Central Bank in the "reform" period following the fall of President Suharto, more and more conventional banks are opening "Syariah branches." This leads not only to more employment opportunities for the alumni of Syariah Faculties, but also to a more intense scholarly discourse on Islamic economics as a whole.

On the other hand, the national legal restructuring since 1989 has put Islamic courts on par with other courts which has led to further demand for Islamic legal studies and provided graduates of IAIN Syariah Faculties with new career opportunities. The position of Syariah degree holders has been further strengthened with the enactment of the new Advocates Law in 2003, which grants graduates of Syariah Faculties the same opportunity to practice before Indonesian courts as graduates of Law Faculties at public universities.

In line with all of these developments, the emergence of the three UINs in Jakarta, Yogyakarta, and Malang has provided Syariah Faculties with even greater opportunities. At UIN Jakarta, for instance, the Faculty of Syariah has become the Faculty of Syariah dan Hukum (Faculty of Islamic and National Law). Within this framework, Islamic law can be studied simultaneously with national law in ways that can serve to facilitate further development toward the development of a distinctly "Indonesian school of Islamic law."

NOTES

Introduction

1. For brief overviews of Islamic religious and legal literatures produced in the Indonesian archipelago during the early period, and the impact of modernization on earlier patterns of scholarship and social organization, see Feener forthcoming a, forthcoming b. We would like to thank Clark Lombardi for his meticulous constructive critiques on an earlier draft of this essay.
2. A landmark in scholarship on this phenomenon, which includes studies of Southeast Asian material alongside treatments of developments in the Middle East and South Asia, is Masud, Messick and Powers 1996a.

Chapter One. R. Michael Feener, *Muslim Legal Thought in Modern Indonesia: Introduction and Overview*

1. The amount of this material has even further dramatically increased since the publication of Karel Steenbrink's survey. Steenbrink 1997.
2. The material covered in broad outline in this chapter is dealt with in considerably more detail in my book, *Muslim Legal Thought in Modern Indonesia* (Cambridge University Press, 2007).
3. See, for example, Eickelman 1992.
4. Martin van Bruinessen notes that works on *uṣūl al-fiqh* first began to attract wider attention by the *kaum muda* reformists in the 1920s. For instance, the reformist magazine *al-Ittifāq wa l-iftirāq* contained numerous writings on *uṣūl* which were excerpted from such works as al-Shāfiʿī's *Risāla* and Ibn Rushd's *Bidāyat al-Mujtahid*. Cit. Schrieke 1921, 298–300; van Bruinessen 1990, 250.
5. A. Hassan, for example, completely rejected the institution of *ijāza* that was such a central part of traditional Muslim education. Hassan 1996, 1179.
6. For an overview of PERSIS and the organization's role in the modern transformation of Indonesian Islam, see Federspiel 2001.
7. *Tarjamah Bulughul Maraam* (Bangil: Pustaka Tamaam, 1991 reprint).
8. This biographical sketch is based largely on his reconstruction of events as outlined in Hamim 1996, 26–56.
9. In the original author's preface to this work, Chalil makes it clear that he intended it as a sequel to his *Biografi Empat Serangkai Imam Mazhab*, as well as a prologue to a larger work of *fiqh*, presumably the *Fiqh al-Nabawwy: Kembali kepada Al Qurʾan dan As-Sunna*. Since that preface was written, the book has gone through at least ten reprints.

10. Here Chalil makes the argument that while *istiṣlāḥ* may be used as a method to guide one's investigations toward a particular ruling, it may not serve as a source of law in and of itself. In doing this he quotes rather extensively from al-Shawkānī's *Irshād*, and then goes on to cite examples in which the Prophet's Companions decided upon certain cases by basing their decisions on considerations of public interest. Among the examples Chalil cites are the compilation of the Qur'an and the establishment of the punishment of eighty lashes for those convicted of drinking wine. Chalil 1956, 259–61. In these discussions, Chalil cites only examples of cases that would be considered as dealing with *muʿāmalāt*, not *ʿibādāt*.

11. For instance, in some places he tends to accept the authority of some later *ʿulamā'* as authoritative without conducting an investigation of their individual rules himself. Thus we often read such statements as, "Imam Suyūṭī delcares this *ḥadīth* sound . . ." etc., in the course of his arguments.

12. The original Indonesian of this clause is itself rather ambiguous and subject to a range of particular interpretations.

13. In 1997, the Semarang publisher Pustaka Rizki Putra reissued over a dozen of Hasbi's most popular works in 'new editions' in which the language, spelling, and style have been updated to make them more accessible to contemporary Indonesian readers. These editions enjoy a wide national distribution and can be found in bookstores throughout Indonesia.

14. For more on the workings of *ijtihād* in Hasbi's system of thought, see Wahyudi 1993.

15. Hazairin completed his dissertation under the direction of Professor Barend ter Haar, one of the most highly regarded scholars in the study of *adat*. The work for this project focused upon the traditional law of the Rejang people inhabiting the hill districts inland of Bengkulu. Hazairin 1936. For a biographical sketch of Hazairin, see Ritonga 1995, 14–37. Other information and anecdotes about Hazairin can be found in the memorial essays of Bismar Siregar, Hasbullah Bakry, Potan Arif Harahap, and S.M. Amin that are included in Thalib 1981.

16. Hazairin discussed his ideas on the subject of inheritance law in a number of publications, including Hazairin 1958.

17. Hazairin's use of the term "bilateral" has led to some misunderstandings, especially by foreign scholars of Indonesian law and society. Some have taken for granted that the concept necessarily implies equal shares of inheritance for both sons and daughters of the deceased, as opposed to the traditional Muslim system whereby daughters receive half-shares, or less, of those allocated to their brothers. However this is not the case. For Hazairin, the Qur'anic stipulation of differential shares to one's male and female children was based upon a clear and authoritative scriptural foundation that could not be neglected or reasoned away. What could be reinterpreted was the extra-Qur'anic system that grew out of traditional Arabian social custom and thence came to be incorporated within the body of laws of inheritance according to the established Sunni schools. Hazairin's ideas on the restructuring of Islamic inheritance law upon a bilateral model focused on these

areas, as well as on other aspects of the system, such as how to distribute residual property after all of the scripturally-determined heirs had received their appointed shares.

18. His dissertation on the subject of Islamic law was published by the Masjumi-affiliated publishing house Bulan Bintang. See Harjono 1968.

19. A helpful collection of Natsir's early writings can be found in Natsir 1954–57.

20. For an introduction to Aquinas' thought on natural law and related issues, see Finnis 1998.

21. It should be noted here that the provisional Indonesian constitution of 1950 was one of the first national constitutions to incorporate the text of the Universal Declaration of Human Rights.

22. Indeed, the roots of Harjono's thoughts on the natural law of God in Natsir's peculiar usage of *ḥudūd* can be seen in Harjono's discussion of *Sunnatullah* as imposing "limits" on the use of reason. Harjono 1995, 27.

23. He further comments, curiously enough, that this is probably what it was that Thomas Aquinas referred to as *lex divina*. Harjono 1995, 26.

24. However soon after the fall of Suharto, the DDII advanced a motion to the national assembly that the national constitution be amended so that the seven words, "with the obligation of Muslims to uphold the Shariʿa" would be included in the preamble and thus established as the law of the land.

25. See, for example, Mahmud 1978, 50–1, 114.

26. For an introduction to Madjid's life and thought, see Barton 1997.

27. For a brief statement of his general argument, see ibid.

28. For more on this organization and its importance to developments in contemporary Indonesian Islam, see van Bruinessen 1994, Feillard 1995, and Barton and Fealy 1996.

29. A more in-depth introduction to these developments can be found in Nelly van Doorn-Harder's contribution to this volume.

Chapter Two. Nelly van Doorn-Harder, *Reconsidering Authority: Indonesian Fiqh Texts about Women*

1. Parts of this article are based on van Doorn-Harder 2006.

2. For a short description of Abdurrahman Wahid's ideas, see Ridell 2001.

3. Ibid., 231. For Nasution's ideas, see also Hooker 2003, 35–7.

4. Amina Wadud (see Wadud 1999) is often mentioned as representative of the reformist interpretation. Several of these writers have articles in Webb 2000.

5. See, for example, Wahid 2001, which contains essays and presentations from the 1970s.

6. For the members of the Forum see n. 10 below.

7. Masdar Masʿudi during a P3M seminar held at the Krapyak Pesantren on *fiqh al-nisāʾ*, September 27, 1997.

8. The information that follows is based on an article published by the P3M staff (Sciortino, Marcoes-Natsir and Mas'udi 1996), the transcripts of P3M meetings, and my own observations when attending some of the workshops and seminars in Yogyakarta and Jakarta during the years 1997 and 1998. Masdar Mas'udi explains the basic human rights in, among others, Mas'udi 1997.

9. See also Mas'udi 1997a, 156–160.

10. The members of the Forum are: Ibu Sinta Nuriyah Abdurrahman Wahid, *kyai* Husein Muhammad, Lies Marcoes-Natsir, Attashendartini Habsjah, Ahmad Lutfi Fathullah, Syafiq Hasyim, Badriyah Fayyumi, Arifah Choiri Fauzi, Juju Juhairiyyah, Djudju Zubaedah, Farhah Ciciek, and Faqihuddin Abdul Kodir.

11. Muhyiddin Sofyan, interview by Nelly van Doorn-Harder, July 12, 1998.

12. Husein Muhammad and Khozin Nasuchah, interview by Nelly van Doorn-Harder, May 25, 1998.

13. Ibid.

14. Husein Muhammad, interview by Nelly van Doorn-Harder, May 25, 1998.

15. An example of a Muslimat grassroots initiative is that of Ibu Ismawati who, like many in Muslimat NU, works mostly in rural areas. While studying for her M.A. at an IAIN she became frustrated with spending much of her energy on counseling women who tried to balance their lives between reality and the preaching of *kyai*s who generously quoted from *Kitāb ʿUqūd*. For her graduate work, Ibu Ismawati decided to combine practice and scholarship by writing a paper about the *Kitāb ʿUqūd*. She looked at its content and the role it played in the lives of village women, translated the text into Indonesian, and pointed out the negative influence it has on the psyche of women in the villages that are under her Muslimat NU branch. Although at the time she wrote her paper, Ibu Ismawati did not have access to the vast knowledge that the research team FK3 brought together in the new edition, she was aware of the fact that several of the *ḥadīth*s quoted were fabricated or weak (Forum Kajian Kitab Kuning 2001). For example, the remark that when a wife refuses to please her husband she will be cursed is based on what Islamic scholars already suspected to be a fabricated report. With her specific religious knowledge—she went through several levels of religious training: the *pesantren*, through the Muslimat-NU and its related organizations for young women, and via B.A. and M.A. studies at the IAIN—Ibu Ismawati embodies the growing group of women whose education has informed them of the influence tradition and culture have on women's lives.

16. To date seven booklets have been published in this series. All are edited by Mukhotib MD and published by YKF in 2002: *KB dan Aborsi* ("Birth Control and Abortion"); *Ketika Pesantren Membincang Gender* ("When the Pesantren Discusses Gender"); *Menghapus Poligami, Mewujudkan Keadilan* ("Do Away with Polygyny, Generate Justice"); *Seksualitas: Menggugat Konstruksi Islam* ("Sexuality: Criticizing the Construction of Islam"); *Menghapus Perkawinan Anak. Menolak Ijbar* ("Abolishing Child Marriage, Rejecting Forced Marriage"); *Menolak Mut'ah dan Sirri. Memberdayakan Perempuan* ("Rejecting the Temporary and the [Illegal] Secret Marriage. Empowering Women"); and *HIV/AIDS: Pesantren Bilang Bukan Kutukan* ("HIV/AIDS: Pesantren Say It Is Not a Curse").

17. Michael Sells observes that the reductionist method of presenting Islam uses the Qur'an as "an abstract filler—a Qur'anic statement is cited to give absolute authority, but the meaning of the statement is left empty, to be supplied with the *ḥadīth*." The *ḥadīth* then is placed in relation to the Qur'an "equal in terms of authority, and dominant in terms of meaning." These observations were posted on the list-serve of the Islam section of the American Academy of Religion, Islamaar@lists. psu.edu, March 24, 2004.

Chapter Three. C. van Dijk, *Religious Authority, Politics, and Fatwas in Contemporary Southeast Asia*

1. In Singapore, which has an Islamic administration comparable to that of the Malaysian states, the mufti is appointed by the president after consultation with the Islamic Religious Council of Singapore (Majlis Ugama Islam Singapura MUIS), which itself was established in 1968 under the Administration of Muslim Law Act.

2. The mufti does not act alone. Before a fatwa is published, it is discussed in the Islamic Legal Consultative Committee or the Syari'ah Committee of the Majlis Agama (or Ugama) Islam dan Adat Istiadat Melayu, the Council of Islam and Malay Custom. The Council of Islam advises the sultans in matters relating to religion and Malay customs.

3. The FPI, with the Laskar Pembela Islam as its para-military branch, was founded in Jakarta on August 17, 1998. Its members are commonly recruited from the community of "traditionalist" Muslims, but not exclusively so. Its Great Leader (*imam besar*) is Al-Habib Muhammad Rizieq bin Husein Syihab, an Indonesian of Arab descent, who had studied Islamic law at the King Saud University in Riyadh. The FPI suspended its activities in November 2002, but was reactivated in March 2003. For a description of its aims and activities, see Purnomo 2003.

4. The MUI guidelines for issuing its fatwas can be found among other places in MUI 1997, 2–12.

5. The article in the Indonesian Constitution of 1945 about freedom of religion states that everybody has the right to practice his or her religion in accordance with his or her religion and belief.

6. The foundation had received Rp. 50 million. The letter from the central board had been signed by its general chairman, Abdurrahman Wahid, and its secretary-general, Ghaffar Rachman. Among those who protested was Ali Yafei, deputy-general-chairman of the Dewan Syuriah (religious advisory council) of the NU, who threatened to resign. Ghaffar Rachman was forced to resign, and Abdurrahman Wahid apologized (Sinaga 1992).

7. Here history has repeated itself. In August 1998, during a meeting of the MUI Fatwa Committee (chaired by Ibrahim Hosen), the MUI spoke out against a sports lottery (Ichwan 2002, 14–5). In February 2004 the secretary-general of the MUI, Din Syamsuddin, rejected a scheme, already approved by the Ministry of Social Affairs at a hearing of the Parliamentary Commission VI, to offer prizes through

tickets sold at tournaments. The proceeds were to be used to finance sports events. The Ministry of Social Affairs claimed that the fatwa committee of the MUI had given its blessing to the lottery. A statement denying this was later issued by Din Syamsuddin. The organizer, Metropolitan Magnum Indonesia, argued that the proposed system was "merely a lucky draw" and that it was intended to induce more people to attend sporting events. Din Syamsuddin countered that it came very close to gambling. Another argument he used was that many poor people would buy a lottery ticket which, according to him, amounted to exploitation. The parliamentary commission eventually adopted this view (thejakartapost.com, February 18, 2004).

8. Such arguments have led some more conservative Muslims to argue, as did the president of the Al-Azhar University during an international congress on Islam and population policy held in Aceh in 1990, that a pregnancy should only be postponed until such time as the mother has recovered fully and her breast-milk is again strong and of excellent quality.

9. For the texts of the statement and the list of signatories, see *Mimbar Ulama* 278 (October 2001): 28–9. The MUI has attempted to galvanize Islamic protests on other occasions. One such occasion was when a medical camp of the Laskar Jihad had been attacked by a newly formed elite unit of the Armed Forces, the Yon Gab (Batalyon Gabungan or Joint Battalion), in June 2001. Twenty-seven organizations co-signed the protest (*Mimbar Ulama* 274 [June 2001]: 24–5).

10. The question was a burning topic during a *Kongres Umat Islam Indonesia* (KUII), Congress of the Indonesian Islamic Community, held in November 1999. One of its committees, which dealt with political and defense issues, spoke out against a female president or vice-president. Another of its committees, that focused on religious questions, could reach no agreement on this point. The final recommendations of the KUII contained no reference to the question whether a female president is allowed. It was decided instead to wait for a decision from the MUI, the institution which, it was argued, had the authority to issue "binding" religious rulings.

11. In September and October 2001, those who called for a jihad almost invariably stressed that their appeal should not be taken as a call for war, though some clearly had war in mind. More often than not reference was to the spiritual "greater jihad" a Muslim had to fight and to the peaceful ways in which Muslims could participate in a physical "lesser jihad," for instance, by equipping medical teams, providing humanitarian aid, and praying. Even the Laskar Jihad emphasized the peaceful aspects of its presence in the Moluccas—the medical care it provided, the community development projects it undertook, and the missionary activities of its members among Muslims. Among the few who do not hesitate to speak openly about the violent aspect of a jihad are Abu Bakar Ba'asyir and those associated with the Jemaah Islamiyah, but even this occurred only after it had become necessary for them to defend their actions publicly.

12. The Nahdlatul Ulama and the Muhammadiyah had not signed the jihad statement, but representatives of Muslimat, the women's organization of the Nahdlatul Ulama, and of the Pemuda Muhammadiyah (Muhammadiyah Youth) did sign.

13. At the same meeting statements were issued to the effect that terrorism is forbidden (*harām*) while a jihad is a religious duty.

14. Earlier, Maʿruf Amin, referring to the April 2000 decision of the DSN, had explained that in view of the growing number of Islamic bank branches in Indonesia the MUI was considering removing the emergency clause (Tempointeractif.com, November 9, 2003).

15. Undeterred, the DSN planned a *Gerakan Ekonomi Syariʿah* (GES), a Shariʿa economic movement. The plan was for Megawati to launch the movement in early 2004. The State Secretariat was informed, but when no reply came, it was decided to delay the launching of the movement until after a new president had been elected.

16. Hamzah Haz also saw no problem with interest. He claimed to follow the opinion of Islamic scholars who argued that interest was not forbidden.

17. One of the times the MUI ventured to draft an opinion on a sensitive and tricky point, on which opinions of mainstream groups differ, was in determining the beginning and end of the fasting month. At the second national congress of the MUI in 1980 it was decided that in the interest of nurturing Islamic brotherhood the opinion of the majority (*jumhūr*) should be followed. However, they added that such a measure would require the setting up of a body with the status of "international qadi," and that as long as this was not yet accomplished, the decision of national governments should be followed (MUI 1997, 41).

18. The official ban on wearing a headscarf with a school uniform is a recurring source of conflict between the government of Singapore and its MUIS on one side and segments of the devout Singaporean Muslim community on the other. It was reported that when Singapore's Prime Minister, Goh Chok Tong, met the Grand Shaykh of Al-Azhar University in February 2004, the latter is supposed to have acknowledged the right of the Singapore government to ban the headscarf from schools. Two months earlier, Ṭanṭāwī had made a similar remark regarding the French plans to bar headscarves in state schools there.

19. The FK-ASWJ was founded in Surakarta on February 14, 1998.

20. A jihad in the Moluccas was even decreed an individual duty (*farḍ ʿayn*).

21. What the insurgents aimed at, Jaʿfar wrote on one occasion, was the establishment of an Alfurese Christian State encompassing Papua, the Moluccas, East Timor, and the Eastern Lesser Sunda Islands (Thalib 2001, 34–5). In this instance he forgot North Sulawesi, which he mentioned in some of his interviews. People like Jaʿfar find strength in their conviction, probably shared by many more Indonesian Muslims, and also present in the highest echelons of the Indonesian Armed Forces, that the United States (sometimes Australia is also mentioned) will not allow an economically and politically strong (Islamic) Indonesia to become a reality, and will do all it can to weaken Indonesia, even working for the disintegration of the country into separate states.

22. The man who received this sentence, Abdullah, was buried as a hero. Posthumously the Indonesian Islamic magazine *Suara Hidayatullah* granted him the "Syariʿah Award." The reason was that he had refused to withdraw his confession and, without the confession, a conviction would have required four male witnesses to testify

that they had seen him commit the rape. Had he retracted, the sentence would not have been executed and his crime would have become a matter "between him and God" (Shoelhi 2002, 75). His decision was said to have been based on a belief that if he were to evade punishment on earth the punishment in the Hereafter would be much more severe. Thus, he reasoned, it "was better to receive the sentence passed here in order to be free from sin and the threat of torture in the Hereafter" (Shoelhi 2002, 73).

23. One of the four girls wore a long-sleeved shirt and a pinafore reaching to her ankles; another one a short-sleeved shirt under a knee-length pinafore; and the other two the ordinary school uniform supplemented with a headscarf.

24. The *Shorter Encyclopaedia of Islam* is more outspoken. It translates *al-Mutakabbir* as "the Haughty" and *al-Jabbār* as "the Tyrant" (Gibb and Kramer 1953, 35).

25. Decisions by the National Fatwa Council have to be endorsed by the Conference of Rulers and, in theory, although politics can interfere, have to be obeyed nationwide.

26. Legal action on the basis of the Penal Code and the Sedition Law against Nik Abdul Aziz Nik Mat was also contemplated. The Kelantan police started an investigation at the end of August after a complaint had been lodged. Nik Aziz was questioned by the police in the middle of September. In his defense he told the police that his words had nothing to do with faith. It was all a matter of language and languages change; they are not static. He preferred to use contemporary parlance and not stick to old-fashioned language used by religious teachers a hundred years ago. Another suggestion was to send Nik Aziz to a religious rehabilitation camp, as had been done in the past with members of the Al Arqam, also accused of harboring deviant ideas.

27. As, for example, when Nik Aziz used the term *ulama barua* (pimp ulama) to describe UMNO religious leaders In the discussion that followed, a PAS leader argued that *barua* was a normal word in Kelantan (the State where Nik Aziz was Chief Minister) and not a term of abuse. This, the UMNO-controlled newspaper *Utusan Malaysia* reported in turn, had angered inhabitants of Kelantan. They were horrified that to defend Nik Aziz, the suggestion was made that *barua* was freely used by people in Kelantan (*Utusan Malaysia* Online, March 22, 2002). *UMNO barua* also seems to be a very popular term in PAS circles. PAS even circulated a VCD with this title.

28. The Election Offences Act was amended in September 2002. One of the amendments prohibits the creation of ill-will, discontent, or hostility among the population of Malaysia in an effort to win votes before, during, and after the election.

29. A similar solution was chosen in March 2004 when Ismail Ibrahim condemned the promises allegedly made by politicians of the PAS that those who voted for that party would be rewarded in the Hereafter with a place in heaven (*Berita Harian* Online, March 5, 2004).

Chapter Four. Michael Laffan, *Lightning, Angels, and Prayers for the Nation: Reading the Fatwas of the Jamʿiyah Ahlith Thoriqoh al-Muʿtabaroh*

1. See Muktamar IX JATMN 2000, 158–62, words in parentheses original.
2. Masyumi (Majelis Syuro Muslimin Indonesia) was formed by the Japanese War administration and forcibly combined reformist and traditionalists under one umbrella, albeit with the reformists being in a dominant position. Of these the most vocal were the members of the Persatuan Islam. On the interrelationship of groups in the Persis/Masyumi axis, see van Bruinessen 2002.
3. For details of various election results from 1955, see Cribb 2000, 163–64, 173–75, 189–90.
4. This is also not to say that the matter was not controversial in the interim. For internal perspectives on the *khittah*, NU's history and stated definitions of Sunni orthodoxy, see the various articles in Yusuf 1994.
5. On the Laskar Jihad and its transnational ideology, see Hasan 2004.
6. Unless otherwise noted, data on the JATM mentioned in this section are sourced from van Bruinessen 1992, 171–73 and the more detailed study of Sujuthi 2001.
7. This was the Badan Kongres Kebatinan Seluruh Indonesia (BKKI). See Howell 2003. In any case NU already had a strong voice within the government given that all Ministers for Religion between 1953 and 1971 were from the movement.
8. This address is reproduced in a collection of Zuhri's speeches. See Zuhri 1965, 155–57.
9. Debate over the exclusive rights to this designation and its definition continue within NU circles, as was evidenced by the Bahsul Masaʾil of 2002, to which Habib Luthfi contributed. See Laffan 2004.
10. The original founder of NU and doyen of Tebuireng, Hasyim Asyʿari (1875–1947), is said to have disapproved of the orders. This tradition seems to have been maintained by his successors, including the current head, Yusuf Hasyim. Then again, a great many other members of the Hasyim line, including Asyʿari's grandson, Gus Dur, are famous practitioners of Sufism. Van Bruinessen observes that 64 out of Romly's 80 representatives came from Tebuireng, and one even taught there. With the shift in political allegiance, one of the Tebuireng representatives, Adlan Ali, was urged to renounce his allegiance to Romly and was granted authority to act as a *murshid* in his own right by Muslih of Mranggen, a senior member of the Qadiriyya wa Naqshbandiyya. Thereafter the Tebuireng followers were urged to shift allegiance to Adlan Ali, which some did, while others moved to Romly's *murshid*, Usman bin Ishaq from Sawahpulo, Surabaya. (I would like to acknowledge here the help of Arif Zamhari confirming the general descriptive outline of these disputes and for recommending the work of Sujuthi.)
11. Van Bruinessen gives Magelang as the location, whereas the documents from the JATMN cited below state that it was at Semarang.
12. I have discussed Habib Luthfi's contributions to the debates of 2002 regarding the juridical identity of NU and its claims to represent the Ahl al-Sunna wa l-Jamaʿa elsewhere. See Laffan 2004.

13. This earlier fatwa is also presented in later NU compilations. See *al-Fuyūdāt*, 109. Equally, JATM fatwas often echo those issued by NU, which had previously issued rulings as to whether certain orders, such as the Tijaniyya, were valid or not. See, for example, fatwas nos. 50 of 1928, 117 of 1931, and 173 of 1935, as presented in Masyhuri 1997.

14. The compilation of all official NU fatwas is currently overseen by Masyhuri. See, for example, Masyhuri 1997.

15. This is rather similar to the case of the collection of Meccan fatwas, the *Muhimmāt al-nafā'is*, given for an Indonesian audience in the 1870s and 1880s, where the original questions (assumedly asked in Malay) were presented in Arabic first. I have discussed the issue of translation of the question and answer elements of Southeast Asian fatwas elsewhere. See Laffan, forthcoming.

16. Here a footnote in Arabic taken from the *Marāqī l-ʿubūdiyya fī sharh bidāyat al-hidāya* of Muḥammad Nawawī of Banten (1813–1897) reads: "The way (*tarīqa*) entails carrying out the duties and precepts [of Islam], abstaining from those things illicit, abandoning the pleasures of things permissible, and the adoption of the limits of piety (*waraʿ*) and the exercises of wakefulness (*sahar*), hunger (*jūʿ*) and silence (*samt*)."

17. The fatwa then continues with quotations from cited Arabic sources: Information is derived from (a) *al-Maʿārif al-muḥammadiyya*, p. 81; and (b) *al-Adhkiyā'* [no p. mentioned]. See *al-Fuyūdāt*, fatwa no. 1.

18. In Sufi parlance *majdhūb* designates a state experienced by a passive mystic as opposed to an active "strider" (*sālik*) on the mystic path. It has also been a key term used to attack Sufi practices in general. See *Encyclopaedia of Islam*, new edition, s.v. "Djadhba" (by R. Gramlich). Understandably, too, it is often disavowed publicly by the Sufis themselves, as in the case of fatwa no. 13 in *al-Fuyūdāt*, "Makmum kepada imam yang jadzab."

19. Those listed in the fatwa were: the (1) ʿUmariyya, (2) Naqshbandiyya, (3) Qādiriyya, (4) Shādhiliyya, (5) Rifāʿiyya, (6) Aḥmadiyya, (7) Dasūqiyya, (8) Akbariyya, (9) Mawlawiyya, (10) Kubrāwiyya, (11) Suhrawardiyya, (12) Khalwatiyya, (13) Jalwatiyya, (14) Baktāshiyya, (15) Ghazāliyya, (16) Rūmiyya, (17) Saʿdiyya, (18) Chishtiyya, (19) Shaʿbāniyya, (20) Kalshāniyya, (21) Ḥamzawiyya, (22) Bayramiyya, (23) ʿUshshāqiyya, (24) Bakriyya, (25) Idrusiyya, (26) ʿUthmāniyya, (27) ʿAlawiyya, (28) ʿAbbāsiyya, (29) Zayniyya, (30) ʿIsāwiyya, (31) Buḥuriyya, (32) Ḥaddādiyya, (33) Ghaybiyya, (34) Khadiriyya, (35) Shaṭṭāriyya, (36) Bayuniyya, (37) Malamiyya, (38) Uwaysiyya, (39) Idrīsiyya, (40) Akābir al-awliyā', (41) Madbūliyya, (42) Sunbuliyya, (43) Tijāniyya, (44) Sammāniyya.

20. The issue of relations with Indonesia's Christian minorities has been frequently addressed by many of the fatwa-giving bodies in Indonesia, including the State Council of Ulama. For an overview, see Hooker 2003, 74–82.

21. The editorial committee comprised Habib Luthfi, Achmad Zaini Mawardi, Luthfi Hakim Muslih, and Abd. Rochim Hasan.

22. The appendix lists 1,947 names from participants from the provinces and special territories of Bali, Bengkulu, Aceh, Yogyakarta, Jakarta, Jambi, West Java, Central Java, East Java, West Kalimantan, South Kalimantan, Central Kalimantan, East

Kalimantan, Lampung, West Nusa Tenggara, Riau, South Sumatra, West Sumatra, and North Sumatra. As might be anticipated, the largest grouping came from East and Central Java. Muktamar IX JATMN 2000, 224–75.

23. "From Sabang to Merauke" is an oft-repeated territorial claim, made famous by Sukarno, of Indonesia's spread from the westernmost town in Aceh to the border with Papua New Guinea.

24. Interestingly the Dutch scholar Martin van Bruinessen (cited by the Minister on p. 50 as "Frans Bruonessen") is given as the authority on the history of the entrance and spread of the first "respectable" orders in Indonesia.

25. These issues are discussed further in Laffan 2004.

26. Here Luthfi spoke of the essential unity of purpose of all the orders and the fact that human devils were far more dangerous than the Jinn in "our times of treachery and evils" and thoughtless emulation of European and Western ways. Luthfi 2000.

27. For a description of this practice, known as *rābiṭa*, rather than the more precise *taṣawwur*, see van Bruinessen 1992, 82–5.

28. *Tawajjuh* involves a student imagining his or her heart to be laid bare before the master, who brings it into the presence of the Prophet. While more usually practiced between teacher and pupil, van Bruinessen noted that it also took place in group meetings in Indonesia. See van Bruinessen 1992, 86–7.

29. Such issues appear, for example, in the fatwas of the Patani scholar and long-time resident of Mecca Aḥmad b. Muḥammad Zayn b. Muṣṭafā al-Faṭānī, written ca. 1905 for the Sultan of Kelantan. See al-Faṭānī 1957.

30. *Allāhummā aʿizz al-islām wa-ijʿal indūnīsiya hādhihi balada ṭayyiba tajrī fīha aḥkāmuka wa-sunnat rasūlik.* See Muktamar IX JATMN 2000, 162.

31. References are made to proceedings of the Mranggen Congress, Central Java, question 8, in addition to supporting texts from *Tanwīr al-qulub* and the *Fatāwā al-ḥadītha li-Ibn Ḥajar al-Haytamī*. See Muktamar IX JATMN 2000, 170–72.

32. According to research carried out in the 1980s, this *ḥadīth* was widely cited by Indonesian *ʿulamāʾ*, despite being regarded as a weak tradition. See van Bruinessen 1990, 52.

33. The issue certainly reared its head again in the last elections of 2004, and the Tebuireng branch of NU issued an advisory statement (*tausiyah*) urging the severing of all political links between the *kiai*s and the national parties. See "Nasional Tausiyah NU Stop Dukung-mendukung," *Tempo*, March 29–April 4, 2004.

Chapter Five. Rifyal Kaʿbah, *Islamic Law in Court Decisions and Fatwa Institutions in Indonesia*

1. An examination of the fatwas produced by a rather different type of modern Indonesian institution can be found in Michael Laffan's contribution to this volume.

2. On this point, Wahba al-Zuhaylī states that "If the jurists are in agreement on a certain matter, then [the judge] decides [the case] based upon it, as was done by the first four caliphs. If they are of differing opinions, then the best of their opin-

ions is taken and [the judge] rules according to what he views as correct, unless there is someone who understands the matter better than himself, in which case he may take the more expert opinion and leave his own opinion on the matter" (al-Zuhaylī n.d., 6289). This position is often justified with reference to Q 39:17–18: "So announce the good news to My slaves, those who listen to the Word [the Qur'an] and follow the best thereof. Those are [the ones] whom Allah has guided and those are men of understanding."

3. The General Explanation of the Compilation of Islamic Law, point 3, states: "Substantive law which has been in effect in the Religious Courts is Islamic law, the bulk of which relates to marriage, inheritance, and endowments." In a Circular Letter to the Religious Courts dated February 14, 1958 (No. B/I/735), the Bureau of Religious Courts within the Department of Religious Affairs specified 13 books to be used by the Courts in deciding cases in the areas of marriage, inheritance, and endowments. All 13 of these texts are from the Shafiʿi school.

4. *Pokok-Pokok Manhaj Majlis Tarjih Yang Telah Dilakukan dalam Menetapkan Keputusan.* Official document of the Majlis Tarjih of Muhammadiyah Central Leadership (Yogyakarta, n.d.), 2–3; Fathurrahman Djamil, *Metode Ijtihad,* 78.

5. Al-Qaraḍāwī calls this *ijtihād intiqāʾī,* that is, "selection of one opinion from among the strongest legal opinions in the inherited corpus of Islamic *fiqh,* which consists of many fatwas and legal verdicts." Al-Qaraḍāwī 1987, 24.

6. H. Imam Muchlas, "Several Challenges for *Ulama Tarjih.*" *Suara Muhammadiyah* 79, no. 14 (1994): 32.

7. In Yogyakarta there once existed the Muhammadiyah Tarjih Academy, which was aimed at equipping LT cadre with knowledge in Islamic disciplines such as *tafsīr, ḥadīth,* and *fiqh,* but which did not last long. Even so, this academy succeeded in producing a number of LT cadre in certain disciplines. Tahir Badri, interview by Rifyal Kaʿbah, May 27, 1997.

8. In 1994, the graduating class of IAIN Jakarta had 25 master and doctoral students, nine of whom came from families belonging to the Muhammadiyah organization. *Suara Muhammadiyah* 79, no. 14 (1994): 29.

9. Cf. Abdurrahman Wahid in *Media Indonesia,* March 17, 1999.

Chapter Six. Mark E. Cammack, Helen Donovan, and Tim B. Heaton, *Islamic Divorce Law and Practice in Indonesia*

1. According to the doctrine of the Hanafi and Hanbali schools, the couple may be reconciled by simply resuming conjugal relations. Likewise according to the doctrine of the Maliki school, provided the intent in resuming conjugal relations is reconciliation (*Ensiklopedi Hukum Islam* 1996, 1777).

2. First, except in rare circumstances, a man can divorce and then reconcile with the same woman no more than twice. The third divorce is irrevocable and there is no right of reconciliation (though the couple may remarry if, following the divorce, the woman marries and is then divorced by another man). Second, the time frame

within which a man may reconcile after the first two repudiations is limited. The husband's right of reconciliation may only be exercised during the wife's waiting period (*'idda*). Unless the woman is pregnant at the time of the divorce, the *'idda* lasts for only three months after the repudiation. If the *'idda* expires without a reconciliation, the only way that the couple can be remarried is by contracting the marriage anew. It is possible for a Muslim husband to recite the *talak* three times on one occasion. Muslim jurists are unanimous in regarding such an act as reprehensible (*makrūh*), however, they are divided on its consequences. Some jurists hold that regardless of how many times the *talak* is recited on a singular occasion it remains equivalent to a single *talak*. Others hold that three *talak*, even if recited on a single occasion, effect a third and final divorce.

3. Other circumstances where *talak* is forbidden include a *talak* performed while the wife is menstruating or in the 40-day waiting period after childbirth or while the wife is not menstruating but has had intercourse with her husband since her last menstruation (*Ensiklopedi Hukum Islam* 1996, 1777).

4. One reason given for the unilateral right of divorce having been given to men is precisely that men, unlike women, are believed to approach problems rationally and to be less easily affected by emotion; thus they are unlikely to repudiate their wives merely because of trivial disputes which are an unavoidable aspect of household life (*Ensiklopedi Hukum Islam* 1996, 1778).

5. The six grounds for divorce include:
   a. one spouse has committed adultery or become an alcoholic, drug addict, gambler, or something of a similar nature which is difficult to cure;
   b. one spouse has deserted the other for a period of two consecutive years without the permission of that spouse and without a valid reason and not because of factors beyond his or her will;
   c. one spouse has been sentenced to a period of five or more years imprisonment after the commencement of the marriage;
   d. one spouse has committed an act of cruelty or serious assault which endangers the other;
   e. one spouse suffers from a physical deformity or illness with the consequence that he or she is unable to perform spousal duties;
   f. between husband and wife there are ongoing differences and disputes and there is no hope that they may live harmoniously in one household.

6. The implementing regulations, and therefore the Marriage Act itself, did not come into force until October 1, 1975, more than a year and half after the Marriage Act was passed by Parliament.

7. Section 45 of the implementing regulations provides that a fine is payable if the following sections are breached: §3 (requiring that 10 days prior notice be given to the Marriage Registrar of intention to marry), §10(3) (requiring that marriage must take place before a Marriage Registrar and in the presence of two witnesses), or §40 (requiring that if a husband intends to take more than one wife he must forward a written request to the court for approval).

8. This interpretation is reflected in an early 1980s account of the typical passage of

talak divorce proceedings through the Islamic court in Purwokerto. The procedure was as follows: A man wishing to divorce was required to submit a notification letter stating his reasons as well as a marriage certificate and a certificate of residence to be examined by the court registry. If the reasons were deemed inadequate, the request could be denied. The registry officials also tried to reconcile the parties before the request was forwarded to the judge. Before the court would hear the husband's *talak*, a hearing was held to determine the husband's income and how much he was to give his wife. The court then determined the amount the husband must pay as maintenance (*nafkah*) during the wife's waiting period. This payment had to be given to the wife at the time the husband pronounced the *talak*. If the husband did not have the money, the pronouncement of the *talak* was postponed by the judge for at most a week while the husband got the money together.

9. The divorce scheme contained in the implementing regulations was similar to the provisions of a Muslim-backed Marriage Bill that failed to win support in 1968 (Cammack, Young, Heaton 1999, 183–84).

10. Indonesian court decisions are not routinely published. Decisions cited here are taken from a variety of compilations of jurisprudence published by the Department of Religion, the Supreme Court, and from private sources. Most of these compilations provide the full text of the decision, but some of the early Department of Religion publications contain relatively brief summaries. The purpose of the compilations is to provide guidance to the lower courts on the law. For that reason, the selection of cases for inclusion reflects the compiler's vision of what the law should be, and does not necessarily mirror what the courts are in fact doing.

11. *Marliah Andriani v Mahakemri Rangkuti*, Islamic High Court, Medan (PTA Medan, No. 14/1977). The Certificate Regarding the Occurrence of a *Talak* was issued on June 2, 1977 by the Islamic court for Rantau Prapat without an accompanying written decision.

12. At first instance the husband had cited as his reason for the divorce the disapproval of the marriage by the couple's parents, which had prevented them from establishing a calm and harmonious household. The wife did not wish to be divorced and claimed that there had never been quarrelling within the relationship so as to justify a divorce. She claimed that the couple had continued to live with their respective parents after marriage because her husband was still looking for work. Her husband visited her nightly and the couple had produced a child. The wife also claimed that her husband had not provided any financial support for herself or the child.

13. With respect to the wife's claim that the lower court had not dealt with her husband's legal obligation towards her, the court stated that the wife was free to press her claim in a separate suit.

14. *Zuarni My B.A. binti Mahya St. Mansur v Roestam Luddin*, Islamic Court, Pekanbaru (PA Pekanbaru, No. 287/1977).

15. *Zuarni My B.A. binti Mahya St. Mansur v Roestam Luddin*, Islamic High Court, Padang (PTA Padang, No. 10/1977).

16. The presiding judge at first instance had even visited the petitioning husband in hospital to verify directly whether, and on what basis, he had repudiated his wife.

17. On the evidence accepted by the first instance court there was inconsistency in the stated grounds for divorce. The reason for divorce, as cited in the petitioning husband's written declaration of repudiation and as explained in court by his representative, was that he was unable to provide spiritual fulfillment/conjugal support to his young wife as a result of his paralysis. However, when questioned by the presiding judge in hospital, the petitioning husband stated that he divorced his wife because she was "bad."

18. In *re Kartak bin Mitpisari*, Islamic Court, Bangkinang (PA Bangkinang, No. 10/1979); *Yulis bin Putih v Kartini binti Nontok*, Islamic Court, Padang (PA Padang, No. 315/1981). The 1981 Padang decision is somewhat unusual in that although the court decreed that the extra-judicial *talak* was valid, it was deemed to take effect from the date of the decree rather than the date of pronouncement. In two further cases, *M. Hasan Abdullah v Sofiah binti Matsyah*, Islamic Court, Bireuen (PA Bireuen, No. 17/1979) and *M. Amin Abbas v Hartinah binti Abdullah Nafi*, Islamic Court, Lhokseumawe (PA Lhokseumawe, No. 8/1979), the court decreed that a *talak* had not occurred when the repudiation formula was recited outside of the court. However, in both cases the court's decision was based on a finding that the recitation did not occur voluntarily with intent. Failure to comply with the Marriage Act and Regulations was not discussed.

19. *Agustinar v Abd. Muluk*, Islamic Court, Lubuksikaping (PA Lubuksikaping, No. 82/1979); *Maryani binti Hanafiah v Syarifuddin*, Islamic Court Meureudu (PA Meureudu, No. 04/1979); *Pasa Harahap v Kamal Tampubolon*, Islamic Court, Padang Sidempuan (PA Sidempuan, No. 209/1981); *Nipah binti P. Rasmoʿi v Asmawi bin P. Tiwar Tayyib*, Islamic Court, Sampang (PA Sampang, No. 50/1981).

20. Penetapan 04/1979 PA/Mahkamah Syarʿiyah Meureudu [Law Report Putusan/ Penetapan Pengadilan Agama Th 1979, 81]. The wife was assisted in that case by the evidence of an official from the Office of Religious Affairs (*Kantor Urusan Agama*, KUA). Her husband had approached the KUA to request a reconciliation with his wife and in the course of examination admitted that he had repudiated her three months earlier.

21. For example, in one decision a text is relied upon that states: "A valid *talak* occurs when it comes voluntarily from a husband of legal age."

22. It should be noted that there are some reported cases from this early period where the court refused to witness a husband's recitation of the *talak*. For example, in two separate cases where the husband had given as a reason for divorce his inability to pay maintenance, and where the wife had testified that despite this inability she did not want a divorce, the court found that there were no grounds for divorce within the meaning of the regulations. *Hartono bin Kasan Asmo v Sukesi*, Islamic Court, Yogyakarta (PA Yogyakarta, No. 61/1979); *Zainuddin bin P. Aliyas v Lilik Suhartatik binti Suryo Atmojo*, Islamic Court, Kraksaan (PA Kraksaan, No. 115/1981).

23. *Cut Satariah v Rasyidin bin Sulaiman*, Supreme Court (MA No. 03/Ag/1979).

24. Petition of Rasyidin bin Sulaimin, Islamic Court, Sigli (PA Sigli, No. 174/1977).

25. *Rasyidin bin Sulaiman v Cut Satariah*, Islamic High Court, Banda Aceh (PTA Banda Aceh, No. 61/1977).

26. *Syafrin bin Intan v Raflaini binti Zuber*, Islamic Court, Padang Panjang, (PA Padang Panjang, No. 03/1978).
27. *Syafrin bin Intan v Raflaini binti Zuber*, Islamic High Court, Padang, (PTA Padang, No. 01/1978).
28. *Raflaini binti Zuber v Syafrin bin Intan*, Supreme Court (MA, No. 04/Ag/1979). In that case the appeals court again acknowledged that the repudiation pronounced out of court was in violation of the statute, but held that such violations were not within the jurisdiction of the Islamic courts. The court stated that the essence of the claim was a request for a decision on the legal status of the *talak*; that the Marriage Law states that a marriage is valid when it is carried out according to the religious law of the parties, and that while the statute requires that divorce be performed in the presence of the court, the statute does not clearly declare non-complying *talak* to be invalid. Given that the statute does not speak to the validity of a *talak* pronounced out of court, and because the Islamic courts do not have jurisdiction over violations of the statute, the court declared the unauthorized *talak* valid in accordance with the "living law." The Supreme Court again overturned the appeals court decision and reiterated that a repudiation is valid only if it has been pronounced in accordance with statutory procedures, that is, in the presence of the court. *Yaneta Hakam binti Hakam v Syafnil bin Ahmad*, Supreme Court (MA, No. 51/Ag/1981).
29. The Circular is titled "Respecting the Requirement for a Decree of a Court in Granting a Request to Pronounce a *Talak*."
30. Of course, Supreme Court circulars did not prevent people from petitioning the court to validate extra-judicial *talak*. One method the courts used in responding to such requests was to essentially ignore the unauthorized *talak* and process the case as a petition for permission to utter the repudiation in court. In that context, evidence of the unauthorized *talak* was often relied upon as an indicator of breakdown in the marital relationship and a clear sign that the couple is no longer able to live together harmoniously. There are practical and potentially significant consequences that follow from adopting this approach. Reciting the *talak* again in court is not merely a matter of procedural formality nor of affixing an official date of divorce for purely bureaucratic purposes. It will affect when the wife's *'idda* is deemed to commence, which in turn affects when she is able to remarry and when her husband's financial obligations towards her cease. Further, if the couple reconcile during the waiting period, having already repudiated his wife twice, the husband would enter into the new marriage with one remaining *talak* instead of two.
31. In addition to these provisions dealing specifically with *talak* divorce proceedings, the Act also contains general provisions governing the procedural law of the Islamic courts. Article 55 states that in order for the examination of a case to commence, a petition (*permohonan*) or complaint (*gugatan*) must be filed and the "parties to the case must be called in accordance with the applicable procedures."
32. If one of the parties is not in the country and unable to attend, s/he may send a representative especially authorized for that purpose, but if both parties are abroad, the husband must attend in person (Art. 82(3)).

33. This inherent contradiction between the language used in the Religious Judicature Act to describe *talak* divorce proceedings and their outcome, and the actual nature of the proceedings, has been the subject of discussion and analysis. In a 1997 article appearing in a journal published by the Department of Religion (Azhar 1997) it is asserted that *talak* divorce proceedings are petition proceedings, that is, *ex parte* (or voluntary) proceedings, in form only. This is evident in a number of factors. The wife is treated as a party to the case, opposing her husband and enjoying equal rights with him before the court. She has the right to file both a response to the petition and a cross claim. As a party, she also has the right to advance a case, to tender evidence in support of her case, and to respond to and rebut the case of her husband. Azhar also observes that the provisions dealing with *talak* divorce fall within a section of the Religious Judicature Act entitled "trying contentious matrimonial disputes." Further, the court is compelled to try to reconcile the parties and may only allow a divorce to occur where these attempts are unsuccessful. Having illustrated the clearly contentious nature of *talak* divorce proceedings, the article considers whether it is appropriate that the document ultimately issued by court is a decree rather than a decision. The article endorses the phased approach ultimately adopted by the Supreme Court, which involved first instructing the courts to issue a final document headed "decision" but with the orders formulated as a "decree" before incrementally moving towards a final product both headed as a decision and entirely framed in the language of a decision.

34. *Ma'rifah Suhuni v Ratman Walahi*, Islamic High Court, Manado (PTA Manado, No. 15/1993).

35. The case went to the Supreme Court on cassation. *Ratman Walahi v Ma'rifah Suhuni*, Supreme Court (MA, No. 210/Ag/1993). The Court delivered an interlocutory decision ordering that the matter be remitted to the court of first instance for further evidence so that the court could call and hear additional evidence from close family and friends of both the husband and wife. The Court then held that on the basis of the additional testimony it was apparent that there was sufficient reason to grant the husband's petition for divorce. In another case *Earnie binti B. Latief v Syafriul bin M. Nu'i*, Islamic High Court, Pekanbaru (PTA Pekanbaru, No. 21/1991), the provincial level appeals court in Pekanbaru also remitted the case to the Court at first instance so that more evidence could be taken before delivering a final decision. In that case, even after further evidence was gathered, the Court was of the view that grounds for appeal had not been made out. The husband's divorce petition was rejected.

36. *Mery Rukaini binti Anton Idris v M. Ramli Budi Setya bin Masrie*, Islamic High Court, Palangkaraya (PTA Palangkaraya, No. 1/1993).

37. The decision of the appeals court was upheld by the Supreme Court, which found that there was no fault in the appeals court's application of the law and that all other matters raised related to the discretionary evaluation of evidence and were therefore not matters to be considered by a court of cassation. *M. Ramli Budi Setya bin Masrie v Mery Rukaini binti Anton Idris*, Supreme Court (MA, No. 113/Ag/1994).

38. In addition to these straightforward means of dissolving the marriage, there were

also available a number of less often used and sometimes more controversial avenues for escaping an unwanted marriage. Wives were able to extricate themselves from an unwanted marriage by persuading or sometimes paying their husbands to repudiate them. The purchase of a *talak* was occasionally carried out under the supervision of the court—a practice referred to as *khulʿ*. Sometimes a wife could obtain a judicial annulment of the marriage based on some technical defect in the marriage, but the most drastic approach was to apostasize from Islam, which effected an automatic termination of the marriage. For a discussion of divorce law and practice in Islamic courts prior to the enactment of the Marriage Act, see Lev 1972, chapter 5.

39. Lev 1972, 163 identifies the doctrinal basis for the practice as a legal maxim contained in a sixteenth-century commentary known as *al-Taḥrīr* by Zakariyyā' al-Anṣārī. According to this maxim, which is frequently quoted in the decisions of Islamic courts: "Whoever makes his *talak* dependent on an action, then the *talak* occurs with the existence of that action, according to the original pronouncement."

40. One of the problems with the *taklik talak* procedure was that a recalcitrant husband could immediately exercise his right to reconcile with his wife upon pronouncement that his *talak* had fallen. Thus the wife's attempts to divorce would be thwarted. To overcome this potential problem it was generally required that the wife pay a nominal amount of compensation so as to effect a non-revocable divorce.

41. For an English translation of this standard provision, see Lev 1972, 163–64.

42. The initial approach of the Islamic courts to the application of the Marriage Act and implementing regulations in *taklik talak* divorce cases is also well illustrated by a 1977 decision of the provincial level Islamic appeals court in Medan *Pangalampoi Harahap v Siti Gabena Hasibuan*, Islamic High Court, Medan (PTA Medan, No. 07/1977). In that case, the court refused to grant a *taklik talak* divorce because there was no evidence that the husband had undertaken to grant a conditional *talak* at the time of the marriage. The marriage had not been officially formalized and there was no marriage certificate. Although the wife was able to satisfy the requirements for divorce as set out in the Marriage Act and regulations, the court denied her a divorce because of a failure to prove the pronouncement of the *taklik talak* at time of marriage.

43. *Abd. Aziz M. bin Laposi v Sitti Hadrah binti H. Abdullah*, Supreme Court (MA, No. 13/AG/1979).

44. In one case (*Zuhroyani binti H. Saleh v Satimin bin Somad*, Supreme Court (MA, No. 25/Ag/1979)) the Supreme Court decided that, in the case of marriages entered into before the Marriage Act came into force, the Islamic courts could grant divorce applications based on breach of the *taklik talak* provisions. Interestingly, in 1981 a matter came before the Supreme Court in which the first instance court had granted a divorce on the grounds that the husband had breached the *taklik talak* provisions though the marriage had been contracted after the Marriage Act came into effect. Irreconcilable differences had also been cited as a basis for seeking divorce, but the court did not call the necessary witnesses to satisfy itself that this ground was made out and, therefore, it could not form the basis of the court's decision.

The appeals court affirmed the decision of the lower court. The husband sought cassation in the Supreme Court but did not raise as an issue the fact that a breach of the *taklik talak* provisions could not per se form a ground for divorce under the Marriage Act. The Supreme Court rejected the husband's request for cassation, but it is not clear whether the Supreme Court declined to deal with the issue because it was not raised by the husband, because the Court was not alive to the possible error in the earlier decisions, or because the Court was satisfied that grounds for divorce, as defined by the implementing regulations, had been made out.

45. In the same case the Supreme Court emphasized that in any case that involves a "dispute," that is, whenever there are "two parties, each of whom may advance arguments and defenses, and each of whom has the right of appeal and cassation, the product of the court must be a decision rather than a decree." *Abd. Aziz M. bin Laposi v Sitti Hadrah binti H. Abdullah*, Supreme Court (MA, No. 13/AG/1979).

46. It is noteworthy that the grounds for divorce listed in the statutory provisions are not grounded in Islamic doctrine but rather evolved from an early Dutch ordinance regulating Christian marriage (Rozak 1991).

47. Lev 1972, 170–72 explains the evolution of *syiqaq* from a procedure to resolve marital problems to a procedure for ending the marriage as motivated by a desire on the part of Islamic judges to prevent desperate wives from resorting to apostasy to escape an unwanted marriage.

48. It is sometimes a condition of repudiation that the wife repay her original bride price.

49. *Nurhasanah binti Samenun v Mistari bin Buhari*, Islamic Court, Probolinggo (PA Probolinggo, No. 133/1981).

50. In another example, after its own repeated attempts at reconciliation failed, the Islamic court in Magelang *Aspijah binti Dulah Setijo v Muchamad Zaini bin Zainudin* (PA Magelang, No. 273/1979) appointed the wife's father and the husband's cousin as mediators. The couple had already been separated for eight months. The wife claimed that her husband had left her after approximately one year of marriage and had not paid spousal support since that time. The husband claimed that the wife refused to move to his house and that if she did so, she would be paid the requisite support. According to the court, the mediation failed because the wife's mediator continued to insist that the husband repudiate his wife while the husband's mediator was only prepared to grant a divorce if the wife were prepared to pay ten times her original bride price. The court subsequently dismissed both family mediators and appointed two new mediators from amongst the judges of the court. The new mediators reached the conclusion that the couple could not be reconciled and recommended that the couple be divorced. Again the court's decision involved a validation of the *talak* pronounced by the husband's mediator and accepted by the wife's mediator. See also *Subandiyah binti Surat Gondoutomo v Sutrisno bin Ponijan*, Islamic Court, Kediri (PA Kediri, No. 60/1979).

51. *H. Abd. Karim bin H. Abd Madjid v H. Maryam binti H.M. Dja'far*, Supreme Court (MA, No. 23/Ag/1979).

52. As described in the decision of the Supreme Court, the first instance Islamic court

in Mejene had appointed mediators to represent the husband and wife. The two mediators were unable to reconcile the couple and concluded that the husband's mediator should repudiate the wife on condition that she return her bride price. The Supreme Court found that the lower court was entitled to conclude, based on the outcome of the unsuccessful mediation, that there was fighting and disagreement between the couple that could not be resolved and that grounds for divorce under Art 19(f) had been established. The Supreme Court considered that, because of the mediation process that was followed, it was immaterial that the lower court had not heard from family members and had not clarified for itself the causes of disagreement between the couple, as required by Art 22(b) in cases where Art 19(f) is relied upon.

53. *Siti Hawa v A. Rahman, Supreme Court* (MA, No. 15/Ag/1980).

54. Similarly, in a second 1980 case, the Supreme Court found that strict compliance with the *syiqaq* procedure prescribed in the Qur'an was not essential in divorce proceedings based on irreconcilable differences. The Supreme Court considered it sufficient that the court at first instance had heard from relevant witnesses and had formed the opinion that the husband and wife were engaged in constant feuding and could not be reconciled. *Djuariah binti Muhammad v Yunus bin Budiman*, Supreme Court (MA, No. 18/Ag/1980).

55. For a comparison between *syiqaq* procedure as prescribed in Islamic doctrine and as applied in Indonesia pursuant to statute, see Manan 1997.

56. *Katini binti Madin v Subari bin Daeri*, Islamic Court Nganjuk (PA Nganjuk, No. 41/1979).

57. *Saidah binti Waim v Kandar bin Kasan*, Islamic Court Tegal (PA Tegal, No. 273/1979); *Komsatin binti Pardi v Bunali bin Kerto Glenter*, Islamic Court, Sidoarjo (PA Sidoarjo, No. 257/1981).

58. For a discussion of Rhoma Irama and the significance of the phenomenon he launched, see Frederick 1982.

59. "Rhoma Irama Kawin di 'Bawah Tangan' dengan Ricca Rahim," *Pos Kota* (Jakarta), May 17, 1985.

60. "Rhoma Anggap Sodaqoh Bathin Baginnya," *Pos Film* (Jakarta), July 7, 1985.

61. "Veronika Kawin Lagi; Suaminya Anak Buah Oma Irama," *Pos Kota* (Jakarta), June 27, 1985.

62. *Dangdut* has found a new superstar and is more popular, and more controversial, than ever. But it no longer fulfils Rhoma Irama's vision of popular Islamic propagation. Twenty-four year old "Inul" surged to *dangdut* stardom in 2003 with her "bump and grind" dance move called the "drill." Both Rhoma Irama, who is still a presence in the Indonesian music scene, and the Indonesian Council of Ulama (MUI) have condemned her dancing as immoral and un-Islamic. Ellen Nakashima, "Muslim Clerics in a Twist over Dangdut Dancer," *The Washington Post*, May 31, 2003.

63. "Rhoma Irama dan Veronica bukan Muslim Sejati," *Barata Minggu* (Jakarta), July 1985.

64. Jusuf M. Wibisana, letter to the editor, *Tempo*, July 13, 1985.

65. "Rhoma Anggap Sodaqoh Bathin Baginnya," *Pos Film* (Jakarta), July 7, 1985.

66. "Menolak Jadi Isteri Tua, Malah Jadi Isteri Muda," *Swadesi* (Jakarta), July 14, 1985; "Rhoma Irama Lumpuh; Vero Balas Dendam," *Terbit Minggu* (Jakarta), July 1985. Yet another legal problem raised by Veronika's marriage to Erwin was that Erwin, as a civil servant employed by the national radio network, had failed to obtain required permission from his superiors to enter into a polygamous marriage. "Perkawinan Veronica Cuma Sensasa, Erwin Tuntut Wartawan," *Sentana*, (Jakarta), July 1985.

67. "Meskipun Kawin Dibawah Tangan Rhoma Irama Masih Kebal Ilmu Tongkat: Perkawinan dengan Ricca tetap Sah," *Inti Jaya* (Jakarta), July 1985.

68. Statistics on the number of cases decided by Islamic courts are from Bisri 1997, 167. We independently confirmed the totals reported by Bisri with statistics we received directly from the Department of Religion. The number of cases decided by Islamic courts is not an exact proxy for the number of court-authorized Muslim divorces, but it is close, because most cases decided by Islamic courts are requests for divorce. In any event, the number of decided cases represents an over-estimate of the number of court-authorized divorces, and therefore strengthens rather than undermines the point being made here, which is that a very large number of divorces occurring each year are unauthorized.

69. Although the government has invested considerable effort to promote awareness of the Marriage Act, the campaign to publicize and enforce the law has not been nearly as aggressive as the government's other major family initiative—the family planning program. The national family planning agency has mobilized thousands of grass roots volunteers across the country who monitor and record the family planning practices of every household in the village.

70. An empirical study of the reasons for underage marriage carried out near Jogjakarta in Central Java in the mid 1990s (Sulistiowati 1995) identified five primary reasons for entering into underage marriage: 39% of respondents reported that they married because they had begun having sexual relations; 34% stated that the husband was working and therefore they were prepared to establish a household; 16% attributed the marriage to "traditional" beliefs about parental authority over the marriage of daughters; 7% because of economic necessity; and 5% because the girl had become pregnant.

Chapter Seven. Siti Musdah Mulia, *Toward a Just Marriage Law: Empowering Indonesian Women through a Counter Legal Draft to the Indonesian Compilation of Islamic Law*

1. The title "Counter Legal Draft" was chosen because, as will be discussed below, the Draft was prepared as an alternative to the "Compilation of Islamic Law," a code of marriage, inheritance, and charitable trust rules that had been applied by the Islamic courts since 1991.

2. The other members of the drafting committee were Marzuki Wahid, Abd. Moqsith Ghazali, Saleh Partaonan, Abdurrahman Bima, A. Mubarak, and Anik Farida.

3. This legal pluralism applied not only to the law governing personal status but also to commercial transactions and public law.

4. For brief, general introductions to women and law in Indonesia, see Ihromi 1997; Mulia 2001b; and Irianto 2003.

5. The Department of Religion has published English and Arabic language translations of the Compilation under the titles *The Compilation of Islamic Laws of Indonesia* (1996/1997) and "*Jama' al-aḥkām al-Islāmiyya al-Indūnisiyya.*"

6. In 1958 the Bureau for Religious Courts within the Department of Religious Affairs, which at that time exercised exclusive control over the Islamic courts, issued a circular letter to the courts with a list of 13 *fiqh* sources to be used in deciding cases coming before the courts.

7. See "Ancaman Pidana Pasal Poligami," *Gatra*, November 28, 2003.

8. Department of Religion data indicate that 48 percent of all marriages are unregistered. This is a crucial issue, since failure to register is highly detrimental to the rights of women and children.

9. The policy was adopted in implementation of Indonesia's ratification of the International Convention on the Elimination of All Forms of Violence Against Women (Law 7/1984) and in response to the United Nations Declaration on the Elimination of Violence against Women.

10. Religion can be the principal source of the patriarchal values that inform and legitimate the law. See generally Ruether 1983; Mulia 2001a; and Faqih 2001. Religious doctrine that has been incorporated in state law is an especially potent force for sustaining social inequality, since the discriminatory values embodied in laws are justified and reinforced by religious authority. Groups that have been working to promote gender equality and fair treatment of women have long regarded marriage law both as a source of social problems and the cause of unfairness and inequality in domestic life.

11. These four regions were chosen for the survey because groups in each of these areas have called for a wider implementation of Islamic law. In addition to judges, the survey focused on state marriage registrars, a sub-district level state official, and local religious leaders.

12. On the need for revising the Marriage Law, see generally Nasution 2002; Afianah 2003; Ritonga 2003; Widyasari 2004; and Nurrohmah 2003.

13. The husband is designated as the "leader" (*pemimpin*) of his wife, though important household decisions are to be made jointly by both parties. It is the obligation of the husband "to provide his wife with religious instruction and the opportunity to study and gain knowledge useful and profitable for religion and the homeland." The husband bears the responsibility to provide his wife and the household with material support. This obligation arises only after the wife submits to her husband sexually, and lapses if the wife is disobedient (*nusyuz*).

14. The day after the Draft was released, representatives from MMI appeared at the offices of the Department of Religious Affairs demanding a meeting with the Minister

of Religion. When the Minister declined to meet with the group, Musdah Mulia agreed to speak with them in his place. She agreed to a meeting to discuss the Draft, but requested that they read the document before the meeting. The next month MMI, HTI, and FPI held an open forum in the city of Yogyakarta. In response to their invitation, she also attended this meeting and responded to questions.

15. "Kerancuan Metodologi Draft Kompilasi Hukum Islam" (http://swaramuslim.net/more.php?id=2443_0_1_66_M/).

16. "Menggugat Draf Kompilasi Hukum 'Ingkar Syariat'" (http://swaramuslim.net/more.php?id=2402_0_1_10_M/). The title of the article plays on the Indonesian initials of the Compilation of Islamic Law to describe the CLD as a "Compilation of Laws Denying the Shari'a."

17. M. Shiddiq Al-Jawi, "Ushul Fikih Palsu Kaum Liberal" (http://hizbut-tahrir.or.id/main.php?page=alwaie&id=7/).

18. See Chamzawi, "Sebuah Catatan Tentang Kontroversi Revisi Kompilasi Hukum Islam" (http://www.yarsi.ac.id/kolom_chamzawi/detail.php?id=26/), discussing criticisms of CLD by retired Supreme Court Justice Busthanul Arifin.

19. See "Women Stall Review of Marriage Law," *Jakarta Post*, May 16, 2005 quoting Nabilah Lubis. See also "Menyosialisasikan 'Counter Legal Draft' Kompilasi Hukum Islam," *Kompas*, October 11, 2004.

20. Menyosialisasikan 'Counter Legal Draft' Kompilasi Hukum Islam, *Kompas*, October 11, 2004.

21. "Prof. Dr. Huzaemah Tahido Yanggo, Ulama Fiqh Perempuan yang Anti Feminisme" (http://www.eramoslem.com/br/pr/56/19255,1,v.html/). See also "Hukum Perkawinan Islam: Kembalilah ke Perspectif Islam," *Republika*, June 24, 2005.

22. Hera Diani, "Revival of Draft Islamic Code Sought," *Jakarta Post*, March 8, 2005.

23. Syafiq Hasyim, "Kebangkitan Sayap Konservatif," *Kompas*, November 26, 2004.

24. "Dinilai Resahkan Umat, Menteri Agama Batalkan Draf Kompilasi Hukum Islam," *Kompas*, February 15, 2005.

Chapter Eight. Mark E. Cammack, *The Indonesian Islamic Judiciary*

1. Parts of this chapter draw on Cammack 1989 and Cammack 1997.

2. The statistics cited in this paragraph are taken from Bisri 1997, 167.

3. It did not take long after the Department of Religion abandoned its opposition to Supreme Court review that appeals from the Islamic system to the Court became routine. In 1989 cassation was requested in 213 cases (Laporan Tahunan 1989/1990, 46); by the year 2000 the number of appeals in cassation had increased to 600.

4. The Supreme Court and the Department of Religion publish and distribute compilations of Supreme Court decisions regarded as particularly important.

5. This change in attitude was a reflection of changes occurring within the Department of Religion. In 1971 Nadhlatul Ulama lost its lock on the Department of Religion when Professor Mukti Ali, a western-trained educator with strong ties to neither

of the country's major religious organizations, was appointed Minister of Religion. An even more significant appointment was made seven years later when the Religion portfolio was given to General Alamsjah Ratu Perwiranegara, a military man and member of the President's inner circle.

6. An initial "academic draft" of the bill on Organization and Powers, completed in early 1984, defined the competency of the Islamic courts as including "the receipt, consideration, and resolution of civil cases involving Muslims in the areas of family law, inheritance, wills, gifts, foundations (*wakaf*) alms (*sadaqah*), the treasury (*baitul mal*), and contracts (*perikatan*) based on Islamic law" (Departemen Agama 2001, 42–3).

7. Supreme Court Order KMA/081/IX/1986. Although the Court's order does not distinguish between marriage and inheritance cases, some courts have apparently limited the use of single judge courts to marriage suits.

8. The total equals more than 100 percent because many of the judges with university degrees also have a Syariah degree from an IAIN.

9. That the number of cases decided each year is small is confirmed by a study carried out by the Islamic law section of the Gajah Mada Law Faculty. The study found that during the six year period from 1993 to 1999, the five Islamic courts within the special administrative region of Yogyakarta received a total of only 52 inheritance filings.

10. Of the 52 cases in the Gajah Mada University study mentioned above, seven were excluded from the analysis because of pending appeals. Of the remaining 42 cases only seven involved disputes.

11. Inheritance cases make up approximately 14 percent of the docket of Islamic appeals courts but less than one-half of one percent of cases before first instance courts.

12. John Bowen's contribution to this volume illustrates the types of difficult legal and factual problems encountered by Islamic courts in inheritance cases and the approach adopted by one court in addressing those complexities.

Chapter Nine. John R. Bowen, *Fairness and Law in an Indonesian Court*

* This chapter is a slightly revised version of my contribution in *Dispensing Justice in Islam*, ed. K.M. Masud, R. Peters, and D.S. Powers (Leiden: Brill, 2006).

1. Given that both the civil court and the town jail had shut down because of the extreme violence, and anyone arrested was promptly released, the cautionary remark was more of a moral nature than a physical threat.

2. If marital property was divided as part of a divorce settlement, as often is the case, then that division is not recorded separately. Therefore, court divisions after divorce are much more common than is suggested by these figures.

3. I drew my sample of cases from the archives of the two courts during fieldwork conducted in July 1985, June–August 1994, and June 2000. For each court, I selected blocks of years, beginning in the late 1940s and including all available

cases from the 1990s. For each sample I read all cases with a bearing on issues of family property.

4. Although bequests to heirs are invalid if contested by an heir, they are valid if all parties agree to them.

5. I translate the Indonesian gloss given in the text of the decision; the Arabic of the first part of the verse is "God commands you concerning your children."

6. Case No. 180, 1991, heard and rejected by the Supreme Court in 1995. Aman Sarana then asked for a judicial review of the case (*peninjauan kembali*) and engaged a lawyer, an action that still is rare in Takèngën. As of June 2000 the file ended at that point.

7. The document was signed in ways that shed light on the probable participation of the various parties in its drafting: the father, Aman Aji, signed "Aman Aji" in Arabic script; his wife, Inën Aji, just made a thumb print. Aji, the defendant in this case, signed in Latin script. Two sisters also signed: Jemilad made a thumb print, and Inën Lukman painfully printed IL. All documents are in Latin script, and by that time, the late 1980s, Arabic-script signatures were rare in the Takèngën area.

Chapter Ten. Moch. Nur Ichwan, *The Politics of Shari'atization: Central Governmental and Regional Discourses of Shari'a Implementation in Aceh*

* I wish to thank Michael Feener for his critical comments on an earlier draft of this chapter, and Arskal Salim for the initial discussion on this subject. The views expressed in this chapter, however, are my own.

1. "*Adat* in the hands of Sultan / Law in the hands of *ulama* / *Qanun* in the hands of Putri Pahang / *Reusam* in the hands of Admiral" is a popular Acehnese proverb, quoted in the *Elucidation of the Qanun on Shari'a Courts and the Implementation of Shari'a*. It ends with: *Hukom ngon adat / Lagee zat ngon sifeuet* ("Law and custom [*adat*] / are like matter [*zat*] and its attribute [*sifat*]"). See Azra 2003, xxvi–vii.

2. Some regencies, such as Pamekasan in Madura; Maros, Sinjai, and Gowa in South Sulawesi; and Cianjur, Indramayu, and Garut in West Java, have demanded the implementation of Shari'a, and in some of these locations Shari'a has begun to be applied in a limited way. See "Syariah Law in Indonesia: Strict only on Paper," *Tempo*, December 10–16, 2002. The situation in Aceh differs from these other areas, however, since in Aceh Shari'a is under the authority of the Provincial government and is implemented province-wide, and because unlike in other regions the central government is involved in its formation.

3. For an anthropological examination of the Shari'a issue in Aceh through 2001, see Bowen 2003. The present chapter deals primarily with the period 2001–2003.

4. I use this term here in the Lacanian sense of a "signifier to which other signifiers refer, and are unified by—and it fixes their identity." Sayyid 1997, 45. For more on this concept as an analytical tool for the study of Muslim discourse, see Lacan 1977 and Sayyid 1997.

5. The official central government discourse can be found in Law No. 18/2001 on the Special Autonomy of the Privileged Province of Aceh as the Nanggroe Aceh Darussalam and Presidential Instruction No. 11/2003 on Shariʿa Courts and Provincial Shariʿa Courts in the Province of Nanggroe Aceh Darussalam. This legislation cannot, however, be dissociated from the issuance of Presidential Instructions Nos. 4 and 7/2001 and No. 1/2002 on the Special Treatment of the Problem of Aceh. In response to the above legislation, the Acehnese regional government, along with the regional People's Representative Council (DPRD), issued several Qanuns ("regional regulations") regarding Shariʿa Courts and on the implementation of Shariʿa in the fields of creed, worship, and Islamic symbolism. In 2000, the Regional Regulation (Peraturan Daerah, Perda) No. 5/2000 on the Implementation of Shariʿa was issued.

6. Tengku Hasan Muhammad di Tiro declared Aceh independent from "all political control of the foreign regime of Jakarta and the alien people of the island of Java" and formed Gerakan Aceh Merdeka (GAM) on December 4, 1976 (di Tiro 1981, 15–18).

7. Presidential instructions, like statutes, regulations, and other enactments, are numbered consecutively throughout the year, and identified by number and year of issuance. The official designation of the April 11, 2001 Instruction is *Instruksi Presiden Republik Indonesia Nomor 4 tahun 2001 tentang Langkah-Langkah Komprehensif Dalam Rangka Penyelesaian Masalah Aceh.*

8. *Instruksi Presiden Republik Indonesia Nomor 7 tahun 2001 tentang Langkah-Langkah Komprehensif Dalam Rangka Penyelesaian Masalah Aceh.* Megawati's instruction does not explicitly acknowledge the existence of Abdurrahman Wahid's instruction, or make clear to what extent it was to be seen as a revision or continuation of the previous policy.

9. See the *Menimbang* (Considering) sections of Presidential Instructions Nos. 4/2001, and 7/2001. The "six comprehensive steps" mentioned in the instructions refer to the proposed solutions to the "six problems" of Aceh in the fields of politics, the economy, society, law and social order, security, and information and communication.

10. *Instruksi Presiden Republik Indonesia Nomor 1 tahun 2002 tentang Peningkatan Langkah Komprehensif Dalam Rangka Percepatan Penyelesaian Masalah Aceh.*

11. *Undang-undang Republik Indonesia nomor 18 tahun 2001 tentang Otonomi Khusus bagi Provinsi Daerah Istimewa Aceh sebagai Provinsi Nanggroe Aceh Darussalam.*

12. On the politics of Islamic law in general prior to the Reformasi era, see Hooker 2003, 33–47 and Lubis 2003, 48–75.

13. On the implementation of Shariʿa during these periods, see van Langen 1997 and *EI2*, s.v. Atjeh (A.J. Piekaar).

14. Dinas Syariat Islam, *Eksistensi Mahkamah Syariyah dalam Rangka Pemberlakuan Syariʿat Islam di Nanggroe Aceh Darussalam* (Banda Aceh, 2003), p. 1.

15. On the role of religious scholars from the sultanate period to the establishment of PUSA, see Saby 2001. On the conflict between the religious scholars and the uleebalang and central-periphery politics, see Morris 1983. On the role of Acehnese religious scholars prior to the 1990s, see Saby 1995.

16. For further information on the history of Shariʿa in Aceh, see Salim 2004.

17. "Keputusan Penguasa Perang No. KPTS/PEPERDA-061/3/1962 tentang Kebidjaksanaan Pelaksanaan Unsur-Unsur Sjari'at Islam bagi Pemeluknja di Daerah Istimewa Atjeh," quoted by Morris 1983.

18. M. Daud Beureueh, "Muqaddimah Pelaksanaan Unsur-unsur Sjari'at Islam," April 9, 1962, quoted by Morris 1983, 243.

19. On the Religious Judicature Act, see Cammack 2003, and Wahid and Rumadi 2001.

20. See *Penjelasan atas Undang-undang Republik Indonesia nomor 18 tahun 2001 tentang Otonomi Khusus bagi Provinsi Daerah Istimewa Aceh sebagai Provinsi Nanggroe Aceh Darussalam*, Part I, *Umum* (August 9, 2001).

21. *Undang-undang No. 18/2001 tentang Otonomi Khusus bagi Provinsi Daerah Istimewa Aceh sebagai Provinsi Nanggroe Aceh Darussalam* (August 9, 2001).

22. For the draft of the Law on NAD, I use the text published as *Rancangan Undang-Undang Nanggoe Aceh Darussalam*, in *Suara Aceh*, February–March 2000, http://www.kimpraswil.go.id/pemdaaceh/buletin/dratf%20RUU%20NAD%20psl.115.htm/ (last accessed January 15, 2004). For the purpose of this study, I will confine my discussion to a comparison of provisions relating to Shari'a and the Shari'a Courts. There are, however, a number of other differences, especially concerning the political, judicial, and economic authority of NAD in relation to the central government, which are beyond the scope of this paper.

23. *Keputusan Presiden Republik Indonesia Nomor 11 Tahun 2003 tentang Mahkamah Syariah dan Mahkamah Syariah Provinsi di Provinsi Nanggroe Aceh Darussalam.*

24. There were 19 Religious Courts in Aceh that were transformed into Shari'a Courts: Banda Aceh, Sabang, Sigli, Meureudu, Bireun, Lhokseumawe, Takengon, Lhoksukon, Idi, Langsa, Kuala Simpang, Blang Kejeren, Kutacane, Meulaboh, Sinabang, Calang, Singkil, Tapak Tuan, Jantho. A total of 121 judges serving on the former Religious Courts were transformed into the judges of the Shari'a Courts by Articles 1 and 2 of the Presidential Decision.

25. "Mahkamah Syariah Aceh Diresmikan," *Suara Aceh*, March 5, 2003.

26. "Presidential Decision No. 28/2003 on the Military Emergency Situation in Aceh," *Kompas*, May 19, 2003.

27. "MA Bentuk Tim Asistensi Mahkamah Syariah di NAD," *Kompas*, July 8, 2003.

28. *Peraturan Daerah Provinsi Daerah Istimewa Aceh Nomor 5 tahun 2000 tentang Pelaksanaan Syariat Islam.*

29. Dinas Syariat Islam, *Eksistensi Mahkamah Syariah: dalam Rangka Pemberlakuan Syari'at Islam di Nanggroe Aceh Darussalam* (Banda Aceh, 2003), p. 5.

30. Prof. Rusydi Ali Muhammad, interview by Moch. Nur Ichwan, October 14, 2004.

31. On the role of Islamic political parties in this case, see, for instance, *Serambi Indonesia*, July 25, 2002.

32. *Qanun Provinsi Nanggroe Aceh Darussalam Nomor 10 tahun 2002 tentang Peradilan Syariat Islam.*

33. *Qanun Provinsi Nanggroe Aceh Darussalam Nomor 11 Tahun 2002 Tentang Pelaksanaan Syariat Islam Bidang Aqidah, Ibadah Dan Syiar Islam.* The absence of any protest against

these actions could be interpreted as signaling acceptance of this policy, but the accuracy of that intepretration would require a survey of Acehnese attitudes on the implementation of Shariʿa. To date, no such survey has been undertaken.

34. *Qanun Provinsi Nanggroe Aceh Darussalam Nomor 12 tahun 2003 tentang Minuman Khamar dan Sejenisnya; Qanun Provinsi Nanggroe Aceh Darussalam Nomor 13 tahun 2003 tentang Maysir (Perjudian); and Qanun Provinsi Nanggroe Aceh Darussalam Nomor 14 tahun 2003 tentang Khalwat (Mesum).*

35. The term "current" (*aliran*) in modern Indonesian refers to a particular body of religious, spiritual or political thought within a broader religious, spiritual or political discourse.

36. These include the festivals of ʿId al-Fitr, ʿId al-Adha, Mawlid al-Nabi, Isra' Miʿraj, and Nuzul al-Qurʾan.

37. The corporal punishment of caning for drinking intoxicants is actually absent from the Qurʾan. However, many later jurists considered drinking *khamr* to be punishable by caning. Forty strokes caning is in accordance with the authoritative opinion of the standard Islamic legal school in Indonesia. See al-Dimashqī 1993, 492.

38. "Pemerintah Provinsi NAD Siapkan Polisi Syariah dan Algojo," *Kompas*, October 24, 2002.

39. "Ibu-ibu dan Remaja Dibagikan Jilbab," *Serambi Indonesia*, May 7, 2002.

40. "Warga Pakai Celana Pendek akan Dirazia," *Serambi Indonesia*, February 3, 2004.

41. "Sosialisasi Busana Sesuai Syariat Islam," *Serambi Indonesia*, August 9, 2002.

42. "Warga Pakai Celana Pendek akan Dirazia," *Serambi Indonesia*, February 3, 2004.

43. "Pelaksanaan Syariat Islam secara Menyeluruh di Aceh," March 6, 2003, http://www.lin.go.id/ (accessed September 20, 2003).

44. *Peraturan Daerah Provinsi Daerah Istimewa Aceh Nomor 5 tahun 2000 tentang Pelaksanaan Syariat Islam secara Menyeluruh di Aceh.*

45. "Lomba Mode Busana Syariʿat Islam," *Serambi Indonesia*, July 25, 2002.

46. In his book, Professor Rusydi Ali Muhammad, rector of the State Institute of Islamic Studies (IAIN) Ar-Raniry, denies that the *jizya* is paid to the Muslim community, since it is paid to the state, for the betterment of all people, like *zakāt* for Muslims. *Jizya*, he insists, is thus just another name for *zakāt*. He further suggests that the amount of *zakāt* could in theory be higher than that of *jizya*. Muhammad 2003, 65.

47. See Salim and Azra 2003b, 11–12. The national system of Religious Courts deal with the first level only, that is, family law matters relating to marriage, divorce, and inheritance. The Compilation of Islamic Law (*Kompilasi Hukum Islam*) is likewise limited to these subjects. In the economic field (second sphere), *zakāt* (alms giving) has been regulated based on Law No. 38/1999 on Zakat Management, and Islamic banking is now authorized under recent legislation on the national banking system. In the wake of these changes, *zakāt* institutions (Lembaga Amil Zakat, LAZ) and Islamic banks have been established in various parts of the country.

48. "Zakat Mengubah Minus Jadi Plus," *Serambi Indonesia*, July 22, 2002.

49. "BPD Buka Empat Bank Syariah," *Serambi Indonesia*, August 7, 2002.

50. "Belum Ada Dasar untuk Mahkamah Syariah," *Kompas*, November 6, 2003.

51. Except, perhaps, in the case of khamr, which is threatened with the *ḥudūd* punishment of forty lashings with a cane (Qanun 12, Art. 26:1).

52. BBC News, March 4, 2003, http://news.bbc.co.uk/go/pr/fr/-/-asia-pasific/2816785.stm (accessed February 2004).

53. *Penjelasan atas Undang-undang Republik Indonesia nomor 18 tahun 2001 tentang Otonomi Khusus bagi Provinsi Daerah Istimewa Aceh sebagai Provinsi Nanggroe Aceh Darussalam*, Part I, *Umum* (August 9, 2001).

54. The change was based on Law No. 35/1999, revising the 1970 Basic Law on the Judiciary, and Presidential Instruction No. 21/2004 (March 23, 2004).

Chapter Eleven. Tim Lindsey and M.B. Hooker, *Shariʿa Revival in Aceh*

1. This distinction has to be treated within caution as *adat* in Aceh usually has significant Islamic content.

2. Dewan Perwakilan Rakyat Daerah.

3. The final detail of the provisions of the Bill will be critical to determining how Aceh's new Shariʿa institutions will develop. Relevant clauses in the current Bill include Arts. 101–106 on the Mahkamah Shariʿa; Arts. 107–110 on the application of Shariʿa; Arts. 111–113 on the MPU; Arts. 157(1) and (4) on the Wilayatul Hisbah; Arts. 158(2) and (5) on the Public Prosecutor; and Art. 176(7)) on human rights.

4. A fatwa is a (usually) non-binding pronouncement by a qualified religious legal scholar on an issue of belief or practice. The decision is made in the context of past interpretations of other scholars of the same school of jurisprudence (Federspiel 1995, 59).

5. Muslim Ibrahim, Chair MPU, interview by Tim Lindsey and M.B. Hooker, February 2003 and December 2005.

6. The Indonesian *Keputusan* (Decision) is often translated as "decree." This is inaccurate, however. The *Maklumat* or Presidential Decree proper was abolished in 1996. See Lindsey 2001, 43.

7. The statistics regarding the system of Religious Courts contained in this and the following paragraph are taken from Anonymous, "Beberapa Informasi tentang Pengadilan Agama di Indonesia" (2005, unpublished paper on file with the authors).

8. See also Nurussalim, "Ho Taba Syariat Islam," http://indomedia.com/ (accessed October 10, 2003).

9. The categories of cases decided by the Religious Courts as determined by the Department of Religion are: permit for polygamy, marriage evasion, marriage repudiation by registrar, marriage annulment, negligence lawsuit over marriage, *talak* divorce (application by husband), divorce (application by wife), division of marital property, child custody, child support by mother, alimony to divorced wife, child's legitimacy, cancellation of parental custody, guardianship, cancellation of guardianship, appointment of new guardian, compensation for guardian, establishment of child's descent, refusal of mixed marriage, formalities for marriage, permission to

marry, marriage dispensation, marriage guardian, inheritance, wills, bequest, charitable trusts, alms (Ar. *ṣadaqa*) and "others."

10. All terms are from the Arabic: *aḥwāl shakhṣiyya*, "personal affairs," is a legal category referring to personal and family law; *mu'āmalāt* is a legal category that includes those aspects of life dealing with human relationships and the physical world, mainly commerce and trade, which do not fall under the category of *'ibādāt* or ritual worship (Federspiel 1995, 166); and *jināya* is a legal category dealing with crime, judgment, and punishment (Federspiel 1995, 117).

11. See also Nurussalim, "Ho Taba Syariat Islam," http://indomedia.com/ (accessed October 10, 2003).

12. Letter from Ewa Wojkowska of UNDP, dated August 27, 2003.

13. "Special purpose laws overrule general laws."

14. Article 24C of the 1945 Constitution vests the Constitutional Court with "authority to . . . make final decisions in the review of legislation against the Constitution. . . ."

15. Letter from Ewa Wojkowska dated August 27, 2003.

16. "Bashir's JI Role Revealed," http://www.theage.com.au/ (accessed November 2, 2003). JI is, of course, the radical Islamist organization believed to be linked to Al-Qaeda and the Bali bombings, which killed over 200 Western holidaymakers and Indonesians on October 12, 2002. JI has been held responsible for subsequent bombing attacks on landmarks in Jakarta, including the Marriott Hotel and the Australian Embassy, as well as church bombings across Indonesia and inter-religious violence in eastern Indonesia (International Crisis Group 2002b).

17. Ar. *'aqīda*, "correct belief, doctrine." The term here includes the key doctrines regarding the nature of God and creation and the necessity for worshipping and acting as God has commanded (Federspiel 1995, 12, s.v. "*akaid*").

18. Ar. *'ibādāt*, "ritual worship, service." The legal meaning is ritual worship, as opposed to *mu'āmalāt* or "worship" in areas thought of as secular in the West. *'Ibādāt* comprises a wide number of matters, especially prayer, pilgrimage, alms giving, and fasting (Federspiel 1995, 86). In Islamic law there is generally much less scope for innovation in matters of *'ibādāt*, as opposed to other areas.

19. The word *syiar* is defined as "magnificence, greatness (of God and religion). *Syiar Allah*: God's greatness," in Echols and Shadily 1989, 538. *Syiar Islam* is most often used to mean the spreading, propagating, reviving, or other means of increasing the greatness of Islam.

20. Ar. *ahl al-Sunna wa l-jamā'a*, "people [who follow] the tradition of the Prophet and the community," a term used by Sunni Muslims to describe themselves, especially to distinguish themselves from Shi'i Muslims (Federspiel 1995, 10).

21. Ind. *shalat* (Ar. *ṣalāt*), the ritual prayer in Islam. Muslims should perform the prayer five times a day at prescribed times. There are also additional, superogatory prayers.

22. Traditionally the Friday prayer is only obligatory for men. However, it may be that in this context being a woman or a child constitutes an excuse allowed in Shari'a, which include ill health, old age, childhood, and travel. The excuses will vary according to which act is being contemplated.

23. "Malay Arab script" is a translation of *tulisan Arab Melayu*, which refers to a script

popular for several centuries throughout the Indo-Malay areas in which Arab letters are used to write Malay. Also known as *jawi*, it has been retained as a script in present-day Malaysia, Southern Thailand, and Brunei (Federspiel 1995, 115). It is mainly of only historical importance in areas of Indonesia outside Aceh, although there are now moves to revive the use of *jawi* in some other provinces where Islamic revivalism is politically significant.

24. Al Yasa' Abubakar, interviews by Tim Lindsey and M.B. Hooker, February 2003 and December 2005.

25. "Tsunami was God's revenge for Your Wicked Ways, Women Told." *Times Online*, December 22, 2005, http://www.timesonline.co.uk/article/0,,25689-1952823,00.html.

26. Ibid.

27. "Acehnese Accuse Religious Police of 'Arrogance' and Thuggery," *Jakarta Post*, February 23, 2006.

28. Ibid.

29. "Tsunami was God's revenge for Your Wicked Ways, Women Told." Supra, n. 25.

30. The rationale is that the passenger on an *ojek* must necessarily embrace the driver. The reports also suggest, however, that this restriction may soon be extended to *becak*, pedal rickshaws, although there is no physical contact between driver and passenger.

31. As is reflected in the stated aims of Qanun 11/2002 (Art. 2), which are:

> to develop and protect the faith and piety (*taqwā*) of individuals and the community from the influence of misguided teachings, to improve the understanding and the performance of *ʿibādāt* and the provision of facilities for it, and to enliven and celebrate activities in order to create an Islamic *atmosphere and environment* [emphasis added].

32. For example, under Art. 21(1):

> Whosoever fails to perform the congregational prayer three consecutive times, with no excuse allowed in Shariʿa as described in Article 8 sub-section (1), shall be punished by discretionary punishment in the form of imprisonment for a maximum of six months or public caning of a maximum of three strokes.

Other sentencing options, such as fines and the revocation of trading licenses are available in specific instances, and the punishment for not adhering to correct belief (*ʿaqīda*) is left to a separate Qanun (Art. 20(2)), which suggests that no agreement could be reached within the DPRD on the punishment to be imposed, perhaps because *ʿaqīda* is by and large a personal matter, including, for example, the religious education of children.

33. Sian Powell, "Aceh Warms to Flogging as Gambler gets Six of the Best," *The Australian*, June 25, 2005, p. 15.

34. Article 23 provides:

> Whosoever does not wear Islamic dress as described in Article 13 sub-section (1) shall be convicted by a discretionary punishment after having undergone a process of warning and guidance by the Wilayatul Hisbah [Islamic police].

35. Al Yasa' Abubakar, interview by Tim Lindsey and M.B. Hooker, February 2003 and December 2005.

36. Sian Powell, supra, n. 33. Another reason often given in Aceh for the absence of appeals from caning sentences is that the way it is administered means that it usually not does not cause severe physical injury and that many convicts would therefore prefer it to imprisonment or fine.

37. Ibid.

38. Muslim Ibrahim, Chair MPU, interviews by Tim Lindsey and M.B. Hooker, February 2003 and December 2005.

39. The Shari'a Courts currently operate with the same procedural rules as those applicable to civil cases in the General Courts. There are currently no provisions for the procedural aspects of criminal trials and therefore new legal procedures will have to be developed in order to hear such cases. Only Qanun 11/2002 regulates the prosecution of Shari'a cases, and it establishes a special prosecutor's office to prosecute violations of Shari'a law (Art. 16(1)). These public prosecutors will have the similar role of investigating, preparing indictments, prosecuting cases, and executing decisions of judges as prosecutors in other courts (Art. 17). Like the civil investigators, the prosecutors also come under the domain of the Governor's office (Art. 16).

40. L. McCulloch, "Aceh asks: Islamic Law for Whom?" http://www.atimes.com/ (accessed on June 12, 2003).

41. Basri Daham, "Setahun Setelah Pemberlakuan Syariat Islam di Aceh Perempuan Diminta tak Berkunjung ke Tempat Berbau Maksiat," http://www.kompas.com/ (accessed June 16, 2003).

42. Ibid. This was presumably done pursuant to Governor's Instruction No. 4/2002.

43. Basri Daham, supra, n. 41. Marijuana is traditionally used in Acehnese cooking. It is easily available throughout most of the province and unlikely to be eradicated.

44. Ibid.

45. Sian Powell, "Aceh Warms to Flogging as Gambler gets Six of the Best," *The Australian*, June 25, 2005, p. 15.

46. Ibid. It is assumed the relevant regulations breached in these cases included Qanun No. 5/2000 and No. 7/2000. Governor's Instruction No. 4/2002 required monitoring and reporting of these activities by provincial authorities.

47. Although the relationship between the Supreme Court and the new Constitutional Court in terms of the overall Court hierarchy remains unclear (Clarke 2003).

CONTRIBUTORS

Azyumardi Azra is Professor of History and former Rector of the National Islamic University (UIN) in Jakarta. Since completing his Ph.D. at Columbia University in 1992, he has been a leading figure in Islamic Studies in Indonesia, founding the trilingual journal *Studia Islamika*, and publishing over twenty books in Indonesian as well as *The Origins of Islamic Reformism in Southeast Asia: Networks of Malay-Indonesian and Middle Eastern 'Ulamā' in the Seventeenth and Eighteenth Centuries* (2004).

John R. Bowen is the Dunbar-Van Cleve Professor of Sociocultural Anthropology at Washington University in St. Louis, Missouri. His research focuses on the role of cultural forms (religious practices, aesthetic genres, legal discourse) in processes of social change. He is the author of six books, including *Islam, Law and Equality in Indonesia: An Anthropology of Public Reasoning* (2003).

Mark Cammack is Professor of Law at Southwestern Law School. His articles and chapters on Islamic law in Indonesia and the Indonesian legal system have appeared in, inter alia, *The International and Comparative Law Quarterly*, *The American Journal of Comparative Law*, and *Indonesia*.

Ross Clarke, BA, LLB (Melb), is a member of the Asian Law Centre, the University of Melbourne. His publications include "Retrospectivity and Constitutional Validity of the Bali Bombing and East Timor Trials," *The Australian Journal of Asian Law* (2003).

Kees van Dijk has been affiliated with the KITLV/Royal Netherlands Institute of Southeast Asian and Caribbean Studies as a researcher since 1968 and Professor of the History of Islam in Indonesia at University of Leiden since 1985. He has published various articles on contemporary politics and violence in Indonesia in journals and edited volumes. Among his publications are *Rebellion Under the Banner of Islam: The Darul Islam in Indonesia* (Martinus Nijhoff, 1981) and *A Country in Despair: Indonesia between 1997 and 2000* (2001).

Helen Donovan has been a researcher at the International Secretariat of Amnesty International since September 2004. Before joining Amnesty International she worked for the Judicial System Monitoring Programme in Dili, East Timor as well as with the Office of the Director of Public Prosecution in Canberra. Her contribution to this volume was written before her appointment at both the DPP and AI and does not reflect the views of either of those organizations.

Nelly van Doorn-Harder is Associate Professor of Theology at Valparaiso University, Indiana. She has taught Islamic Studies at a university in Yogyakarta, Indonesia where she helped establish an Institute for Interfaith and Religious Studies. Prior to that she was the director of a refugee agency in Cairo, Egypt and a lecturer of Middle Eastern Studies at the University of Leiden in the Netherlands. Her publications include *Women Shaping Islam: Indonesian Muslim Women Reading the Qurʾān* (2006).

R. Michael Feener is Associate Professor of History at the National University of Singapore, and a Research Fellow at the Asia Research Institute. He has published articles on jurisprudence, Orientalism, mysticism, hagiography, diaspora studies, and Qurʾanic interpretation in academic journals from Asia, Africa, Europe, and the United States. His books include *Muslim Legal Thought in Modern Indonesia* (2007) and *Islam in World Cultures: Comparative Perspectives* (2004).

Tim B. Heaton is Professor of Sociology at Brigham Young University. His research focuses on changing patterns of family behavior in the United States, Latin America, the Middle East, and Southeast Asia. His publications include "Socioeconomic and Familial Status of Women Associated with Age at First Marriage in Three Islamic Societies," in Xuanning Fu, *Interracial Marriage in Hawaii, 1983–1994* (1997), and (with R. Forste) "Education as Policy: The Impact of Education on Marriage, Contraception, and Fertility in Colombia, Peru, and Bolivia," *Social Biology* 45 (1998), 194–213.

M.B. Hooker is Adjunct Professor, Law Faculty, Australian National University and a Senior Associate of the Asian Law Centre, the University of Melbourne. His recent publications include *Indonesian Islam: Social Change through Contemporary Fatwāwā* (2003), "The State and Syariah in Indonesia 1945–1995," in Tim Lindsey, ed., *Indonesia: Law and Society* (1998) and (with Tim Lindsey) "Public Faces of Syariah in Contemporary Indonesia: Towards a National *Mazhab*," *The Australian Journal of Asian Law* 4 (2003).

Moch. Nur Ichwan obtained his Ph.D. from the International Institute of Asian Studies (IIAS) in the Netherlands in 2006. His work concentrates on Indonesian state discourse on Islam both during and beyond the Suharto years, and his dissertation is entitled "Official Reform of Islam: State Islam and the Ministry of Religious Affairs in Contemporary Indonesia, 1966–2004."

Rifyal Kaʿbah is a Justice on the Indonesian Supreme Court (Mahkamah Agung) and a lecturer in the Law Faculties of the University of Indonesia and YARSI University. He received his Doctor of Laws degree from the University of Indonesia, and has also studied at the Higher Institute of Islamic Studies, Jakarta, and at al-Azhar University in Cairo. He has authored numerous books and articles on Islam and law, including *Indonesian Legal History* (2001) and *Penegakan Syariʾat Islam di Indonesia* (2004).

Jeremy Kingsley, BA, LLB (Deakin), LLM (Melb) is a Principal Researcher in the Asian Law Centre and a Ph.D. candidate at the University of Melbourne. His publications include "Legal Transplantations: Is This What the Doctor Ordered and Are the Blood Types Compatible?" *Arizona Journal of Comparative and International Law* (2004).

Michael Laffan is Assistant Professor of History at Princeton University. He earned his BA at the Australian National University in Canberra (1995) and his Ph.D. in Southeast Asian History at the University of Sydney (2001). He is the author of *Islamic Nationhood and Colonial Indonesia: The Umma Below the Winds* (2003).

Tim Lindsey is Professor of Asian Law and Director of the Asian Law Centre as well as Deputy Director of the Centre for the Study of Contemporary Islam at the University of Melbourne. His publications include the edited collections *Indonesia: Law and Society* (1998) and (with Helen Pausacker) *Chinese Indonesians: Remembering, Distorting, Forgetting* (2005), and, with M.B. Hooker, "Public Faces of Syariah in Contemporary Indonesia: Towards a National *Mazhab*," *The Australian Journal of Asian Law* 4 (2003).

Musdah Mulia is former head of the Special Research Staff and Lecturer on Religion at the Indonesian Department of Religious Affairs. She has studied at the IAIN Alauddin in Makassar, South Sulawesi, and completed her dissertation at IAIN Syarif Hidayatullah (Jakarta) in 1997.

GLOSSARY

Many of the terms used to discuss Islam and Islamic law in modern Indonesian (*Bahasa Indonesia*) are derived from Arabic. In this glossary, such terms are presented with full Arabic diacritics for the benefits of students of Islamic law who are unfamiliar with the Indonesian language. In vernacular publications, however, these terms appear without diacritics, and often in variant spellings. Thus, the most popular Indonesian forms of such terms are included in the entries as well.

adat	Ind. (< Ar. *ʿāda*); "custom" or "local tradition"; during the colonial period the Dutch often appealed to "customary law" (*adatrecht*) to counter the implementation of forms of Islamic law in various parts of the archipelago
akad nikah	Ind. (< Ar. *ʿaqd al-nikāh*); contract of marriage under Islamic law
ʿālim	Ar. (pl. *ʿulamāʾ*); a Muslim scholar trained primarily in the traditionalist milieu of traditional jurisprudential (*fiqh*) scholarship
asbāb al-nuzūl	Ar. "the occasions of revelation"; the traditional method of textual analysis used to interpret the particular circumstances in which various Qurʾanic verses were revealed to Muḥammad
āya	Ar. (pl. *āyāt*); literally "sign"; also the common term used to refer to Qurʾanic verses
bidʿa	Ar. (> Ind.) "innovation [in matters of religion]"; generally used by Muslim reformists in a pejorative sense
cendekiawan	Ind. "intellectual," in the sense of one enjoying a modern education, rather than one who is solely *pesantren*-trained
dalīl	Ar. "indication"; used in this volume more specifically to refer to the "legal indicator" upon which a given ruling is based
daʿwa	Ar. (> Ind. *daʿwa, dakwah*) "call"; Islamic religious propagation; in modern Indonesia this became a primary field of activity for politically disenfranchised Islamists under the New Order (1965–1998)
fatwa	Ar. *fatwā* (> Ind.); the judicial opinion issued by a mufti in response to a specific question by a given petitioner
fiqh	Ar. (> Ind. *fikih*) "understanding"; traditional Muslim jurisprudence
furūʿ	Ar. (> Ind.) "branches"; rulings on specific *fiqh* issues, as opposed to the study of the sources and methods of jurisprudence (*uṣūl al-fiqh*)
ḥadīth	Ar. (> Ind.) "reports" of the words and deeds of Muḥammad; a primary source of Islamic law after the text of the Qurʾan
halqah	Ind. (< Ar. *ḥalqa*) "circle"; used to refer more specifically to study groups dedicated to religious learning
hikmah	Ind. (< Ar. *ḥikma*) "wisdom"; refers in this volume to the inner meaning of religious texts

ʿibādāt   Ar. (> Ind.) "[acts of] worship"; refers to those areas of *fiqh* concerned specifically with matters of religious observance

ʿidda   Ind. (< Ar.) "number"; the prescribed waiting period before which a widow or divorcée can remarry under Islamic law

ijmāʿ   Ar. (> Ind.) "consensus"; used in the technical sense as a source of law comprising the past agreement of authorities on a particular issue

ijtihād   Ar. (> Ind.) "independent jurisprudential reasoning"

ikhtilāf   Ar. (> Ind.) "difference, diversity"; used to refer to the study of variant legal rulings on a given issue

isnād   Ar. (> Ind.) "chain of transmission"; intended to insure the reliability of transmitted religious knowledge

istiṣlāḥ   Ar. (> Ind.); the consideration of public interest (*maṣlaḥa*) as a source of law

Jāhiliyya   Ar. (> Ind.) "the Age of Ignorance"; used classically to refer to pre-Islamic Arabian society; in the modern period it has come also to be used polemically against the modern "pagan" West in Islamist polemics

kiai   see *kyai*

kitab kuning   Ind.; books on the Islamic religious sciences composed in Arabic, or Arabic-script forms of Malay and Javanese that were traditionally taught in the *pesantren* milieu

kyai   J. and Ind. (also *kiai*); a Javanese Muslim teacher trained in the "traditionalist" milieu of Indonesian *pesantren*

liʿan   Ind. (< Ar. *liʿān*) "condemnation"; allegation of adultery under Islamic law

madhhab   Ar. (> Ind. *madhab, mazhab, madzhab*); used to designate a "school of thought" or "methodology" within *fiqh*

mahar   Ind. (< Ar. *mahr*); "dower" or "bridal money" stipulated in a Muslim marriage contract (*akad nikah*)

maqṣūd   Ar. (pl. *maqāṣid*) "goal"; used to refer to the "aim" or "intention" behind the law

maṣlaḥa   Ar. (> Ind.) "that which is beneficial, or promoting advantage"; the consideration of such factors in the formulation of rulings on a particular question of *fiqh*

matn   Ar. (> Ind.) "core text"; in *ḥadīth* studies comprising the actual message delivered by a chain of transmitters (*isnād*)

muʿāmalāt   Ar. (> Ind.); referring to the sphere of "worldly transactions" as opposed to more specifically "religious" issues (*ʿibādāt*) in the context of *fiqh*

mufassir   Ar. (> Ind.); a practitioner of Qurʾanic exegesis (*tafsīr*)

mufti   Ar. (> Ind.); see fatwa

mujtahid   Ar. (> Ind.); a practitioner of independent jurisprudential reasoning (*ijtihād*)

muqārana   Ar. "comparison"; of the rulings on a given issue between the various legal schools (*madhhabs*)

naskh   Ar. (> Ind.) "abrogation"; referring to that of one verse of the Qurʾan by another, subsequent one. The sub-discipline of Qurʾanic studies that is used to determine such cases is referred to in Arabic as *al-nāsikh wa l-mansūkh*, or "the abrogator and the abrogated"

nusyuz	Ind. (< Ar. *nushūz*) "animosity", "discord"; used to refer in Islamic law to the violation of marital duties on the part of the wife
Pancasila	Ind.; the official Indonesian State ideology, consisting of "five principles": belief in one God, humanitarianism, national unity, democracy, and social justice
pesantren	J. and Ind.; "traditionalist" Indonesian Muslim religious school, often specializing in the study of *fiqh*
Pembaharuan	Ind. "Renewal"; used to refer to the "neo-modernist" reform movement in Indonesia
qanun	Ind. (< Ar. *qānūn*, < Gk.); "canon" in English, this term is often used to refer to formalized code or statute law in Muslim societies
qaṭ'ī	Ar. (> Ind.); knowledge that can inform an Islamic legal ruling with "certainty", as opposed to *zannī*
qiyās	Ar. (> Ind.) "analogical reasoning"; considered as a source of law supplementing those of the Qur'an and *ḥadīth* in most of the "classical" schools of *fiqh*
Reaktualisasi	Ind.; a program for the "re-actualization" of Islamic law in Indonesian society promoted in the 1980s by then-Minister of Religious Affairs Munawir Sjadzali
sūra	Ar. (> Ind.); a "chapter" of the Qur'anic text
Sunna	Ar. (> Ind.) "the Way"; generally used to refer to the example set for the community by the Prophet Muḥammad
tafsīr	Ar. (> Ind.) "interpretation"; Qur'anic exegesis
talak	Ind. (< Ar. *ṭalāq*) "divorce"; esp. the unilateral declaration of divorce by the husband by repeating a formula of verbal repudiation
taqlīd	Ar. (> Ind.) "imitation", or the "following" of established rulings on issues already considered conclusively resolved in the traditional corpus of fiqh literature
tarekat	Ind. (< Ar. *ṭarīqa*); a term used to refer to Sufi orders, and sometimes Sufism more broadly, in Indonesia
tarjīḥ	Ar. (> Ind.); "to make outweigh"; choosing from the most convincing of various possible legal rulings on a given issue of *fiqh*
tawḥīd	Ar. (> Ind.); the central Islamic doctrine of the "oneness of God"
'ulamā'	see *'ālim*
uleebalang	Acehnese; a term referring to a category of traditional local elites
umat	Ind. (< Ar. *umma*); the [Muslim] community
'urf	Ar. "custom, usage"; established local practice considered by some to be a supplementary source of law in *fiqh*
uṣūl al-fiqh	Ar. (> Ind.); the "roots" or "sources", a term used to cover the theoretical and methodological aspects of *fiqh*
wali nikah	Ind. (< Ar. *walī al-nikāḥ*); used for the male guardian of a bride contracting a marriage under Islamic law
zakāt	Ar. (> Ind.); "obligatory almsgiving"; one of the five pillars of Islam
zannī	Ar. (> Ind.); knowledge that can inform an Islamic legal ruling only on the level of "probability", as opposed to *qaṭ'ī*

BIBLIOGRAPHY

Abaza, Mona. 1993. "Changing Images of Three Generations of Azharaties in Indonesia." Occasional Paper No. 19. Singapore: Institute of Southeast Asian Studies.

———. 1994. *Islamic Education, Perception and Exchanges: Indonesian Students in Cairo.* Paris: Cahier d'Archipel.

Abou El Fadl, Khaled. 2001. *Speaking in God's Name: Islamic Law, Authority, and Women.* Oxford: Oneworld Publications.

Abū Ṭālib, Shūfī Ḥasan. 2001. *Taṭbīq al-sharīʿa al-islāmiyya fī l-buldān al-ʿarabiyya.* Cairo: Dār al-Nahḍa al-ʿArabiyya.

Achmad, Nirwanto Ki S. Hendrowinoto and Gunarso T.S., eds. 2001. *Osama Vs Bush: Perang Jihad.* Jakarta: Gria Media Prima Jakarta.

Afianah, Yayuk. 2003. "Pola Penyelesaian Hukum Tindak Kekerasan Dalam Rumah Tangga." MA thesis, IAIN Syarif Hidayatullah.

El Alami, Dawoud Sudqi, and Doreen Hinchcliffe. 1996. *Islamic Marriage and Divorce Laws of the Arab World.* London: CIMEL/Kluwer Law International.

Ali, Kecia. 2003. "Progressive Muslims and Islamic Jurisprudence: The Necessity for Critical Engagement with Marriage and Divorce Law." In *Progressive Muslims: On Justice, Gender, and Pluralism*, ed. Omid Safi, 163–89. Oxford: Oneworld Publications.

Amal, Taufik Adnan and Samsu Rizal Panggabean. 2003. "Syariat Islam di Aceh." In *Syariat Islam: Pandangan Muslim Liberal*, ed. Burhanuddin, 84–128. Jakarta: Jaringan Islam Liberal/Asia Foundation.

Anam, Choirul. 1985. *Pertumbuhan dan Perkembangan Nahdlatul Ulama.* Surakarta: NST Offset Sala.

An-Naʿim, Abdullahi Ahmed. 1990. *Towards an Islamic Reform: Civil Liberties, Human Rights, and International Law.* Syracuse: Syracuse University Press.

Anwar, Syamsul. 2002. "Pengembangan Metode Penelitian Hukum Islam." *Profetika* 4/1: 123–36.

Arian, Cut. 1982. "Perkawinan dan Perceraian Pada Masyarakat Aceh." Yogyakarta: Center for Demographic Research and Studies, Gadjah Mada University.

Arifin, Jenal. 2003. "Konsorsium Ilmu Ke-Syariʿatan dan Struktur Kurikulumnya." Unpublished paper available at Office of the Rektor, UIN Syarif Hidayatullah.

Asad, Talal. 1986. *The Idea of an Anthropology of Islam.* Washington, DC: Georgetown University CCAS Occasional Papers.

———. 2003. *Formations of the Secular: Christianity, Islam, Modernity.* Stanford: Stanford University Press.

Asia Foundation/A.C. Neilson. 2001. *Survey Report on Citizens' Perceptions of the Indonesian Justice Sector: Preliminary Findings and Recommendations.* Jakarta: Asia Foundation.

Aslan, Reza. 2005. *No God but God: The Origins, Evolution, and Future of Islam.* New York: Random House.

Azra, Azyumardi. 2002. *Islam Nusantara: Jaringan Global dan Lokal*. Bandung: Penerbit Mizan.

———. 2003. "Implementasi Syari'at Islam di Nanggroe Aceh Darussalam." In *Revitalisasi Syariat Islam di Aceh: Problem, Solusi dan Implementasi. Menuju Penerapan Hukum Islam di Nanggroe Aceh Darussalam*, ed. Rusydi Ali Muhammad, xix–xxxii. Jakarta: Logos/IAIN Ar-Raniry.

———. 2004. *The Origins of Islamic Reformism in Southeast Asia: Networks of Malay-Indonesian and Middle Eastern 'Ulamā' in the Seventeenth and Eighteenth Centuries*. Canberra: ASAA & Allen-Unwin, Honolulu: University of Hawai'i Press, and Leiden: KITLV Press.

Baker, Jacqueline. n.d. "Laskar Jihad dan Mobilisasi Umat Islam dalam Konflik Maluku." http://www.acicis.murdoch.edu.au/hi/fieldḥtopics/jbaker.doc.

Barlas, Asma. 2002. *Believing Women in Islam: Unreading Patriarchal Interpretations of the Qur'an*. Austin: University of Texas Press.

Barton, Greg and Greg Fealy, eds. 1996. *Nahdatul Ulama, Traditional Islam and Modernity in Indonesia*. Clayton: Monash Asia Institute.

Barton, Greg. 1997. "Indonesia's Nurcholish Madjid and Abdurrahman Wahid as Intellectual *Ulama*: The Meeting of Islamic Traditionalism and Modernism in Neo-Modernist Thought." *Studia Islamika* 4/1:29–82.

Behrend, Timothy. 2003. "Preaching Fundamentalism." *Inside Indonesia*, April–June. http://www.insideindonesia.org/.

Bisri, Cik Hasan. 1997. *Peradilan Islam dalam Tatanan Masyarakat Indonesia*. Bandung: Remaja Rosdakarya.

Bolland, B.J. 1971. *The Struggle of Islam in Modern Indonesia*. The Hague: Martinus Nijhoff.

Bowen, John R. 1998. "'You May Not Give it Away': How Social Norms Shape Islamic Law in Contemporary Indonesian Jurisprudence." *Islamic Law and Society* 5/3:1–27.

———. 1999. "Legal Reasoning and Public Discourse in Indonesian Islam." In *New Media in the Muslim World: The Emerging Public Sphere*, eds. Dale F. Eickelman and Jon W. Anderson, 80–105. Bloomington: Indiana University Press.

———. 2000. "Consensus and Suspicion: Judicial Reasoning and Social Change in an Indonesia Society, 1960–1994." *Law and Society Review* 34/1:97–128.

———. 2003. *Islam, Law and Equality in Indonesia: An Anthropology of Public Reasoning*. Cambridge: Cambridge University Press.

Brenner, Suzanne. 1998. *The Domestication of Desire: Women, Wealth, and Modernity in Java*. Princeton: Princeton University Press.

Bruinessen, Martin van. 1990. "Indonesia's Ulama and Politics: Caught Between Legitimizing the Status Quo and Searching for Alternatives." *Prisma* 49:52–69.

———. 1990. "*Kitab Kuning*: Books in Arabic Script Used in the *Pesantren* Milieu." *Bijdragen tot de Taal-, Land- en Volkenkunde* 146/2–3:226–69.

———. 1992. *Tarekat Naqsyabandiyah di Indonesia: Survei Historis, Geografis dan Sosiologis*. Bandung: Mizan Publishers.

———. 1994. *NU: Tradisi, Relasi-relasi Kuasa, dan Pencarian Wacana Baru*. Yogyakarta: Lembaga Kajian Islam dan Sosial.

———. 1995. *Kitab Kuning, Pesantren dan Tarekat: Tradisi-Tradisi Islam di Indonesia*. Bandung: Mizan Publishers.

————. 2002. "Genealogies of Islamic Radicalism." *South East Asia Research* 10/2:117–54.

Bustamam-Ahmad, Kamaruzzaman. 2002. "Law and Culture in Islam: The Case of Western Scholars Perception on Islamic Law and Its Effect to Islamic Law Studies [sic] in State Institute of Islamic Studies (IAIN) of Indonesia." *Profetika* 4/1:71–93.

Butt, Simon. 1999. "The *Eksekusi* of the *Negara Hukum*: Implementing Judicial Decisions in Indonesia." In *Indonesia: Law and Society*, ed. Timothy Lindsey, 247–57. Sydney: Federation Press.

Cammack, Mark. 1989. "Islamic Law in Indonesia's New Order." *International and Comparative Law Quarterly* 38:53–73.

————. 1997. "Indonesia's 1989 Religious Judicature Act: Islamization of Indonesia or Indonesianization of Islam?" *Indonesia* 63:143–68.

————. 1999. "Islam, Nationalism, and the State in Suharto's Indonesia." *Wisconsin Journal of International Law* 17:27–63.

————. 2002. "Islamic Inheritance Law in Indonesia: The Influence of Hazairin's Theory of Bilateral Inheritance." *Australian Journal of Asian Law* 4/3:295–315.

————. 2003. "Indonesia's 1989 Religious Judicature Act: Islamization of Indonesia or Indonesianization of Islam?" In *Shari'a and Politics in Modern Indonesia*, eds. Arskal Salim and Azyumardi Azra, 96–124. Singapore: Institute of Southeast Asian Studies.

Cammack, Mark, Lawrence A. Young, and Tim B. Heaton. 2000. "The State, Religion, and the Family in Indonesia: The Case of Divorce Reform." In *Family, Religion, and Social Change in Diverse Societies*, eds. S.K. Houseknecht and J.G. Pankhurst, 175–204. New York: Oxford University Press.

————. 1996. "Legislating Social Change in an Islamic Society: Indonesia's Marriage Law." *American Journal of Comparative Law* 44:45–73.

Chalil, Moenawar. 1955. *Biografi Empat Serangkai Imam Mazhab*. Jakarta: Bulan Bintang.

————. 1956. *Kembali kepada Al Qur'an dan As-Sunna*. Jakarta: Bulan Bintang.

Cholidul, Azhar. 1997. "Kontroversi Seputar Keputusan Perkara Cerai Talak: Penetapan atau Putusan." *Mimbar Hukum* 32:71–86.

Clarke, Ross. 2003. "Retrospectivity and the Constitutional Validity of the Bali Bombing and East Timor Trials." *The Australian Journal of Asian Law* 5/2:128–59.

Cribb, Robert. 2000. *Historical Atlas of Indonesia*. Honolulu: University of Hawai'i Press.

Crowe, Michael Bertram. 1977. *The Changing Profile of the Natural Law*. The Hague: Martinus Nijhoff.

Departemen Agama. 1983. *Standarisasi Pengadilan Agama dan Pengadilan Tinggi Agama*. Jakarta: Direktorat Jenderal Pembinaan Kelembagaan Agama Islam, Departemen Agama R.I.

————. 1984. *Statistik Peradilan Agama*. Jakarta: Direktorat Jenderal Pembinaan Kelembagaan Agama Islam, Departemen Agama R.I.

————. 1989/1990. *Laporan Tahunan Direktorat Pembinaan Badan Peradilan Agama*. Jakarta: Direktorat Jenderal Pembinaan Kelembagaan Agama Islam, Departemen Agama R.I.

————. 1996/1997. *Kompilasi Hukum Islam di Indonesia*. Jakarta: Direktorat Jenderal Pembinaan Kelembagaan Agama Islam, Departemen Agama R.I.

————. 2000. *Sketsa Peradilan Agama*. Jakarta: Direktorat Jenderal Pembinaan Kelembagaan Agama Islam, Departemen Agama R.I.

————. 2001. *Peradilan Agama di Indonesia: Sejarah Perkembangan Lembaga dan Proses Pembentukan Undang-Undangnya*. Jakarta: Direktorat Jenderal Pembinaan Kelembagaan Agama Islam, Departemen Agama R.I.

————. 2004. *Profil Peradilan Agama*. Jakarta: Direktorat Jenderal Pembinaan Kelembagaan Agama Islam, Departemen Agama R.I.

di Tiro, Tengku Hasan. 1981. *The Unfinished Diary of Tengku Hasan di Tiro*. National Liberation Front of Aceh Sumatra.

Dijk, Cornelius (Kees) van. 1981. *Rebellion Under the Banner of Islam*. The Hague: Martinus Nijhoff.

————. 1991. "The Re-Actualization of Islam in Indonesia." *Review of Indonesian and Malaysian Affairs* 25/2:75–84.

————. 2001. *A Country in Despair: Indonesia between 1997 and 2000*. Leiden: KITLV Press.

————. 2002. "Is God a Gangster? Political and Religious Authority and Religious Sentiments." Paper presented at the conference "Fatwās and Dissemination of Religious Authority in Indonesia," Leiden, October 31, 2002.

al-Dimashqī, Muḥammad b. ʿAbd al-Raḥmān al-Shāfiʿī. 1993. *Rahmatul Ummah: Berbagai Masalah Hukum Islam*, trans. by Sarmin Syukur and Luluk Rodliyah. Surabaya: al-Ikhlas.

Djamil, Fathurrahman. 1995. *Metode Ijtihad Majelis Tarjih Muhammadiyah*. Jakarta: Logos Publishing House.

Djamil, Fathurrahman and Jenal Arifin. 2003. "Pembidangan Ilmu-ilmu Syariʿah: Sebuah Tinjauan Filosofis." Unpublished paper on file at Office of the Rektor, UIN Syarif Hidayatullah.

Dupret, Baudoin. 2000. *Au nom de quel droit*. Paris: Maison des Sciences de l'Homme.

EI² = *Encyclopaedia of Islam*. New Edition. 1960–2004. 12 vols. Leiden: Brill.

Eickelman, Dale. 1992. "Mass Higher Education and the Religious Imagination in Contemporary Arab Societies." *American Ethnologist* 19/4:643–55.

Engineer, Ashgar Ali. 1992. *The Rights of Women in Islam*. New York: St. Martin's Press.

Ensiklopedi Hukum Islam. 1996. Jakarta: Ichtiar Baru van Hoeven.

Ensiklopedi Islam. 1993. Jakarta: Ichtiar Baru van Hoeven.

Faqih, Mansour. 1997. *Analisis Gender: Transformasi Sosial*. Yogyakarta: Pustaka Pelajar.

al-Faṭānī, Aḥmad b. Muḥammad Zayn b. Musṭafā. 1957. *al-Fatāwā al-Faṭāniyya*. Siam: al-Maṭbaʿa al-Faṭāniyya.

Federspiel, Howard M. 1994. *A Dictionary of Indonesian Islam*. Athens: Ohio University, Center for International Studies.

————. 2001. *Islam and Ideology in the Emerging Indonesian State: The Persatuan Islam (PERSIS), 1923–1957*. Leiden: Brill.

Feener, R. Michael. 2001. "Indonesian Movements for the Creation of a 'National Madhhab'." *Islamic Law and Society* 9/1:84–113.

————. 2007. *Muslim Legal Thought in Modern Indonesia*. Cambridge: Cambridge University Press.

————. forthcoming a. "Southeast Asian Localisations of Islam and Participation within a Global *Umma*, c. 1500–1800." In *The New Cambridge History of Islam*, vol. 3., eds. Anthony Reid and David Morgan. New York: Cambridge University Press.

————. forthcoming b. "Islam, Technology, and Modernity in the Nineteenth and Early Twentieth Centuries." In *The New Cambridge History of Islam*, vol. 6, ed. Robert W. Hefner. New York: Cambridge University Press.

Feillard, Andrée. 1995. *Islam et armée dans l'Indonésie contemporaine*. Paris: Editions l'Hartmann.

Finnis, John M. 1998. *Aquinas: Moral, Political, and Legal Theory*. Oxford: Oxford University Press.

Forum Kajian Kitab Kuning (FK3), ed. 2001. *Wajah Baru Relasi Suami-Istri. Telaah Kitāb ʿUqūd al-Lujjayn*. Yogyakarta: Lembaga Kajian Islam dan Social.

Frederick, William. 1982. "Rhoma Irama and the Dangdut Style: Aspects of Contemporary Indonesian Popular Culture." *Indonesia* 34:103–30.

al-Fuyūdāt al-rabbāniyya fī muqarrarāt al-muʾtamarāt li-jamʿiyyat ahl al-ṭarīqa al-muʿtabara al-nahdiyya, n.d., n.p.

Gautama, Sudargo. 1991. *Essays in Indonesian Law*. 2nd ed. 1993. Bandung: Citra Aditya Bakti.

Gibb, H.A.R. and J.H. Kramer. 1953. *Shorter Encyclopaedia of Islam*. Leiden: E.J. Brill.

Glenn, H. Patrick. 2000. *Legal Traditions of the World: Sustainable Diversity in Law*. New York: Oxford University Press.

Hamim, Thoha. 1996. "Moenawar Chalil's Reformist Thought: A Study of an Indonesian Religious Scholar, 1908–1961." Ph.D. diss., McGill University.

Harahap, M Yahya. 2001. *Kedudukan, Kewanangan, dan Acara Peradilan Agama*. Jakarta: Sinar Grafika.

Harahap, Zainabun. 1965. *Operasi-operasi Militer Menumpas Kahar Muzakkar*. Jakarta: Mega Bookstore.

Harjono, Anwar. 1968. *Hukum Islam: Keluasan dan Keadilannja*. Jakarta: Bulan Bintang.

————. 1995. *Indonesia Kita: Pemikiran Berwawasan Iman-Islam*. Jakarta: Gema Insani Press.

Hartini and Yulkarnain Harahab. 2000. *Pengaruh Kompilasi Hukum Islam dalam Penyelesaian Perkara Warisan pada Pengadilan Agama di Daerah Istimewa Yogyakarta*. Yogyakarta: Universitas Gajah Mada.

Hasan, A. 1928. *Al-Boerhan*. Bandung: Persatuan Islam.

————. 1996. *Soal-Jawab Masalah Agama*. 4 vols. Bangil: Penerbit PERSIS.

Hasan, Muhammad Tolchah. 2000. "Ceramah Tashowwuf Menteri Agama Republik Indonesia." In *Hasil-hasil Muktamar IX Jamʿiyyah Ahlith Thoriqoh al-Muʿtabaroh an-Nahdliyyah*, 42–52. Pekalongan: Sekretaris Muktamar IX, JATMN.

Hasan, Noorhaidi. 2004. "Between Transnational Interest and Domestic Politics: Understanding Middle Eastern *Fatwā*s on Jihad in the Moluccas." *Islamic Law and Society* 12/1: 73–92.

Hazairin. 1936. *De Redjang: De volksordening, het verwantschaps-, huwelijks-, en efrecht*. Batavia: Universitas Indonesia.

————. 1951. *Hukum Islam dan Masjarakat*. Jakarta: Bulan Bintang.

————. 1958. *Hukum Kewarisan Bilateral Menurut al-Qurʾan dan Hadith*. Jakarta: Tintamas.

al-Hibri, Azizah Y. 1982. "A Study of Islamic Herstory: Or How Did We Ever Get Into This Mess?" In *Women and Islam*, ed. Azizah al-Hibri, 207–20. Oxford and New York: Pergamon Press.

Himpunan Putusan Tarjih. n.d. *Himpunan Putusan Tarjih Muhammadiyah*. Yogyakarta: Pimpinan Pusat Muhammadiyah.

Hisyam, Muhammad. 2001. *Caught Between Three Fires: The Javanese* Pangulu *Under the Dutch Colonial Administration 1882–1942.* Jakarta: INIS.

Hooker, M.B. 1984. *Islamic Law in South East Asia.* Singapore: Oxford University Press.

———. 1986. "The Law Texts of Muslim South East Asia." In *Pre-Modern Texts.* Vol. 1 of *Law of South East Asia,* ed. M.B. Hooker, 347–433. Singapore: Butterworths.

———. 2003a. "Submission to Allah? The Kelantan *Shariʿa* Criminal Code (II) 1993." In *Malaysia: Islam, Society and Politics,* eds. Virginia Hooker and Norani Othman, 80–98. Singapore: Institute of South East Asian Studies.

———. 2003b. *Indonesian Islam. Social Change through Contemporary* Fatāwā. Honolulu: University of Hawaii Press.

———. 2003c. "Introduction: Islamic Law in South-East Asia." *Studia Islamika* 10/1: 1–22.

———. 2005. "The State and *Shariʿa* in Indonesia." In *Shariʿa and Politics in Modern Indonesia,* eds. Arskal Salim and Azyumardi Azra, 33–47. Singapore: Institute of Southeast Asian Studies.

Hooker, M.B., and Timothy Lindsey. 2003. "Public Faces of *Shariʿa* in Contemporary Indonesia: Towards a National *Madhhab?*" *Studia Islamika* 10/1: 23–64.

Hosen, Ibrahim. 1987. *Apakah Judi Itu?* Jakarta: Lembaga Kajian Ilmiah Institut Ilmu Al-Qurʾan (IIQ) Jakarta.

Howell, Julie D. 2003. "Modernity and the Borderlands of Islamic Spirituality in Indonesia's New Sufi Networks." Paper presented at the conference "Sufism and the 'Modern' in Islam," Bogor, Indonesia, September 4–6, 2003.

Ibn Taymiyya. 2000. *Majmuʿ Fatāwā Ibn Taymiyya,* topic *al-Fiqh al-tamādhhub,* CD-ROM Cairo: Ḥarf.

Ichwan, Moch. Nur. 2003. "The Seven-Word Controversy." *IIAS Newsletter.* March 30.

———. 2005. "'Ulamāʾ, State and Politics: Majelis Ulama Indonesian 'Ulamāʾ after Suharto." *Islamic Law and Society* 12/1:45–72.

Ihromi, T.O. 1997. *Wanita dan Hukum Nasional.* Jakarta: University of Indonesia Press.

Ihza, Yusril. 1995. "Modernisme Islam dan Demokrasi: Pandangan Politik Mohammad Natsir." In *M. Natsir. Sumbangan dan Pemikirannya untuk Indonesia,* ed. Anwar Harjono, 143–54. Jakarta: Media Dakwah.

Inkiriwang, Justus. 1983. *Perkawinan dan Perceraian Pada Masyarakat Minahasa.* Yogyakarta: Center for Demographic Research and Studies, Gadjah Mada University.

International Crisis Group. 2001. "Aceh: Can Autonomy Stem the Conflict?" Jakarta/Brussels: I.C.G.

———. 2002a. "Aceh: A Slim Chance for Peace." Jakarta/Brussels: I.C.G.

———. 2002b. "Al-Qaeda in Southeast Asia: The Case of the 'Ngruki Network' in Indonesia." Jakarta/Brussels: I.C.G.

Irianto, Sulistyowati. 2003. *Perempuan di antara Berbagai Pilihan Hukum.* Jakarta: Yayasan Obor Indonesia.

Jamhari. 2002 "Indonesian Fundamentalism." *Studia Islamika* 9/3:183–89.

Jones, Gavin. 1994. *Marriage and Divorce in Islamic Southeast Asia.* Kuala Lumpur: Oxford University Press.

Jusoh, Hamid. 1991. *The Position of Islamic Law in the Malaysian Constitution with Special Reference to the Conversion Case in Family Law.* Kuala Lumpur: Kementerian Pendidikan Malaysia, Dewan Bahasa dan Pustaka.

Ka'bah, Rifyal. 1999. *Hukum Islam di Indonesia: Perspektif Muhammadiyah dan NU*. Jakarta: Universitas Yarsi.

Kamali, Mohammad Hashim. 1998. *Freedom of Expression in Islam*. Kuala Lumpur: Ilmiah Publishers.

Kasim, Massuana, and Rachmatiah B. Idrus. 1983. *Perkawinan dan Perceraian Pada Masyarakat Bugis*. Yogyakarta: Center for Demographic Research and Studies, Gadjah Mada University.

Kasto. 1982. *Perkawinan dan Perceraian pada Masyarakat Jawa*. Yogyakarta: Center for Demographic Research and Studies, Gadjah Mada University.

Keputusan Muktamar Tarjih XXII. n.d. *Keputusan Muktamar Tarjih Muhammadiyah XXII*. Yogjakarta: Pimpinan Pusat Muhammadiyah.

el Khalieqy, Abidah. 2001. *Perempuan Berkalung Sorban*. Yogyakarta: YKF/Ford Foundation.

Kiprah Kemasyarakatan Alumni Fakultas Syari'ah dalam Pentas Nasional. 1999. Jakarta: Fakultas Syari'ah IAIN Syarif Hidayatullah.

Lacan, Jacques Lacan. 1977. *Four Fundamentals of Psychoanalysis*. Harmondsworth, UK: Penguin.

Laffan, Michael Francis. 2003. *Islamic Nationhood and Colonial Indonesia: The Umma below the Winds*, London-New York: RoutledgeCurzon.

———. 2004. "The *Fatwā* Debated? *Shūrā* in an Indonesian Context." *Islamic Law and Society* 15/1:93–121.

———. Forthcoming. "*Iftā'* as Translation Represented: Implicit Hierarchies of Language and Script." In *A History of Translation in Southeast Asia*, ed. H. Chambert-Loir.

Lev, Daniel S. 1972. *Islamic Courts in Indonesia: A Study in the Political Bases of Legal Institutions*. Berkeley: University of California Press.

———. 1996. "On the Other Hand?" In *Fantasizing the Feminine in Indonesia*, ed. L.J. Sears, 191–202. Durham: Duke University Press.

———. 1999. "Between State and Society: Professional Lawyers and Reform?" In *Indonesia: Law and Society*, ed. Timothy Lindsey, 227–46. Sydney: Federation Press.

———. 2000. "Comments on the Course of Legal Reform in Modern Indonesia." In *Indonesia: Bankruptcy, Law Reform and the Commercial Court*, ed. Timothy Lindsey, 74–93. Sydney: Desert Pea Press.

Libson, Gideon. 1997. "On the Development of Custom as a Source of Law in Islamic Law." *Islamic Law and Society* 4/2:131–55.

Lindsey, Timothy. 1999. "From Rule of Law to Law of the Rulers—to Reformation?" In *Indonesia: Law and Society*, ed. Timothy Lindsey, 11–20. Sydney: Federation Press.

———. 2001. "Abdurrahman, the Supreme Court and Corruption: Viruses, Transplants and the Body Politic in Indonesia." In *Indonesia: The Uncertain Transition*, eds. Damien Kingsbury and Arief Budiman, 43–67. Adelaide: Crawford House.

———. 2002. "Indonesian Constitutional Reform: Muddling Towards Democracy." *Singapore Journal of International and Comparative Law* 6:244–301.

Lubis, Nur A. Fadhil. 2000a. "Mengembangkan Studi Hukum Islam." In *Problem dan Prospek IAIN: Antologi Pendidikan Islam*, eds. Komaruddin Hidayat and Hendro Prasetyo, 273–94. Jakarta: Departemen Agama R.I.

———. 2000b. *A History of Islamic Law in Indonesia*. Medan: IAIN Press.

———. 2003. "The State's Legal Policy and the Development of Islamic Law in

Indonesia's New Order." In *Shariʿa and Politics in Modern Indonesia*, eds. Arskal Salim and Azyumardi Azra, 48–75. Singapore: Institute of Southeast Asian Studies.

Luthfi, Habib. 2000. "Khuṭbat al-iftitāḥ li-raʾīs al-ʿāmm [li-]jamʿiyyat ahl al-ṭarīqa al-muʿtabara al-nahḍiyya." In *Hasil-hasil Muktamar IX Jamʿiyyah Ahlith Thoriqoh al-Muʿtabaroh an-Nahdliyyah*, 31–6. Pekalongan, Indonesia: Sekretaris Muktamar IX, JATMN.

MacIntyre, Aladair. 1988. *Whose Justice? Which Rationality?* Notre Dame, Ind.: University of Notre Dame Press.

Mahfudh, Sahal. 1994. *Nuansa Fiqih Sosial*. Yogyakarta: Lembaga Kajian Islam dan Sosial.

———. 2000. Interview published in *Sufi*, 1–1, April 2000.

Mahfudz, Gusti. 1982. "Perkawinan dan Perceraian Pada Masyarakat Banjar." Yogyakarta: Center for Demographic Research and Studies, Gadjah Mada University.

Mahmud, Said Mahmud, ed. 1978. *15 Tahun Institut Agama Islam Negeri Jamiʿah Ar-Raniry Darussalam Banda Aceh*. Banda Aceh: Panitia Harijadi ke-XV IAIN Jamiʿah Ar-Raniry.

Mahmud, Syoib M. 1982. "Perkawinan dan Perceraian Pada Masyarakat Ogan Ilir." Yogyakarta: Center for Demographic Research and Studies, Gadjah Mada University.

Majelis Ulama Indonesia (MUI). 1997. *Himpunan Fatwa Majelis Ulama Indonesia*. Jakarta: Majelis Ulama Indonesia.

Manan, H. Abdul. 1997. "Syiqaq dalam Hukum Perkawinan di Indonesia." *Mimbar Hukum* 31:61–71.

Maritain, Jacques. 2001. *Natural Law: Reflections on Theory and Practice*. Edited and introduced by William Sweet. South Bend, Ind.: St. Augustine's Press.

Masʿudi, Masdar F. 1991. *Agama Keadilan: Risalah Zakat (Pajak) dalam Islam*. Jakarta: P3M.

———. 1997. "Halqah: Nafkah dan Dilema Perempuan Pekerja." Paper prepared for "Workshop on Provisions for the Wife and the Dilemma of Woman's Work," July 17–19, 1997, Tasikmalaya, Indonesia.

———. 1997a. "Perempuan dalam Wacana Keislaman." In *Perempuan dan Pemberdayaan*, eds. Smita Notosusanto and E. Kristi Poerwardari, 53–64. Jakarta: Program Studi Kajian Wanita and Program Pasca Sarjana, Universitas Indonesia.

Mastuhu, 2004, "Fiqh Teaching in the Pesantren and Its Inevitable Development." Paper prepared for the conference "Islamic Law in Modern Indonesia," Harvard Law School, Cambridge, MA, April 17–18, 2004.

Masud, Muhammad Khalid, Brinkely Messick, and David S. Powers, eds. 1996a. *Islamic Legal Interpretation: Muftis and their Fatwas*. Cambridge, Mass.: Harvard University Press.

———. 1996b. "Muftis, Fatwas and Islamic Legal Interpretation." In *Islamic Legal Interpretation: Muftis and their Fatwas*, eds. Muhammad Khalid Masud, Brinkley Messick, and David S. Powers, 3–32. Cambridge, Mass.: Harvard University Press.

Masyhuri, K.H. Aziz, ed. 1997. *Aḥkām al-fuqahāʾ fī muqarrarāt muʾtamarāt nahḍat al-ʿulamāʾ wa-mushāwarātihā: Masalah keagamaan hasil Muktamar dan Munas Ulama Nahdlatul Ulama*. Surabaya: Dinamika Press.

———. n.d. "Kata Pengantar." In *al-Fuyūdāt al-rabbāniyya fī muqarrarāt al-muʾtamarāt li-jamʿīyyat ahl al-ṭarīqa al-muʿtabara al-nahḍiyya*, iii–vi. N.p.

Mattalioe, M. Bahar. 1965. *Kahar Muzakkar dengan Petualangannja*. Jakarta: Delegasi.

Mawardi, Ahmad Imam. 2003. "The Political Backdrop of the Enactment of the Compilation of Islamic Laws in Indonesia." In *Shariʿa and Politics in Modern Indonesia*, eds. Arskal Salim and Azyumardi Azra, 125–47. Singapore: Institute of Southeast Asian Studies.

Melucci, Alberto. 1996. *Challenging Codes: Collective Action in the Information Age*. New York: Cambridge University Press.

Merryman, John Henry. 1985. *The Civil Law Tradition: An Introduction to the Legal Systems of Western Europe and Latin America*. 2nd ed. Stanford: Stanford University Press.

Millie, Julian. 1999. "The *Tempo* Case: Indonesia's Press Laws, the *Pengadilan Tata Usaha Negara* and the Indonesian *Negara Hukum*." In *Indonesia: Law and Society*, ed. Timothy Lindsey, 269–78. Sydney: Federation Press.

Moors, Annelies. 1995. *Women, Property and Islam: Palestinian Experiences, 1920–1990*. Cambridge: Cambridge University Press.

Morris, Eric Eugene. 1983. "Islam and Politics in Aceh: A Study of Center-Periphery Relations in Indonesia." Ph.D. diss., Cornell University.

Mudzhar, Mohammad Atho. 1993. *Fatwas of the Council of Indonesian Ulama: A Study of Islamic Legal Thought in Indonesia 1975–1988*. Jakarta: Indonesia-Netherlands Cooperation in Islamic Studies.

———. 2002. "Studi Hukum Islam dengan Pendekatan Sosiologi." In *Antologi Studi Islam, Teori dan Metodologi*, ed. M. Amin Abdullah, 239–71. Yogyakarta; IAIN Sunan Kalijaga.

———. 2003. "The Study of Islamic Law in Indonesia Islamic Universities." In *Islam and Islamic Law in Indonesia*, 177–91. Jakarta: Office of Religious Research and Development, and Training, Ministry of Religious Affairs of Republic of Indonesia.

Muhammad, Rusydi Ali. 2003. *Revitalisasi Syariat Islam di Aceh: Problem, Solusi dan Implementasi Menuju Penerapan Hukum Islam di Nanggroe Aceh Darussalam*. Jakarta: Logos/IAIN Ar-Raniry.

Muktamar IX, JATMN. 2000. *Hasil-hasil Muktamar IX Jamʿiyyah Ahlith Thoriqoh al-Muʾtabaroh an-Nahdliyyah*. Pekalongan, Indonesia: Sekretaris Muktamar IX, JATMN.

Muladi, Maulana. 2004. "Peran Ulama dalam Mensosialisasikan Bank Syariah." *Mimbar Ulama* 306:21–2.

Mulia, Siti Musdah. 2001a. *Kesetaraan dan Keadilan Gender: Perspektif Islam*. Jakarta: Departemen Agama R.I.

———. 2001b. *Posisi Perempuan Dalam Undang-Undang Perkawinan Indonesia dan Kompilasi Hukum Islam*. Jakarta: LKAJ.

Muliakusuma, Sutarshi. 1982. "Perkawinan pada Masyarakat Betwai: Suatu Studi Kasus di Desa Balekambang, Jakarta." Yogyakarta: Center for Demographic Research and Studies, Gadjah Mada University.

Nasution, Khoiruddin. 2002. *Status Wanita di Asia Tenggara*, Leiden-Jakarta: INIS.

Nasution, Yasir, 1998. "IAIN dan Kajian Hukum Islam di Abad Moderen: Peluang dan Tantangan." In *Perguruan Tinggi Islam di Era Globalisasi*, ed. Syahrin Harahap, 93–113. Yogyakarta: IAIN Sumatera Utara/Tiara Wacana.

Natsir, M. 1954–57. *Capita Selecta*. Jakarta: Pustaka Pendis.

Nurdin, Faisal bin Hj. Muhammad Ali. 1996. "Sadd al-dharaʾiʿ: Pemakaiannya dalam Fatwa Majelis Ulama Indonesia." M. Shariah diss., University of Malaya.

Nurrohmah, Leli. 2003. "Pengalaman Perempuan Dalam Menjalani Perkawinan Poligami." M.A. thesis, University of Indonesia.

Pedoman Fakultas Syariah dan Hukum Tahun 2003/2004. 2004. Jakarta: Fakultas Syariah dan Hukum, UIN Syarif Hidayatullah.

Pinardi. 1964. *Sekarmadji Maridjan Kartosuwirjo.* Jakarta: P.T. Aryaguna.

Pokok-Pokok Manhaj. n.d. *Pokok-Pokok Manhaj Majlis Tarjih Yang Telah Dilakukan dalam Menetapkan Keputusan.* Yogyakarta: Pimpinan Pusat Muhammadiyah.

Powers, David S. 1994. "Kadijustiz or Qāḍī-Justice? A Paternity Dispute from Fourteenth-Century Morocco." *Islamic Law and Society* 1/3:332–66.

Price, Daniel E. 1999. *Islamic Political Culture, Democracy, and Human Rights: A Comparative Study.* Westport: Praeger Publishers.

Purnomo, Alip. 2003. *FPI Disalahpahami.* Jakarta: Mediatama Indonesia.

al-Qardawi, Yusuf. 1995. *Ijtihad Kontemporer.* Jakarta: Bulan Bintang (Ind. trans. by Abu Barzani of: al-Qaraḍāwī, Yūsuf. *Al-Ijtihād al-muʿāṣir.* Cairo: Dār al-Tawzīʿ, 1994).

Ricklefs, Merle C. 1993. *A History of Modern Indonesia Since c. 1300.* Hampshire: MacMillan.

Ridell, Peter. 2001. *Islam and the Malay-Indonesian World: Transmission and Responses.* Honolulu: University of Hawaiʾi Press.

Ritonga, Iskandar. 1995. "Pemikiran Hazairin tentang Pembaharuan Hukum Islam di Indonesia." M.A. thesis, IAIN Syarif Hidayatullah.

———. 2003. "Hak-Hak Wanita Dalam Putusan-Putusan Peradilan Agama DKI Jakarta, 1990–1995." Doctoral diss., UIN Syarif Hidayatullah.

Rofiq, A.H. et al., 1995. *Pelajaran KeNUan Ahlussunnah wal Jamaʿah.* Yogyakarta: LTN.

Rombe, Popaun, and A. Mukri Agafi. 2001. *Implementasi Hukum Islam.* Jakarta: PT Perca.

Rozak, Abd. 1991. "Perzinaan Sebagai Alasan Perceraian." *Mimbar Hukum* 4:31–7.

Rozehnal, Robert. 2004. "Debating Orthodoxy, Contesting Tradition: Islam in Contemporary South Asia." In *Islam in World Cultures: Comparative Perspectives*, ed. R. Michael Feener, 103–32. Santa Barbara: ABC-CLIO.

Ruether, Rosemary R. 1983. *Sexism and God-Talk: Toward a Feminist Theology.* London: SCM Press.

Saby, Yusny. 1995. "Islam and Social Change: The Role of the "Ulamā" in Acehnese Society," Ph.D. Diss., Temple University.

———. 2001. "The ʿUlamāʾ in Aceh: A Brief Historical Survey." *Studia Islamika* 8/1:1–54.

Saleh, Fauzan. 2001. *Modern Trends in Islamic Theological Discourse in 20th Century Indonesia: A Critical Survey.* Leiden: Brill.

Salim, Arskal. 2003. "*Zakat* Administration in Politics of Indonesian New Order." In *Shariʿa and Politics in Modern Indonesia*, eds. Arskal Salim and Azyumardi Azra, 181–192. Singapore: Institute of Southeast Asian Studies.

———. 2004. "'*Shariʿa* From Below' in Aceh (1930–1960): Islamic Identity and the Right to Self-Determination with Comparative Reference to the Moro Islamic Liberation Front (MILF)." *Indonesia and Malay World* 32/92:80–99.

Salim, Arskal and Azyumardi Azra, eds. 2003a. *Shariʿa and Politics in Modern Indonesia.* Singapore: Institute of Southeast Asian Studies.

————. 2003b. "Introduction: The State and *Shariʿa* in the Perspective of Indonesian Legal Politics." In *Shariʿa and Politics in Modern Indonesia*, eds. Arskal Salim and Azyumardi Azra, 1–16. Singapore: Institute of Southeast Asian Studies.

Sayyid, Bobby S. 1997. *Fundamental Fear: Eurocentrism and the Emergence of Islamism.* London: Zed Books.

Schrieke, B.J.O. 1921. "Bijdrage tot de Bibliographie van de Huidige Godsdienstige te Sumatra's Westkust." *Tijdschift voor het Bataviaasch Genootschap* 59:249–325.

Sciortino, Rosalia, Lies Marcoes-Natsir, and Masdar Masʿudi. 1996. "Learning from Islam: Advocacy of Reproductive Rights in Indonesian Pesantren." *Reproductive Health Matters* 8 (November 1996): 86–93.

al-Shāfiʿī, Muḥammad b. Idrīs. 1979. *al-Risāla.* Cairo: Dār al-Turāth.

Shoelhi, Mohammad. 2002. *Laskar Jihad Kambing Hitam Konflik Maluku.* Jakarta: Pustaka Zaman.

————. 2002a. *Laskar Jihad Kambing Hitam Konflik Maluku. Suplemen.* Jakarta: Pustaka Zaman.

Sinaga, Anthon P. 1992. "SDSB Diguncang Demonstrasi." In *Rekaman Peristiwa 1991*, ed. Albert Hasibuan, 154–55. Jakarta: Pustaka Sinar Harapan.

Sisters in Islam. 1993. "Memorandum on the *Shariʿa* Criminal Code (II) 1993 State of Kelantan," http://talk.to/sistersinislam/.

Sjadzali, Munawir. 1998. "Reaktualisasi Ajaran Islam." In *Polemik Reaktualisasi Ajaran Islam*, 1–11. Jakarta: Pustaka Panjimas.

Smith, Jonathan Z. 1978. *Map is Not Territory.* Leiden: E.J. Brill.

————. 1982. *Imagining Religion.* Chicago: University of Chicago Press.

Steenbrink, Karel. 1997. "Recapturing the Past: Historical Studies by IAIN-Staff." In *Toward a New Paradigm: Recent Developments in Indonesian Islamic Thought*, ed. Mark R. Woodward, 155–92. Tempe, Ariz.: Arizona State University Program for Southeast Asian Studies.

Sujuthi, Mahmud. 2001. *Politik Tarekat Qadiriya wa Naqsyabandiyah Jombang: Hubungan Agama, Negara dan Masyarakat.* Yogyakarta: Galang Press.

Sukarsi. 1992. *Nasihat-nasihat C. Snouck Hurgronje Semasa Kepegawaiannya kepada Pemerintah Hindia Belanda 1889–1936.* Jakarta: INIS (Ind. trans. of E. Gobée and C. Adriaanse, eds. *Ambtelijke adviezen van C. Snouck Hurgronje, 1889–1936.* The Hague: Martinus Nijhoff, 1957).

Sulistiowati. 1995. "Praktek Perkawinan dibawah Umur: Studi Kasus di Desa Wukirsari, Kabupaten Bantul." *Mimbar Hukum* (UGM) 21:65–76.

Tapol. 2002. "The Indonesian Human Rights Campaign: Background on Aceh, Indonesia," http://tapol.gn.apc.org/.

Thalib, Jaʿfar Umar. 2001. "Laskar Jihad Ahlus Sunnah Wal Jamaʿah Mempelopori Perlawanan terhadap Kedurjanaan Hegemoni Salibis-Zionis Internasional di Indonesia." [Jakarta?]: DPP Forum Kominikasi Ahlus Sunnah Wal Jamaʿah Divisi Penerangan.

Thalib, Sajuti, ed. 1981. *Pembaharuan Hukum Islam di Indonesia, In Memoriam Prof. Mr. Dr. Hazairin.* Jakarta: Penerbit Universitas Indonesia.

Tucker, Judith E. 1998. *In the House of the Law: Gender and Islamic Law in Ottoman Syria and Palestine.* Berkeley: University of California Press.

United Nations Development Program. 2003. "Aceh Regional Public Expenditure Review," unpublished report on file at the Asian Law Centre, University of Melbourne.

Doorn-Harder, Nelly van. 2006. *Women Shaping Islam: Indonesian Muslim Women Reading the Qur'an*. Urbana-Champaign: University of Illinois Press.

van Langen, K.F.H. 1997. *Susunan Pemerintahan Aceh Semasa Kesultanan*. Translated by Aboe Bakar. Banda Aceh: Pusat Informasi dan Dokumentasi.

van Nieuwenhuijze, C.A.O. 1958. *Aspects of Islam in Post-Colonial Indonesia*. The Hague/Bandung: W. van Hoeve.

Wadud, Amina. 1999. *Qur'an and Woman: Rereading the Sacred Text from a Woman's Perspective*. New York: Oxford University Press.

Wahid, Abdurrahman, ed. 2001. *Menggerakkan Tradisi: Esai-Esai Pesantren*. Yogyakarta: Lembaga Kajian Islam dan Social.

Wahid, Marzuki and Rumadi. 2001. *Fiqh Mazhab Negara; Kritik atas Politik Hukum Islam di Indonesia*. Yogyakarta: Lembaga Kajian Islam dan Social.

Wahyudi, Yudian. 1993. "Hasbi's Theory of Ijtihād in the Context of Indonesian Fiqh." Ph.D. diss., McGill University.

Webb, Gisela, ed. 2000. *Windows of Faith: Muslim Women Scholar-Activists in North America*. Syracuse, NY: Syracuse University Press.

Wheeler, Brannon. 1996. *Applying the Canon in Islam: The Authorization and Maintenance of Interpretive Reasoning in Hanafi Scholarship*. New York: SUNY University Press.

Widyasari. 2004. "Meninjau Undang-Undang Perkawinan No. 1 Tahun 1974, Dalam Perspektif Feminisme dan Hukum Islam." M.A. thesis, UIN Syarif Hidayatullah.

Yayuk, Afianah. 2003. "Pola Penyelesaian Hukum Tindak Kekerasan Dalam Rumah Tangga." M.A. thesis, UIN Syarif Hidayatullah.

Yusuf, H.A. Nasir. 1994. *Menggugat Khittah NU*. Bandung: Humaniara Utara.

al-Zuḥaylī, Wahba. n.d. *al-Fiqh al-islāmī wa-ʿadillatuhu*. CD-ROM. Damascus: Dār al-Fikr.

Zuhri, Saifuddin. 1965. *Agama: Unsur Mutlak dalam Nation Building*. Jakarta: Api Islam.

INDEX